Also available from Bloomsbury

The Holocaust in Eastern Europe: At the Epicenter of the Final Solution,
by Waitman Wade Beorn
*The League of Nations and the Refugees from Nazi Germany: James G. McDonald
and Hitler's Victims*, by Greg Burgess

A Polish Woman's Experience
in World War II

A Polish Woman's Experience in World War II

Conflict, Deportation and Exile

Irena Protassewicz

Edited by Hubert Zawadzki

With Meg Knott

Translated by Hubert Zawadzki

BLOOMSBURY ACADEMIC
LONDON • NEW YORK • OXFORD • NEW DELHI • SYDNEY

BLOOMSBURY ACADEMIC
Bloomsbury Publishing Plc
50 Bedford Square, London, WC1B 3DP, UK
1385 Broadway, New York, NY 10018, USA

BLOOMSBURY, BLOOMSBURY ACADEMIC and the Diana logo are trademarks of
Bloomsbury Publishing Plc

First published in Great Britain 2019
Reprinted 2019

ISBN: HB: 978-1-3500-7992-2
ePDF: 978-1-3500-7993-9
eBook: 978-1-3500-7994-6

Typeset by Newgen KnowledgeWorks Pvt. Ltd., Chennai, India
Printed and bound in Great Britain

To find out more about our authors and books visit www.bloomsbury.com
and sign up for our newsletters.

'Though the thorn wounds'

To the grandchildren and great-grandchildren of Irena Protassewicz

Contents

Foreword *Robert Evans*   ix

Acknowledgements   xii

Notes on Polish Terminology, Names and Pronunciation   xiii

List of Illustrations   xv

Protassewicz Family Tree   xvi

Maps   xviii

Prologue *Hubert Zawadzki*   xxiii

Part 1 1910 to 1939

1   Wars and reconstruction (1914 to 1925)   3

2   Education, home and the stirrings of love   19

3   All not quiet in the distant provinces   35

4   Warsaw: Relatives, love and a brush with dangerous politics   49

5   Wacław Protassewicz: The last squire of Borki   59

6   Before the storm   73

Part 2 1939 to 1945

Introduction to Part Two *Hubert Zawadzki*   83

7   'The end of our world'   95

8   Under Soviet occupation (1939 to 1941)   105

9   Siberia   121

10 Joys and sorrows in Central Asia   133

11 From Persia to the Holy Land   147

12 From Egypt to Scotland   161

Part 3 1945 to 2016

Epilogue: Exile and resettlement in Britain *Hubert Zawadzki*   169

Postscript: Tying up some loose ends *Hubert Zawadzki*   203

Notes   207
Bibliography   242
Index   247

Foreword

Robert Evans

Never was there a greater need than now to present real stories of human migration, of refugees in the past. Today's levels of dislocation are terrifyingly high, but they have their antecedents. Typically the stories are of forced removal; of physical and mental stress; of prolonged displacement and extended travels. They culminate in some kind of new life: any earlier status quo is rarely recovered, wherever resettlement eventually occurs. But the bitter experience of exile can also be enriching for those involved, both the migrants and those who deal with them.

All this is abundantly illustrated by tales of the Polish émigrés of the Second World War: one of the most extraordinary of collective odysseys, which began in mass coercion and was accomplished by a myriad remarkable examples of individual enterprise. It also served as striking evidence of the global implications of twentieth-century conflicts exported from Europe.

Poles, notably those in the privileged society recaptured at the start of this memoir, long tended to be rooted in their native soil, whereas neighbouring communities, of Germans and Jews in particular, were more mobile over the centuries. Gradually the Polish nation extended eastwards to dominate also the Kresy, or 'borderlands', of historic Lithuania and Ukraine, although it did so mainly by assimilating the local elites there. This is where Irena Zawadzka, née Protassewicz, lives in the early chapters of the present book. That process long took place in tandem with an expansive 'migration' of the borders of the state: at its prime, the composite monarchy of Poland-Lithuania was the largest country in Europe.

In the late eighteenth century, borders migrated again; but now they were lines of partition, such that the historic Polish polity was effaced from the map and Poles found themselves living inside other states. All this still without their having moved physically, at least until participants and victims of the great insurrections of 1830–1 and 1863–4 needed to flee abroad, mostly to France, a few already to Great Britain. Trust in the heritage of their own sovereign statehood was startlingly and dramatically vindicated at the end of the First World War, when the partitioning empires collapsed. An independent Poland could be restored and was able to reincorporate much of the former Kresy.

Envisaged by the victor powers as a bastion against both Bolshevik-led Russians to the east and Prussian-led Germans to the west, this old-new Poland seriously overplayed its hand. It was not inherently weak, as Poles' open resistance at home, and their military engagement abroad throughout the next world war would show. However, after a few years of domestic experiment with unstable representative institutions, Poland's government fell into the hands of the comparatively benign, but increasingly rudderless, semi-military dictatorship of Józef Piłsudski, a leader much admired by Irena and her family. By 1939, the country had lost its way on the international stage, and its moral compass too, as was shown by its neglect of the growing threat from Nazism, which culminated in Poland's egregious share in the dismemberment of Czechoslovakia after Munich. It was woefully unprepared for the *coup de théâtre* of the Nazi-Soviet pact.

Irena's world was transformed on 18 September 1939, when Soviet troops arrived in her village. There followed nearly two years of tense and often desperate uncertainty before her deportation to Siberia. Many of her compatriots suffered yet worse from the bestiality of Stalin's regime. Irena's involuntary migration began on 20 June 1941. Just a few days later, German troops, in their turn, occupied the Kresy as the first stage of their invasion of the USSR. Ironically, this surprise Nazi-Soviet war proved to be Irena's salvation, just as the unexpected pact between those two parties had earlier ruined her prospects. Propelling Stalin into an alliance with the West, it now liberated many exiled Poles, Irena among them, to return to Europe, if they could organize the journey and survive its rigours. The epic trek of the Anders's Army is a central theme of this book.

In 1945, as Irena and many other Poles settled in Britain, the next wave of East European migration began. It proceeded pari passu with the enforced migration of borders again, this time dictated by the Soviet Union, with the connivance of the West. The German inhabitants of almost all the restored countries of the region were brutally expelled. Some found themselves banished from territory that had been ethnically and politically German for centuries, but which was now assigned to Poland. They were replaced in their former motherland by Poles deported from the eastern borderlands that henceforth were incorporated into the USSR.

As is clear from Hubert Zawadzki's Epilogue, Polish migrants had ambiguous feelings about post-war Britain. Their émigré government in London was tolerated but not recognized; and there was often only grudging acceptance of their claims, even of those who had fought with British forces through all or much of the war, to domicile in the United Kingdom. Nevertheless, massive provision was made for them at length, by the terms of the Polish Resettlement Act of 1947, the first legislation of its kind, which applied to over 200,000 people (and one brown bear). Now across the whole country, from Scotland to Cornwall – as Irena's family themselves experienced – dozens of makeshift and spartan residential camps sprang up to accommodate them in the decade and more after the end of the war. Springhill, in the Cotswolds, where the Zawadzkis settled longest, was utterly typical. And most of those who passed through these camps, especially those who (like Hubert) grew up in them, remained in Great Britain.

Poles were by some way the largest group among wartime influxes, the harbingers of waves of immigration to the present day, partly from Europe (including many more Poles after the turn of the twenty-first century), but mainly from the wider world: India, Pakistan, the Caribbean, East Africa, alongside continuing arrivals from the White Commonwealth. Together they have rendered Britain far more diverse and multicultural, even as Poland and other east-European homelands have grown more restrictive, introverted and monochrome.

This book is much more than just a memoir; it's a duly authenticated historical source. Personal reminiscences are often committed to writing through the promptings of younger family members. In Irena's case her firstborn, 'Wacio' to her but Hubert to his British contemporaries, became a historian. Having coaxed his mother into telling her story, he felt it a professional challenge as well as a filial duty not only to translate and edit the text for publication, but to provide a full context for the events it relates.

Of course, memoirs, like any other literary creation, have their own validity. Their opinions, prejudices maybe, were true for the author, and perhaps for many others at the time of writing. It's important to record them. Even clear errors of fact may be as significant in popular memory as a more accurate version of events. But it's a huge enhancement of this text that it has been set against the facts as reconstructed by historians.

Some might think that Hubert's meticulous and thoroughgoing reality-check risks limiting the scope of the memoir, clipping its imaginative wings, correcting and amending its emphases. Yet surely the historical framework rather universalizes the memoir, setting it within a clear interpretative scheme which furthers relevant comparison. Thus this finely worked jewel of a text should appeal to a wide audience as it illustrates the generalities as well as the particularities of migration, exile and reintegration.

Acknowledgements

It is always a pleasure to acknowledge and thank individuals who, since the project's inception, have offered practical help, advice, information and, not least, encouragement.

First of all, I would like to thank my daughter Meg Knott who, despite her very busy life, found the time to assist me as co-editor. Professor Robert Evans offered invaluable support and advice on how to improve the structure of the text, and very kindly wrote the Foreword to the book. Over many months at his Oxford home, the late Michał Giedroyć answered scores of detailed questions about people and events which feature in the book, and shared his own life story which in some instances ran parallel to Irena's. I also thank Dr Michael Laird and Professor Jerzy Lukowski, both of whom read the entire text and offered helpful comments.

I am grateful for the help provided by archivists and other academics, including Jane Anderson (Atholl MSS at Blair Castle), Barbara Kroll (Polish Army Records, RAF Northolt), Dr Maciej Siekierski (Hoover Institute, University of Stanford) who provided permission to quote from Irena's deposition of 1943, Dr Andrzej Suchcitz (Polish Institute and Sikorski Museum, London), the late Dr Zbigniew Brzeziński, Professor Norman Davies, Dr Olesya Khromeychuk, Dr Martin Kroeger, Robert Ostrycharz, Dr Jan Tarczyński and Dr Nina Terlecka-Taylor.

Warm thanks are due to friends who assisted in various ways, including Janina Mineyko (née Niezabytowska), Terence Dooley, Rosy Giedroyć, Ania Walles and Jacquie Worswick. I am also grateful to the numerous audiences who heard my talks about Irena's life story, asked searching questions and by their positive response encouraged me to continue with the project.

This was, in many ways, a family effort. I owe a great debt to my wife Francesca and, in addition to Meg, my other children: Helen von der Osten, Anna Zawadzki-Brown, William Zawadzki, Alice Zawadzki and Charlie Zawadzki. I thank my sons-in-law, Ben Knott, Ulf von der Osten and Gareth Brown, who supported the project in many ways. Working on Irena's account has deepened my understanding of my parents' generation's tumultuous life and experience. To share this insight with my sisters Anna Zawadzka and Helen Péchon (née Zawadzka), and sister-in-law Grace Zawadzki, has been tremendously valuable.

Piecing together the fragments of Irena's life has also been possible thanks to members of Irena's extended family abroad: the late Zofia Jamontt, Aleksandra Kucz (née Kostrowicka), Lech Kontkowski, Kasia Pereira, Zofia Popiołkiewicz, Zbigniew Protassewicz, the late Halina Skrzyńska (née Jamontt) and Maciej Skrzyński.

Last but not least, I wish to thank my editor at Bloomsbury, Rhodri Mogford, for his enthusiastic support for the project, and Beatriz Lopez for her help in the final stages of bringing the manuscript together.

Hubert Zawadzki
Abingdon, 2018

Notes on Polish Terminology, Names and Pronunciation

Some Polish terms used in the text require further detail:

- *inżynier* = chartered engineer: a scientific-technological degree acquired at a polytechnical institute, and a title much prized by Poles and used in social intercourse.
- *szlachta* = nobility, although it must be borne in mind that the *szlachta* of the former Polish-Lithuanian Commonwealth was a very large socio-legal estate, comprising about 7 per cent of the country's population: probably the most numerous nobility in Europe. In law (until 1791) all the nobles were equal citizens, but in economic, social and cultural terms they ranged from wealthy owners of vast estates to smallholders (akin to English yeomen) and impoverished 'barefoot' *szlachta*. The Protassewiczes were substantial landowners, akin to the English gentry, although the inheritance of land by all sons and daughters (according to Polish and Lithuanian law) had led to the fragmentation of much of the family's landed property.

After Poland-Lithuania was dismembered by Austria, Prussia and Russia at the end of the eighteenth century, the governments of the partitioning powers employed different measures to deprive the mass of the *szlachta* of their special legal status. Many of the dispossessed or impoverished ex-*szlachta* either moved into the ranks of the intelligentsia or merged with the peasantry, the urban artisanate or the new industrial working class. The absence of a Polish state with its own civil service and army (except for the period 1807 to 1831) deprived many of the poorer *szlachta* of career opportunities, unless, of course, they entered the service of the partitioning powers – which many did.

- Peasantry: the term 'peasant' (*chłop*) is not used by Irena in any pejorative sense. The term, used objectively in historiography, social studies and literature, refers to a specific social group of smallholders who cultivated their own soil and to landless farmworkers. In Irena's district, most peasants (the largest part of the population) were descendants of serfs; serfdom there was only abolished in 1861.
- Pan/Pani/Panna = Mr/Mrs/Miss. Originally 'Pan' and 'Pani' meant Master/Sir/Lord, and Lady (like the French *Monsieur/Madame*). The appellation 'Pan' is also frequently used just with the first name, for example Pan Wacław or Pani Zofia.
- Irena's use of the diminutives when writing about her parents ('Tatuś' and 'Mamusia') is preserved.

- Polish surnames ending in -ski, -dzki, -cki have male and female forms: e.g. Pan Strawi**ński** but Pani Strawi**ńska**; Zabło**cki** and Zabło**cka**. Some surnames even distinguish between married and unmarried women: for example a married woman can be Pani Protassewicz or Pani Protassewicz**owa** (ending -**owa** indicates married status), and an unmarried woman can be Panna Protassewicz or Protassewicz**ówna** (ending -**ówna** indicates unmarried status).
- With the exception of Warsaw, the Polish versions of place names in interwar Poland are used. Russian names of people or places are transliterated phonetically.
- The territory of the Second Polish Republic (1918–39) was divided into fifteen provinces (*województwa*) which in turn were subdivided into districts (*powiaty*). The government-appointed official at the head of a *województwo* was a *wojewoda* (provincial governor) and the chief official in a *powiat* was a *starosta* (district governor). The city of Warsaw enjoyed the status of a separate province under a government commissioner.
- Polish currency: in 1924 the złoty (= 100 groszy) was introduced. As for monthly salaries in the 1930s: a village postmaster earned 75 złotys; a district governor 600 złotys; a member of the Polish Parliament 1,000 złotys in 1930; a high civil servant or judge in Poland in the late 1930s earned 3,000 to 4,000 złotys. In 1939, 1 US dollar was worth 5.31 złotys.
- All English-language biblical quotations are from *The Holy Bible. Revised Standard Version. Catholic Edition* (London: Catholic Truth Society, 1966).
- The abbreviation IP used in the endnotes refers to Irena Protassewicz's correspondence and papers.

A short guide to approximate Polish pronunciation will be useful to the reader:

ą – similar to French *on* as in *bon*
c – *ts* as in *its*
ć, ci, cz – *ch* as in *chop*
ch – *ch* as in Scots *loch*
dź, dzi, dż – *g* as in *George*
ę – similar to French *in* in *fin*
g – *g* as in *go*
i – *ee* as in *meet*
j – *y* as in *year*
ł, Ł – *w* as in *water*, although traditionally pronounced as *ll* in *ill*
ń – *n* as in *new*
ó, u – *oo* as in *took*
ś, si, sz – *sh* as in *shop*
w – *v* as in *vest*
y – *i* as in *bit*
rz, ż, ź – *s* as in *pleasure*

Illustrations

All the photographs come from Irena Protassewicz's private collection.

1 Borki manor before 1914   4

2 Wacław and Zofia Protassewicz with their daughters (left to right: Hania, Irena and Jula) in front of Borki manor, c. 1919   9

3 Irena in class 4 at the convent school run by the Sisters of Nazareth in Wilno, 1924   21

4 Three sisters (left to right): Irena, Jula and Hania in Warsaw, 1936   52

5 Irena at work as a beekeeper in Borki   71

6 Irena after typhus, Kazakhstan, 1942   140

7 Irena (standing 4th from left) with other members of the Polish Women's Auxiliary Service in Uzbekistan, 1942   143

8 Irena (2nd row from top, 3rd from left) with staff and boys at the school for Polish young soldiers in Nazareth, 1943   151

9 Irena and Michał Zawadzki on their wedding day at the Polish military hospital in Taymouth Castle, Scotland, 28 January 1945   164

10 Irena with husband Michał and three of their children (left to right: Wacio/Hubert, Anna and Helen) in front of their Nissen hut in the Polish resettlement camp in Springhill, Gloucestershire, c. 1953   193

Maps

1 Borki estate   xviii

2 Borki and district   xix

3 Northeastern Poland (1922–39)   xx

4 Partitioned Poland (1939–41)   xxi

5 USSR and the Middle East (1941–44)   xxii

Eustachy PROTASSEWICZ (1832–1896) m. Apolonia ŻÓRAWSKA (c.1841–1905)

(1) Maria Protassewicz (Marynia)
(1867–1953)
m. Aleksander Świackiewicz
(1849–1903)

Witold Świackiewicz (Wicio)
(1887–1974)
m. Sabina Czajkowska

Marian Świackiewicz (Maniuś)
(1888–1969)
m. Zofia Bozyczkówna
2 children

Jadwiga Świackiewicz (Jadzia)
(1889–1957)
m. Maciej Jamontt
(1881–1940)
Halina Jamontt (1911–2011)
m. Henryk Skrzyński (1913–2008)

Wanda Świackiewicz
(1898–1966)

(2) Wacław Protassewicz
(1868–1938)
m. Zofia Żórawska
(1884–1957)

Irena Protassewicz
(1910–1994)
m. Michał Zawadzki
(1909–1963)
Wacław/Hubert
Helena
Michael
Anna

Julia (Jula) Protassewicz
(1911–1980)
m. (1) Jan Karczewski
(1908–1943)
2 children
m. (2) Ferdynand Prange
(1915–2009)
1 child

Anna (Hania) Protassewicz
(1915–1987)
m.(1) Ryszard Baczyński
(d. 1944)
m. (2) Stefan Protassewicz
(1905–1946)
m. (3) Janusz Jaroszyński
(c.1925–1995)

(3) Wilhelm Protassewicz (Wiluś)
(1870–1921)
m. Zofia Stabrowska
(1872–1961)

Kazimierz Protassewicz (Kazio)
(1896–1946)
m. Joanna (Janka) Łysak
(1906–1975)
2 children

Zygmunt Protassewicz
(1899–1991)
m. Jadwiga Smosarska
(1900–1971)

Apoloniusz Protassewicz (Polik)
(1902–1984)
m. Helen Rockey
(1908–1999)

Stefan Protassewicz
(1905–1946)
m. Anna (Hania) Protassewicz
(1915–1987)

(4) Piotr Protassewicz
(1874–1932)
m. Kamilla (Kama) Morska
(1883–1969)

Kamilla Protassewicz
(1909–1990)
m. Zygmunt Zbroja
(1905–1940)
2 children

Wacław Protassewicz
(1912–1935)

(5) Salomea Protassewicz (Salunia)
(1876–1954)
m. Mieczysław Połubiński
(1863–1919)

Emilja (Mila) Połubińska
(1902–1984)
m. Wiktor (Witek) Kontkowski
(1897–1962)
3 children

Eustachy PROTASSEWICZ (1832–1896) m. Apolonia ŻÓRAWSKA (c.1841–1905) *(cont.)*

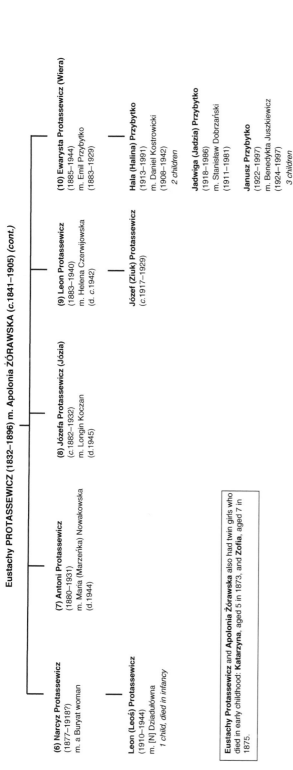

(6) Narcyz Protassewicz
(1877–1918?)
m. a Buryat woman

Leon (Leoś) Protassewicz
(1910–1944)
m. [N] Dziadułówna
1 child, died in infancy

(7) Antoni Protassewicz
(1880–1931)
m. Maria (Marzeńka) Nowakowska
(d.1944)

(8) Józefa Protassewicz (Józia)
(c.1882–1932)
m. Longin Koczan
(d.1945)

(9) Leon Protassewicz
(1883–1940)
m. Helena Czerwijowska
(d. c.1942)

Józef (Ziuk) Protassewicz
(c.1917–1929)

(10) Ewarysta Protassewicz (Wiera)
(1885–1944)
m. Emil Przybytko
(1883–1929)

Hala (Halina) Przybytko
(1913–1991)
m. Daniel Kostrowicki
(1908–1942)
2 children

Jadwiga (Jadzia) Przybytko
(1918–1986)
m. Stanisław Dobrzański
(1911–1981)

Janusz Przybytko
(1922–1997)
m. Benedykta Juszkiewicz
(1924–1997)
3 children

Eustachy Protassewicz and **Apolonia Żórawska** also had twin girls who died in early childhood: **Katarzyna**, aged 5 in 1873, and **Zofia**, aged 7 in 1875.

Protassewicz Family Tree

Maps

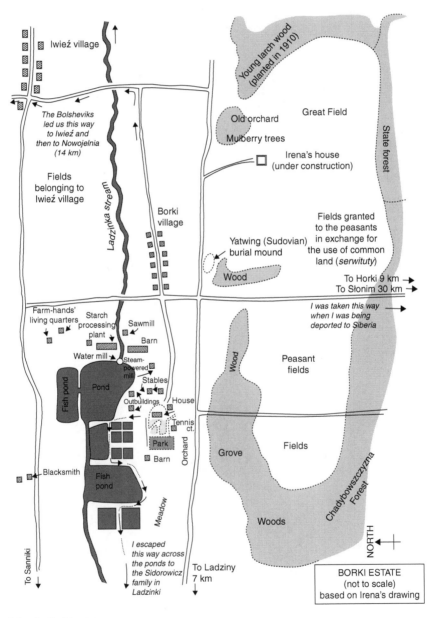

Iwieź village

Young larch wood
(planted in 1910)

Great Field

The Bolsheviks
led us this way
to Iwieź and
then to Nowojelnia
(14 km)

Old orchard

Mulberry trees

State forest

Fields
belonging to
Iwieź village

Ladzinka stream

Irena's house
(under construction)

Borki
village

Fields granted
to the peasants
in exchange for
the use of common
land (serwituty)

Yatwing (Sudovian)
burial mound

Wood

To Horki 9 km →
To Słonim 30 km →

Farm-hands'
living quarters

Starch
processing
plant

Sawmill

Barn

I was taken this way
when I was being
deported to Siberia →

Water mill

Steam-
powered
mill

Wood

Peasant
fields

Stables

Fish pond

Pond

Outbuildings

House

Tennis
ct.

Blacksmith

Park

Orchard

Barn

Grove

Fields

Chadybowszczyzna Forest

Fish
pond

Meadow

Woods

NORTH

To Sanniki

I escaped
this way across
the ponds to
the Sidorowicz
family in
Ladzinki

To Ladziny
7 km

BORKI ESTATE
(not to scale)
based on Irena's drawing

Map 1. Borki estate.

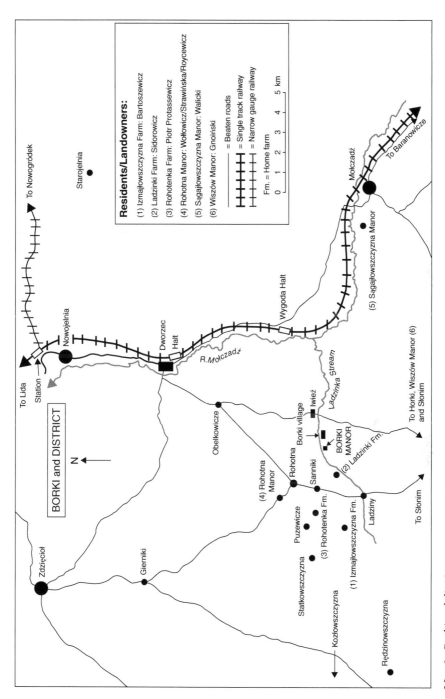

Map 2. Borki and district.

Residents/Landowners:

(1) Izmajłowszczyzna Farm: Bartoszewicz
(2) Ladzinki Farm: Sidorowicz
(3) Rohotenka Farm: Piotr Protassewicz
(4) Rohotna Manor: Wołłowicz/Strawińska/Roycewicz
(5) Sagajłowszczyzna Manor: Walicki
(6) Wiszów Manor: Gnoiński

Fm. = Home farm

= Beaten roads
= Single track railway
= Narrow gauge railway

0 1 2 3 4 5 km

BORKI and DISTRICT

N

To Nowogródek
Starojelnia
To Lida
Station
Nowojelnia
Dworzec Halt
R.Mołczadź
Wygoda Halt
Mołczadż
To Baranowicze
(5) Sagajłowszczyzna Manor
Ladzinka Stream
Iwież
Borki village
BORKI MANOR
(2) Ladzinki Fm.
To Horki, Wiszów Manor (6) and Słonim
Obelkowicze
(4) Rohotna Manor
Rohotna
Sanniki
Puzewicze
(3) Rohotenka Fm.
Ladziny
To Słonim
(1) Izmajłowszczyzna Fm.
Statkowszczyzna
Kozłowszczyzna
Zdzięcioł
Gierniki
Rędzinowszczyzna

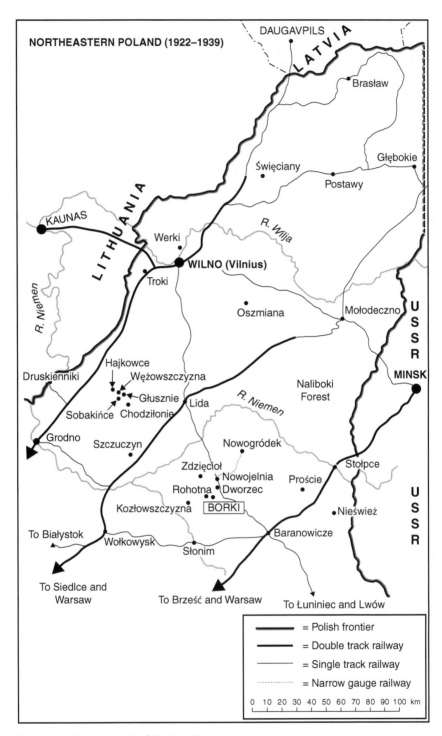

Map 3. Northeastern Poland (1922–39).

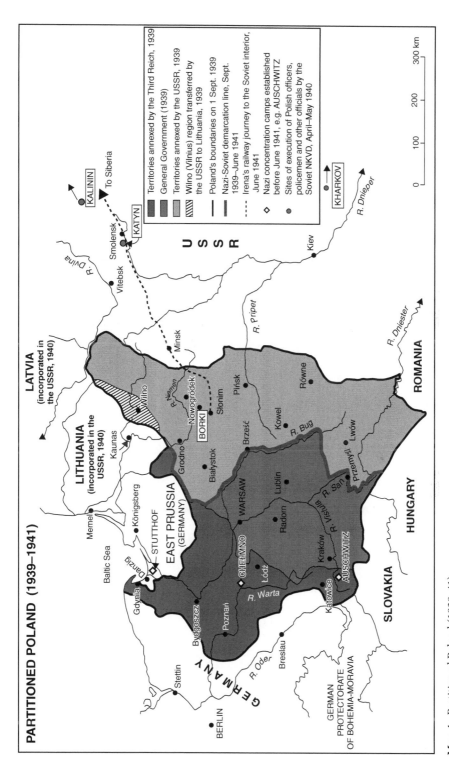

Map 4. Partitioned Poland (1939–41).

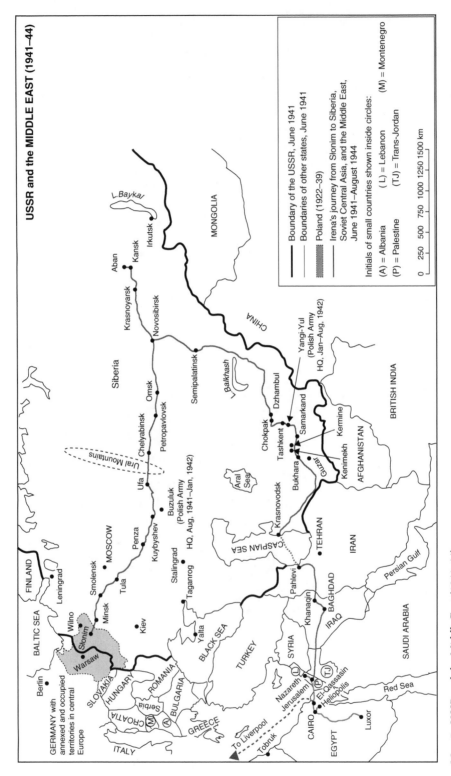

Map 5. USSR and the Middle East (1941–44).

Prologue

Hubert Zawadzki

For many years the inhabitants of the south Warwickshire village of Lower Quinton would have observed an elderly widow shuffling between her nondescript red-brick council house and the local shop or the village post office. Sometimes she would be seen using the mobile library that came to the village every fortnight, or waiting for a bus to Stratford-upon-Avon. She cultivated her fruit and vegetable garden intensively, and lived frugally. She seemed tense, even highly strung, and rather scatty in her manner. She spoke adequate English with a strong foreign accent, and would throw in foreign words when her English vocabulary failed her. Her husband had died in 1963, leaving her with four children, the eldest only sixteen. By the early 1970s, her children had flown the family nest. They visited her often, and she would spend the winter months with her elder daughter in London. But she felt at her best in Lower Quinton and would return with the first sign of spring.

Irena, for that was her first name, was not the only 'stranger' in the village. Hers had been just one of a dozen foreign families that had somehow landed in this attractive corner of Warwickshire in the 1950s and 1960s. What the local villagers made of her is difficult to tell. Few of them would have known who she was, what she had been and what she had lived through and witnessed before arriving among them in 1956. For Irena had a remarkable story to tell: of wars and revolutions; of invasion and deportation; of the death of many relatives and friends; of the loss of her home and country; and of the destruction of an entire social order into which she had been born.

During the Russian Revolution, when Irena was seven, she miraculously avoided a sniper's bullet. As a ten-year-old she lived through the period of conflict and anarchy that accompanied the Polish-Soviet war of 1919–20. Her years of adolescence and early adulthood in interwar Poland were by no means uneventful. She yearned for true love and adventure – and soon got the adventure of a lifetime. Her world was destroyed when the armies of Nazi Germany and of the Soviet Union invaded Poland in September 1939, and she feared for her life when the Red Army arrived in her district of eastern Poland. Irena survived the ensuing chaos and class warfare fomented by the Soviets, and found herself working as a nurse in her own house which the Soviets had turned into a hospital. In June 1941 she was deported to Siberia and sent to work on a collective farm where she was told she would have to stay for twenty years. But events soon took an unexpected turn: the Nazi invasion of the USSR altered the status of the thousands of Polish prisoners and deportees trapped there. Irena was freed and set off to join the Polish Army that was being formed in Soviet Central Asia. As a military nurse she witnessed horrific scenes of disease and death, and herself fell victim to typhus in early 1942. Her situation seemed hopeless, but she recovered. In August 1942 she was evacuated with the Polish Army to the Middle East where she looked after young Polish soldiers, many of them orphans, who had succeeded in leaving the USSR. Based in Palestine, Irena took every opportunity to visit as much as possible of the Holy Land. In August 1944 she was despatched to a Polish military hospital in Scotland and served as a ward sister until early 1945. There she met her future husband.

Irena often told her children episodes from her previous life: about her idyllic existence in her country home in eastern Poland; about her mother playing Chopin; about encounters with wolves; about some remarkable people that she had met; about the Soviet secret police (the NKVD) and her 'adventures' in the USSR; about her work as a military nurse; and about the wartime fate of her family. She would show them old photographs of relatives with strange names. She would mention exotic-sounding places in the east of Europe, in Asiatic Russia and the Middle East. Several military uniforms could be seen hanging in her wardrobe, while a casual search of the chest of drawers in her living room would reveal two stiletto daggers which she had purchased in Cairo in 1944. Each of these objects had a dramatic story to tell. But there was no chronological or coherent sequence to much of her storytelling. For her British-born children, these tales seemed a world away from their modest but secure life in England.

It was I, her elder son Hubert (but known in the family as Wacio), by then a postgraduate history student, who encouraged her to write down an account of her life. Irena did this in 1968–9: she was in her late fifties and her memory was still remarkably good. Neglecting housework, she applied herself with great industry to recreating her life story on paper. The net result was a text nearly 100 foolscap pages long, typed with a fading ribbon, with single spacing and hardly any margins. Squeezed between the lines were scrawled later additions made with a black ballpoint pen. The emotional effort she put into this project took its toll: Irena had always had frequent nightmares brought about by her wartime ordeals and privations, but in the summer of 1969, on finishing her account, she suffered a breakdown which required lengthy hospitalization.

In the early 1970s her grown-up children were all trying to make their way in the wider world and their thoughts lay elsewhere: studies, seeking careers for themselves, and then marriage and parenthood. Irena's typescript lay largely unread by the time of her death in 1994. It was only in 2006, on reaching retirement, that I was able to devote myself properly to the text. My mother had written her account largely at my prompting, and I now felt a moral responsibility and an obligation not to allow her record to be forgotten. My initial aim was to translate the text into English for the benefit of the family in England, but as I started working on the text I quickly realized how engaging and vivid, and how candid, my mother's story was, and that it deserved a wider readership. I acquired supplementary information from various public records and publications, and explored the hundreds and hundreds of letters that Irena had received since 1939 from her extended family and numerous friends, and which, unknown to us her children, she had kept hidden away in a large bin liner and a collection of old cardboard boxes. Among them were also drafts of letters she had written. Of great value were also Irena's long letters to her cousin in Australia. All these sources provided important additional information and, like pieces of a jigsaw, they often filled gaps in Irena's story or elucidated key events in her life and the lives of her relatives.

Like much of her storytelling, her text was not always chronological nor strictly thematic in the section covering the period before 1939; she sometimes added afterthoughts with bits of information she had forgotten earlier. It was therefore necessary to impose some order on her material, to avoid occasional repetition and to create coherent and manageable chapters. For instance, very early in her account Irena produced portraits, some longer, some shorter, of numerous members of her extensive family: grandparents, aunts, uncles, cousins. Having to face such a dense phalanx of individuals at the start of her story, and without having them placed in the necessary chronological and historical context, would have discouraged many a prospective reader from continuing. I have therefore relocated the individuals concerned, while of course preserving Irena's descriptions, to where they would sit more comfortably in Irena's chronological narrative. I was assisted in this process by my daughter and Irena's granddaughter, Meg Knott. By the same token, Irena's many references to her father were scattered throughout the first half of her original typescript. I have brought these pieces together to create a coherent separate chapter about him as he was such a key figure in her life.

Her account of the events of 1939–45 was chronological and thus much easier to deal with. The outbreak of war in 1939 is a clear watershed in Irena's story, and this is why I have also structurally divided her material into two parts, the first dealing with the pre-war period and the second with the wartime years. In Part One, the reader learns how Irena's identity and values were shaped by her social and cultural background, of considerable importance to understanding her reactions to her dramatic experiences during the war as related in Part Two. I have also supplied Part Two with an introduction in order to contextualize this pivotal period in Irena's life. Part Three (the Epilogue) covers the post-war period in Britain based on her surviving letters, documents and information from members of her family. Significantly, this illustrates how her wartime experiences affected her during her remaining long life after the war. In addition, Irena's typescript also contained examples of her poetry as well as two poems by one of her uncles and one of her aunts. While few of these poems would have added much to her narrative and may instead have been a distraction, five are relevant and it is only these that I have included in the text. One of these, published in a Warsaw newspaper in the 1930s, encapsulates Irena's romantic attitude to life. Where particularly relevant to Irena's story, extracts from her earlier accounts (in letters and depositions of 1940 and 1943–5) have been inserted in italics in Irena's text with the appropriate annotation, or in the notes.

Irena's story needs a wider context, and a few introductory remarks about her family's earlier history might be helpful for readers not familiar with her part of Europe. She was born Irena Protassewicz. On her father's side, Irena was descended from an old landed (*boyar*) family whose distant roots lay in what today is Belarus, part of the Orthodox Slavonic lands that had once formed Kievan Rus. During the course of the fourteenth century, the lands of Belarus (and much of what today is Ukraine) were absorbed into the Grand Duchy of Lithuania, the last pagan state in Europe. At its greatest extent, the grand duchy, a vast sprawling polity, stretched from the Baltic to the Black Sea, and it became in some respects a successor to Kievan Rus, a status that was later to be challenged by the emerging Principality of Moscow. In 1386 the

Grand Duchy of Lithuania entered into a dynastic union with the Catholic Kingdom of Poland. Its hitherto pagan rulers adopted Roman Christianity and shifted their multi-ethnic and multi-religious principality into the orbit of Western Christendom. In 1569 this partnership was transformed into a federal state: the Polish-Lithuanian Commonwealth. The Grand Duchy of Lithuania adopted many Polish representative institutions of government and saw the spread of Catholic influence in its Slavonic lands. In 1598 most of the Orthodox bishops in the grand duchy accepted the supremacy of the Roman Pontiff while retaining their Orthodox liturgy and married parish clergy; thus came into being the Greek Catholic or Uniate Church. Many of Irena's ancestors, like numerous others of the grand duchy's Orthodox nobles, went even further, abandoning Orthodoxy for Roman Catholicism and gradually adopting Polish culture.

The Protassewicz family made its mark on the public life of the Grand Duchy of Lithuania. It produced two eminent churchmen in the second half of the sixteenth century: Irena's direct ancestor Jonasz, the Orthodox metropolitan of Kiev, and his distant cousin Walerian, the Roman Catholic bishop of Wilno (Vilnius) who helped found the university in that city.[1] At the turn of the sixteenth and seventeenth centuries, the family could also boast several royal secretaries and judges, a distinguished soldier, a classical scholar and a deputy to the Polish-Lithuanian parliament.[2] However, despite this sprinkling of talent, the family failed to secure its position among the grand duchy's elite, and gradually settled for the life of country squires, significant in their locality but not at a national level.

A series of devastating wars in the mid-seventeenth century, combined with an increasingly ineffective political system at home, led to the rapid decline of the Polish-Lithuanian Commonwealth as a leading power in central eastern Europe. In the early 1700s it was overshadowed by Muscovy which Peter the Great was brutally transforming into a new military power in the northeast: the Russian Empire. By the end of the eighteenth century, the Polish-Lithuanian Commonwealth, once one of the largest states of Europe, had been partitioned by its more powerful neighbours and had ceased to exist. Russia took the lion's share, while Prussia and Austria grabbed the remainder.

When Irena's paternal grandfather was born in 1832, the homeland of Irena's ancestors (the territory of present-day Lithuania and Belarus) had been a part of the Russian Empire for nearly four decades. But conquest by Russia in those days did not mean social revolution. Catherine the Great and her imperial successors recognized the status of the local elites, provided they remained loyal to the ruling Romanov dynasty. However, dreams of resurrecting the former Polish-Lithuanian Commonwealth were still strong; many of the inhabitants of Lithuania and Belarus took up arms against tsarist rule during Napoleon's invasion of Russia in 1812, and in particular during the two Polish insurrections of 1830–1 and 1863–4. The insurrections had started in the neighbouring 'Congress' Kingdom of Poland centred on Warsaw, which Russia had acquired as a distinct but dependent state at the Congress of Vienna in 1815 at the end of the Napoleonic wars.

All these attempts to overthrow tsarist rule failed and were followed by increasingly severe measures taken by the tsarist authorities to reduce Polish and Catholic influence in Russia's western governorates. This included the closure of the University of Wilno in 1832. By the time Irena's father was born in 1868, there were no longer any state-maintained Polish-language schools in the region. The centuries-old Lithuanian legal code had been replaced by Russian law, while several million Greek Catholics (Uniates) had been forced to return to the Orthodox fold. The use of the Polish language in public was forbidden, and Polish Roman Catholics were barred from buying land. On the other hand, Tsar Alexander II had emancipated the serfs of the Russian Empire in 1861. As a result, part of the land belonging to the Polish-speaking landed class in the western governorates was transferred to peasant ownership. Despite that, and despite punitive confiscations of other property following the insurrections, the Polish-speaking landed class remained in possession of about 60 per cent of all land in Lithuania and Belarus on the eve of the First World War. It is also important to note that, even after losing its autonomy, the 'Congress' Kingdom of Poland remained a distinct administrative unit of the Russian Empire until 1915, different in many respects from the empire's western governorates. Irena refers to it simply as the 'Kingdom' (*Królestwo*), as opposed to the lands further east which she calls the 'borderlands' (*Kresy*).

Irena's home, Borki manor, lay in a district with a very diverse ethnic and religious composition. Most of the rural population spoke Belarusian; there were numerous Jewish traders and shopkeepers, descendants of the world's largest Jewish community which had flourished in the former Polish-Lithuanian Commonwealth; there were many Polish speakers, major landowners as well as yeomen and all sorts of déclassé gentlefolk; and even some Muslim Tartars. The village of Borki was predominantly Orthodox, but some neighbouring villages were Roman Catholic.[3] The nearest town of any significance was Słonim, 30 km to the southwest, which had a predominantly Jewish population (78 per cent of 12,800 inhabitants in 1900; and 53 per cent of 16,300 in 1931). But it was the city of Wilno, the multicultural heart of the former Grand Duchy of Lithuania, about 120 km to the north, which remained the main cultural and social centre for Irena's wider family. The city became more accessible from Borki with the opening of the Wilno-Baranowicze railway in 1884. And it was in Wilno that Irena was born in 1910.[4]

The four decades after the 1863–4 insurrection had been relatively quiet in Irena's district, which remained something of a backwater. At the beginning of the twentieth century, this part of the Russian Empire was still an overwhelmingly rural world with few railways, poor roads, extensive forests and a largely illiterate population. But change was on the way. There were modest improvements in agriculture, some urban growth and echoes of developments in the wider world: the rise of modern nationalism, of socialism and even the Dreyfus Affair which so bitterly divided France at the end of the nineteenth century. Local wealthy Poles of course had the means to travel widely within the Russian Empire and abroad. Several of Irena's uncles found lucrative work in Siberia and the Far East, while other relatives were sent to study in Galicia (Austria's share of old Poland), where the Poles enjoyed extensive autonomy under the Habsburgs and where Polish educational institutions flourished. The Russian Revolution of 1905 signalled some improvements: restrictions on the use of the Polish language were relaxed and the building of new Catholic churches was permitted. Local Poles could now also be represented in the newly created Russian Parliament (*Duma*).

The relative calm of the region came to an abrupt end with the outbreak of the First World War which saw the German Army penetrate deep into Russia's western governorates, including the area around Borki. The war and all the horrors associated with it brought about the eastward exodus of hundreds of thousands of people from Belarus; refugees as well as villagers were forced to leave by the Russian authorities. Some retreating Russian units employed a scorched earth policy to deny the Germans the resources of the region. Many local landowners, such as Irena's father and his family, were also pressured to depart for the Russian interior. As a result, Irena spent two and a half years in Taganrog (1915–18). Although Russia was allied to France and Great Britain, she could not ultimately bear the heavy brunt of modern industrialized warfare. In a series of revolutionary convulsions, the Romanov dynasty was overthrown in February 1917 and was replaced by a Provisional Government; this in turn was toppled when the Bolsheviks seized power in October 1917 and engulfed Russia in a terrible civil war. Two of Irena's uncles died in Russia as a result of the Bolshevik coup, while another joined the pro-independence socialist movement led by Józef Piłsudski (the future Polish Head of State and Marshal) and fought in the Polish Legions alongside the Austrians against the Russians in 1914–17.

At the peace treaty signed at Brest-Litovsk in March 1918 the Bolsheviks surrendered a vast swathe of the former Russian Empire (including the area around Taganrog) to the Central Powers, and Irena's family was able to return home. But the German victory in the east was short-lived. The Germans failed to achieve the decisive breakthrough in the west and were forced to sign an armistice in November 1918. One of the demands of the victorious Allies was that the German Army should withdraw from Russia. With the defeat of Germany and the collapse of both the Russian and Austrian empires, the Poles declared their independence (November 1918), although it would take four years of diplomatic and military effort before Poland's borders were settled. And it was in the east, where rival national movements laid claim to the same territories and where Bolshevik Russia soon made its hostile presence felt, that the Poles faced their greatest challenge. Irena's district now became part of a battleground between the rival armies of resurgent Poland and the new Bolshevik state which criss-crossed the area in 1919–20. Two of Irena's first cousins participated in the military conflicts of those years.

Between May 1919 and July 1920, the area around Borki was under Polish occupation. Indeed, by December 1919 the Poles had occupied all of Belarus as far as the Beresina river. In May 1920 the Poles and their Ukrainian allies (Petlura's units) had reached Kiev with the objective of consolidating an independent Ukrainian state. The situation then changed dramatically: a Bolshevik counter-attack in June 1920 forced the Poles to retreat along the whole front between the Dvina and Dniester rivers. The Red Army was soon pouring westwards towards Warsaw. Its objectives reflected Lenin's large-scale ambitions: to carry the torch of communist revolution over the body of 'White' Poland to Germany and beyond. The existing social order in the borderlands, especially its propertied upper strata, was now again in mortal danger. Irena's childhood memories include vivid episodes from the Bolshevik presence in Borki in 1920, what she refers to as the 'first' Bolshevik period, in contrast to the 'second' in 1939–41.

A Polish counter-attack east of Warsaw in August 1920 stemmed the Red Army's advance, and the Bolshevik rout was confirmed by a subsequent Polish victory on the Niemen river in September. The war ended with the Treaty of Riga signed on 18 March 1921. The Polish-Soviet border established by the treaty ran well to the east of Borki which now found itself within the frontiers of the reborn Polish state. There remained the problem of the contested city of Wilno. The new Lithuanian state claimed Wilno as its historical capital (although most of the city's inhabitants spoke Polish or Yiddish) while the Lithuanian-born Piłsudski, the Polish head of state, had hoped to include the Wilno region in a latter-day version of the former multi-ethnic Grand Duchy of Lithuania. It would consist of three ethnic cantons (Lithuanian with a capital in Kaunas; Polish with a capital in Wilno; and Belarusian with a capital in Minsk) and would join Poland in a federal relationship. In October 1920, in pursuit of this project, Piłsudski informally authorized local Polish units under General Żeligowski to 'mutiny' and to seize the city from the forces of the new Lithuanian state. The Wilno region was then proclaimed as 'Central Lithuania' (*Litwa Środkowa*) which was to be one of the three cantons of a larger multi-ethnic Lithuania. But neither Polish nor Lithuanian nationalists, determined to create new national states, were willing to compromise on the city's future and claimed it exclusively for themselves. Piłsudski's complex federal plan, harking back to a pre-nationalist age and opposed by the nationalist majority in the Polish Parliament, was doomed; with it disappeared 'Central Lithuania'. In March 1922 Wilno was simply incorporated into the Polish state.[5]

In the meantime, further south, the region around Borki, with its finely balanced and mixed social and ethnic composition, was gradually settling down to a period of stability. After six years of warfare and turmoil, peace finally arrived (or so many hoped) to Poland's eastern borderlands, and reconstruction could begin. Irena's family's fortunes were much depleted and its properties largely devastated. However, through ingenuity and hard work, Irena's father succeeded in restoring the Borki estate as a viable economic enterprise. The rebirth of an independent Poland also offered to some of Irena's relatives career opportunities in the Polish civil service, the armed forces and in other professions.

All this came to a tragic and brutal end with the Nazi-Soviet invasion of Poland in September 1939 and the dismemberment of the country between the Third Reich and the USSR. Although occupied by the two totalitarian powers, Poland did not capitulate, and Polish forces continued to fight alongside their French and then their British allies in the west, until the end of hostilities in 1945. In Poland itself, an impressive resistance movement was established in the form of the Polish Underground State, owing allegiance to the exiled Polish government in London. Irena deals in some detail with several of these events, many of which affected her personally. She also describes the fate of some of her close relatives during the dark years of the Second World War: the deaths of several aunts and cousins, the dispossessions and the final dispersal of her family. An independent Poland was not restored after the Second World War, while Stalin kept most of pre-war eastern Poland (including the area around Borki), his share in the original pact with Hitler. Those of Irena's relatives who had survived the war in the east had to find new homes and start new lives after 1945 in the new Poland controlled by the communists. As for the Polish servicemen and other Polish exiles in the west, many did not return home; this applied to Irena herself as well as to one of her aunts and two cousins.

Irena's account offers an insight into the lives and mores of the landed gentry of northeastern Poland in the interwar period, shortly before the violent destruction of this class in 1939. Her narrative is interspersed with character sketches of numerous diverse and engaging individuals: relatives, friends, neighbours and various eccentrics; artistic and literary figures she encountered; as well as her numerous suitors. There also feature ordinary countryfolk from her village and district as well as many local Jews, as seen from the perspective of the daughter of the manor.

She writes extensively about the repressive religious climate of her convent school and about her religious and philosophical doubts. Irena's frank depiction of her religious upbringing, of her patronizing approach to Orthodoxy and some of her social attitudes should be seen as very much of her time and of her social milieu. Indeed, her candid remarks about the social divisions in her district are one of the strengths of Irena's account. At the same time, one can also trace how some of her perceptions on all these matters, whether it be the nature of authority in the Roman Catholic Church, her attitude toward other Christian churches or her views of the Jews and other social groups, evolved in a distinctly liberal direction during the war and then with additional momentum in exile in Britain. Indeed, by the late 1960s her theological views could be labelled 'radical'. And it is clear that by then she was more understanding of the complexities of human nature and was less willing to condemn what she had considered as 'immoral' behaviour in her puritanical youth.

Irena's devotion to her father, a figure larger than life, is unquestioned although it is clear that he had little understanding or appreciation of his eldest daughter's intellectual interests and aspirations. And it is unfortunate that he discouraged Irena from attending university, which is what she hoped to do, and which would have sharpened her sceptical and inquisitive mind and given her a more thorough academic grounding. As it is, she had to rely on her own extensive autodidactic reading. On the one hand, she laments the 'complete intellectual loneliness' on the family estate, and it is clear that it was her long stays in Warsaw, Wilno and Kraków that provided her with varieties of intellectual stimulation. On the other hand, she extols her love for Borki manor and its natural surroundings, with its ponds, fields and especially its forests with their wild animals. In addition, Irena's happiness is further enhanced by her enthusiastic beekeeping which provided her with the financial independence she craved.

One individual to whom Irena found herself drawn was the spiritualist philosopher Wincenty Lutosławski, and her relationship with him merits further comment. For many years the polymath Lutosławski (1863–1954), an international authority on Plato, was the best-known Polish philosopher in the English-speaking world (and uncle of the composer Witold Lutosławski). He was also interested in psychic phenomena and mysticism. A central feature of his spiritualist system was the idea of reincarnation and the existence of a hierarchy of spirits – individual, national and cosmic – with the Polish nation playing a special role![6] It is not clear how much influence Lutosławski's ideas had on Irena, but there are certainly echoes of his spiritualist system in some of Irena's passages and in her surviving correspondence. She had been going to write a separate account of his work, but no such text has been found in her papers. What is however apparent is that Lutosławski regarded the twenty-five-year-old Irena as worthy of his guidance. In September 1935 he wrote to her:

> You need not worry at all about my feelings towards you. Your first letter was already sufficient evidence that from birth you belong to my spiritual family. Your further three letters have confirmed this, and now I long for a meeting with you, not to check further your intellectual worth, about which I cannot have any doubts, but in order to lay out as speedily as possible a plan for our joint action.[7]

Irena spent a month during the winter of 1935–6 with Lutosławski and his wife in Kraków. In the summer of 1936 the philosopher even visited Borki. A year before the war, Irena sought his advice about studying psychology abroad; he suggested Grenoble or Geneva.[8]

Sometime in the 1930s Lutosławski asked Irena (so she told me) to become his wife in the next life. Irena resumed contact with Lutosławski after 1945 and corresponded for many years with his daughter, Janina Lutosławska, who even visited Irena in England in 1964. Janina mentioned her father's bizarre marriage proposal to Irena in a letter of 22 October 1989. Lutosławski's first wife was the Spanish writer Sofia Pérez Eguia y Casanova (1861–1958); they separated in 1911–12. Hispanic scholar Roberta Johnson notes: 'Lutosławski was a womanizer, probably the model for the Slavic Don Juan that Casanova describes in her book on Russia. Like Unamuno's Avito Carrascal of *Amor y pedagogia* Lutosławski harboured the quixotic desire to father a son in order to raise a genius.'[9]

Other men and women would also influence Irena's experiences and ideas. Some appear in her story as minor characters, but there were several significant figures, in addition to Lutosławski, about whom the reader may wish to know more. An intellectual with whom Irena had dealings, and who visited Borki on several occasions in the 1930s, was the political writer and activist Władysław Studnicki (1865–1953). Originally a socialist, Studnicki had been exiled to Siberia in 1890–6. By the time of the First World War he had become an active Germanophile conservative and served on the German-sponsored Temporary Council of State in Warsaw in 1917–18. In the interwar period, he considered the USSR as Poland's main enemy, and consistently advocated that Poland should form a close political alliance with Germany. An energetic man possessing great civic courage, Studnicki often went against the mainstream of public opinion and was viewed by some as an *enfant terrible* of Polish political life. He remained an incorrigible Germanophile during the Second World War and attempted to persuade the Nazis to abandon their policy of terror in occupied Poland; for his pains, he was twice imprisoned by the Germans, including a long spell (fourteen months) in the Gestapo Pawiak prison in Warsaw. He arrived in London, via Rome, in late 1946. Irena was able to re-establish contact with him shortly afterwards.[10] Studnicki wrote a warm appreciation of Irena's father, after his death, in an article entitled 'Parę słów wspomnienia o ś.p. Wacławie Protasewiczu' (Some Memories of the Late Wacław Protasewicz) in the Wilno newspaper *Słowo*. He applauded Wacław's exceptional enterprise and industry in rebuilding the family estate after the wars of

1914–20, and praised Borki as a beacon of Polishness among the local Belarusian population.

A very different individual who, after a rocky start, also became a friend of the family and who appears at various intervals in Irena's story was Melchior Wańkowicz (1892–1974), an immensely popular and prolific writer, journalist and war correspondent. His witty newspaper articles and published sketches about Irena's father and Borki, which he visited on several occasions, have been carefully preserved by Irena's family. Irena was also to meet him in Palestine and possibly towards the end of the war, in London. Wańkowicz's style is characterized by a lively picturesque narrative and owes much to the storytelling traditions of the *szlachta* (nobility) in the former Grand Duchy of Lithuania (he was born on the family estate of Kałużyce near Minsk). His autobiographical *Szczenięce lata* (Puppy Years) (1934) is considered the most beautifully written account in Polish literature of the decline of the Polish gentry class in the east. His most important work is the three-volume *Bitwa o Monte Cassino* (The Battle for Monte Cassino) published in Rome in 1945–7; an abridged censored version appeared in Poland in 1957. His *Ziele na kraterze* (Greenery on the Crater) (1951) is part autobiography, part family saga and part tale covering the pre-war and wartime years in Poland. At odds with the Polish exile establishment in post-war London, Wańkowicz moved to the United States in 1949. He was to return to Poland from exile in 1958 but eventually got into trouble with the communist authorities over censorship and received a suspended three-year prison sentence in 1964.[11]

Among artistic figures with a national reputation who feature in Irena's story is Jadwiga Smosarska (1900–71), one of pre-war Poland's leading theatre actors and film stars who married Irena's cousin Zygmunt Protassewicz in 1935. Irena last saw Smosarska and Zygmunt in September 1939 in Borki shortly after the outbreak of the war but was able to resume contact with them in 1944, by which time they were safely in the United States while Irena was in Palestine. Another was the modernist Polish-Czech painter Wlastimil Hofman (1881–1970), who with his wife Ada had fled from Poland to Palestine in 1939. It was in Palestine that Irena befriended Hofman; Irena devotes quite a long section to his work and life there. Not only did Hofman paint an excellent portrait of Irena, but both he and his wife were to maintain an occasional correspondence with her after their return to Poland in 1946. It was Hofman who introduced Irena to the religious history of the Czech people.

Standing quite apart from all the individuals above, and an even more controversial figure in Polish political history than Studnicki, was Bolesław Piasecki (1915–79), whom Irena encountered in Warsaw in 1933–4 through her cousin Hela Jamontt. Piasecki, a law student at Warsaw University, was not yet twenty years old but had already gained notoriety as an extreme nationalist. In 1934, following a split from the mainstream nationalist National Democratic Party, Piasecki joined the fascistic ONR (*Obóz Narodowo-Radykalny*; National Radical Camp) which enjoyed most support among university students. Banned by the authorities, the ONR continued to function illegally. In 1935 the ONR split, with Piasecki creating the National Radical Movement (RNR; although the public referred to it as 'ONR-Falanga') which advocated a totalitarian model for Poland. During the Second World War, Piasecki fought the Germans and the Soviets. It appears that in 1944 the Soviet NKVD spared his life in return for his proposal to undermine the Catholic Church in Poland by establishing a rival 'Catholic' organization. Recent research suggests that at that time he had come to the conclusion that it would be possible to reconcile his version of nationalism with communism, and that eventually the former would become dominant. His pro-regime pseudo-religious organization 'PAX' was an important and influential institution in communist Poland. During the political crises in Poland in 1956 and 1968 he supported the hard-line elements of the Polish Communist Party, and was appointed member of the State Council in 1971.[12] Irena did not join the ONR but with her cousin attended some of their meetings and, with her romantic taste for adventure, found herself drawn into the conspiratorial world of extreme right-wing politics, which she recounts with some candour. Fortunately, she was able to escape unscathed from this brush with danger.

Some comments also need to be made about political events in 1938–9. In her account of her planned but abandoned trip to Berlin at the end of 1938 to visit the family of her German friend Hans Albert Reinkemeyer, Irena makes no reference to politics. Nor does the subject figure in Hans Albert's surviving letters from November 1938 dealing with the visit. Irena seemed quite happy at the prospect of attending lectures at the University of Berlin. Was Irena, in the light of her friendship with Hans Albert, well disposed to Germany at this stage of her life? How much did she know about the Nazi regime? How well informed was she about foreign affairs? Or was she just naive in matters political, viewing individuals and public events through an unworldly romantic prism? Was she too preoccupied with events at home: the consequences of her father's death for the family and the estate; pressures put on her to marry; the ruin of the rye harvest in 1938? Would a trip abroad have been a welcome distraction? Or did she simply feel, when writing her account thirty years later, that a commentary on international relations in 1938–9 was unnecessary, unless it directly affected her and her family? In the absence of any evidence we shall probably never find out. And yet it would be intriguing to know what was discussed in Borki during the visit of the Germanophile Studnicki at this time. In any case, official relations between the Third Reich and Poland, based on a non-aggression treaty between the two states signed in 1934, were still formally correct. Indeed, Poland had 'benefited' from the Munich Agreement of October 1938 by annexing the Teschen (Cieszyn) district from the prostrate Czechoslovakia, which gave the misleading and highly damaging impression that Warsaw was acting in collusion with Berlin. Furthermore, German demands for Danzig and overtures to Poland to join the Anti-Comintern Pact against the USSR (October 1938 and January 1939) were still conducted in secret and were unknown to Polish public opinion.

Similar thoughts occur on reading Irena's account of her journey to Italy in the spring of 1939. There is much there on culture and religion but no comment on Mussolini's regime, and the only mention of Hitler is that he had forbidden any Germans to attend the first Easter celebration of the newly elected Pope Pius XII. There is admittedly a brief reference to 'talk of war', for by then Hitler had occupied Prague (15 March) and the Polish government had finally declined Hitler's 'magnanimous' offer of an alliance (26 March), while Chamberlain had publicly declared British and French support for Poland (31 March). And it was during Irena's stay in Rome that Britain offered a formal guarantee of Polish independence (6 April). By the time Irena was back in Poland, Hitler had publicly repudiated the German-Polish treaty of 1934 (28 April). It was then Poland's turn to face Hitler's wrath.

What Irena does affirm strongly in her writings is that her romantic political views were formed under the influence of both the patriotic tradition of the Polish insurrections of the nineteenth century and Piłsudski's struggle for Polish independence. There is no evidence to establish exactly what Irena's attitude was to Piłsudski's socialist past or to his role during the 1905 revolution in Russian Poland when his socialist fighting squads confronted the tsarist police and army, and clashed with rival squads raised by the nationalist National Democratic Party, in what began to resemble a Polish civil war.[13] What certainly did meet with Irena's admiration was Piłsudski in his post-Marxist phase after 1908 in Galicia, where he attracted many students and youngsters to his military wing of a broad pro-independence association, and then in his role during the First World War as commander of a Polish Legion fighting on Austria-Hungary's side against Russia. His exploits on the Galician front, followed by his long imprisonment (July 1917 to November 1918) by the Germans for refusing to cooperate with them unless they permitted the restoration of a genuine Polish state, only added to his aura of heroism in the national cause. With his left-wing background, which earned him wide support among a population desperate to escape wartime privations yet euphoric about the imminence of independence, and his readiness to rise above party factionalism, Piłsudski was able to make a decisive contribution to the establishment of an independent Polish state in 1918–19. His role (much resented and even questioned by his nationalist opponents) in the defeat of the Red Army in 1920 proved to be a crowning moment in the emergence of a legend that elevated Piłsudski to the status of Poland's man of Providence. Indeed, the cult of Marshal Piłsudski, shared also by some of her relatives, features prominently in Irena's text. There is much to suggest that Irena's view of Piłsudski was influenced by her uncle Leon Protassewicz, who served in Piłsudski's Legions and who, with his wife Helena, remained on close terms with the future Marshal. Irena's romantic attachment to the former Grand Duchy of Lithuania also made her sympathetic to Piłsudski's federal schemes in the east. It is perhaps not surprising that Irena makes only an incidental reference to Piłsudski's coup of 1926, which led to the authoritarian regime that was to dominate Polish political life until 1939.[14]

Does all this underline Irena's romantic rather than democratic values? And where could she have learnt about democracy in her social milieu and in her part of the world? Within her family, it was with her progressive-minded uncle Leon and his wife that Irena might have been able to discuss the merits of democracy, although both of them were, when all is said and done, devoted followers of the Marshal. If anything, it was the menacing spectre of godless Bolshevism just over the not too distant border of Soviet Russia that shaped attitudes within her social class in Poland's eastern borderlands. Irena's cultural, religious and political values were to be put to the test when she found herself under Soviet rule in 1939 and when in 1941 she was forcibly transported deep into the militantly atheistic and repressive world of Stalin's Russia, 'this land clasped in Satan's embrace', as she describes it. Irena's confrontation with the

Soviet 'other', which was to affect her for the rest of her life, is an important theme in Part Two of her account.

To be employed as a 'Soviet' nurse in her former home which had been expropriated by the Soviets and converted into a hospital was probably a rare if not unique experience for someone of her background after the Soviet invasion in 1939, during which landowners either fled from their properties or were arrested. Her vivid account of her subsequent life as a military nurse with the Polish Army in the USSR, the Middle East and then in Britain is a valuable contribution to the remarkable story of the Polish war effort during the Second World War. No other witness account of Polish military nurses at work in those regions has yet appeared in print in English, and I am not aware of any in Polish. Narrated from direct personal experience in a clear and engaging style, Irena's is also a female voice, so often missing in accounts of war.

Part One of the text (Chapters 1 to 6) deals with the period 1910–39, the first twenty-nine years of Irena's life. Part Two (Chapters 7 to 12) focuses on the war years 1939–45. Part Three comprises the epilogue covering 1945–2015 in which I describe Irena's search to discover the wartime and post-war fate of her family and friends on both sides of the Iron Curtain, and the challenges of exile in Britain. It should be added that like many continental Europeans, Irena uses the term 'England' and 'English' indiscriminately for 'Great Britain' and 'British' – even when she has Scotland in mind. When referring to her parents, Irena uses the Polish diminutives *Tatuś* and *Mamusia* for her father and mother.

Other people may have different perspectives on the events and individuals she describes, but what follows is her story. And it is now time for Irena's voice to be heard. She begins with a message to me.

Part One

1910 to 1939

1

Wars and reconstruction (1914 to 1925)

Evacuation to Russia – Taganrog – Revolution in Russia – Return to Borki – Wężowszczyzna and my Żórawski aunts – Starting from scratch – Bolshevik War 1920 – Bandits – Cousin Kazio, two swapped letters and the ensuing tragedy – The bizarre story of Klemens Minasowicz – Hunting wolves and wild boar – Borki back on its feet – Pan Wincenty the estate administrator

25 January 1968

Dear Wacio!

Your letters urge me to start writing. Yesterday, while listening to the record 'The Magic of Polesie' (*Polesia czar*) at the Zielińskis, I happened to glance at a large portrait of Józef Piłsudski hanging on their wall.[1] What an impact it made on me! It was as if his deeply thoughtful face spoke to me and tugged at some long-forgotten heartstrings. No, just as a tree cannot forget its roots, so one cannot forget the *Kresy* which have produced people of such calibre.

I once experienced two calamities within the course of one year. The death of my father, Wacław Protassewicz of Borki, brought the world of my childhood to an end. The destruction of Poland removed the ground from under my feet, not only in a literal sense through the loss of Borki, but also because Poland had totally disappeared into a bottomless pit.

My parents, Wacław Protassewicz of Borki and Zofia Żórawska of Wężowszczyzna, were married on 9 September 1909. I was born in Wilno on 4 August 1910 according to the Julian calendar (17 August 1910 according to the Gregorian calendar). Mamusia breastfed me, but because she did not have enough milk I cried all the time. Apparently, she was not able to breastfeed her babies well; those were not our modern times. Perhaps this early undernutrition affected my health in later life, as I turned out to be weak and anaemic. When my sister Jula was born in 1912, my mother employed a healthy strong peasant wet nurse for her. As a result, Jula was always healthier than I was. My youngest sister Hania was also not strong as a child. For example, once when Hania and I had a bad case of dysentery, Jula was unaffected, and she hardly ever caught colds after running around barefoot. Perhaps a reason for falling ill was the existence of numerous ponds for breeding carp which my father established near our house, as well as the natural lake. The surrounding air was damp and the house stood in the shadow of ancient lime trees. We always went to bed to the distant accompaniment of croaking frogs. Through the open windows of the drawing room came the scent of the lime trees, to be met by the beautiful tones of Chopin's Preludes played by my mother who ended her working day in such a way.

In 1914, war broke out between Russia and Germany. We left for Russia in September 1915. I remember how, before our departure, Tatuś shot an apparently mad dog outside the windows of our 'blue room', at the back of the house. It turned out that the dog's body was to mislead thieves. In a deep hole in the garden Tatuś buried the family porcelain, some of Mamusia's trousseau and her memoirs, sealed in an iron box. These items were covered with a layer of soil on top of which he placed the dead dog to deflect any unwelcome attention, and covered it with soil. After we left, local peasants looking for signs of disturbed earth found the dog and then stopped looking any further. Tatuś had the moving parts of the two steam engines thrown into the pond; this saved the machines because later the Germans could not take them. In addition to this, my mother removed the family portraits from their frames. Adam Skorochod, our groom, geared up four horses into the beautiful Cracovian harness (a wedding gift from Uncle Wiluś Protassewicz) and placed the rest of the harness with the silver fittings along with our luggage. Then off we set into the unknown to escape the advancing German front line.

We spent the first night with a hospitable Orthodox priest. I remember, as if it were yesterday, the tasty fruit preserves we children were offered and the picture books we

Figure 1. Borki manor before 1914.

were given to look at. I think it was in Minsk that Tatuś decided to sell our fine horses; we then boarded a train bound for Taganrog, a seaport on the northern shore of the Sea of Azov. We took up residence in a house on Petrovskaya Street (no. 97) in an ugly part of town, but it was chosen for its proximity to the railway station. In addition to our coachman Adam, our servant Helenka came to nurse my newborn sister Hania. Helenka later married Adam and they both moved out of our house since Adam had found a job as a cabby. By 1918 Adam and Helenka had a son Staś whom my father held at the christening. Staś Skorochod was to become quite Polonized during his service in the Polish Army in the interwar period, and was to opt for Poland after the great reshuffling of borders in 1945. He now lives in Sopot in Poland, and makes a good living as a mechanic, having learnt smithing on the Borki estate. The rest of his family continues to vegetate in poverty in *Kresy* (Soviet Belarus).

I have very pleasant memories of Taganrog. It was a beautiful seaside town with a lovely climate. Mamusia would take us to the beach where we swam, holding on to her arms, in the section reserved for women, and collected shells. There were also many delicious tropical fruits. We gorged ourselves on peaches, heavenly aromatic melons, not to mention watermelons which we ate as the third course for lunch. Mamusia would buy delicious *fosfatynka* drinks for Hania, the sight of which made my mouth water.[2] Our neighbours in Taganrog, the Kufszyniec family, lived in the courtyard with their four charming daughters who performed gypsy dances while playing their castanets. The poor things were later forced to marry some primitive Bolsheviks and life did not turn out well for them. Pani Kufszyńcowa was very wealthy and gave me her portrait which I took back to Borki.

Mamusia always attached great importance to education and so we were immediately sent to Madame Mamol's nursery school. We learnt to read and write there, as well as to dance, and we played the piano during school performances. I remember how Jula and I once appeared as angels wearing beautiful dresses covered with silver stars, and how we performed some folk dances with flowery *sarafans* (folk dresses) over our shoulders. The Polish evacuees in Taganrog also formed a landowners' association which held various meetings. Tatuś went there to play *vint*, a Russian card game, while Mamusia was twice invited to give Chopin recitals. Incidentally, it was between these performances that Mamusia gave birth to my future singer sister Hania.

Then, out of the blue, revolution broke out.[3] Dreadful things began to happen. It was rumoured that the Bolsheviks were throwing young officer cadets into roaring furnaces. Some cadets barricaded themselves in the railway station: the end of the line there was perpendicular to the station and the Bolsheviks directed a train straight at them. Terror prevailed. Men hid. We soon felt hunger, and it was dangerous to appear on the streets. Once Mamusia sent me to run across the courtyard to get some potatoes from a neighbour. Running, I tripped over something in the middle of the road and fell on the ground. At that very moment I heard the whizz of a rifle bullet passing over my head. This was my first miraculous escape. There were to be many during the Second World War.

It was hardly surprising that in 1918 the inhabitants of Taganrog greeted the Germans with flowers. Two friendly moustached soldiers were billeted with us. They occasionally gave us sugar cubes which had become a rarity by then. Sugar jokes appeared: for example, sugar was to be eaten '*v prygladku*', that is looking at a sugar cube which lay on a table, or '*v prylizku*', where a sugar cube was suspended on a string over a table so that everybody could touch it with his or her tongue before pushing it to the person seated next to them. Of revolutionary songs I remember 'O rise, working people ... to the factory let's go, let's go' (Russian: *Vstavay podnimaysya rabochyi narod ... idyom, idyom v zavod*). Another song, a rhyme for older children, went 'A giant crocodile was moving along the street, it, it ...' (Russian: *Po ulitsy khodila bolshaya krokodila, ona, ona ...*). The rest I can't remember. Those were my memories from when I was seven years old.

In 1918 the Germans allowed us to leave Taganrog by train. We had received news that the house in Borki had survived the war; Adam, Helenka and baby Staś travelled back with us. What was now of great importance was to avoid the quarantine post near Baranowicze where the Germans, fearing the spread of Spanish influenza, dispatched trains with 'evacuees', but where the sick infected the healthy. In fact, that is how the mother of Aunt Kama Protassewicz of Rohotenka died. Tatuś approached a German officer in charge of the station with a request to be exempt from the quarantine. However, out of meanness, the officer summoned a railway worker and instructed him to make a special note of our carriage number and to make sure that it should be immediately moved onto the track leading to the quarantine. For a bribe the railway man revealed all this to us and advised us to move to another carriage. That is how we finally reached Nowojelnia, the nearest railway station of significance to Borki. From there Tatuś sent a runner to our neighbours, the Sidorowiczes of Ladzinki, who then sent horses for us.

The house in Borki was completely denuded of furniture and was inhabited by a German who later sold Tatuś various kinds of nails and some barbed wire. There was also nothing left of the family library. As for Mamusia's memoirs, the damp soil had dissolved all her handwriting: we could only stare at the blank pages. On the other hand, the Sidorowiczes had looked after Mamusia's grand piano, which had been part of her trousseau, as well as a beautiful glass chandelier from the drawing room. While the family stayed with the Sidorowiczes, Tatuś made repeated trips across the ponds to Borki and restored some order to the house. New window panes were fitted and temporary beds were made from planks. Fortunately, the beautiful large round table from the dining room had survived in somebody's care. It was several years later that we inherited a whole suite of red furniture pieces from my great-aunt Ewarysta Żórawska in Wilno. Later some inlaid tables and other fine furniture were made for us by the Salesian Fathers who ran a carpentry school in the former Zawisza mansion in Dworzec (9 km north of Borki). On a subsequent visit there, my heart bled at the sight of what had been done to this palatial building by the philistine administration of the monks. There was no trace of any of the mansion's original beautiful furniture which had gone no one knew where; nor was there any trace of old mementoes. The area around the house was neglected and the interior was a ramshackle carpentry shop.

It is interesting to note that many landowners in the district of Słonim who had stayed behind during the war of 1914 to 1918 managed to save their possessions because the front line did not run across the whole region. When we eventually returned to our empty house and had to start from scratch, we discovered that the residence of our distant neighbour, Jan Strawiński of Mirowszczyzna, had survived with all its mementoes and furniture. It was with a touch of envy that we once saw all the treasures that had been accumulated in his house over the centuries.

Indeed, even my mother's family home in Wężowszczyzna, with its furniture and portraits, survived when the area was occupied by the Kaiser's army.[4] This was because while in 1915 the Russians forced us, at Borki, to leave for the Russian interior, my maternal grandmother Antonina Żórawska stayed in Wężowszczyzna with her remaining daughters. Indeed, one might say they spent this time 'pleasantly', since a group of German staff officers was billeted in the house. The officers treated the Polish ladies with courtesy, and one of them, von Brück, a wealthy industrialist from near Berlin, fell in love with my aunt Janka, a beautiful and slim brunette with a nightingale voice, and proposed marriage. Not keen on marrying a German, Aunt Janka diplomatically played for time. After the war she sent her Polish fiancé to see von Brück to settle some financial accounts. Von Brück took the hint, and so the prospect of that Polish-German marriage came to nothing.[5] The house even survived the Bolshevik war of 1920, although the estate was largely devastated. During that time my grandmother and her younger daughters found shelter somewhere in Warsaw. After the end of hostilities they returned to face the difficult task of reconstruction.

It was the unmarried Aunt Mania who then took over the running of Wężowszczyzna, which she did with great charm and in great style. She played the piano beautifully, and the house remained a centre of music during her residence there, as it had been in my grandfather's time. Her guests included the pianists Wojtkiewicz and Heintze;[6] the latter, poor soul, died prematurely from multiple sclerosis. At a time when many landowners in the region had lowered their standards, Wężowszczyzna was able to maintain its high artistic, cultural and culinary level. One unexpected guest of Aunt Mania's was none other than Marshal Piłsudski whose car once broke down in the neighbourhood and who spent a night at the house.

Living for a time in Wężowszczyzna was also Mania's younger sister, my aunt Irena Żórawska. She was continually involved in a long line of affairs and once revealed to me a whole chest of love letters from her admirers. I remember one of the letters starting with the phrase: 'My dearest piggy!' (*Najdroższa świneczko!*). Never in my life have I come across such a beautiful deep voice, with such a wide range and tone, the only exception being the silken voice of my sister Hania.[7] Aunt Irena started her career as an opera singer in Warsaw, performing first in Moniuszko's *Halka*. Other operas followed. However, owing to her laziness, she later opted for an independent life on the family estate and only gave solo performances. She once performed in Druskienniki[8] and was honoured there by the presence of Marshal Piłsudski, with whom she claims to have drunk whisky!

Aunt Irena was not suited to being a reliable wife and mother and only married late in life. With her husband Stefan Gołębiowski, a military officer, she led a rather hedonistic existence in great comfort. Stefan was a divorcee, which greatly distressed my very devout grandmother, although she did all she could to conceal her feelings from them. Aunt Irena impressed me with her vitality and good health. She was nineteen years old at my parents' wedding, but she passed herself off as someone much younger. Even before the war she and her equally long-lived sister Mania (who remained socially in Aunt Irena's shadow and hence never married) demanded that I, their niece, call them by their first names in order to rejuvenate themselves by a generation.

When my sister Jula and I were teenagers, our mother took us on a tour of the district where she had spent her youth. The high point of our trip was of course to visit my grandmother in Wężowszczyzna. For us children, Wężowszczyzna was a fairyland. The manor house was a most attractive building picturesquely situated among fertile fields. One approached the house through a fine whitewashed stone gateway in front of which played a fountain. The porch was made of elaborately carved panelling and painted white. It was designed by grandfather Stanisław who also, I seem to remember, designed the nearby church in Sobakińce.[9] Behind the house, through a dense thicket with trees, a long path led to a large tennis court situated on the edge of a cornfield. Not only was there the excitement of exploring a place unknown to us and devouring cherries straight off the trees for hours on end (surprisingly with no ill effect to our health), but we had the entire enormous attic to ransack. And what did we not find there! Apart from old dresses and hat boxes, there were, in my eyes, priceless treasures everywhere: old letters and scattered ancestral papers. Just over a decade later, during the Second World War, this beautiful and delightful manor was burned to the ground by the local peasants. They ploughed over the terrain and planted potatoes. *Tout passe, hélas …*

But let us go back to Borki in 1918. We lived in conditions of extreme poverty with not a single cow or horse. We had to start from scratch, for my father's pre-war fortune had been exhausted by our move to Taganrog. Furthermore, the thousands of roubles of compensation he had received from the tsar became worthless after the revolution and lay scattered in our cupboard. Eventually we bought a cow and some horses formerly owned by Germans, including two beautiful saddle-horses: *Iskra* (Spark) and *Hetman* (General). *Hetman* died a dozen years later from glanders, despite the injection I administered to his neck. *Iskra* was full of charm and Tatuś or I would often ride her. I even have a photo of her by the well. *Iskra* survived bravely until the Second World War before being taken as pillage. People in the countryside become attached to animals just as they do to people, and become fond of them. I clearly remember how often as children we mourned the death of a dog, the death of my rabbits or the death of a trapped wolf cub.

In addition to the thoroughbred horses, Tatuś was able to buy a half-dead horse which was so weakened through hunger that it was unable to stand on its legs, and whose bare coat was completely covered with scabs. Adam enabled the horse to stand by supporting it with belts in the stable. He then rubbed it with birch sap until it grew a beautiful coat. It recovered its health and strength and also worked hard until the Second World War. Tatuś purchased other horses with money earned from the sale of fox skins, for which Jewish dealers paid handsomely. Tatuś killed the foxes by using strychnine that he inserted inside yew berries which were then encrusted with suet. A roller smelling of suet and camphor (I think) was attached to the rear end of a sleigh which would then be driven over the snow-covered fields to leave a scent. Morsels of bread covered with fat would then be scattered and at intervals the poisonous balls would be dropped. Just before daybreak, armed with a shotgun, Tatuś would set off

Figure 2. Wacław and Zofia Protassewicz with their daughters (left to right: Hania, Irena and Jula) in front of Borki manor, c. 1919.

with Adam to collect the valuable dead foxes. Adam carefully skinned them, stuffed them with straw and dried them out for the dealers. On one such early outing, by the light of the moon, Tatuś observed something moving around like ants on the raised flat ground of the Great Field – it turned out to be scores of wolves. Adam turned the horses around and in great haste they miraculously managed to escape back to the house. Adventures of this kind happened all the time in the countryside. Once Tatuś saw with his own eyes how wolves tore out the guts of several cows.

But before normal life could be fully restored, we had to endure the arrival of the Red Army. In 1920 Tatuś had four nephews in the Polish Army, and used this fact to frighten the peasants, saying that if they even tried to do something wrong during the conflict with the Bolsheviks, their whole village would go up in smoke. It helped then, but not in 1939 when the Bolsheviks not only seduced the local peasants with hollow promises to improve their lives, but represented a real power and provided real backing for the peasants' struggle for the lords' land.

I remember the following scenes from the 'first' Bolshevik period (1920): Cossacks sleeping in a row on the floor of our house; hungry soldiers banging on our windows and pressing their noses against the glass, and calling 'Bread! Bread!' Somehow they did nothing terrible to us then. Tatuś and Mamusia never showed any fear and always spoke calmly to them. One Bolshevik, who said he was fond of music, asked Mamusia to play some Chopin; she agreed and, calmly as ever, sat down at the piano. It was worse when the Bolsheviks were in flight after the defeat of the Red Army outside Warsaw in August 1920. They seized and took away with them male landowners, and there was a rumour that they had buried alive a large number of Jews in Słonim. It was then that Tatuś went into hiding. Whenever any of the Bolshevik soldiers arrived to see him, Mamusia would reply that he had just left for the commune office in Rohotna. 'Where is the *barin* (squire)?' they would ask. Supplied with adequate furs and food, Tatuś hid in a boat that was concealed among the reeds in the lake. Only at night did he creep up silently to the house: when the flowerpot was not on the windowsill it was a signal that he could enter safely, have something to eat and relax.

At this time my father's sister Salomea (Salunia) Połubińska was with us, along with her adolescent daughter Mila whom she hid in the attic. Barefoot and disguised as a peasant, Aunt Salunia would make her way to Rohotenka, over 3 km away, to find out if there was any news of Uncle Piotr's family. She discovered that they had hidden in a cavern where potatoes were kept. Only ten-year-old Leoś remained in the house with a servant; he even played a trick on the Bolsheviks by cutting their telephone wires. Leoś was the orphaned son of Uncle Narcyz Protassewicz (who had died in unknown circumstances during the Russian Revolution) and was now being looked after by Uncle Piotr and his wife Kamilla (Kama), a great beauty. At one point, one Bolshevik took Leoś into a *bryczka* (britzka; an open horse-drawn carriage), saying that he was going to take him to Russia. Leoś said yes, but added that he wanted to take his clothes and toys with him. The Bolshevik agreed, and Leoś escaped through the window of the house into the park and the forest beyond. In the van of the Bolsheviks roamed peasants armed with rifles. Once two such men were trying to get through barbed wire to pick some apples. Jula and I (aged nine and ten) approached and lowered the raised wire thus trapping them in the barbs; we then ran away. Such were our adventures. On another occasion a couple of Cossacks galloped in and ordered the cook to catch some chickens for them. Anna, the cook, pretended to call the chicken but in such a way that she could not actually catch them. The Cossack then drew his sword, and slew a couple of ducks which he then attached to his saddle by the legs. One day, out of the blue, Polish lancers arrived. What joy there was. Unfortunately, they stole many hens from the peasants, and trampled a lot of our hay.

Of Tatuś's three brothers who were involved in railway construction in Siberia, two did not return from the east: Uncle Wilhelm (Wiluś) and Uncle Narcyz. Uncle Antoni (Antoś) did escape with his life, although his health was seriously undermined by a spell in prison. That his wife Aunt Marzeńka was able to rescue him from the clutches of the Cheka was a miracle. In the meantime, a chest of gold which Antoni had expedited with his batman disappeared. Antoni and Marzeńka returned to Poland without any means of livelihood, so to support his wife Antoni took on whatever jobs he could. For a time he had the lease of a horse-drawn railway in the district of Lida and also manufactured hollow clay bricks. He died suddenly in Borki (in 1931). Antoni and Marzeńka had no children. Several years later the widowed Aunt Marzeńka married Konstanty Bielon, a Russian living in Warsaw. Marzeńka radiated warmth and kindness. She had beautiful large blue eyes with long dark eyelashes, a beautiful mouth with lovely teeth, a small nose and a fine complexion. She was very tall, but later put on too much weight. She was killed by a bomb during the Warsaw Uprising while carrying food to an elderly uncle.

During the period of the Polish-Bolshevik war and its immediate aftermath, our region swarmed with real bandits. The most notorious were Komar (Gnat) and Mucha (Fly). Once, Komar robbed passengers on the horse-drawn railway run by Uncle Antoś. Komar was apparently caught by a mounted policeman, the late Starczewski, who told us the story himself in 1963. The policeman discovered that Komar was going to go drinking during Whitsun with some woman in a cottage near the forest. The policeman then devised a plan in collusion with the peasant living in this cottage. Komar would keep an axe by his feet when sitting at the table. The peasant borrowed the axe on the pretence of needing to chop some wood. At that moment Starczewski entered the cottage: 'Hands up!' he called out, and then handcuffed Komar. On being asked by the policeman if he was angry with him for having caught him, Komar replied: 'No, not with you, no! No one could ever catch me, and only you were clever enough to do it. You have my brigand's respect!'

And it was probably Mucha who raided the manor house in Wężowszczyzna. It happened to be 13 June, my grandmother Antonina Żórawska's name-day. This was after the Bolsheviks had been expelled and a greater sense of freedom had returned to the district; as a result many of the local gentry were able to gather for the occasion. Among the men present was also Uncle Piotr Protassewicz. All of a sudden the door to the drawing room opened and in came Mucha pointing a revolver at the assembled company. Everybody raised their hands and Mucha proceeded to relieve all the ladies of their jewellery; he also removed Uncle Piotr's watch. Uncle Piotr did have a revolver in his pocket, but no resistance was offered as it was feared that the house was surrounded by a whole gang of robbers. My grandmother was actually ill that day and lying in bed; Mucha went to her bedside and looked under the mattress to see if any money was hidden there.

Another landed lady in the Słonim district (I forget her surname) reacted very differently in similar circumstances. A gang of bandits started banging on her door. Although she was alone, she let them in. Seeing they were dealing with only a woman they began to enter 'gently'. All of a sudden she produced a revolver and shot dead all four intruders. How remarkable was the courage of these Polish Amazons of the eastern borderlands, worthy adherents of the best traditions of Emilia Plater.[10] Indeed, Emilia Plater was a model and inspiration for me when I decided to stay behind alone in Borki in 1939 and to remain 'on guard'.

In the period 1920–1, Tatuś received several rifles from the district authorities; we were then constantly 'under arms' until all the bandits had been caught by the police or by the army. Lesser thieving continued for longer. Sometimes, when the night watchman heard some noise near the grain store suggesting that thieves were about to help themselves, Tatuś would take his revolver (by then the rifles had been returned) and together with his farmhands he would drive away the prospective burglars. With all these childhood memories, I am still surprised that in 1939, after the Soviets had occupied our district, I was not afraid to be alone at night for three weeks when our house was deserted.

Soon after the end of the Bolshevik war, a railway wagon arrived with gifts from America which were given out to the peasants.[11] Local landowners immediately formed a cooperative (which later went bankrupt), and thus cultural life returned. The first artistic performance was organized in the home of Pani Wanda Strawińska in Rohotna. Pani Bartoszewiczowa of Izmajłowszczyzna played 'Dziad i baba' (The Old Man and the Old Woman). Panna Mania Kozłowska looked delightful in her large hat as she went around with a collection box. Mania Kozłowska later became a nursery maid in our house, and my cousin Kazio Protassewicz, still a student in Wilno, fell in love with her. Mania was the daughter of peasants from the nearby village of Ladziny. It is only by chance that she had managed to finish five classes in a grammar school in Russia; as a result she blossomed like a beautiful flower (she was beautiful and delicate like mimosa) in what were otherwise primitive surroundings. Just as one remembers flowers, it was just such a memory that she left with us children who, although small, could sense the attraction of the intellect and the grace of this lovely girl. If any romanticism still remains from those days it is the recollection of Mania Kozłowska standing in the drawing room and singing *Chylisz główkę* (Bow Your Little Head) with a delightful and attractive voice, to Mamusia's piano accompaniment.

But fate destroyed this flower. Everyone around was guilty: we too, the children, who spied with curiosity through the openings in the loft as she went on walks together with Kazio. It became clear to my parents that Kazio was enraptured with her; they were obliged to send her away. She then worked as a teacher and Kazio visited her at her parents' home and planned how he could marry her in the face of my father's opposition to such a misalliance. At the time Kazio was still without a permanent post. In addition to this, Kazio's brother Polik, in his concern to prevent his brother marrying a peasant girl, swapped two unsealed letters written by Kazio. Tatuś received a letter beginning with 'My dearest ...', while she received Kazio's letter to my father in which he reassured him that it was nothing serious. The result was a scandal. Sometimes the best people in the world, acting allegedly in good faith, like Tatuś and Polik, can be cruel.

Matters were not helped when Mania's parents brazenly started to lord it in certitude of their daughter's marriage. Her mother arrived unannounced in Borki and proceeded to embrace Mamusia, like a relative; her father, who was on bad terms for some reason with Pan Herubowicz from Redzinowszczyzna, loudly proclaimed that he would 'smash his snout' as soon as his Mania wedded young master Kazio. Buckling under the pressure of events, Kazio broke off with Mania, but never ceased to regret it. Heartbroken as a result, and after suffering from headaches for several years, Mania lost all hope. She was eventually persuaded to marry a simple local official, only to die in childbirth. Some years later, I was travelling with Kazio in a *bryczka*; as we passed a fine and stylish smithy (designed by Uncle Antoś) near our lake, he told me that by now he could have had a fourteen-year-old son, and added that it was we the children who were to blame by blabbing about his courting of Mania. It was over a dozen years after the tragic love affair that Kazio fell in love with Janka Łysak, a charming woman of great inner qualities who was employed in a pharmacy. They married in 1936 and enjoyed several years of happiness before the Bolsheviks arrested him in 1944.[12]

I regret that while staying with the Lutosławskis in Kraków during the winter of 1935–6 I did not visit Kazio who was then the municipal governor (*starosta*) of Lwów, which was not far away. He invited me, mentioning that I would be looked after by a company of the city's most elegant male youth; with my provincial timidity I took fright and instead of going to Lwów I went to Zakopane. As a result I was never to see Lwów in all its beauty during the period of Poland's independence between the wars. In life one must not miss opportunities that arise for they may never return. One never re-enters the same river, as a Greek philosopher once said.

According to documents in my father's possession, the Borki estate was acquired by the Protassewicz family over 350 years ago. A splendid house was then built with a roof in the style of a Chinese pagoda. A similar house belonged to the Walicki family in neighbouring Sągajłowszczyzna, although its surroundings were not as beautiful. A lime tree as well as a semi-circle of lilacs were planted in front of our house. Beyond were stables and farm buildings. During repairs done to the house in 1909, a copy of the Four Gospels was discovered bricked up in the foundations. They were put back in the same spot. Not surprisingly, Borki manor became known as 'The House on the Four Gospels' (*Dom na Czterech Ewangeliach*).[13] Despite many wars and insurrections, the house had survived intact, and it was a listed building in my day.

My grandfather Eustachy Protassewicz was released from the Imperial Guard well before the Insurrection of 1863 and returned to live in Borki, although as a former military officer he had not the faintest idea about farming.[14] But he had a courageous wife who not only bore him twelve children, two of whom died in infancy, but also ran the entire estate and the adjacent farms at Wielkie Pole (Great Field) and Chadybowszczyzna. Their marriage was entirely accidental. The matchmaker was a local Jew who, while on a business trip to Countess Zawiszyna in Starojelnia, spotted there a hitherto unknown young lady. 'Oh, sir! What a pretty young lady has come to visit Countess Zawiszyna!' My grandfather immediately got into his *bryczka* and so met Miss Apolonia Żórawska of Wężowszczyzna in the district of Lida.[15] Eustachy took great care to maintain high standards at home. He had beautiful hands and refined manners, and always created a good impression. My grandmother was responsible for everything else.

And times were difficult. During the Insurrection of 1863, Eustachy had given shelter on his property to anti-tsarist insurgents. As a penalty, the tsarist authorities imposed heavy fines on the estate, just when the family was beginning to grow in size. The burdens on the estate were compounded by a fire (sometime in the 1870s) that destroyed the distillery.[16] Little wonder that grandfather Eustachy was not considered to be very wealthy, despite the additional inheritance of Rohotenka from his brother, and of Hajkowce in the district of Lida from his wife.[17]

The atmosphere in my grandfather Eustachy's home had been patriarchal. The children, that is my father and his siblings, were never allowed to sit down at the table before their parents and Eustachy's two sisters, for whom an annexe was built to the house. On entering the extensive dining room, the aunts would approach a large picture of Christ on the Cross which hung in the room and would kiss the feet of the Crucified Saviour; then they would take their place at the table.

In the house in Borki, there were just three old paintings: a small miniature of an unnamed Protassewicz who had held the office of *cześnik* (cup-bearer);[18] a life-size portrait of *Hetman* (General) Makowiecki, related to us on the distaff side of the family; and a fine portrait of Bishop Walerian Protassewicz with a long beard and wearing a biretta. He was the ancestor we always mentioned with pride.

In the summer, I slept in a small room over the porch which in wintertime served as a store for apples. I then moved to the 'blue' room on the ground floor next to the drawing room. Guests to the house used to sit in the drawing room on a sofa placed below portraits of the Minasowiczes, painted by Klemens Minasowicz, and below his fine self-portrait ('se ipsum fecit Anno Domini 1830' was the inscription on the reverse side) painted in a French style.[19] Looking at this handsome young man's self-portrait brought to mind a very shocking tale. The story goes that when he was studying in Paris, Klemens fell in love with a waitress at a café, but his parents forbade him to marry her. She died unexpectedly, and Klemens had her head embalmed and kept it in a glass vessel. I was surprised to discover in an illustrated article by Gomulicki, published in a journal in Poland, that Klemens actually loved someone else, a beautiful young married woman – someone he loved from a distance. He would creep into a church in Warsaw to watch her during services. After her death he had her body disinterred and removed her head which a doctor friend of his embalmed for him. It was to be expected that Klemens subsequently invented the story that this was the head of his Parisian love, for how else could he have concealed his conspiracy with the doctor and kept secret the sacrilegious decapitation of a corpse of a woman from Warsaw's high society?[20] As for the doctor, after his death a large number of plaster casts of naked women, his beautiful patients, were found in his attic. He clearly knew how to make moulds of living women. This was his secret hobby which, after his death, caused an incredible scandal in Warsaw. After the looting of our manor house in 1939, I managed to save the portrait of Klemens by giving it for safekeeping to the Tarasik family in Borki village. They hid it in the attic of their cottage, but it has probably been eaten by rats.

To return to Borki manor, there was a circular bower (*altana*) and a quadrangle of 300-year-old lime trees behind the house. The area immediately around the house was full of charm: ponds and meadows stretched across the lower ground, while on the right and the northern side the fields were enveloped by wooded hills. The old grove extended almost around the house and was separated from it only by a narrow field. Located there was the mysterious 'Devil's Hill' surrounded by old pine trees where a summer picnic was sometimes organized for guests. I loved to wander in the forests armed with a revolver in my belt or with an air gun, or a knife and whistle. At the foot of 'Devil's Hill' we searched for glow worms or picked beautifully scented wild flowers. Wild nature held the charm of divine secrets, and the peasants were also sensitive to this. I fully understand therefore why ancient oaks were venerated as sacred objects;

they spoke of the eternity of God's creation. Among the peasants there survived the tradition of celebrating Kupała, a pagan god, with popular festivities involving bonfires on the hill tops. Christians later adopted this tradition and turned it into St John's Eve.[21] Near the road towards the Great Field, on an overgrown hillock, was a Yatwing burial ground.[22] Before the First World War, an archaeologist came from Moscow and dug up the graves. Apparently all the skulls lay in the same position and were of a longish shape.

There was a beautiful old pine forest separating the Great Field from Chadybowszczyzna, a nearby farm. I sometimes explored these mysterious places on horseback. Unfortunately my father had the forest cut down and gave the cleared land to the peasants in return for the abolition of their rights to use the common land pasture (the so-called *serwitut*) situated on the best soil of the Great Field.[23] After the First World War the Borki estate was 800 *desyatins* (2,112 acres) in size.[24] Before the emancipation of the peasants in 1861, it must have been at least 1,000 *desyatins* (2,750 acres) since an enormous area just behind the house was cleared for the use of the village. Thanks to this policy of the tsarist authorities, the Borki manor house was situated on the lower part of the estate and the manorial lands stretched in a semi-circle around the village lands for a distance of 3 km, ending with the common land (*serwitut*). This half-moon shaped estate was awkward to farm. After the ending of the *serwitut*, Borki had 660 *desyatins* (1,794 acres), including 200 *desyatins* of forest. Also beyond Rohotna there were over a dozen hectares of good meadow which belonged to us. In my grandfather's time there were outbuildings on the Great Field and an orchard of which only some old mulberry trees remained. We used to ride up there to feast on the sweet fruit. One year, I even amused myself by breeding silkworms, and every day a farmhand would bring mulberry leaves from the Great Field. I made no money out of this. The experimental station for the production of silk at Milanówek (west of Warsaw) gave me mere pennies for the silk cocoons.

After the First World War the harvested grain used to be brought up to the manor. It was only after my father's death in 1938 that we started the construction of separate farm buildings on the Great Field. In the planned division of the estate, I chose this piece because it was on higher ground in a better location. Chadybowszczyzna would probably have been sold to benefit Hania who, as a singer, had no desire to live in the country. Jula was to receive the manor house.

In the early post-war period, we also had to deal with the large numbers of wolves in our area. The wolves were hunted by being driven towards the guns; they were then trapped by long pieces of rope to which red ribbons were attached. There was something exciting and romantic about hunting. Many neighbours would join us, while Mamusia ordered the preparation of a large vat of superb *bigos* which was transported into the forest with supplies of vodka.[25] Countless numbers of beaters would be drafted in from the village; they were spread out in the forest and moved forward making a din with wooden rattles. From their appointed positions the hunters fired at whatever animals ran out of the trees; sometimes it was no more than a dozen hares or a fox. Once, some years later, I took part with a shotgun, but I missed a hare which then escaped ...

Later, wolves became more of a rarity, but the population of large wild boars increased instead. They would emerge from a state-owned forest near Słonim and raid our fields. Uncle Wilhelm Protassewicz's son Apoloniusz (Polik), the airforce instructor at Dęblin,[26] was an accomplished hunter; his great passion was hunting for wild boar. One summer, together with Tolik Stabrowski, his cousin on his mother's side, he killed thirty wild boar. I had several skins tanned and used them to embellish the floor in my 'blue' room where I slept and which I arranged as a hunter's den – this was after completing my secondary education in 1930. Through my aunt Jadzia Jamontt, I was also able to make contact with Pan Marylski, a traveller, who was in the process of selling his property which included a large collection of antelope heads and horns, snake skins and so on. I persuaded Witek Kontkowski, my cousin Mila Połubińska's husband, to buy this collection for about 300 złotys. He then presented me with a couple of antelope horns and snake skins which I displayed in my room.

Going back to the wild boar, we once had an extraordinary adventure. We were driving to church on Easter Day when a large herd of boars suddenly shot out from behind the cottage of the blacksmith's wife. The herd then rushed into the stream flowing from Ladzinki into our pond. Our horses reared and wanted to bolt. Seeing that the giant boar, large sow and the young boars had already rushed by, our coachman Adam passed the reins to us and jumped off the vehicle in an attempt to catch a pair of young piglets – which he failed to do. As a coachman, Adam had no equal. He was always elegantly dressed in navy blue livery (to match the coach) with red braid. There is no denying it, he was tall and handsome, blessed with a fine healthy complexion and for a coachman he had a lordly style. Indeed, he was the last coachman with style in the land of historic Lithuania. Mamusia remembered well the high standards maintained by her own father in his stables, and saw to it that Adam's livery was always *comme il faut*.

Adam was the only groom who still possessed the art of cracking his whip when approaching the manor. He kept the four coach horses in peak condition. We often used them to pull the coach during trips with my father, for instance to balls in Słonim or to meetings of local landowners. Adam solicitously looked after the splendid silver-embossed harness for six horses as we sometimes travelled with six horses for display when visiting neighbours. Once, when we had gone to a names-day party at the Gnoińskis in Wiszów, Adam was given a lot to drink. On the way back he was swaying in his saddle, to the horror of all the occupants of the coach, for it was impossible to jump out of the closed moving vehicle. Fortunately, the six horses reached the house by themselves by following the roads and crossing bridges. Tatuś was the last of the local gentry to travel in a coach after the First World War; he even managed to acquire a spare one. Here and there the odd coach had survived the wartime destruction, but no one possessed as fine a harnessed coach as we did. Some landowners either became totally impoverished and travelled any old how – most changed to travelling in a *bryczka* – or the wealthy ones, such as the Godlewskis, abandoned old habits for new, and acquired motor cars.

It so happened that during the First World War many beautiful and prosperous manors had been burnt down, such as Wiszów of the Gnoiński family. Many old landowners had also died. Their sons, many with their education unfinished, led lives with lower aspirations. They drank away their inheritance or incurred numerous debts which increased manifold during the Great Depression and brought about the financial collapse of their landed fortunes. Decline and general downfall was the characteristic of the landed class of our district in the post-war years. Bad times and eventual ruin even hit the Rohotna estate of the Wołłowiczes, once so self-confident and proud.[27] Except for such affluent people as the Strawińskis of Mirowszczyzna, who owned distilleries, or our more distant neighbours the Godlewskis of Synkowicze and Count Emeryk Hutten-Czapski in Synkowicze-Las, we enjoyed the highest financial and cultural status in the district.

With all the wars over, we were quickly able to prosper materially. Tatuś restored the two steam engines after recovering the moving parts of these machines from the lake. One steam engine powered the saw mill, which provided a large income, and even greater profits were generated by our grain mill, powered by the second engine. Watermills were cheaper, but after the war only a few remained, so most people in the neighbourhood brought their grain to us for milling. Tatuś also established a model carp farm which was to give him a large income.

In addition, we were very fortunate to have the assistance of a new estate administrator Pan Wincenty Wilniewszczyc, an upright man. Tatuś did not like subordinates who were too clever, and hence after exchanging a few sentences with him at the job interview he had decided not to employ Pan Wincenty. At this, tears appeared in Pan Wincenty's eyes – Tatuś gave in. Pan Wincenty was a young armigerous yeoman (*szlachcic zagrodowy*) who dreamt of becoming a priest, but his mother's small home farm did not bring in enough profit to enable him to enter a seminary. For a while he worked as a teacher before coming to us.

Observing this young man as a schoolchild, I came to the firm conclusion that there can exist such a thing as a divine calling for service in the priesthood. He turned out to be a resourceful administrator and Tatuś raised his monthly pay from 40 to 100 złotys. Years later Pan Wincenty was called back home by his elderly mother who wanted him to marry; he left with a wagon full of possessions. Apart from his paid work, he helped our farmhands to improve their reading and frequently recited his Latin, hoping that he might yet enter a seminary. He was also our moral confidant and kept a caring eye on us; for instance, he once appeared by the lakeside when we and our cousins took it into our heads to go boating by moonlight. He told us that it is better to love than to be loved, because being loved carries with it responsibilities and duties to the other person. Unfortunately, he was also an admirer of the books of Rodziewiczówna who in her novels instilled in her readers not only the love of one's ancestral soil but also the readiness to sacrifice all one's strength and even one's life to preserve one's patrimony.[28] In the period after the 1863–4 uprising, when the Russians confiscated so many landed estates, the sale of the land of one's fathers was regarded as tantamount to treason. This deeply held belief also nearly cost me my life when I remained in Borki in 1939 in order to 'watch over' our land.

Wincenty Wilniewszczyc abandoned any hope of finding personal happiness through an outlet for his soul in the priesthood precisely because it did not even enter his head to sell his smallholding to finance his education. And so he returned to his mother. Despite his mother's insistent pressure, it emerged that he had not married before the outbreak of war in 1939. I know this because my husband met him later, quite by chance, when he was an officer in General Anders's Army in Russia. We agreed as to his identity, because in the army he insisted that soldiers should always say grace before meals; it was his pious father who had instilled in him the belief that only pigs get down to their trough without praising the Creator. I do not know what happened to him subsequently. At any rate he was a shining light set against the background of the ignorant local Belarusians. Wincenty's departure coincided with the Great Depression, and he was to be succeeded by dishonest administrators. Never again was Tatuś to do so well financially as in the period around 1925.

Education, home and the stirrings of love

Convent school in Wilno – A pleasant year with Aunt Marynia Świackiewicz – Miseries of boarding school – Studies – Religion and attitudes to sex and fasting – Temporary loss of religious faith – Childhood and adolescence in Borki – The sculptor and matters of love

Mamusia and Aunt Kama Protassewicz of Rohotenka came to the conclusion that we, the children, could not be educated at home. In 1921, the decision was taken to send us to the school run by the Sisters of Nazareth in Wilno. It was felt that the state grammar school (*gimnazjum*) in Słonim was attended by the dregs of society. Nor was there any question of us being sent to the state *gimnazjum* in Wilno for fear of the bad moral influence of the youth there.[1] On the other hand, the convent school was comfortable and old-fashioned. At first, we lived in rather poor conditions with our elderly great-great-aunt Bronia Żórawska who lived in a dreadful slum-like street in the Skopówka district of central Wilno; food was supplied from home by Mamusia and Aunt Kama. Aunt Bronia's apartment was primitive in taste, and generated within me a sense of spiritual degradation and aesthetic suffering. The furniture in the drawing room had been moved to Borki after the death of Bronia's half-sister Ewarysta Żórawska. I have unpleasant memories of that year for by nature I cannot bear living in conditions of cave-like ugliness. It was also a long way to the school: we had to walk the whole length of Mickiewicz Street uphill, and then turn left into Piaskowa Street where the school buildings were situated.[2]

The standard of education we had received at home from resident tutors was inferior to that offered at the convent school; French, for instance, with its awful grammar, was taught at the school to a high standard by a demanding red-haired female teacher. But we were clearly able, for I soon joined the top stream. I was in the same class as Aunt Kama's daughter Mila.[3] At a time when my sisters and I were little more than small, uninteresting girls, she was like a doll with beautiful features, exuberant charm and an incomparable complexion. Somehow she already had the appearance of a young lady. Furthermore, she possessed a rare talent for relating each lesson afterwards as if it were some lovely story. I well remember how the nature studies teacher gazed with delight at this thirteen-year-old girl when she was called up to the blackboard and answered questions in a stream of vivid words, with the full conceited consciousness of her charm and eloquence. Later, however, Aunt Kama transferred her to Słonim, due to lack of funds, I think, since the school of the Sisters of Nazareth was expensive. In the meantime, Jula and I continued at the convent school as the steam-powered mill in Borki was still generating a healthy income.

During my third year, when I was still a day pupil, I spent a pleasant time living with Aunt Marynia Świackiewicz, my father's elder sister. She was very good-looking and family-oriented by nature, but also a worldly lady from high society. She had rejected one suitor, whom she found attractive but who was a rake, and instead, at the age of seventeen, married her wealthy cousin Aleksander Świackiewicz because, as she explained, she preferred to wipe her tears in a grand carriage. They had two sons and two daughters. Aunt Marynia had frequently travelled abroad with her children, having first obtained a medical certificate (to show to her husband) that such travel was essential for her health.

Aunt Marynia's apartment was located in a courtyard on Garbarska Street, not far from Cathedral Square.[4] Its drawing room had beautiful old-fashioned furniture and was adorned with paintings and rich brocade door-curtains, perhaps originating from the manor house in Dębinki. Displayed in the living room were albums with photographs of foreign journeys and of her late husband's estates. Aunt Marynia left her estates to her sons, while Dębinki had to be sold after her husband's death (in 1903) because of disastrous mismanagement by the land steward. The remaining rooms of the apartment were somewhat cluttered with thousands of odds and ends. Aunt Marynia had a small separate bedroom decorated with beautiful boudoir pictures; there was also a variety of old-fashioned screens and porcelain ewers. I have to admit that I found some of the baroque or rococo style in her home oppressive and stifling. Nonetheless, Jula and I were very happy with our aunt. She extended to us a family love characteristic of all Protassewiczes who were, in general, devoid of egotism. But the food at Aunt Marynia's was much worse than in Borki, for there were still many post-war shortages, and it was difficult to bring all supplies from the country. Once I gave a cabbage as a present to our kindly maths teacher, an elderly lady who lived in some crowded street – such were the conditions then. Despite this, Aunt Marynia never lost her old, lady-like spirit.

As a widow, Aunt Marynia lived independently in Wilno, and spent her inexhaustible energy on social life and community welfare work. During the fighting against the Bolsheviks in 1919, she was in charge of feeding wounded soldiers in the Wilno hospital. I saw a splendid photograph of her wearing a white apron, standing next to cousin Kazio Protassewicz who was then serving in the Polish Army and undergoing treatment for a deep wound to his hand. Later, she was very actively engaged with the so-called Vincentines, a Catholic charitable society, who looked after an old people's home. At the same time, she showed great talent as a hospitable lady of society. Wilno's entire elite attended her name-day party on 2 February, starting with pompous handsome prelates in purple and ending with Wacław Iszora, the governor of the Wilno district, who was to remember me from that occasion and who ten years later wanted to marry me. But my nature made me unsuitable for that role. I was rather a suffragette type. I was seeking Love, rather than the position of wife of a district governor, a role that required one to be responsible for running a home to a high standard. Aunt Marynia's son always brought along supplies of ducks, turkeys, hams and patés. With the help of a servant, my aunt would prepare *faworki*[5] and doughnuts. Various side dishes, such as fish in aspic, were also prepared in the home. Although her drawing room was not large, there was enough space for dancing mazurkas, obereks, polonaises and waltzes – which swept everyone into a whirl of delight.

A later resident in Aunt Marynia's apartment was our charming cousin Wicio (Witold) Pilecki, a student of fine arts at the university.[6] He was blond, slim, outgoing and full of vigour, cheerfulness and verve. His hobby was drawing with charcoal and chalk, and many of his sketches adorned our aunt's walls. He once said that he had the feeling that he would perish in a war, but I could never have envisaged that instead of a lancer's death on a battlefield, he was to suffer great tortures. As a member of the Home Army (AK),[7] he volunteered in 1940 to infiltrate Auschwitz in order to organize resistance within the concentration camp. Later he was dispatched from Italy to Poland by General Anders; after three years of torment in a communist jail, he was shot by the UB (the Polish communist security police).[8]

Living with Aunt Marynia on Garbarska Street, I was fortunate to be able to accompany her to High Mass in Wilno cathedral where we heard Władysław Bandurski, the inspired bishop of the Legions, preach from a suspended pulpit. Even small children are capable of sensing the genius of a soul specially favoured by God. Bishop Bandurski was the reincarnation of Skarga, the great sixteenth-century preacher, and at the same time a true saint.[9]

Figure 3. Irena in class 4 at the convent school run by the Sisters of Nazareth in Wilno, 1924.

After our stay with Aunt Marynia, our parents transferred us to the school as boarders. The fees for boarding and lessons amounted to something in the region of 180 złotys; with personal expenses it was 200 złotys per month for each of us (we were joined later by little Hania). As a boarder with the Sisters of Nazareth, I had to attend Sunday worship in the convent, and those first moving experiences in the cathedral soon faded into the past. I was hidden away behind convent walls, and everything that was human was made alien. There was nothing else but boarding and strict discipline; it was not always possible to leave the prep room after finishing homework. Having led an exuberant life in Borki, where slides, horse riding or boating brought one closer to nature and gave one a sense of freedom, I now found myself in a prison. At night I cried for my lost freedom, but it was impossible to escape. Tatuś was worried that living privately we might be in danger of getting run over by a horse-cab. There was money, so for the sake of safety we were put into a convent; thus, our joy of youth was lost.

How fondly I remember the pleasant times we had earlier spent with Aunt Marynia: we used to go for walks in the park, and in winter, when all the lanes were covered with ice, we would skate in the company of large groups of young people and to the sound of a live band! Now, two years older, we were not allowed to go anywhere alone; outside the convent we had to go in pairs under the supervision of a nun. Furthermore, I was never able to get used to barrack life and to being driven like a sheep. The food was also unpalatable: the cocoa was watery, the bread thinly spread with butter. We were not even allowed to have our own apples, although they were good for us. Indeed, fruit rarely appeared on our dining tables, and any apples sent from home were immediately distributed among all the pupils. I was anaemic and undernourished, and having tasted delicious home cooking I found it difficult to swallow the unknown stews or the thick cereals (*krupy*) served with plums. Awful Galician cuisine, I thought to myself.

On one occasion, by chance, I happened to enter a room where the religious supervisor had just been served dinner. I saw a splendid cut of roast meat served with a generous helping of currants. I was shocked and outraged by this, for I realized that unappetizing food was served only to the pupils, although one paid heftily for it. The principles of the Catechism were instilled in us; one of these principles was that to backbite and to criticize was a sin. Determined never to commit such a sin by complaining to my parents, I continued to suffer eating such tasteless meals. It sometimes happened that a cockroach fell from the inside of the dumb waiter onto the food itself. With my lips sealed, I could not speak about this either. My sister Jula enjoyed better health than I did; she ate everything and felt happy in the organized life of the convent. Her favourite saint was Saint Teresa. Jula slept well; she played at school performances; and she had a good friend, Ola. On the other hand, I was nervous and weak and found it difficult to fall asleep while, night after night, the other girls in the dormitory continued whispering in bed after lights out. Our beds were also hard. I was always short of sleep. I dreamt of being able sometimes to sit comfortably on a sofa or lie on a bed with a book. To enter the dormitory in daytime was out of the question; we had to be at school all day long. Having to sit on hard benches even after completing one's prep was sheer agony. I sometimes felt that my head would drop off, and my back hurt. I was academically gifted and it took me only half an hour to complete my homework. My body yearned for movement, but I had to remain seated at the desk because other girls were still doing their work. It was then that I wrote my first poem about freedom and Borki, where 'No-one imprisons you, no-one forces you to do anything; / where everyone cries out: you are a Free Spirit'.[10] Hania made a scene in front of our parents so they transferred her to the Ursuline Sisters where the regime was milder, and she started attending their *lycée*. I did not want to worry my parents and continued to suffer torments as a boarder.

I boarded again in my fifth year and had to endure the physical misery brought about by the unsuitability of my delicate health to the rigours of barrack-like life and by the insipid food which completely killed my appetite. On the other hand, I felt much better spiritually because during this period we had a Mother Superior who possessed personal charm and created feelings of family warmth and confidence, so indispensable for a child's spiritual equilibrium. The headmistress was also charming and motherly. Later came a new Mother Superior, short in height and cold in personality, the incarnation of the letter of canon law. Being sensitive, I began to suffocate in the new atmosphere of chilly and impersonal discipline. Boarding ceased to bear any similarity to family life; I felt I had been banished. Then a new headmistress arrived, an American, intellectually interesting but rather masculine. She introduced educational methods more reminiscent of a military cadet school. Mentally, this was the final straw for me. The remaining years spent there were a torment.

My constant slight temperature meant that there was a one-year break in my schooling after I had finished the fifth class; on medical advice, my parents took me back home to recuperate. At last I was back, among wild but beautiful surroundings! When I returned to school after my year's absence at home, it was not as a boarder: I now lived in Aunt Salunia Połubińska's house on Wielka Pohulanka Street,[11] not far from the school. I was delighted with the arrangement of her home which was full of elegant furniture, simple but artistic in its design, while the splendid high windows and ceilings created the sensation of a third spiritual dimension. There I felt happy. Aunt Salunia, my father's second sister, was a puritan and the family's female philosopher. She sternly disapproved of her worldly elder sister Marynia ever since the episode in their youth when she had observed Marynia secretly applying some light rouge to her already beautiful and youthful face. Once, under the influence of a deeply religious aunt who had looked after her upbringing, Salunia even wanted to become a nun. Aunt Salunia's religiosity was not expressed by frequent 'running' to attend church services, but in the depth of her experiences. She was equally puritanical in her manners, a quality which arose, I later concluded, from a simple lack of temperament. Her husband Mieczyś Połubiński[12] adored her and spent a fortune on curing her from tuberculosis by sending her repeatedly to health resorts in Switzerland and on the Adriatic coast. But she always remained delicate, as did her daughter Mila who herself was nursed all her youth. Suffering from poor health by nature, they all clung to domestic tranquility and immersed themselves in the world of books.

I was also always enchanted by Wilno, the Polish Athens and the city of Gedymin.[13] My memories and associations with the city are manifold. Wilno in winter: skating on ice in Skaraszewski Park. Wilno on 4 March: the colourful *Kaziuk* (St Casimir) fair which fascinated us as children. Wilno in the summer meant wonderful school river trips in June to Werki, the eighteenth-century residence of the Catholic bishops of Wilno, and the nearby pine forests. Wilno in the winter also meant Osterwa's theatre. I doubt whether anyone who has not lived through Osterwa's performances in the Great Theatre on Wielka Pohulanka[14] can ever understand what it means to be enraptured by art, to be in ecstasy and at the same time to be torn apart by all the sufferings worthy of a Judym or a Werther.[15] The menfolk preferred to watch lighter plays in the theatre on Mickiewicz Street as a form of relaxation after work.[16] Women, on the other hand, including Aunt Salunia's daughter Mila, sought greater depth which would fill their quiet domestic lives. Later, after I had finished school and had settled permanently in Borki, and right up to the outbreak of war in 1939, I would occasionally receive invitations from Aunt Salunia to come to Wilno in order to see this or that play in the theatre on Wielka Pohulanka.

I studied hard at school, and the new battleaxe headmistress who was in love with classical culture succeeded in implanting the same enthusiasm in our minds. I remember what a thrilling experience it was to work through Shakespeare's *Julius Caesar*. But this classical atmosphere was a little too pagan, and the Order instructed the headmistress to go on a long 'retreat'. She refused and left the Order. Many years later, after the Second World War, my old school friend Myszka Malinowska wrote to me that the headmistress later returned to convent life in the United States with one of my school friends (once an unruly and rebellious person), and died there.

I never liked any games. Cards bored me, and I could on no account force myself to concentrate on chess. However, I was deeply moved by the delights of the inner harmony of Horace, and I relished in reciting the works of classical poets, such as 'Exegi monumentum aere perenius'.[17] I was fascinated with classical prose, so full of logic which was victoriously deployed in the struggle for the domination of minds on paper, through the medium of the ear. I cannot forgive myself for having neglected my Latin for the past forty years and, as a consequence, for having completely forgotten it. Had I dipped into my school textbooks even a few times a year, I would have retained the language in my memory, as has been the case with my French. I use French rarely now but returning to it now and then has enabled me, after so many years, to read easily and to understand French works.

Nature study was of a poor standard and was taught only in the lower classes, as a less important subject. Originally, we had a male teacher. Then came a quiet and melancholic lady, of a dull disposition and appearance. The poor thing, probably well aware of her own unattractiveness, apparently drowned herself in the river Wilja out of despair because no one loved her. I cannot forget this tragedy. Our maths teacher, in class eight, was the pleasant and elderly Pani Daszkiewicz. I liked mathematics, algebra and physics. History too: in class eight it was taught by Pan Puciata, who was tall and thin like Sancho Panza. His namesake was the previous classics teacher, Father Leon Puciata, who once brought some reproductions of classical works of art from Rome. With the approval of the headmistress, but to the indignation of the puritanical Sisters, he displayed them in the corridors of the school.

The school chapel was pleasant and full of flowers. The chaplain, Father Jan Kozak, was slim and Christ-like in appearance. He officiated at the marriage of my cousin

Halina Przybytko to Daniel Kostrowicki and at the marriage of my sister Jula to Janek Karczewski; of course, being kind and unselfishly devoted to his mission, he did not charge anything for his services. In some ways he was a true tutor and pedagogue, and his lectures had some valuable qualities, but otherwise he exerted a harmful influence on my psyche. His pedantry, exactitude and precision in everything generated in me qualms of religious conscience and removed the freedom of inner development, while church rules bristled all over with venial sins. For example, teaching us once about the wording of Baptism (which I was later to find useful in Russia), Father Kozak mentioned that the word 'Amen' should be omitted at the end because it was contrary to regulations and would be a venial sin.

I also suffered much harm from the pious books of devotion which we used to read in the convent. I recollect the life of one female saint who was punished by God with purgatory for having looked at the beauty of her hands; I recollect also that this saint had a vision of millions of people pouring into hell and only very few, rarely, entering heaven. Such material created in my soul the image of a cruel and not a merciful God, to the extent that walking once near one of our ponds I thought that if God was so terrible then it would be better to drown myself. I consider the distortion of the image of God, and the representation of God as someone little different from an executioner of the Inquisition, to be the greatest heresy; it was this heresy which was inculcated into us during lessons of religious instruction. Can there be a greater affront to God than a parody of Him? Even now I still sometimes find I cannot rid my subconscious of the spiritual wounds which I had incurred in the convent, particularly as a result of reading the lives of saints. That is why I would like to see the day when it is forbidden to give such literature to children.

With their puritanism, the Sisters also deformed a healthy approach to the body and to sex. Wearing flesh-coloured stockings was a sin, while holding a man's hand was no less than a mortal sin. At the school ball, the girls had to dance together or with their male teachers, which looked comical since watching us all around were numerous acquaintances and relatives. The body was evidently the work of Satan; sex also his invention – and not created by God. The slightest deviation from the sixth commandment, whether in thought, look or behaviour, was a mortal sin; for this, one went to hell. In the countryside I encountered what I then regarded as the primitive naturalism of the peasants, and these two contrasts were not conducive to the formation of a balanced view on matters of sex.

When I was in class eight, our parents lodged us with the Byszewski family who lived near the school. The food there was not tasty because everything was fried in some cheap and horrible margarine or oil; but the rissoles (*kotlety*) made from brain were excellent. There, I also met the future musician Jeśman, a delightful pupil of short stature who attended the School of Music. Wanda, the daughter of the Byszewskis, was taking singing lessons and later, in Borki, taught us how to sing. She had a strong but terribly shrill voice. Also living in that house was Antoni Gołubiew, the future writer who looked mysterious in his student cap,[18] and Antoni Maruszkin, a law student who had a lovely tenor singing voice. We (that is, my sister Hania and I) were secretly in love first with Jeśman; and then Maruszkin won all our hearts. We once invited Maruszkin to Borki where he sang beautifully to Mamusia's accompaniment. It is a pity that he did not marry Hania, who was then head over heels in love with him. Perhaps then her spiritual life would have developed along a deeper path, for Maruszkin was a very worthy and religious person of integrity. I think he was subsequently a judge in Postawy or some such place.

Shortly before the outbreak of war, by chance, I visited the school for some meeting of former pupils; it was a time when Jola Kontkowska, the daughter of Mila Połubińska, had started attending the school. Two Sisters appeared at the meeting: the Mother Superior and the headmistress. Both were slim, beautiful aristocratic ladies, full of goodness, cheerfulness and moderation – what a contrast to my unhappy time at the school. I understood then, in the light of what seven-year-old Jola revealed to me, that she adored these Sisters. I was overwhelmed then by a sense of sorrow for the lost happiness of my childhood days there, and by a sense of envy that it was not given to me to end my school days in such a spiritual atmosphere. Let us not mince words: every system of morals and of religiosity is repellent and oppressive unless it is enveloped with external personal charm and grace, that scent of the inner soul.

At the centre of the world of religion was an obsession with fasting. Not once during a sermon did I ever hear a priest speak about problems such as the welfare of servants, or about taking a piece of rarely seen bacon to hungry families in the countryside during the period of penitential fasting of Holy Week, or bringing something else for the numerous children. Instead, during Lent, whole hours were spent on announcements, issued with the full authority of the church, of precise instructions: that it is forbidden to taste meat even once on Wednesdays, Fridays and Saturdays; that on other weekdays meat can be served only once; but that on Sundays it could be eaten as one wished. The preoccupation with what enters the stomach overshadowed all other aspects of Christianity, although it was Christ himself who said: 'not what goes into the mouth defiles a man, but what comes out of the mouth, this defiles a man'.[19] Earlier, in my great-aunts' lifetime, it was even worse: there was strict fasting for seven weeks.[20] This tradition survived for a long time as an obsession among the peasants. Peasant women who were exhausted, short of sleep, continually breastfeeding or pregnant, starved themselves and their children during Lent. *Cui bono?* I myself observed how peasant women would scrupulously buy oil (instead of using butter), and if that was lacking they would sprinkle puréed linseed on potatoes served for the family. And one old Polish woman – Pani Jałowiecka, who today lives next door in Quinton – told me how in her district of eastern Poland all the milk used to be turned into cheese which was then dried on shelves, because even children were not allowed to eat noodle soup with milk during Lent. I include this among the scandals of applied Christianity, modelled on sadistic hermits who wanted to do penance in order to overcome their sexual urges with such discipline.

Peasant women, sensitive to religious romanticism, found an outlet for their natural emotions in religious singing in church; their prayerful wailing at the feet of the Mother of God gave them relief from the crushing burden of ceaseless pregnancies, broken nights and so many other misfortunes experienced in the lives of women. The men were healthier and stronger; even during the exhausting period of the harvest, they did not give their wives respite at night, arousing sometimes in their wives' hearts a hatred of their ruthlessness. The men were also more sceptical in matters of religion which, in their minds, was identified with fasting and with the tribute paid to the priest every year on the occasion of their children's baptism, or with greater offerings at weddings or funerals. The church did little to prepare the Belarusian peasants spiritually for the challenges of modern times; its priests were indifferent to social problems, and treated their parishioners as a source of income in return for carrying out liturgical rites. Let us hope that devotion to Mary may preserve something of Christianity in those parts during the present dark night of Soviet rule.

In my view, parish priests need first to have basic instincts of humanity, such as sensitivity to human poverty, developed during their time in seminaries; only then should the letter of canon law be crammed into their minds. Sometimes the very opposite happened. It took one sentence from a bishop's mouth directed at our kindly parish priest in Rohotna, Father Goj, to kill in him his spiritual idealism and sow the seeds of materialism. Father Goj told me with what earnestness he had been approaching his future mission, and the church as God's throne on earth. After completing his studies at the seminary, he was summoned by the bishop and informed that he would receive his first parish. The bishop added that Father Goj should be pleased because it was a wealthy – that is, a profitable – parish. The kindly little man was shocked and blushed at the mention of this fact, as if someone had hit him in the face. Such an introduction to administering a parish flock exerted, over the years, a pernicious influence. However, our parish priest was no longer aware of it when he considered it quite normal to demand 1,000 złotys for Tatuś's funeral. The funeral took place in the country, where a plot in the cemetery and other necessities cost nothing. Kazio Protassewicz was hard put to persuade the priest to lower his fee to 700 złotys. To press for a further reduction seemed improper, since Kazio had given in to Father Goj's argument that 'he [Father Goj] would never again in his life have the opportunity to bury a gentleman of such substance'. Father Goj admired Tatuś, but because of this, felt he had an almost filial claim to 'a drop from his legacy …'. But do such methods assist with the spreading of the Gospel? I doubt it.[21]

Another telling episode comes to mind. There lived in Sanniki, a village just to the west of Borki, a lonely old cobbler by the name of Wincenty who once, during the presence of the Soviets (in 1939–41), repaired some shoes for me for nothing. He was such a kind and fair man, and I was puzzled why he never attended church. I learnt the reason. He began to tell me how during the first Bolshevik occupation in 1920 he appeared at the presbytery and offered to save the priest's horse from the Bolsheviks. The poor man spent three weeks sleeping in the forest, suffering from cold and hunger. The Bolsheviks left and, looking haggard but triumphant, he led the uninjured horse back to the parish. The priest took the horse and, in recognition of all of Wincenty's efforts, said just one word: 'thanks'. Wincenty was left standing in the courtyard. This very likeable priest was not ungenerous in his dealings with the peasantry, but clearly considered that every parishioner should be satisfied merely with an expression of the word 'thanks'.

Monasteries also permeated with materialism. Kazio Protassewicz told me how, when he was already a district governor, he had been informed that the inmates in a certain orphanage were being poorly fed. In the manner of Premier Składkowski, he made an unannounced inspection of that institution during dinner time. First, he demanded entry into the nuns' dining room. There he found the nuns quite happily tucking into all sorts of titbits given to them as presents by devout landed ladies. Next, he went into the children's dining hall and observed that the food there was quite poor. He rebuked the nuns with great force, whereupon the nuns began to explain that they were eating all the delicacies by themselves since each of the donors sent, for instance, only a couple of small jars of mushrooms or preserved fruit, and there was not enough to divide equally among all the orphans. The nuns therefore ate the delicacies themselves in order not to favour only some of the children. And so the poor orphans were never to discover the taste of preserved fruit, because to maintain justice and equality among the children, the nuns devoured the treats themselves. But let us not be unfair to the generality of the clergy by citing such examples. They were people who approached their work with devotion and self-sacrifice; perhaps the enjoyment of the little titbits sugared their difficult life, which was full of work and which was deprived of the greatest good, namely that of a family life. We complain about materialistic priests or at the defects of nuns, but it is thanks to them, and despite their shortcomings, that the continuity of Christian learning has been preserved; it is probable that, in a state of dispersal and without such an ecclesiastical organization, this learning would not have reached our times.

Although by nature I was inclined to self-denial and asceticism, and would give any tasty morsel of food to my children instead of eating it myself, my artistic side rejected a hair-shirted existence in ugly surroundings. Once, in exchange for two pine trees from the grove, I ordered a dressing table to be built for use in my room as well as a decorated bed made out of a nut tree. Uncle Leon from Belweder was scandalized by my actions as he felt this was contrary to what the Gospels preach; yet he himself, in one year, smoked cigarettes to the value of several pine trees, and considered this as natural because it did not bring beauty and aesthetics to one's surroundings. His actions were therefore not an expression of ostentation bordering on wickedness. External ugliness was considered a virtue. Even an ordinary bee is an artist when it makes its honeycomb. One is overwhelmed when looking through a telescope, and even more so through a microscope, when the smallest cells are visible in their unending artistry. I rebelled against the idea of God as expressed by pillar saints, flagellators and saints mortifying their body with dirt and asceticism. I found confirmation for my internal intuition in Słowacki's poem: 'I see that He is not only the God of worms / And of creatures that creep and crawl upon the dust. / He likes the booming flight of great birds; / Does not bridle wild horses.'[22] With this maxim in the background, I was able, from then on, to understand the beauty of man's spirit and of his body. I was drawn to people of genius, and disgusted by limited narrow minds even if they were the most orthodox in their Catholicism – and perhaps even more so on account of it.

Although I have always possessed a natural religious predisposition, I lost my religious faith when I was in the sixth class at school. It happened after I had bought my own copy of the Gospels, and when I reached the section on the Pharisees, those who extort the homes of widows.[23] In a flash, I perceived all village priests precisely like a new version of the Pharisees, and I became doubtful of their teaching, suspecting that the priests had falsified the pure message of the Gospels into one of profit. And my spiritual world collapsed entirely one Sunday as I was returning from church through

Sanniki village. I heard terrible crying and wailing coming from one of the cottages. I stopped and asked what was happening: it emerged that the father of a large family had died. I observed with my own eyes the priest's plump farmhand calmly leading away the distressed family's remaining calf from their cowshed, as payment to the priest for the funeral. It was only *The Foundations of Christianity* by the communist Kautsky, a book I came across by chance sometime later, which enabled me to accept the historicity of Christ and set me on the path to seek for myself the Profundity of fundamental truths.[24] Nonetheless, when I left school I felt that my mouth was gagged, that my brain was fettered and that my heart was squeezed as if in a vice. I was spiritually much too subjugated to be able to find another way out except to suppress within me all doubts, even if just to avoid corrupting the 'little ones' and to avoid the disapprobation of my superiors. I envied those of my school friends who were so naively devout and happy, and who had no intellectual-religious problems. It was only during the Second Vatican Council (1962–5) that my soul recovered its freedom and I reclaimed the right to my own brain and to my own conscience.

Although my school days were not always happy, life at home as a child and adolescent had its drawbacks. All my life I delighted in the beauty of Borki, the manor house, and its setting in the midst of venerable lime trees and girdled by forests; but it did bring about problems for my outlook on life. Living in the country with my parents, as natives of the region and independent of anyone else, gave one freedom in the primitive surroundings in which we lived, but it did not prepare us for life in an urban civilization. Jula was also affected by this, and always felt at a loss after she married and went to live in ugly Warsaw. Every year as soon as May arrived, she would escape to this sea of sweet-scented bird cherry trees and to the singing nightingales in the park. I too could not have been happy if I had married a townsman. On the other hand, living in the country would have meant an emptiness for the mind and the lowering of one's sights to matters merely economic. That is why I feel so well now in England, because here towns blend in with the countryside; living far from the smells and bustle of streets, I can still easily travel to town for books and shopping. I also had a difficult life on account of my weak health. I was constantly worn down by throat infections, and it was only after finishing my *matura* (secondary education certificate) that my parents decided to send me to hospital to have my tonsils removed. The tonsils were full of cavities and the hotbed of infections that caused frequent bouts of fever.

Despite my pleasant life with the family in the country, I was nevertheless condemned to complete intellectual loneliness. My parents, happy in each other's company, kept us at a distance according to the precepts of upbringing of that time: the children's place was in the children's room. Mamusia did not like to favour her own children and did not permit us to complain about others. The result was that I experienced all my pains of childhood in complete isolation, forced to rely on myself alone. I wept in loneliness since there was no one to whom I could turn. Other mothers always stood up for their children; whereas, if we started to complain about some event, instead of defending us, Mamusia immediately would shout at us that complaining was disgraceful and so on, give us a slap and that was that. Once when I asked her where children come from, she related a story about the stork, which I did not believe; as a result I lost trust in my mother, assuming that she was hiding something and that this something could be immoral. It is difficult to imagine what a burden it is for a child to hew out by herself knowledge of the facts of life without having the close and emotional support of her mother; to learn these things by overhearing whispers of the servants or of peasant children. The issue of sex was taboo in the family, and taboo in the convent school. Knowledge acquired secretly carried with it the stamp of a forbidden fruit or sin, while everything that came from the mouths of peasant children sounded coarse and left an aesthetic distaste.

At home we were always treated like children and had no voice at all in decision-making, even as adolescent young ladies. Mamusia's maxim, probably inherited from her despotic father, was that 'children and fish have no voice'. This was not at all helpful in developing any independent standpoint when facing life. It affirmed in us naivety and immaturity, all the more so since no conversations were held in our presence that dealt with events of doubtful morality or about scandals in society. It was from other quarters and much later that I supplemented my knowledge of the 'reality' of life in such matters. I remained in this state of unreality until war flung me, in a brutal manner, out from my 'home oasis' into the wider world. My encounter with unfamiliar surroundings in Wilno sharpened my critical judgement, because it created comparisons, but I was never quite able to get rid of my naivety.

As I grew older, my loneliness became greater, because each one of us had a different temperament. Jula had the qualities of a 'domestic hen'. Her approach to everything was practical: she was not particularly interested in reading books and was scared to go into the forest. Hania was five years younger than I was; she possessed an artistic soul and was Mamusia's favourite. Already at the age of twelve she could easily work out by ear the accompaniment to dance melodies; she had perfect pitch and dreamt one day of becoming a singer. With Mamusia she lived in a world of music and harmony. Being less gifted in this respect, I was unable to break into the orbit of their world. After leaving school at the age of seventeen, Hania went to live in Warsaw to study singing under Wacław Brzeziński,[25] and was able to establish herself as a professional singer, choosing the name 'Borey' after Borki. Mamusia played Chopin beautifully, and I sometimes accompanied her on the piano, not showing much talent at it, while she played on the violin. Jula's fingers moved deftly among the piano keys, but she never reached the level of Art with a capital A. Today, she earns a living by playing at dances and in schools, or by singing while playing the piano; but it is not great artistry, only an aptitude. Hania spent most of her time at the piano or pottering about the house; she never had the courage to go into the forest for fear of the wolves. And so I used to go to the forest alone, equipped with a whistle and a knife, because there was no one else with such rather boyish interests.

On one occasion, during our school holidays, I was alone in the forest of Chadybowszczyzna, to the south of the house. I happened to hear something rustling. Thinking that it was some woman stealing mushrooms, I turned around; just beyond a fir tree I noticed an enormous he-wolf. Terror wrung my heart. I overcame my fear, but I had nothing with me other than my knife which I had brought along to cut some mushrooms. But I had my whistle. I started to blow it, all the time looking to see if the wolf would attack me. I was no more than ten steps from him and afraid to move. At the sound of the whistle, the wolf turned around and started to move into the centre of the copse. I shot out of the forest onto peasant fields as fast as my legs could carry me, and then ran like mad, occasionally glancing back. Our house was about 3 km away, but I reached the road, and there I felt safer.

On another occasion, also in a grove, I spotted an entire flock of tiny grey chicks on the ground. I had scarcely bent down to catch one of them when I heard a rustle. An enormous dark grey bird the size of a turkey, probably a capercaillie, was rushing at me with its wings fully spread in fury. I aimed my air rifle at the bird in case it attacked me. But when it was no more than three steps from me, the bird leapt sideways. I then turned to look at the chicks; there was no trace of them, nor of their mother.

Once, also during my schooldays, I set out at night into the forest with my Morski cousins from Poznań who used to come to Rohotenka for the summer.[26] We took a puppy with us and then squeezed its neck to see if its squealing would attract a wolf. Nothing happened, and so in the end, quite frightened, we ran back home. Gienio Morski, who had recently returned from Russia with his parents, was strongly Russified, as was his brother Henryk. Gienio would often recite Pushkin's poems and those of other Russian poets in his beautiful, resounding voice. He also penned his own poems and enjoyed hunting, and we girls idolized him. I remember him declaiming while standing in the thicket of the park in Rohotenka; all the young people present listened intently with bated breath to the beauty of the poetry. He hunted birds professionally and sold them stuffed to various scientific collections in Poznań. With the help of an enormous encyclopaedia he brought from Russia, he had learnt how to recognize every type of bird. He once shot and wounded a giant eagle; not wanting to damage its skin with another shot, he started to gouge out its brain with a needle. We were horrified by this act of cruelty, but at the same time were amazed by the pride of the bird which stood fiercely, held by its wings, and did not move, suffering in silence and in dignity. In its inner self it remained the unconquered ruler of the skies.

One day (around the year 1927) we were visited by my cousin Halina Jamontt; she was aged sixteen and very beautiful.[27] I was struck by her exuberant good looks. She slept in my room above the porch. For us, buried in the Belarusian countryside, she was a vision from another world, some sort of goddess with her long plaits reaching the ground, and with her elegant female figure. She was strong and athletic, and went skiing in Zakopane and rode on horseback. At the same time, she was girlish and full of romantic charm. I could not take my eyes off her. For me, she was the personification of the 'Great World Beyond', for she often travelled with her mother to various spas, to the seaside, to the mountains and all the places frequented by Warsaw's rich elite. Although her mother, my aunt Jadzia, had been forced to agree to divorce her husband-cousin (the barrister Maciej Jamontt), she continued to receive from him vast sums of money in order to enable her and her daughter to maintain an appropriately high standard of living. Much taller than her mother, Halina was a modern version of Diana, the goddess of hunting. Never having met anyone like this before, Gienio Morski fell in love with her at first sight. She was pressured to address him by his first name, for he was a sort of relative, although, as she disclosed to us, she had first consulted her horoscope to see what might befall her. Then, out of the blue, Aunt Jadzia arrived from Warsaw, descending on Borki like some royal hawk. In time she sensed the atmosphere and tone of adoration in the conduct of the 'cousin'. 'This is a scandal. A misalliance could very well come from this', she announced to all and sundry in Borki, and with great clamour she whisked Halina away into the unknown.

Sometime later, Gienio wrote a satirical poem about us. This was after we had returned to the convent school and when my sisters and I decided to address him as 'Pan', because it was improper not to do so. He also mentioned Halina in this poem: 'and another had the name Halina – I like that name very much. Yet I do not know whose fault it is that this friendship brought about ill …'. And spitefully about me: 'Irenka was of a different mind, within her love of nature throbbed. Now that Irenka is no more, now a bigot stares from her'. That was the end of our romantic adventures with Gienio, who at one time was also a little in love with me – he would have eyes only for me when reading poetry. Later, I too was a little in love with him, but on the quiet so that he would not suspect it. However, my sister Jula revealed her interest in him openly. Realizing that, after all, it was Halina Jamontt who had enraptured Gienio, Jula made a scene and had it out with Halina in the children's room. She drove Halina into a corner with the words: 'Do you love him? If not, then don't get in my way, because I'm in love with him'. Horrified, Halina did not know how to respond to such a demand; somehow she extricated herself diplomatically. After Halina's departure, we all forgot about our Shakespearian *Midsummer Night's Dream*, and Gienio sank into the shadows of oblivion, until Tadeusz Stulgiński, the future sculptor, one of cousin Leoś' friends, came to visit us …

I found myself very much interested in Tadeusz's unusually rich personality, his talent (he had just made a bust of Tatuś), his integrity, his generous character and his intellect. A bond developed between us. Tatuś and Mamusia quietly observed the unfolding of events with Tadeusz and, thinking highly of him, were not opposed to our friendship. Who knows, it might have led one day to marriage had it not been for the indoctrination I had received at the convent. All feelings of attraction to the opposite sex struck my conscience as a Sin – with a capital S. Within myself I fought to suppress the feeling that I was increasingly attracted to him. In the end I burnt his photograph which had caused such anxiety in my heart. Once, Jula (aged thirteen) had a childhood crush on Jurek Bartoszewicz of Izmajłowszczyzna (a nearby farm) and wrote a letter to him from the convent, addressing him as 'Darling Jurek' and ending with the words: 'I kiss you 100 times a 100'. She presented this letter to the religious tutor, who was also her confessor, for censoring. 'What', he remarked, 'do you wish to marry him?' 'Marry him? But I'm not even thinking about that', replied Jula. 'In that case cross out the words "Darling" and "100 times a 100"'. Jurek, who was far away in Warsaw, was so distressed that he started to smoke cigarettes, and by the time summer came his love for Jula had been stifled. I too, despite the fact I was already eighteen, stifled my love in a similar way and, it seemed, with effect. After he had completed his secondary schooling, Tadeusz unexpectedly appeared in Borki to formally propose to me. Suddenly, I felt all my attraction disappear. I was therefore very sad when he wanted to kiss me and I froze in silence like a stone. All he said was: 'You don't love me!' and then left forever.[28]

It was, I think, good that it ended that way, for I would have probably become so engrossed in his world of art that I would have had no time for any children. Later, in

Palestine, during the war, Wlastimil Hofman would say that artists' wives ought not to have children. Be that as it may, such methods of upbringing as practised in the convent kill all spontaneity of feeling, and constantly cast a shadow of sin. Burdened with such an outlook, I consider it a miracle that eventually at the age of thirty-four I decided to get married. I might not have dared to venture into the forbidden domain of sex had it not been for a psychological compulsion not to delay, for happiness does not always return, and it might soon be too late to have children. Only thirteen-year-old Hania, indignant that none of the men were paying her any attention, uttered her opinion that Tadeusz was of no interest to her because 'one day all men are going to be at my feet'.

A few years later (around the year 1931) Jula got engaged on impulse to a certain officer from Wilno after he had suddenly kissed her during a dance; this first sensation in her life seemed to her to be love. He wrote long romantic letters. It later appeared that this came easily to him, for he always used to get top marks for essay writing. He was simply eager for a good dowry combined with a good-looking girl. He came to Borki. Tatuś could not bear empty-headed officers, but what could he do since Jula was keen? By now, however, Hania had reached the age of sixteen; when the young man noticed her, he secretly revealed to her that he preferred her to Jula, although he had no idea how to extricate himself from his fiancée. Tatuś learnt of this, and in an abusive and devastating letter informed the young man that he would get neither of his daughters. In this way, both Jula and Hania were spared a disaster. The unfortunate dowry-hunter was sadly later killed in Katyn, leaving a blind sister in Wilno. How difficult it is to know when one encounters true love and a person suited to one's character. There was a time when my great-great-aunt Ewarysta Żórawska used to fly into a rage whenever anyone in her company mentioned the word 'love'. All love ended in disaster, she would argue, unless one was fortunate to meet a person with a suitable character. Tatuś also used to say how fortunate he was that he had found a wife who did not try to 'fashion' him after her own mould, and who enabled him to feel unfettered – unlike the case of many men who had married 'battleaxes'.

And indeed we, the three sisters, were to have contrasting attitudes to love. The artistic Hania could not do without the love of a devoted man. She could never live with an empty heart. Once love, the soul of a marriage, has evaporated, Hania is incapable of living in wedlock just based on reason, money and obedience to canon law. My sister Jula was not capable of experiencing great deep love; she was rather a maternal figure. As for myself, I daydreamed too much in a world of unreality, loving a variety of ideal individuals from a distance, romantically, like Don Quixote.

All not quiet in the distant provinces

Reflections on crime and punishment – A confidence trickster – Servants and village life – The Red Cross – The duel that never was and the scandal that followed – Eccentric neighbours – Sister Jula marries Jan Karczewski

In general, the peasants usually stole from the forest and the fields. This was a habit they inherited from the period of serfdom when the manor supplied them with free firewood and allowed free use of the meadows. Now these arrangements no longer existed, so one could hardly be surprised if the poor smallholders tried to make up their shortages wherever they could. However, some villages were the haunts of professional thieves, such as Obelkowicze near Dworzec (about 6 km north of Borki); the thieves from there would scour the district in search of loot. There was also the case of a young peasant from nearby Iwież, who had been hired to whitewash the walls in Rohotenka and Borki. He stole all of Aunt Kama's supply of smoked meat kept in her loft and also broke into our loft. Somehow, I happened to witness the police making an entry into his home. He was not there, or perhaps he had already been taken and the police were merely seeking information as to where the meat had been hidden. His foul-mouthed wife hurled herself at the constables like a lioness.

Moving closer to home, I have a childhood memory of little Anna, our cook, well known for her cleanliness and skill in making excellent meals. She occasionally liked to pilfer, but whenever she was sent away for this we had to bring her back, for no one else cooked as well as she did. Once Mamusia sent me to keep an eye on Anna when the bread dough was put in the oven. While my back was turned I heard a splash. Instead of sliding it into the oven, Anna had deliberately dropped a lump of dough into a can of water in order to steal it. I was too embarrassed to make a scene. When the Soviets arrived in 1939 and when our house was looted, it was the elderly Anna who appeared first and handed us a loaf of her own bread. The peasants stole because they were poor, while we, the owners, ever protecting our property, developed the idea that even small thieving brings disgrace. To become a 'thief' was tantamount to being excluded from polite society. That loaf of Anna's opened my eyes and taught me to look for humanity in everyone. In the end, it turned out that those who sometimes stole from us looked after me discreetly in 1939; sometimes they would bring me a piece of smoked bacon fat as a gift. Those people were somehow linked by sentiment to their 'masters', whereas those who did not steal remained emotionally detached from them and did not feel obliged to do anything to help during the ransacking of the manor house. Every stick has two ends. And I had always associated the word *zbój* (bandit) with something diabolical in man: they were monsters who rightly had to be shot.

Once before the war, in Zakopane, I met Pan Szurlej, a charming barrister from Warsaw who acted as defence counsel for many a notorious murderer.[1] I was surprised by this, not knowing how to reconcile his personal integrity and moral standing with his role as a defender of 'Crime', with a capital C. Asked about this, Pan Szurlej replied that it was not such a simple issue. He explained that such a murderer might have acted on a sudden impulse, without premeditation. Every murderer has a mother or a wife who would suffer after the passing of the sentence, and who, perhaps with children, would lose all means of livelihood. Every murderer, he continued, is also a human being, and not always a monster. One has to delve more deeply into each case, and one must not condemn every transgressor beforehand, for there are always some extenuating circumstances.

My distant uncle Janusz Jamontt also influenced me. He was a judge in the Supreme Court and had worked on the codification of Polish criminal law; he was even offered the post of minister of justice.[2] He was also offered a chair in law in Greece. Well, not once did he condemn anybody to death. If the case was hopeless, he would pass it on to other judges. He told me that he could not have a death sentence on his conscience. He frequently spoke to me about the genetic discoveries of Lombroso who believed that a crime is usually linked to some hereditary factor. It is worth adding in this context that I was once robbed of my purse in Zakopane and witnessed the police questioning a well-known young pickpocket. What a pathological type he was, with his restless and wily eyes; the album with photographs of various thieves at the police station was like something lifted straight from Lombroso's diary. Under the influence of these two men of the legal profession (barrister Szurlej and judge Jamontt), I discovered the law of relativity in the field of morality, and understood the profundity of Christ's words: 'Judge not, that you be not judged' and 'Father, forgive them; for they know not what they do.'[3]

This brings to mind an incident in 1920[4] when one evening a couple of lancers, escorting some prisoners, arrived at our house and asked to spend the night. 'It's only for one night', they explained, 'for tomorrow on our way to Słonim we're going to shoot these bandits.' Tatuś's heart sank. To receive condemned men under his roof was something he could not contemplate. He agreed to give shelter to the soldiers, but on condition that they would not shoot their prisoners and would hand them over to the judicial authorities. And so it happened. Indeed, ten years later the blacksmith (whose wife used to iron our dresses) and his son returned home from prison. It was they who had killed some bandit, thinking that he probably had some money on him. They then threw his body into a nearby river. This murder was soon uncovered – a most foul business. And Tatuś, who was sensitive to human suffering, was pleased that by intervening he did not have those deaths on his conscience – even indirectly.

Thinking of the issue of crime in our district brings to mind an exciting event from the 1930s. Every couple of years, military manoeuvres used to take place in our district. One morning a *bryczka* arrived in front of the house. Out of it alighted a tall handsome man with dark hair, of military deportment, aged about thirty. He introduced himself as Lieutenant Brzoza, serving as a deputy quartermaster in the army. He explained that, in preparation for the approaching manoeuvres, he would like to make direct purchases of oats and hay from the local landed gentry and so avoid using Jewish middlemen. It was May, before harvest time, and as usual in this period there was a shortage of cash at home. My parents entertained the visitor most hospitably, offering him our tastiest delicacies. I remember how Mamusia herself went to the greenhouses to pull a bunch of fresh radishes for the occasion. It was said that Lieutenant Brzoza was related to the parish priest in Starojelnia, a village 18 km northeast of Borki. He was certainly very familiar with all sorts of local connections. He began to show an interest in our photo albums, which were on display in the house; Jula even explained who the people on the photographs were.

The quartermaster, a captain, was to arrive with the cash after lunch in order to leave a deposit, or even pay in advance for the oats. Every time there was the sound of a carriage, Lieutenant Brzoza would peer through the window. In the meantime, Tatuś showed him around all the barns, and the visitor revealed a professional knowledge when looking at different varieties of hay. A proper contract was drawn up which the lieutenant and Tatuś signed. But there seemed to be no sign of the expected captain. The lieutenant in civilian clothes was therefore offered the use of our *bryczka*, and the next day Adam took him to Rohotenka and elsewhere in the neighbourhood where he made further purchases of supplies and signed contracts to that effect. On his return, he went for a walk with Jula around the park. He talked about one thing and another; at one point he produced a revolver bullet which he started to throw up and down, asking Jula casually whether we had any weapons that might fit this bullet.

The evening of 15 May arrived, the feast day of St Sophia, when we annually celebrated Mamusia's name-day in some style. Many of our neighbours were there; so were we, the girls. The guests made themselves comfortable at the big table, and began to partake of the splendid dishes that were served on Mamusia's silver dining set for twenty-four people, all embellished with the Żórawski coat-of-arms. At one point our servant Gienia Tarasik (whom we liked very much because she was warm-hearted and devoted, and also used to make dresses for us), who was bringing the dishes from the kitchen, approached Tatuś and told him that Pan Aranowski, the teacher in Iwień, had arrived with an urgent message. Tatuś got up and left the room. Shortly afterwards Brzoza excused himself, got up and went into the drawing room; it was assumed he was going to the toilet. Then all of a sudden Tatuś rushed into the dining room brandishing a revolver and searching with his eyes for Lieutenant Brzoza. His seat was empty. 'Where is he? After the bandit!' The gentlemen produced their revolvers and rushed out into the park. The bravest of all during this chase was Ksawuś (Ksawery) Gnoiński. The whole park was searched, as was the garden and the area around the ponds. But there was no sign of the villain. He had probably jumped out of the drawing room window into the park. There was also some concern in case Brzoza had a gang, or some 'back-up', lurking in the forest.

The assembled guests quickly left the house, but the younger men, armed with revolvers, spent the night guarding the house against a possible attack. In the meantime, Tatuś quickly dispatched Adam on horseback to the police station in Rohotna. It eventually transpired that Lieutenant Brzoza, calmly as ever, had set out on foot to Aunt Kama's house in Rohotenka. For some reason she was not present at the party. Perhaps she was still in mourning for her son Wacio who had died from tuberculosis, or for her husband who had died earlier, also from tuberculosis which he had caught after not treating an inflammation of the lungs.

The police caught Brzoza near Rohotenka and took him, handcuffed, to Aunt Kama's house for identification. Aunt Kama opened her door, surveyed the whole scene and asked caustically: 'Is that you?' 'Yes, it's me', he replied with a scowl. It appears that the teacher from Iwież had just returned from Nowojelnia where the whole district was in uproar because some bandit, claiming to be a relative, had insinuated himself into the favour of the local parish priest and had stolen a coat. We were alarmed at the thought of what could have happened subsequently in our house. The police enquiry revealed that the whole affair was not as dangerous as it may have seemed. It emerged that Brzoza was no lieutenant, but some NCO in the army commissariat who had been thrown out of the army for stealing. A brilliant idea occurred to him how to turn his expertise in the field of supplies into cash. He therefore travelled from manor to manor, was everywhere entertained and then disappeared having stolen something. Perusing family albums in different manor houses he learnt a lot about the landed families he visited. Then, using this information, he would present himself as a close relative in other neighbouring houses, thus gaining the confidence of his unsuspecting hosts. He admitted to the police that he did not steal anything in Borki only because he had been genuinely moved by the hospitality he had received there.

Returning to the servants, for many years my parents employed an old woman, Katarzyna. Right up until her death, she had daytime use of a small room near the hall. She helped around the house and did some spinning. Often she could be seen shedding silent tears as she lamented that she had been left an orphan and that her uncle had dismissed the only suitors who came to see her. She remained an old spinster and thought that, when her time came, she would be denied a proper burial. In fact she was buried properly in the cemetery. Afterwards, I occasionally said a Hail Mary for her soul. She was the talisman of our home. Unfortunately, her eyes were always red. It did not occur to my parents that she had trachoma, like many of the inhabitants of her cottage in the village. Not surprisingly she infected us, the children. Later at school we suffered torments from the pain under our eyelids, and even worse tortures when the surgeon had to scrape away and cauterize the granular excrescences from underneath. Ignorance in matters of health was terrible in those days.

At one time Katarzyna shared her cottage with another of our servants, Malwina, who was later seduced by our estate steward Felix. He left, and she poisoned herself. It was a great shock for the entire household when her blue corpse was carried out with the help of the police who found a phial of copper sulphate by her body. Malwina was ugly as sin. Looking at little Hania's doll, she would often sigh that had she been as pretty as the doll all the boys would have run after her. Social disapproval and the stigma of unmarried motherhood were sufficiently instilled in Malwina that she could not summon enough courage to bear the consequences of her affair with Felix. Besides, she may indeed have fallen in love with the handsome steward, and being abandoned, out of quiet despair, she purchased the poison somewhere. I sometimes pray for her too.

It was usually the case that we had new servants every few years; once they had saved several hundred złotys, they normally found a prospective bidder for their hand. There was one particularly beautiful and buxom lass by the name of Maryla, I think. The good-looking young Heljasz, our barn-keeper, fell in love with her. They made a handsome pair, but were terrorized afterwards, until his death, by their miserly father-in-law who lived in Borki village. Other handsome couples that caught one's eyes were the high-minded Wojciech and Jan Zych with their wives. Our Gienia Tarasik also married happily. She said later that 'my husband felt sorry for me', by which she meant that he took care that she did not work too hard so that she would be happy with him. Not all peasant marriages turned out like this. One heard stories of a woman who scraped her husband's bald head with a grater, and so on.[5] Besides, there were some unfeeling men who treated their women as slaves. How often did one hear the confidences of such wronged women who breathed hatred for their brutish spouses. On one occasion a dreadful tragedy befell the village of Borki: a rejected suitor broke into a cottage with an axe and killed everyone inside outright.

On the whole, however, the families of the peasants made a positive impression as they toiled all their lives, through thick and thin, and managed to create close family units, something that is not easy in our times. Everyone in the family had his or her own area of work, and from earliest childhood, everyone was in some way occupied. Small children even nursed younger ones. Young lads looked after cows and sheep, and later were drawn into doing heavier work in the fields. The women wore long skirts to the ground (without underwear) and garments of heavy homespun cloth. It was only after the First World War that village women in the area began to wear shorter skirts and purchase colourful scarves from Jewish dealers. All woollen and linen cloth was woven at home during the winter. That was the women's task. During the winter months the men would spend a lot of their time lying on the great stoves in their cottages unless they went to chop wood in the forest.[6] Only in spring would ploughing commence, as well as the removal of manure and other jobs in the fields.

Every Wednesday, or another designated day, a market was held in nearby Mołczadź or Dworzec, where everyone went to sell sheep and pigs, or to buy a new cow. Eggs and bacon were also on sale. Many swindlers mingled with the crowds at these markets. Gypsies or Jews would sometimes sell stolen horses, which were then disguised either by using paint or by creating additional 'stars': a splinter would be driven into the hide and left long enough to create an abscess. A white patch would then appear on that spot. One day Marcin from Rohotna, known for his beetroot-coloured face, was at such a market when he noticed a throng of people. Among them stood a Jewish pedlar who was secretly showing some golden crosses tucked under his sleeve; other Jews were crowding around and running up the bidding, as at auctions in England. Marcin had just sold a cow and, aware of the money in his pocket, he found himself overwhelmed by gold fever! He paid 100 złotys and took the crosses. He then brought them to my father to sell them. It turned out to be gold from who knows where, and without any hallmarks – and so worthless. In despair Marcin hanged himself. His daughter later worked as a servant in a presbytery. When the priest learnt that she had not been conducting herself morally, in his outrage he gave her a sound kicking and threw her out. When the Bolsheviks arrived in 1939, aggrieved people submitted complaints to them. Marcin's daughter lodged such a complaint as a result of which the priest was arrested; he then disappeared without trace.[7]

Wiera was another servant with whom we used to play as children. She was persuaded to convert from Orthodoxy to Catholicism, and later married Borodziuk from Borki village. I was godmother to her son Janek (Jan), and I gave him a hive of bees as a christening present. Jan was killed a year ago in a coal mine in the Urals; he had moved there after the Second World War to earn more money.[8] He left a daughter. He used to write warm letters to us in England, in Russian, even inviting us to his wedding; he told us that the orchard and the manor house were still standing. His body was returned to the family in February of last year; Wiera sent us a photograph of Jan lying in an open coffin, surrounded by his daughters and sons-in-law. Poor Wiera was heartbroken because of this blow and has not written for a year. I have ordered a Mass to be said in Stratford for the soul of my godson.[9]

I took under my wing a young servant by the name of Mania. She had a very pleasant disposition, and I prepared her for Holy Communion. It all started when I was approached by an unknown woman, who turned out to be Mania's mother. With a degree of servility to which I was quite unaccustomed, she begged me to take Mania into service at the manor. I got to like her and later used to hand down many of my dresses. I once tried to save her mother's life when she was ill with intestinal swelling, but she did not possess a rubber tube such as those used in hospitals with which I could treat her. Twisting in agony, she crawled about on all fours, thankfully with the expected result: she recovered. She had a healthy-looking husband and another daughter Jula who was prettier than her pale-looking self. But I was to be shocked by Mania's mother's behaviour at an assembly of peasants, organized by Soviet soldiers and held after the Borki manor had been sacked in 1939. She stepped forward and greeted them, saying that she had been waiting for them for a long time. I simply froze on seeing the falsehood of this woman who had grovelled before me earlier. Since then I have regarded with the greatest suspicion people who show an inclination to be servile.

My father had a cabinet with medicines in his office and used to treat peasants for all sorts of illnesses. How he learnt such skills, I do not know. He always had a supply of castor oil, opium, iodine, zinc ointment, birch-tar ointment and linseed oil with lime water for treating scalds. On one occasion he was able to save my sister Hania's face from disfigurement after she was scalded by boiling water from a *samovar*. She was treated by the application of poultices with lime water and linseed oil. Potassium permanganate was used for everything: to cleanse cuts, to soak ulcers on legs and so on. On another occasion Hania fell on a bed frame and bit her tongue right through the middle. Again, miraculously, and without a doctor, Tatuś was able to save her; I think he rinsed her tongue in potassium permanganate until the wound healed.

As a result of all this, I decided to attend a course organized by the Polish Red Cross, in order to be able to treat peasants and to help ourselves and others living there in the remote countryside. Aunt Marzeńka, the widow of Uncle Antoś Protassewicz, invited me to stay in her sister's house in Saska Kępa in Warsaw; the modernist house, which looked like a ship, was built by the architect Bohdan Lachert. From there I attended a six-month course in medical theory and practice.[10] The smells in the wards of the Piłsudski Hospital where ulcers were treated were horrible, because penicillin had not yet been discovered and most of the patients soaked their legs and hands in various basins and jugs containing solutions of the ubiquitous potassium permanganate. I observed various operations, including a failed one: an incorrect diagnosis on a female patient led to the dissection of her kidney, followed a month later by further dissection. It turned out however that she had gallstones. The patient died. Appendix operations ceased to interest me, and I waited for more unusual cases. Most important was that I learnt how to give injections. Later, back in the village, I administered them to anyone with a doctor's prescription. I also bought a tube with ethyl chloride, which I used to freeze the skin of my buttock in order to give myself injections of liver extract (*hepatogen*) for my anaemia. I was also able to save a peasant's finger. He had a wooden splinter buried deep under his fingernail; I froze his finger, cut the fingernail in the middle with Tatuś's razor (which I had disinfected) and then removed the splinter.

On another occasion (this was already after our house had been sacked in 1939) I was able to save the sight of another peasant. A microscopic spike of corn had dug itself into his cornea. What to do? There was no doctor. How could I remove the invisible thorn, and with what? I could hardly use metal tweezers on his cornea. But I remembered how some time earlier a shepherd had been injured by a bull. Staying with us at the time was Dr Ostaszewski, a dentist from Warsaw,[11] who used a solution of potassium permanganate to wash the shepherd's wounds and to soak the bandages, made from a torn sheet. By some miracle, a box with potassium permanganate had survived the devastation of the house. I took a stick, wrapped one end with cotton wool and soaked it in potassium permanganate. I then wiped the surface of his cornea with this swab. It caught the thorn and pulled it out. Had the thorn not been removed an abscess would have formed on his cornea, and the peasant would have become blind in one eye. On the strength of my Polish Red Cross certificate I was able to work officially in the hospital the Bolsheviks were to establish in our house in 1939, and to be enrolled later as a nurse in the Polish Army in the USSR and in the Middle East.

I feel I should raise the subject of duels: my father nearly ended up having to fight one![12] How did it all start? There was at the time the widespread practice of 'honest thieving' among the gentry which brought no loss of face in society. This involved drawing bank loans against the accounts of their wealthier brethren or naive neighbours who acted out of 'courtesy', and then not honouring these debts. Well, a supply of artificial fertilizer had been ordered by the Landowners' Association in Słonim. Jeśman, the association's chairman at the time, asked my father to underwrite the bill. Tatuś did so with confidence that it would be repaid. The result was that Tatuś had to pay 4,000 złotys out of his own pocket to the association for the fertilizer. He then called the chairman a thief and with much ado withdrew from the association. An offended Jeśman dispatched his two nephews, as seconds, with a duel challenge. They knocked on the door of Borki manor, but refused to enter or sit down. They issued the challenge and left, their swords jingling as they went. There was consternation at home. Tatuś travelled to Wilno where he purchased a copy of the *Code of Honour*.[13] Somehow, in the end, other landowners were able to straighten things out amicably. It was, in fact, someone else who had stolen the funds belonging to the Landowners' Bank (a certain dishonest Mr K was implicated in this), but Tatuś felt that the chairman should have borne the consequences, rather than overlook it in a swinish way and land Tatuś with paying the bill.[14]

A distorted version of this incident, written by Melchior Wańkowicz in an article entitled 'Domejko and Dowejko', appeared in the *Kurjer*.[15] The story ended up in the press in the following way. One day, Melchior Wańkowicz's car appeared on the drive of Borki manor. Wańkowicz was accompanied by his daughter and by our distant neighbour Senator Józef Godlewski.[16] The writer was looking for material about the landed gentry, and Godlewski wanted him to meet Tatuś, the last true landed gentleman of the old school. Pan Józef had recently been elected chairman of the Landowners' Association. No sooner had he greeted my father than he immediately started persuading Tatuś to rejoin the association. Tatuś responded with one sentence: 'Yes, but on condition you expel all the thieves from the Association.' Melchior picked up that fragment of the conversation, and embellished the story to produce his article. He presented a caricature of Tatuś and poked fun at him a little. At the same time he made Tatuś appear as a speaker of the 'Wilno dialect' mixed with Belarusian, yet at home everyone used purest literary Polish.

A scandal erupted. Zygmunt Protassewicz, my father's nephew and the renowned *inżynier*, telephoned Wańkowicz and threatened him with a duel.[17] Pan Faustyn Czerwijowski, the director of Warsaw's public library and father of Aunt Hela Protassewicz of Belweder, also threatened Melchior over the phone with unpleasant consequences. My father's sister Aunt Marynia Świackiewicz of Wilno threatened to batter Melchior with her umbrella. Even Pani Roycewiczowa, the formidable mistress of Rohotna manor, defended Tatuś and admonished Wańkowicz in a beautiful article in a Wilno newspaper. Pani Bartoszewiczowa of Izmajłowszczyzna proudly informed Wańkowicz, who asked to visit her, that she would not receive him. Pani Żółtowska of Bolcieniki, a landed lady of distinction, also spoke out to the effect that she would not allow into her home anyone who sullied the reputation of the landowners and fouled his own nest. Melchior was beset on all sides; seeing no escape, he decided to go to Canossa… to Borki, to seek Tatuś's forgiveness.

Tatuś was magnanimous, and held a different opinion of the affair. He did not think that any article could do him any harm. On the contrary, he felt that poor Melchior, who had lost his family estate in the Minsk region,[18] and who now had to maintain his family through his pen, had to make a living somehow! Tatuś received Melchior warmly. He showed him around the ponds, and explained how he provided the fish with extra tasty food by suspending lights over the water and thus luring midges onto the surface. There were other amusing anecdotes. Charmed by Tatuś's personality, Melchior then wrote a new article entitled 'The House on the Gospels' (*Dom na Ewangeliach*) and in this way calmed all the seething relatives and neighbours.[19]

Melchior told me that one day his book about the landed class would be as valuable as Pasek's memoirs.[20] He was right: the landed caste of our parts was destroyed by the Second World War, and Melchior's accounts are a contribution to the history of the customs of this vanished stratum of society. Numerous manor houses, great and small, were burnt down by the Germans, the peasants or the Soviets. In social terms everything has been wiped clean – a tabula rasa – in Poland's former eastern borderlands. We shall have to see whether the future history of those lands will be created by God's hand or by that of Satan. Knowing Tatuś's attitude to Wańkowicz, and being aware that Tatuś did in fact consider most landowners in our district to be dishonest, it was with some distress that I acted 'against my heart' when I agreed to support Senator Godlewski in his conflict with Wańkowicz in London in 1946. Godlewski wanted to force Wańkowicz to stop writing unfavourably about the landowners of our region. The result was that in his book Melchior withdrew everything about Tatuś, and that is a pity.[21] Pan Godlewski had officially confirmed my identity before my marriage in 1945, and I felt unable to turn down his request, all the more so since he came out passionately in defence of the landowners, of whom, after all, I too was one.

Once Pani Lala Kutkowska of Podłuże near Słonim caused great confusion at a landowners' meeting. She had written such a hard-hitting letter to the relevant official of the association that, as Tatuś later related, the chairman did not dare to read it out loud. He passed it to his immediate neighbour at the meeting who then read it holding it under the table, and then passed it on to the next person who also read it unofficially in the same way. The letter was thus circulated among all those present. There was complete silence, which in all dignity was not broken. Everyone parted without speaking. Pani Lala Kutkowska was a courageous person, and acted in a manly fashion. One by one she threw out each of her three husbands once they started to get at her forests in order to squander their value. At her third wedding, she received a telegram from her first husband (in Russian): 'Best wishes to you with number three – from number one' (*pozdravlayu z tretim – pervyi*). She built for herself a small castellated manor house in Podłuże and managed her estate herself, doing the rounds with a shotgun and a pack of dogs. She owned beautiful meadows and her land was fertile. Living very near Słonim, Pani Lala could have had a considerable income from supplying milk to the town. However, she could not find a Jewish dealer brave enough to do business with her, for as one of them said: 'Well, she's so wild with that gun there's no reason why she wouldn't shoot me.'

I called on her once in Podłuże with Witek Kontkowski who was giving me a lift from Warsaw by car. Our car was immediately surrounded by a pack of dogs. Pani Lala invited us inside and told us the history of the building of her castellated manor house, which had cost her a fortune. It was an identical copy of the wing of a palace she had once seen and admired. She befriended Aunt Kama and was going to leave Podłuże to her god-daughter. In the meantime, this god-daughter did not marry a landed gentleman but a tax inspector of rather common appearance; once in the office of the commune, I could not distinguish him from other officials there. However, Pan Zygmunt, for that was his first name, was very friendly. He came up to see us in Borki after Tatuś's death, and even drew a plan for me of the house I wanted to build for myself on the Great Field from the proceeds of the wood there. Pan Zygmunt was very much a businessman. When he discovered that Pani Lala Kutkowska had left her much-neglected estate to her god-daughter, his wife, in her will, it occurred to him that it would be wasteful to wait, possibly many years, before Pani Lala died. Would it not be better to transfer the estate immediately to his wife, with the provision that Pani Lala would receive several hundred złotys monthly for the rest of her life?

Pani Lala was dreadfully indignant on hearing this. She threatened to throw Pan Zygmunt out by the scruff of his neck if he ever dared to appear before her in person. I do not know exactly what happened next, but it is clear that relations between them were broken off. But this still left Pani Lala at a loss as to who should inherit her extensive property. During my visit there she seized upon the idea to make me the beneficiary, on condition I married Doboszyński, probably a distant relative of hers, for that was her own maiden name. Not long before, this Doboszyński had physically attacked the district governor in Myślenice, an event which delighted Pani Lala enormously. She spoke of this assault on a state official as the 'last foray'.[22] Then war broke out in 1939. Pani Lala escaped with some gold to Warsaw and disappeared without trace.[23]

Indeed, in the old days our rural district was teeming with all sorts of eccentrics. One such person was the former captain Rahoza. Tatuś often related the story of how he had once witnessed Rahoza's attempt to bring about the ruin of a crooked timber merchant. Rahoza's forest, rather poor in quality, bordered a splendid state-owned forest. The merchant in question was coming to buy some of Rahoza's timber, but before his arrival Rahoza had marked whole rows of trees in the state forest as his own. Seeing these magnificent trees, the merchant left a substantial deposit. He brought along woodcutters and the state-owned pines began to fall. State foresters soon rushed to the scene and drove the merchant away. The timber merchant then turned up at Rahoza's manor house with a grievance. Captain Rahoza ordered his servant Filip to give the merchant a beating. The merchant fell lifeless by the porch. Rahoza immediately ordered other servants to play something loud on various instruments in order to drown out the wailing of the merchant's wife who had run up wringing her hands in great distress. At that point Tatuś observed an approaching turkey about to peck the face of the motionless merchant. He then saw the seemingly dead merchant gently move his hand to keep the turkey away from his face. The whole incident ended with Rahoza giving the merchant some alder trees as compensation; but they were so heavy that when the merchant had them lowered into a river to raft them away, they sank. In this way, the merchant, who used to swindle everyone everywhere, was tricked himself.[24] Captain Rahoza liked to stroll into the fields when the corn was beginning to germinate. He walked around the corn making mysterious movements of his hands, whispering something, and then proclaiming around, in Russian: 'get level' (*ravnyaysya*). Whenever he came on a visit to Borki, he would help his wife descend from the carriage while whispering to himself: 'If God permits it, she will get out of the carriage; but if He does not permit it, she will not.'

Another eccentric was the old Pani Wołłowicz of Rohotna, of the old historic Wołłowicz family. A physically intimidating woman, she reminded me of Horpyna.[25] She adored the company of men and spent much of her time hunting. On one occasion a group of men visiting her sneaked into an outbuilding to have a game of cards on the quiet. They had barely sat at the table, when the door of a cupboard opened and out jumped Pani Wołłowicz with the words: 'You rascals, do you think you can play without me?' Tatuś told me how on one occasion he saw her wading across a river in her boots. On reaching the meadow on the other side, she fell onto her back and emptied her boots of water simply by raising her legs. She then calmly resumed hunting. She was a jealous woman. Once she imported some pedigree pigs. Tatuś asked her if he could buy a couple of piglets from her. She agreed, but had the piglets slaughtered before sending them to him. Tatuś was warm-hearted by nature and such personality traits upset him very much.

Pani Wołłowicz's daughter was Wanda, a woman of monumental beauty who had once enchanted Tatuś in his youth.[26] Before the First World War Mamusia and Tatuś often used to visit her in Rohotna; Mamusia played Chopin there and was referred to as 'Pani Zo'. Wanda Wołłowicz was later to acquire the nickname 'Cleopatra' on account of her eastern looks. Indeed, she moved like an Egyptian goddess and had in fact once purchased live crocodiles from Egypt! In Rohotna I once saw a beautiful alabaster bust of her sculpted by an Italian artist. Her first husband was Pan Ksawery Strawiński, a man as ugly as night, who owned thousands of hectares of forest in Polesie.[27] However, the beautiful Wanda treated her husband with indulgence, as a kind uncle. The marriage, entered into out of calculation, was later dissolved by the church. Wanda's second husband was the handsome horse-riding hero Henryk Roycewicz.[28] Long spells in Warsaw, travels to championships in Milan, nursing her husband who was badly injured while jumping and later a divorce, all consumed the Wołłowicz fortune. Indeed, at one stage, Wanda Roycewicz (to use her second married name) even fed her husband's entire lancer regiment – until she threw him out with all his cavalrymen. Up to her ears in debt, Wanda was reduced to selling off her furniture. Intellectually, Wanda was a refined woman of letters and modelled herself on Sappho or George Sand. She wrote poems and prose, and surrounded herself with literary critics and writers. Once she entertained Józef Wittlin, the author of *Sól ziemi*.[29] But Wittlin quarrelled with his hostess and had to flee to Borki with his wife. Another writer was Sergiusz Piasecki, the author of *Kochanek Wielkiej Niedźwiedzicy*, after his release from the Holy Cross (Świętokrzyskie) prison.[30]

Also among our interesting neighbours was Pani Maria Bartoszewiczowa of nearby Izmajłowszczyzna. At the tender age of fifteen, she had married a rake, the handsome Bartoszewicz, who then abandoned her and her young son. She was an aristocratic lady descended from an ancient Spanish family, and her full surname was: Suza Muza La Perusa Paraguay de Grico, Esterhaze Colorado Monte Ponte Cyro Cera Graf Mendoza de Butello. Pani Maria Bartoszewiczowa's ancestor had emigrated to Poland from Spain because of political persecution. We memorized her full surname, although I'm not sure about its correct spelling. We used all parts of it when counting persons in our games. She was a great admirer of Eliza Orzeszkowa[31] and was something of an intellectual in those days. She had an unusually long and narrow head, while her mouth was so small that her doctor found it difficult to look into her throat. I used to visit her sometimes to give her injections. She assumed that she would die at any time and would constantly call for priests or for the doctor. Once she gave all her clothes away to her servants, but the following day she was worried about what she would wear if she did not die soon. Her grandson Jurek fell in love with my sister Jula. After a visit to Borki, he refused to return home and spent the night at the top of a lime tree in our park. In the morning, our watchman brought a letter from Jurek to Tatuś in which he apologized for his behaviour. Jurek was then loaded onto a wagon and taken home.

Pani Maria Bartoszewiczowa owned a marvellous set of family silver with her family crest which, after her death, passed to her son's family. Her daughter-in-law Franciszka was to take the silver with her when she was arrested and deported to Siberia in 1941. There, in Siberia, our paths were to cross, as I shall relate later. Suffice it to say for the moment that Franciszka Bartoszewicz was to be my companion during our journey in 1941–2 from Siberia to Soviet Central Asia. There, in Dzhambul, in Kazakhstan, I saw with my own eyes a porter run off with her suitcase which contained all the silver. Pani Franciszka's husband (who was Pani Maria Bartoszewiczowa's only child) somehow avoided deportation by the Soviets. He was later shot dead by mistake, through a window somewhere in German-occupied Poland, by someone evidently trying to shoot at a group of Germans sitting in the same room. The aristocratic Pani Maria disliked her daughter-in-law's pretentious behaviour as of someone without proper upbringing and, as long as she could, she administered her small estate by herself. She did give Franciszka 30 hectares of land in perpetuity but, wishing to remain in charge to the very end, refused to part with the rest of her property during her lifetime. Eventually, Pani Maria leased the rest of her estate to Abramek.[32] Franciszka, the daughter-in-law, wanted to get rid of Abramek and to run the estate herself; she would often call on Tatuś to get his support in this matter. At one point, Franciszka exclaimed vehemently: 'Pan Wacław! I see that you are my enemy!' 'That's not true', Tatuś replied, 'when you are in the right, I shall be on your side; but because you're not in the right, I am on the other side'. Tatuś tried to persuade Franciszka to let the aged Pani Maria live out her remaining days in peace: the contract with Abramek had only two more years to run, by which time the mother-in-law was likely to have departed this life. And that is how things turned out. But the energetic Pani Franciszka benefited only briefly from running the estate. Before long the Bolsheviks arrived (in 1939), and all was lost. Previously Franciszka had worked somewhere in Wilno, and later ran a house for a relative in Warsaw. Thanks to this, she was able to pay for the university education of her daughter Fela and her son Jurek.

We also used to visit the Goebel family. They had a son, Stefan, and three daughters. Stefan studied medicine but fell out with his professor and abandoned his studies. Back home, he worked in his own mill. He intended to court my sister Jula, but that was just as she got married. Once, while dancing with him I was surprised when I felt the iron-like muscles of his torso. Until then I had found men rather flabby, but he had the physique of a gladiator, naturally as a result of his physical work, in which he gave vent to his disappointment in his studies. He was to lose an eye during the Warsaw Uprising, but did eventually complete his medical training.

Old Pan Goebel played the cello beautifully; it was later stolen from him when he was escaping with it from the Bolsheviks in 1939. By profession he was a bookkeeper. As a person of transparent honesty, he was employed by a wealthy Jewish firm. His Jewish employer was certain that nothing would disappear and that no commercial information would leak out to rival Jewish businessmen. For this he paid Pan Goebel like Croesus: what in those days was the enormous monthly salary of 1,000 złotys. It was then that Pan Goebel was able to educate his daughters at the convent school of the Sisters of Nazareth and to send his son to university. When he retired, the good times came to an end. As a pensioner, he was tied to his wife's apron strings, and the whole family found themselves in straitened circumstances. His wife, Pani Melania, was very hospitable but was another Horpyna who terrorized the entire household.

We also visited the Walicki family in Sągajłowszczyzna; Pani Walicka was Pan Goebel's sister. Her three children were not particularly robust. Sadly, they were all shot by the Bolsheviks in 1939.

Our visits also included the Bilczyński family. The interior of their house gave the appearance of a ramshackle dwelling and was unbelievably cluttered; it was as if they lived in a warehouse full of nails and bits of iron. Pani Julia Bilczyńska still possessed traces of her former beauty, and her husband, a former general, was a dignified personage. Pani Julia died from cancer in Wilno after spending a long time in a wheelchair. She resisted all the efforts of my devout aunt, the wife of Wiluś Protassewicz, to persuade her to receive the Last Sacrament. Her only response was: 'Don't torment me'. Her mother was a Protestant. The entire Bilczyński family exuded warmth and hospitality, and that is why Tatuś willingly spent time with them. All the more so, since he also had memories from his youth when fifty years earlier he had been in love with the charming Julia. I think that some of the men of the family, the old general and one of his sons, were later shot by the Germans because a revolver was found hidden in their piano. The oldest son lived elsewhere and so survived. The other surviving son was an excellent farmer and beekeeper, and a carpenter too. He was known for his honesty, which was in contrast to the overall decay and drunkenness of the impoverished landowners of the district. The beekeeper son once told me that he lived like this so that after his death the peasants would be able to say: 'Here lived and died a decent man.'

Their father, General Bilczyński, was full of Tolstoy's ideals of 'returning to nature', a bit like Rousseau. The whole family worked hard on the land like smallholders, with very little help from any farm hands. Their ideas may have been high-minded, but by suppressing all social aspirations they reduced the appearance of the house to that of a farmer's tool shed, and lowered the family's standards to one that was not much above that of the peasants. And yet they were descendants of a once wealthy and educated landowning family. This acquisition of rustic manners grated on my feelings. That is why it was totally out of the question for me to accept a proposal of marriage from the young Bilczyński who, seeing that I had taken up beekeeping, wanted to combine our fondness for this work with a matrimonial link.

Although during the period of the Great Depression we were short of cash and had to count everything we spent carefully, we did not allow our standards to fall at home, where Mamusia also created a musical atmosphere. The same applied even to Rohotenka: circumstances there were even more difficult, but Aunt Kama continued to nourish her cultural interests. Her daughter Mila Zbroja wrote recently from Zabrze, that even now (1968), as a partially blind old lady, Aunt Kama spends most of the day listening to radio programmes about science with great interest; she is particularly absorbed by the latest discoveries in physics and engineering. How wonderful for an eighty-four-year-old woman!

It was because of the general cultural decline among the local landowners that it was difficult for us to meet suitable male company. Naturally, we had to travel to the larger cities because there one found those ambitious enough to enter the wider world and seek education. After finishing my secondary education (in 1930) I busied myself with beekeeping because I wanted to be financially independent of my parents, and because

I wanted to have freedom to travel and spend winters in the city. Whatever profits Tatuś made during the Great Depression he ploughed back into new investments and innovations on the estate; hence we were short of ready cash. And so beekeeping was for me the only means of independence. Furthermore, I was proud and did not like asking for money. In the meantime, Mamusia sold the farm at Zosin which she had acquired from the division of her parents' property. Persuaded by Janek Górski, her brother-in-law, she bought a flat in a housing cooperative in Warsaw, and advised by Jadzia Jamontt, she placed the rest of the money in a Warsaw bank. The flat was still being built, while all the interest from the bank account was committed to my sister Hania's training in Warsaw as a singer. Lack of money in this profession could easily lead one down a slippery slope, and so my parents were anxious to protect her from this.

Jula remained in the country. Then she married Janek Karczewski – which led to other expenses. Janek had inherited a boarding house in central Warsaw from his parents, but was preoccupied with his law studies. The woman managing the guest house was owed 4,000 złotys as arrears in her salary, and this had to be settled straightaway. Janek's father had once won a million złotys on a lottery. Although this occurred during a period of currency devaluation, he was still able to buy a plot of land near Warsaw, lots of jewellery and hundreds of Chopin records. He also travelled abroad. Janek had Hungarian ancestry, and that is why Jula's and his daughters had swarthy complexions and dark eyes.

Both Janek and his father looked handsome in photographs, although their eyes revealed something of a quick temper. Janek was a well-built and good-looking man with dark hair and splendid strong teeth. He possessed a great musical talent, but unfortunately had decided against studying musicology, which was the only subject that interested him, and chose law as more useful for making a living. Indeed, he was to work as a lawyer for the Polish State Railways. Whenever he stayed in Borki, he would play Chopin beautifully on Mamusia's splendid grand piano. He also had a gift for languages. As for his character, he had a generous heart, and I noticed that he provided extra food free of charge for an old artist residing in the boarding house. But Janek was also irritable and had fits of anger. This I found shocking for I had an even-tempered father at home, who always showed moderation and elegant polished diplomacy; I was not accustomed to scenes at home. My father only scolded peasants, which he did through a window, and always with great charm.

Tragedy was to strike Jula's family during the war. Janek offered shelter in his Warsaw guest house to a number of Jewish friends from his university days. But someone betrayed him. He was sent to the Nazi concentration camp at Auschwitz where he died.[33] To think that only ashes remained of this physically impressive man! I remember him sometimes in my prayers. His good looks and talent have passed on to Jula's two daughters, Marysia, my god-daughter, and Basia. At least, by moving out of the city earlier, Jula and the children were spared the horrors of the Warsaw Uprising (August–October 1944) which saw their home, with all its contents, destroyed by fire.

4

Warsaw: Relatives, love and a brush with dangerous politics

**Uncle Leon – Cousin Zygmunt – Aunt Jadzia Jamontt – The engineer –
The army captain – Two poems – Hela Jamontt and the National Radicals
(ONR) – Governor Boldok**

My bees kept me at Borki during the summer months, but during the rest of the year I was able to visit relatives and friends in other parts of the country, including Warsaw. Relatives living in Warsaw included Tatuś's youngest brother Uncle Leon Protassewicz. Before the First World War he had been sent to the Polytechnical Institute in Lwów (in Austrian Galicia), but did not finish his studies; instead he joined Piłsudski's conspiratorial organization.[1] Shortly after the outbreak of the First World War, Uncle Leon married Hela Czerwijowska, the daughter of Facio (Faustyn) Czerwijowski, a one-time member of the Polish Socialist Party, who had spent some time with Piłsudski in London. A librarian of note, Faustyn Czerwijowski had co-founded Warsaw's public library.[2]

Leon and Hela were married in unusual circumstances. Aunt Hela had been in the conspiracy for a long time. She was a friend of Piłsudski's first wife and lived in the future Marshal's house. She was very young. One evening, overwhelmed by the imminent departure of the First Brigade of the Legions into battle, she stood in Piłsudski's drawing room, engrossed in thought. Uncle Leon entered the room, also excited by the prospect of departure for the front the next day. He suddenly approached Hela, whom he did not know at all, and ardently proposed marriage to her: 'I'm about to leave for the front, and if I'm killed no one will weep for me. Would you agree to become my wife today?' My future aunt replied 'Yes' without hesitation. During his address at the altar, Bishop Bandurski (the legionaries' bishop) announced that he was marrying a Polish woman with an unknown soldier; that it was a symbolic wedding, a soldier's marriage with the idea of Poland. During the ceremony Piłsudski apparently sat looking very pale, concerned for the future of his beloved Hela who firmly believed in his 'star', that he would make Poland free again.[3]

After returning from the front, Uncle Leon could not trace his wife. She had run away to her parents to escape from the husband whom she could barely remember. In a moment of romantic elation, she had married the apotheosis of the struggle for freedom. 'You took an oath, so you must return to him', declared her parents, and so Aunt Hela returned to share her fortune and misfortune with the legionary. Józef Piłsudski was godfather to their son Józef (known as 'Ziuk'). After the war Uncle Leon and Aunt Hela withdrew to Hajkowce, but both remained in contact with Piłsudski. On one occasion Piłsudski arrived unannounced to see Aunt Hela, of whom he was very fond, at my aunt Salunia Połubińska's apartment in Wilno. Due to post-war shortages there was no ordinary tea in the house; nervously Aunt Salunia instead made some camomile tea for the eminent visitor. Also, before his coup d'état (of May 1926), Piłsudski went on a tour of visits to his loyal former legionaries. He then called on Uncle Leon in Hajkowce. Aunt Hela was apparently so overcome with emotion that she rushed out to meet the Marshal in her nightdress.

Uncle Leon ran his Hajkowce estate with limited success since he attached little importance to material things. He intended to write his memoirs. Aunt Hela also said that she would record on paper important events about which only she knew. They did not find the time to write anything as tragedy struck. Jumping across the cog wheels of a threshing machine, their only son fell in and was crushed to death. I saw Ziuk only once, and will never forget him. He was about twelve years old and had the exuberant good looks of a Cossack commander with dark fiery eyes. One day, while playing, he overheard the grown-ups arguing about something and that Poland would perish. On hearing this, Ziuk started to shout: 'I don't want Poland to perish!' Everyone fell silent, amazed by the child's pained cry. Ziuk's death broke Uncle Leon's heart.

After the tragedy (in 1929), Piłsudski immediately brought Uncle Leon to Warsaw and put him in charge of the administration of the Belweder, the Marshal's official residence. Aunt Hela did voluntary social work in the city. In our family Uncle Leon and Aunt Hela soon became known as 'the Belweder philosophers'. I once visited them in Warsaw where they lived modestly in a small detached house. Uncle Leon worshipped the Marshal and arranged all sorts of surprises for him. For example, one springtime, the Marshal found primroses and violets growing by the side of the bench he liked to sit on. When the Marshal died, Leon and Hela travelled with his coffin all the way to Kraków where the Marshal was buried in the crypt of Wawel cathedral. Uncle Leon received a pension (about 600 złotys per month) and returned once more to Hajkowce. He translated Pushkin's poetry in verse and wrote poems himself.

My cousin Zygmunt Protassewicz, the second son of Uncle Wiluś who had died in Russia, also lived in Warsaw. Zygmunt had been a star pupil at his secondary school in Moscow which he left with a gold medal before securing a place (in August 1917) at the Moscow Institute of Roads and Communication; however he had to break his studies when the family returned to Wilno. He served as a cavalry lieutenant during the Polish-Bolshevik War. After the war Zygmunt resumed his studies at the Warsaw Polytechnical Institute and graduated as a construction engineer. He was responsible for the building of a hotel in Krynica for Jan Kiepura. The Hotel 'Patria' project enhanced his national reputation as a construction engineer, and he was then commissioned to supervise the building of a military hospital in Warsaw, named after Marshal Piłsudski. Zygmunt also met his future wife, Jadwiga Smosarska, one of Poland's leading theatre and film actresses, through Kiepura.[4]

In Warsaw, I often visited Aunt Jadzia Jamontt in her apartment at number 10, Krucza Street. Aunt Jadzia was lady-like and beautiful. She had lovely green eyes, an animated face and was full of life; she was always cheerful and hospitable. Her beautiful hair was always arranged in a coiled plait, and she had fine hands and shapely legs. I remember her when she was no longer young; even in her late forties, her appearance was regal. She had something of the dignified and elegant bearing of the present Queen Mother (widow of George VI). She married her cousin Maciej Jamontt, a well-known barrister in Wilno and legal counsellor in one of the city's banks, a man of senatorial bearing, enormous height and broad shoulders. The largest part of his income came from his work as the plenipotentiary to Marchioness Janina Umiastowska who owned substantial landed estates in Poland and property in Italy. Maciej had played an important role in the formation of Polish military units in Russia after the February Revolution, and later in the Polish administration of the region around Minsk. Maciej's character was despotic. When, twenty years later, the Bolsheviks entered Wilno in 1939, he continued to go for strolls down the main street with a cigar in his mouth, and scolded the Bolsheviks like dogs. It was hardly surprising that he was eventually arrested. He died from tuberculosis in Siberia.[5]

In her Warsaw apartment, Aunt Jadzia entertained the cream of society and members of the 'jeunesse dorée'. I remember how I once committed a faux pas there during the visit of Stefan Ossowiecki who had acquired a European-wide reputation as a psychic-clairvoyant. I asked Ossowiecki, a portly gentleman surrounded by adoring ladies, whether he 'still possessed his powers of clairvoyancy'. On hearing this, Ossowiecki shot up and almost spun around in mid-air. Jadzia was horrified and was at a loss how to cover up my tactless utterance. Needless to say, by that stage I was already rather sceptical.

And it was in Warsaw that I also encountered further emotional experiences. Once, during a longer stay in the city in 1936, Aunt Marzeńka (the widow of Uncle Antoni Protassewicz and now remarried with the surname Bielonowa) invited me to her home in Żoliborz in north Warsaw. There I first set eyes on the tall and good-looking *inżynier* Adolf Skwarczewski who was standing in front of a table covered with magnificent oriental fruit which he used to bring with him. He seemed to me the personification of Vinicius in *Quo Vadis?* His face had wonderful fine masculine features; his beautiful green eyes expressed high-mindedness; his hair was black as night; his complexion was dark, almost Italian in appearance. Immediately *inżynier* Skwarczewski began to court me. I shall never forget the beautiful sonorous male voice which I heard on the telephone every day. It emerged that he had broken up with his fiancée and in all haste wanted to marry me.

I spent Christmas Eve that year in Warsaw with Jadzia Jamontt; the atmosphere there was pleasant and warm. I suggested a meeting with *inżynier* Skwarczewski in Jadzia's residence, for indeed I eventually moved in there. I remember the occasion as if it was today. We were sitting on a sofa in the dining room. He took my hand and asked me if I wanted to be his wife, and to marry in two months' time. I was dumbfounded. He seemed to me some unreal prince from a fairytale, from *One Thousand and One Nights*. I said that ... I didn't know ... although I was perfectly and deeply in love with him. He bade me farewell and I was never to meet him again. No sooner had he

Figure 4. Three sisters (left to right): Irena, Jula and Hania in Warsaw, 1936.

left when Jadzia, who had been eavesdropping through the door, rushed out of her bedroom and assailed me with all her fury: 'How could you possibly say something like that!!!' She scolded me from the heart. 'I spend so much money here leading a social life on a grand scale to find a suitable match for my Halina. Many people have passed through my drawing room, and I have not yet met anyone like your *inżynier*, such a wonderful and charming man. You're an utter idiot for not having said "Yes". I too suffered terribly that it all came to nothing. In any case, news reached me that Mamusia had had a heart attack and was in a clinic in Wilno. My sister Hania had travelled there immediately. I therefore had to return to Borki forthwith, to be with my father.

That same winter my Babcia (granny) Antonina Żórawska (née Romanowicz) died. She was staying with us in Borki when she caught a chill sitting on the porch. I happened to be sitting with her in her room when I noticed her face turn increasingly pale, while retaining a calm expression, full of kindness. She passed away quietly in my arms. I have never witnessed such a beautiful death. Babcia was about eighty-two years old when she died, yet she always worried that in old age a person does not look as pretty as when young. In her youth she used to be concerned about her freckles. I therefore powdered her face to make it look prettier. Aunt Mania Żórawska arrived, broken-hearted by her mother's death. Adam, our coachman, transported the coffin to Wężowszczyzna. Mamusia, who was still in hospital, was not informed, for fear that she might have another heart attack. With her character, Babcia soothed all family disputes. She used to tell me that her mother Helena Romanowicz (née Thugutt) had been impatient, while her father counsellor Franciszek Romanowicz, who admired Ruskin's philosophy, always calmed her down and tried to bring cheerfulness and harmony into their home. Babcia had a great devotion to The Sacred Heart and taught us a prayer to it. She went through life like an angel of kindness, which was no mean feat when married to a despotic husband who sowed fear all around.

In the meantime, *inżynier* Skwarczewski's former fiancée, a divorcee, returned to him. There was a reconciliation between them and they got married. It was good that I did not marry *inżynier* Skwarczewski, for it turned out that he was a Russian; when he did marry, it was in an Orthodox church, which would have been unthinkable for me.[6] Besides, he was a townie, and told me that my Borki was a drawback in his eyes, for of what concern to him was our family tradition. As the representative of Ford cars in Poland he travelled abroad every year, and in the summer earned about 70,000 złotys from the sale of cars at his Warsaw office on Kredytowa Street.[7] He was not for me.

In a similar way I once found myself attracted to the wonderful Captain Kazimierz (Kazik) de Latour, and also found, with the passage of time, that it was fortunate that cousin Leoś successfully prevented a marriage.[8] De Latour was a dashing society man and was unsuited to be a husband or a father to any children. Furthermore, life in the army would not have been for me. But to go back to the beginning of the story: our meeting was arranged secretly by Judge Janusz Jamontt and his wife, the parents of my friend Hela, who lived on Aleje Niepodległości (Independence Avenue) in Warsaw.[9] The Jamontts invited me one evening. I knocked on the door, entered and was greeted by an army captain of unusual charm and elegance. It transpired that he was the brother of Panna Marysia who lived with the Jamontts. I had never before seen such graceful movement, such a fine figure of a man, such a lively face with eyes like emeralds. Captain de Latour looked very different when compared to *inżynier* Skwarczewski, who was dark and had the heavy build of an athlete. Pan Kazik was light in build and narrow in the waist, like a wasp; he was blond and his graceful bearing was worthy of the salons of his ancestors, the marquises de Latour. Apparently one of his forebears had settled in our country during the Napoleonic wars. To be in his company was true romanticism.

We agreed to meet at 'IPS', an artistic café, the evening my sister Hania was to sing there.[10] I wore a black satin dress (the top was like a dress coat) with a bunch of pink roses pinned on. Pan Kazik was in his elegant uniform. The room was full of Warsaw's fashionable society. I also noticed Aunt Jadzia Jamontt dressed exquisitely and with company. Hania's slim silhouette appeared on the stage; she was wearing a long cherry-coloured silk dress with a rectangular low-cut neck. She began to sing about love; the most wonderful songs she could find. She sang with a beautiful and melodious, velvet voice, and always kept her eyes on us, giving to understand that she was indeed singing for us. It is simply difficult to describe the magic of that evening. Everything was beautiful, and I was happy sitting at that table with my black coffee.

At that time I was living in my brother-in-law Janek Karczewski's boarding house on Widok Street, and so I invited cousin Leoś to visit me there. I told him that I was enchanted by the handsome de Latour. Leoś then called on his friend Tadeusz Stulgiński who had known Pan Kazik since the time they both lived in Grodno; Stulgiński's uncle and de Latour's father were high-ranking army officers stationed there. Tadeusz and Leoś came to the conclusion that if I married de Latour that would be the end of Borki. Leoś then informed me that Pan Kazik would come to Borki 'over his dead body'. My sister Hania indiscreetly blurted this out to her friend Panna Marysia, who in turn passed this on to her brother Kazik. A scandal erupted. Not wanting to challenge Leoś to a duel, Pan Kazik immediately left Warsaw and I was never to see him again. During the war, he was captured by the Germans and was to spend many years as a prisoner of war. Pretending to be my brother, Pan Kazik then tried to find me through the Red Cross. His letter reached me too late, for it was several days after Michał and I had got engaged.[11]

At key points in my life I have been moved to write poetry. Aunt Marzeńka arranged for two of my poems to be published in *Kurier Warszawski* (Warsaw Courier).[12]

'Longing' ('*Pragnienie*')
I am filled with sudden longing
For life, for room, for wings
To the brim of suffering
Oh plenitude of joy, of all things

I'll snap a hundred winds
I'll bend them in my hands
Between my teeth rose-wands
Though the thorn wounds

Like fistfuls of cherries I cram
Lifeblood for my limbs
Into my mouth, into my craw
They blossom as the Aurora

'Happiness' ('*Szczęście*')
(**written in Borki when I was in the senior form at school, aged 18–19**)
Happiness deep and tender wafted through my window
like a stand of lilies, like rain-dewed narcissi …
All had been gloom and swoon and twilight,
Silence draped the walls and shrouded the ceiling,
A nightmare spider madness tore its webs,
A spiritless void yawned from dark corners,
and this was neither swoon nor wakefulness.
When, with a sweet radiance, suddenly …

Because of my poor health, I was unable to go to university, although I always dreamt of studying philosophy or something in the field of the social sciences. I catered for my intellectual needs through my friendship with Hela Jamontt, a person of exceptional talent who had finished law at the University of Warsaw with the highest marks, and was now studying philosophy, with the expectation of achieving something in that field.

Hela was short in height, and with her round smiling face resembled that of a Japanese girl. Unfortunately, through her association with Bolesław Piasecki, she got entangled with the ONR . Hela Jamontt was unusually religious and challenged the psychological materialism propounded by her lecturer Professor Kotarbiński.[13] She went to Holy Communion daily, yet somehow, strangely, was able to reconcile this with a blind faith in Piasecki and his world-shaking views.[14] She even managed to persuade me to pawn my splendid flared astrakhan fur coat and lend Piasecki 450 złotys – which were never repaid to me.

Hela was very much impressed by Piasecki who at one point even proposed to her: nothing came of this. Once, at an ONR meeting to which Hela invited me, I spotted an unusually tall brunette with the good looks of Juno. Her name was Halina. I have never encountered a woman of such dignity and beauty, almost born to be a queen. I think that it was she whom Piasecki later married, no doubt considering her as more suitable to be the wife of the leader of the nation, which he dreamt of becoming, rather than the diminutive figure of my Hela Jamontt who was full of enthusiasm but who combined it with a convent-like puritanism.[15] I once saw a magnificent bouquet of flowers from Piasecki in Hela's apartment, and he later used to visit her in a sanatorium in Zakopane where she was being treated for the tuberculosis she contracted in the dreadful smoke-filled atmosphere of the ONR premises. The summer of 1939 proved to be stormy in the relationship between Hela and Piasecki: I had the feeling that it was then that the final rupture between them occurred. Hela Jamontt was to die later, heroically, during the Warsaw Uprising, and ended up buried under the rubble.[16]

Piasecki exploited my presence in Warsaw (in 1933–4) to use me as a messenger. On one occasion I was 'ordered' to meet some mysterious character with a false beard by a lamp post, and to whisper to him instructions for some secret meeting. The person I met turned out to be Wojciech Wasiutyński, now a writer.[17] At that time I lived separately, opposite Hela Jamontt, and it was in my landlady's drawing room that I arranged a meeting between Bolesław Piasecki and Count Emeryk Czapski, the parliamentary deputy for the Słonim district.[18] I used to carry a dagger in my fur coat. Despite all this, I was unaware that I was being followed by the police. I only discovered this later, in Palestine, from the charming and good-looking General Zamorski himself, the chief of the State Police, and Marshal Piłsudski's confidant.[19]

In view of this, I should not have been surprised by the considerable excitement generated in the summer of 1934 when Hela Jamontt came to stay with me in Borki. She was a regular summer visitor and used to sleep in a room in the extension to the house, with a wall separating our two rooms. One evening I heard knocking on Hela's door, and the entry of police officers, accompanied by Tatuś, into her room. The officers were very apologetic to Tatuś but told him they had received orders from Warsaw to search Hela's belongings. Pieracki, the minister of interior, had just been murdered, and it was suspected that the ONR were responsible. Further investigation was to reveal that the assassination was the work of Ukrainian nationalists.[20] It was fortunate that Hela had just given me all her subversive literature, which I was then studying in bed. I was frightened to move in case I betrayed my presence in the adjacent room; I also had no idea how to destroy these papers. Fortunately, the police did not look into my room – and that is how it ended. Hela tried to persuade me to organize public meetings and to explain to the peasants the erroneous policy of the government, but I did not consider this to be right.

I was reminded of this later, in exile in Britain, by Pan Wacław Boldok, a former district governor in Polesie in the east of Poland, who told me the story of the local bishop Łoziński.[21] The bishop was an ascetic individual and was considered as a saint; he always travelled third class by train and led a life of mortification. An example of the latter could be provided when he got an attack of appendicitis; he demanded from the doctors that he should be operated on without any anaesthetic because he wanted to suffer for Christ. The surgeons cut open his abdomen. The bishop's face remained composed; he was evidently praying. But his intestines started to convulse terribly, and the operation could not continue until he had finally agreed to have the anaesthetic. Just as Bishop Bandurski had been an enthusiastic supporter of Piłsudski's Legions, so was Bishop Łoziński an inexorable enemy of Piłsudski's followers who were in power after the 1926 coup. 'They're socialists and they're godless', Bishop Łoziński used to preach. It was one thing to spread such propaganda in a region such as the province of Poznań where the population was overwhelmingly Polish, ultra-Catholic and with a nationalist tinge. But to fulminate against the political party in power in Polesie of all places, with its Belarusian inhabitants, and with a population more than half Orthodox, unfavourably disposed to the Poles and undermined by Bolshevik propaganda, was not only highly unwise but was simply destructive of the social order and would have dangerous long-term political consequences. Bishop Łoziński was so dogged in his ultra-Catholic and nationalist patriotism that he failed to see the danger and the consternation which his Savonarola-like sermons produced. Governor Boldok was charged with the task of curbing the bishop's folly and political fanaticism. Pan Boldok described to me how he had to employ all his diplomatic skills in order to persuade the bishop, without offending his high episcopal dignity, of the negative effects of his sermons. The bishop listened, understood and abated his violent anti-government stance. After the war, in 1948, much was said in the Polish resettlement camp near Morpeth in Northumberland about the possibility of canonizing Bishop Łoziński. Pan Boldok told us in confidence: 'If they're going to canonize him, it will follow that I had given lessons to a Saint, that I had admonished him ... indeed.'

When I first met him, Governor Boldok was an unusually charming and agreeable elderly man. Although quite rounded in overall appearance, his fresh ruddy complexion testified to a life led honestly but with good food. He was frank and hospitable, and he inspired feelings of affection among people whose company he kept. Indeed, the local Jews of Polesie were able to appreciate the fairness of his administration, so much so that when he arrived in Palestine after leaving Russia (in 1942), many Jews there tried to persuade him to settle in their country, saying he would have guaranteed hospitality there for the rest of his life. Such was their gratitude. In the end, Pan Wacław came to England where he mastered the craft of watchmaking. However, he declined the invitation from an English owner to remain in his firm; he wanted to spend the last years of his life among his own people. A few years later he moved from Morpeth to the Polish resettlement camp in Northwick Park in Gloucestershire where he found genial company for himself in his post as the doctor's secretary. He unexpectedly fell ill with cancer of the liver and died much lamented by everyone. One woman who worked there as a nurse described how beautiful his death was. As a result of some injection his body swelled up terribly, and the poor man sought help. The doctors and nurses were evasive and did not want to reveal the nature of his illness. Suddenly, a moment came during a conversation with friends when he understood that he had to die. It was with great poignancy that he took leave of all his associates, thanking everyone for their kindness and friendship. Such was the manner of death of a true gentleman who remained such until the very end. His wife, who remained in Poland, was able to arrange for a gravestone to be put up in the Roman Catholic cemetery in Chipping Campden. On All Souls' Day, I always place flowers on his grave. I cannot forget how, when I was expecting my daughter Helenka, he presented me with a bunch of Alpine violets and compared me to Połaniecka.[22] He was very fond of my two-year-old Wacio and gave him a toy hammer as a present; it now lies broken somewhere in the shed.

5

Wacław Protassewicz: The last squire of Borki

Late marriage – Love of music – Family responsibilities – Cousin Leoś – Aunt
Józia – A generous and even-tempered personality – A wise counsellor –
Abramek and the Dreyfus Affair – Cousin Polik – Views on peasants – Incident
in Warsaw – Gourmet – Model carp farm – Religion – Production of starch –
Stories of ghosts – Russo-Japanese War – Invited to stand for Parliament –
Persuades Irena to take up beekeeping

My father spent two years courting my mother. My maternal grandfather, Stanisław
Żórawski, was at first against such a marriage because Wacław and Zofia were cousins.[1]
On the day of their wedding (9 September 1909) my father was forty years old and my
mother was twenty-five. They were married in Sobakińce, in the local parish church
which served Wężowszczyzna, after which the newly-weds set out by carriage to Borki
which was to be their home. My mother was thrilled by the great bonfires which
Uncle Antoś had lit on various hills along the route to Borki. The entry to Borki was
triumphal. Eventually all the guests departed and all went quiet .... My mother told
me, with great feeling, of her happiness on being gradually and very gently introduced
into the secrets of marital life.

My father was a typical true landed gentleman (*szlachcic*) with handsome features,
an aquiline nose and a finely shaped head. When as a child I sometimes saw him in the
morning, lying in bed with his chest uncovered, he seemed to me like a Slavonic God
the Father. In his youth he was very handsome with slightly feminine looks. Later he
acquired a more manly appearance and sported a short beard and an upwardly pointed
moustache. His beautiful bright green eyes were lively and jocular.

I must add that my father was born in 1868, in an era when only wax candles
and rushlights were used in kitchens and cottages. The railway line from Wilno to
Baranowicze was constructed during his lifetime (in 1884). Then suddenly news burst
forth that in Wilno someone was transmitting the sound of a bell by means of a wire.
Tatuś got his *bryczka* ready, or perhaps he dared to get on the first train, to reach a
house where it was demonstrated how one presses a button in one place and a ringing
sound is emitted in another. It did not take long before local landowners were seized
by a mania to erect telegraph poles and to connect their homes with those of their
neighbours by wires: the telephone had been invented. No taxes were imposed on this

by the Russian authorities, so whoever could afford wire and poles could spend hours chatting happily and exchanging all the gossip with the most beautiful ladies in the area. Holding intellectual sway among the ladies was Wanda Wołłowicz (later Strawińska, and then Roycewicz), the 'sophisticated' heiress of Rohotna. The war of 1914, or was it the peasants being keen on the timber, brought about the end of these marvellous poles. During Poland's twenty-year period of independence, the bureaucrats were always on the lookout to tax any luxury; as a result no one in our district had the temerity to run such a wire cobweb for their own amusement.

Interest in the telephone ceased, but eventually there was a rush in the large cities to purchase the wireless. News of this invention reached Borki. So, for the sum of 450 złotys, and while remaining in the distant provinces, Tatuś and Mamusia were able to satisfy their greatest pleasure: music. It was no longer necessary to travel all the way to Warsaw to listen to Paderewski, something my grandfather Żórawski once did when he took the entire family in his horse-drawn coach and raced to hear the maestro play in Chopin's birthplace. We now had broadcast music at home, and Hania's first radio performances delighted my parents. The servants too gathered in the dining room, where the four-valve radio was kept, to listen to the young lady. My father was very fond of music and it gave him great pleasure that my mother played the piano beautifully. She had been taught by my grandmother Antonina Żórawska who had graduated with distinction from the Warsaw conservatoire, where she had been a contemporary of Ignacy Paderewski. However, being a woman, she was forbidden by her parents to go to Paris to continue her further musical training and to make a name for herself.

Tatuś understood what it meant to struggle for survival and to be anxious to secure the welfare of the family; indeed, he spent most of his life battling for a better future. From his early childhood the family was forced to exercise ceaseless vigilance on account of a variety of burdens and expenses: heavy fines imposed by the tsarist government on the estate after the Insurrection of 1863–4; the destruction by fire of the distillery; and the arrival of a large number of children at home. On several occasions Tatuś mentioned how his mother (my Babcia Apolonia) was often deprived of a tasty morsel. Only bare bones remained by the time even the largest roast hare had been divided among ten children at the table. Like termites, the voracious tensome devoured everything to the last mouthful. Furthermore, the children had to be educated and set up in the world. The eldest daughter Maria (Marynia) managed to get married before my grandfather Eustachy's death in 1896. After this, responsibility for the younger girls rested awith Tatuś, Eustachy's eldest son. After Eustachy's death, Tatuś's brother Piotr received Rohotenka, 4 km from Borki, while the youngest brother Leon acquired Hajkowce, which further reduced Tatuś's resources. It all explains why my father married very late in life – and why his earlier hopes of marriage had come to naught.

As a twenty-year-old youth, Tatuś had fallen in love with Julia Gnoińska of Wiszów. Many, many years later he told us: 'You have no idea how beautiful she was!' She was not only beautiful and rich but also warm-hearted and kind. Alas, Tatuś was twenty and had eight younger siblings, while there appeared from Russia a handsome and wealthy Colonel Bilczyński. And so Julia Gnoińska married him (it is after her that my sister was named Julia). Ultimately, it proved to be a good marriage because this wealthy tsarist officer was attractive and proved to be a loving family man. Tatuś also succumbed to the charm of beautiful Wanda Wołłowiczówna of Rohotna, but his prospects of wooing her proved equally fruitless when the wealthy Ksawery Strawiński arrived on the scene. Wanda's mother, who had a good head for business, took aside my charming twenty-year-old but penniless father and put the question to him: 'Tell me, isn't my daughter beautiful?' 'Yes', replied Tatuś. 'Could one make a "good match" with such a beauty?' she continued. 'Yes, one could', replied Tatuś. 'So, my dear Wacio, I beg you, don't prevent her from making a good match.' Tatuś understood and withdrew, only to hear her add: 'Oh, yes, my dear, I would have no objection if you were to marry my second daughter.'

As for Pani Wołłowiczowa's second daughter, Tatuś soon discovered that she was not for him. Tatuś once told me how he was travelling in a *bryczka* with this second daughter. They were crossing over a bridge when suddenly something splashed in the water below: it transpired that her false plait had fallen off. Tatuś, who could not stand any kind of falsehood, was deeply shocked by this. In any case, he caught the young lady out in a lie on more than one occasion. It was therefore not surprising that when he once had a dream that he had married her, he awoke in horror, bathed in sweat. In fact, Wanda's sister married Bolesław Połubiński, the brother of my aunt Salunia's husband. Sadly, after giving birth to a daughter she went insane and was to spend the rest of her life in an asylum. It seems her lies had a pathological basis. Her daughter Ninka (Antonina) Połubińska later married Tolik (Antoni) Stabrowski. Tolik was a good husband and had a talent for mechanics, but he also had a weakness for alcohol. After the Second World War they both left for Argentina.[2]

To cope with his family responsibilities, Tatuś built a starch-processing plant on the estate. Since the Russian market was virtually limitless, this gave him a substantial income. He was then able to pay off those of his brothers who had left the estate to seek their fortune building railways in Siberia, namely Wilhelm, Antoni and Narcyz. Tatuś was also able to provide dowries for all his remaining sisters. His sense of responsibility for his younger siblings helps to explain why Tatuś was forbearing towards Wańkowicz who provided for his own family with his pen, and also why Tatuś had sympathy for the Jews, those landless and eternal wanderers. For the Jews too had to find whatever means they could to feed their families.

Tatuś's concern for those closest to him developed loyalty and warmth among all the children; with it also came a willing readiness to make sacrifices for the others, and to show openhanded generosity when the financial situation improved. Some years later, Tatuś financed a gathering of the Protassewicz family held in Wilno in connection with the unveiling of a plaque, dedicated to Bishop Walerian Protassewicz, in the university hall, and contributed 500 złotys to the making of this plaque. He also paid for his niece Mila from Rohotenka to attend a beauty contest in Warsaw, and so on. Mamusia was also generous, and I remember how she always reminded Tatuś to give 100 złotys to each of his fatherless nephews when they were leaving Borki to attend school in Wilno. The four nephews were known collectively as the 'Wiluś-ites' (*Wilusiucy*), that is the sons of the late Wiluś (Wilhelm) Protassewicz. Uncle Wiluś had been building railways in Siberia but found himself trapped in Russia after the Bolsheviks seized power. Wiluś lost not just his fortune there; he was detained and died later from throat cancer in a Cheka prison.[3]

My orphaned cousin Leoś (son of Uncle Narcyz who also died in Russia) was brought up in Borki and also enjoyed Tatuś's support. He attended a military college, after which he was appointed second lieutenant in the signals corps. He was tall and had raven black hair, like his Buryat mother. He had an exceptionally pleasant personality; no one disliked him. My sisters and I loved him like a brother. He was always full of fun. As a child I remember when he once jumped into a pond to save my boat from drifting into the deep end. He loved hunting and always took our coachman's son Staś Skorochod with him.

Leoś had a noble character and a great sense of honour. He was once invited by a young countess, whose fancy he had caught, to visit her at her residence in Zatrocze, by a lake near Wilno.[4] He never called there again. His manly pride was offended when the countess, showing him around the estate, kept on saying 'These are my horses. This is my coachman' and so on. Leoś was poor but proud. He later became engaged to Alina Jankowska, the daughter of the governor of Wilno province. Leoś became very attached to the Jankowski family, as both the mother and daughter were so full of warmth. Leoś and Alina were to get married as soon as Alina finished her law studies. But the war shattered their plans.

In 1939 Poland was invaded by the Germans and by the Soviets (Bolsheviks). Leoś took part in fighting the Bolsheviks near Lida. He was wounded in the head, but was able to withdraw with his unit to the German zone of occupation. His betrothed, on the other hand, remained in the east under Soviet rule. Leoś joined the Home Army. At one stage he was caught by the Germans but somehow managed to escape. At some point during the war he married someone else. Sadly, he was killed in December 1944 by an incendiary bomb at the railway station in Częstochowa.

By nature, Tatuś could not bear selfish people. For example, he did not visit his relatives, the Mik[…],[5] because they had once refused him some milk; their excuse was that it was intended for the cheese dairy. Like Piłsudski, Tatuś sought the company of those who really loved him, even if they were young small fry. He suffered most when someone to whom he had been generous proved mean-spirited in return. For instance, Tatuś had always shown kindness to his brother Uncle Piotruś of Rohotenka, who did not possess my father's business acumen and was less well-off financially. And yet when Piotruś's wife Aunt Kama once lent Tatuś a sheaf-binder, she did so on the condition, which she stipulated in a letter, that it should not be damaged.

Indeed, all my father's siblings possessed an expansive temperament, with the exception of Aunt Józia (Józefa). Before the First World War her husband, *inżynier* Longin Koczan, had been engaged in the construction of railways in Siberia and Manchuria. Aunt Józia was fussy over details, pedantic about tidiness and could not stand Jews. That is why she and her husband moved to Poznań.[6] There Józia belonged to various nationalist-catholic organizations which, when she died, bade her farewell to the next world with flags and banners. I spent eight months with Aunt Józia in Poznań, right up to her death (it must have been in 1932). She remained cheerful during the eight months she had to spend in bed under the care of a nurse. When she died it was noticed that cancer had gnawed away at her leg bones to such an extent that they could be bent. Death came kindly. A few tears appeared in her eyes, and she was gone.

Tatuś considered himself as one of nature's noble-minded persons; he said that such people could not be corrupted by any company they found themselves in. He told us about the various shady landowners he had come across. He even spent time in the company of crooks and drunks, yet nothing ever 'stuck' to him. In a letter to Mamusia, in which he proposed marriage, he emphasized that she would never experience any unpleasant surprises with him for he was an even-tempered person. Indeed, noble-mindedness and an even temper were my father's foremost qualities, and of course his innate wisdom and common sense. His ability to make a fair judgement was sought not only by lonely landed ladies but also by local Jews. The latter even came to seek advice on family matters; for instance, in one case, a Jewish man consulted my father about his unfaithful wife who preferred young peasants to himself, her skinny husband.

During the Dreyfus affair, the local Jewish community in a forsaken corner of our district and in our distant part of the world imposed heavy contributions on its members. Poor Abramek, a Jewish leaseholder in neighbouring Izmajłowszczyzna, was tearing his hair out with worry as to how to find so much money. Abramek looked very much like a patriarch and was distinguished by his impeccable honesty. Tatuś was moved by Abramek's story and helped him to make this payment. This is an interesting footnote to Jewish history: even poor Abramek was not exempt from having to contribute to the collection of funds from all over Europe in order to defend Dreyfus.

On one occasion, many years later in the interwar period, Abramek learnt that my cousin Polik, the airman, had come to visit us. Abramek then turned up to inform Polik that two old Mikulski spinsters, 'who would die soon', had many square kilometres of forest on their estate Litwa near Słonim. He advised Polik: 'Well, would it not be a good idea for Sir to marry one of them, and then to be able to fly above your own forests rather than above someone else's?' However, Polik evidently preferred to fly over other people's forests. Once during air force manoeuvres in Lida, Polik unexpectedly appeared in his aircraft over Borki and started to circle the house very low. Tatuś loved Polik very much, but got very agitated by these acrobatics. He rushed out and started to scold him, shouting towards the clouds: 'What the devil, you're mad! You might break my lime trees!' Tatuś waved his stick furiously in the direction of Polik's visible silhouette leaning out of the fighter plane. Polik just waved back.

Polik had earlier joined the Polish Air Force – to his mother's despair. He graduated from the Officer Cadet School at Dęblin in 1929 and returned there at one stage as an instructor. After Poland's defeat in 1939, Polik managed to escape to France and was later evacuated to Britain. He served as a major and flew on bombing raids over Hamburg.[7] He was subsequently appointed Head of Intelligence at the Polish Air Force headquarters in London. I met Polik in London at the end of the war, and I remember him telling me that during the raid on Hamburg he was so scared by the German night fighters that were attacking them all around that it did not occur to him that he was murdering people on the ground below.

It was in his views of the local peasantry that Tatuś was less generous. Once, after I had treated Staś Skorochod's injured finger and had visited the village with medicines, my father commented: 'Don't think that the peasants are capable of feeling gratitude. I know them well and I prefer that they should fear me rather than love me.' He often told us the story of a very wealthy landowner in Volhynia who had given away all his land to the local peasants and had decided to spend his old age living modestly in a little house. The peasants killed him in case he should decide to alter his will. Tatuś spoke of the peasants as 'cattle' who could only be kept under control through fear. Tatuś mentioned to me only one example of a peasant who was a gentleman by nature: that was Jan Zych. He was a fine figure of a man, and indeed his behaviour was beyond reproach during the Bolshevik upheaval. It was hardly surprising since he had been 'inoculated' against Bolshevism. He had earlier married a beautiful and wealthy woman from Estonia. When the Bolsheviks came, they threw him out and appropriated his house.[8] There was the case of Heljasz, our barn-keeper, for whom Tatuś had built a cottage on the edge of Borki village as a gift. During the Bolshevik period in 1920, Heljasz drove us children to work at harvest time. When the Bolsheviks arrived in 1939 he took away my father's portrait and put it up in his cottage. Nevertheless, it has to be acknowledged that soon after that, with his wagon, he helped Mamusia and Jula with her children to catch a train and escape from the Soviets to Warsaw.

Tatuś loved to tell stories about his adventures in Warsaw, when as a young bachelor he made his début in the wide world. At a ball he met an adorable sixteen-year-old debutante. Because this was her first ball, he sent her a large basket of roses as a surprise with an anonymous message: 'To the Queen of the Ball'. She guessed who had sent the flowers and waited for a visit and a proposal of marriage. But Tatuś disappeared from Warsaw; he was to learn subsequently that she had apparently cried as a result of his actions.

Many years later, after Marshal Piłsudski's coup of May 1926, Tatuś went on some business to Warsaw when there was still some unrest in the city. Walking at night in his beaver fur coat and his tall Persian lamb hat, he spotted a group of rough characters, looking in his direction and whispering among themselves. Eventually, one of the group approached Tatuś and asked him for a light. Tatuś had a feeling that they wanted to rob him of his coat, but he did not have his revolver with him. So he hit on another idea. Instead of replying in Polish, he responded in some gibberish which he invented on the spot. 'That's the Swedish envoy', muttered the thieves, 'or some foreign baron', and they walked away. After this incident Wanda Roycewicz endowed Tatuś with the title of 'Baron by the will of the people', and attached some baronial coat-of-arms at the rear of Tatuś's sleigh.[9]

How unforgettable is the splendid figure of my father. How I enjoyed his stories, his sense of humour in company and sitting down with him at the table at meal times. I have never met anyone who ate with such grace and with such appetite, which in turn so effectively stimulated the appetite of others. Indeed, Tatuś was a gourmet, and with such style in company that it appeared to be a virtue, an embellishment of the table. He contributed wit to all conversation; without his presence one simply did not want to eat. He loved fish of all kinds. Mamusia, on the other hand, was not particularly keen, so during our stay in Taganrog, when for a time we had no servant, Tatuś would set out specially to the railway station where the restaurant served a famous fish soup (*ukha* in Russian). The food at home in Borki was not particularly exquisite, as it was in Wężowszczyzna for instance, but everything was prepared with butter, and there was pure cream in the sorrel soups (half and half proportions). And no one could stuff chicken or roast piglets as well as our cook Anna. What a delight were her various *bliny*, and even more so her *pierogi* stuffed with all kinds of berries and served with whipped cream. I don't expect to eat anything so tasty again in my life. Food in England is dreadful and monotonous, while at home now I have neither the time nor the inclination to spend the whole day in the kitchen. Today one eats only to live, and as cheaply as possible.

Tatuś loved farming, and the breeding of fish was a real hobby of his. It is difficult to calculate all the time that he spent by his ponds overseeing the catching of the fish, or checking that sufficient lupin flour had been provided for the carp, or whether the females were spawning, or whether the young fry had grown. In the spring, during the fishing season, sometimes whole boatloads of green frog tadpoles were collected; these were then boiled in a pot, turned into a thick jelly, and fed to the fish. Other harmful larvae were also thus destroyed.

Tatuś was able to establish his model carp farm by resorting to an old legal document, for the project involved the Sidorowiczes's farm at Ladzinki, just over 2 km west of Borki, which my grandfather Eustachy had once given as a present to a loyal steward. The house at Ladzinki was delightfully situated on a hill with open fields and a wood above, and with a small pond and meadows on the Ladzinka stream lower down. The stream then flowed down into our pond at Borki. On making the gift, my grandfather stipulated one condition: that he would retain the right to raise the level of the Borki pond, and this would involve flooding the Ladzinki meadow. And it was on the basis of this document that Tatuś was able to enlarge the pond for his carp. Jews eagerly bought the carp, but the greatest profit probably came from the sale of fry. Sometimes Adam Skorochod transported barrels full of fry by rail in the direction of Wilno. Tatuś started the trend of breeding carp which was copied by many landowners, some even in distant parts, who began to set up their own breeding ponds. For one fish show in Słonim, Tatuś instructed Adam to make some long boxes with nets on top and special compartments in which the different stages of a carp's development were displayed: from the fry to the full-grown carp ready for sale, and ending up with enormous pregnant 'mothers'.

Displayed on a board attached to a pole was cousin Leoś's hand-drawn map of the ponds, as well as my schoolgirl doggerel rhyme which amused everyone:

'Carp for Your Table Makes You a Lord' (*'Kto ma karpia w wodzie – równy wojewodzie'*)
When the taxman voids your pockets
you can wriggle from his harness
and you'll save a heap of złoty
when you buy these carp from Borki
renowned through Słonim for their cheapness
and the speed with which they grow,
as if they fed on yeast; at morning spawn,
by evening they've already grown,
and next-day grace your breakfast table.

As for the Jewish traders who came to buy the carp, Tatuś dealt with them in a firm but jovial manner, for he liked them. One trader, for example, always liked to press the scales gently with his foot so that he would get more fish. Tatuś knew this trick of his and would say to him 'Hey, hey'. The trader would then move away from the scales. On one occasion, aware that they had a virtual monopoly over the sale of fish, the Jews started to offer prices that were too low. Tatuś got angry and threw them out. He ordered Adam to load up the boxes with the carp on a horse-drawn wagon, and to proceed to the market in Słonim. He accompanied this fish caravan in his *bryczka*. Every now and then, Adam would stop the horses and pump air into the water in the boxes, and then he would continue. The Jewish traders were determined not to give up and organized a fake crush of people at the market. Jewish women, pretending to want to buy the fish, began to press onto the wagons; they grabbed the carp and started running off with them. Tatuś took out his revolver and began to shout. The Jewish women threw themselves on the ground, letting the fish fall out of their hands. Calm was restored. The traders approached Tatuś, accepted defeat and paid the higher prices. Tatuś sold the whole lot in bulk and departed. From then on the traders showed good manners, for they knew that they could neither trifle with nor blackmail Tatuś.[10]

Before it was turned into a reservoir for the commercial breeding of carp, the large pond had been a wild expanse of water. Preying in its depths were powerful old pike, the size of small crocodiles. They were hunted at night-time, during their spawning season. The hunting party, carrying flaming torches, would set out in boats which had hanging lights attached to the rear. A rifle would be fired in the spot where the swirling pike could be seen. The stunned pike would surface, whereupon they were harpooned and pulled into the boats.

Later, Tatuś kept enormous pregnant female carp in that pond. In early spring they were caught and placed in small fishponds where they laid their eggs. One year the females spawned prematurely in the large pond. Without the fry, the threat of a financial disaster loomed large, for Tatuś sometimes earned about 7,000 złotys in the autumn from the fish. What was to be done? Tatuś turned to old Sidorowicz for help and asked him if he could borrow some of his female carp which were not commercially exploited and which lived in a wild state in his small ponds. Our neighbour from Ladzinki obviously did not want to bother to lower the water levels of his fishponds so that his carp could be caught. He sent his brother-in-law to the ponds, and he apparently reported that the carp had already spawned. Tatuś became angry in a way I had never before seen. He wrote to Pan Sidorowicz announcing that he was breaking all relations with him. He ended his letter with the words: 'We shall meet in the valley of Jehosophat.'[11]

Mamusia was as upset by this incident as by the earlier affair of the would-be duel. Eventually, after several years, we resumed visits to Ladzinki, although without Tatuś. Fortunately, Aunt Kama came to our rescue. She had her large millpond lowered and lent us female carp for spawning. Naturally, as always, Tatuś repaid the kindness. The breeding of the fish had been saved.

The Borki ponds were very much a part of our lives. As children we were taught how to swim by lying on floating bunches of reeds. We used to go boating, and on the eve of the Feast of St John we placed small wreaths with candles on the water. In the winter we skated on the frozen ponds or travelled on skis beyond the forest. We also used to shoot the green frogs which gobbled up the carp fry; for this, Tatuś used to give us a few *groszy*. Once I fired so accurately with a revolver that I hit a frog right in the eye. There was also a cheaper way of killing frogs. Planks were placed on the water; the frogs then sat on them in large numbers. We approached the planks with oars in our hands and massacred the frogs en masse. Today I would be unable to carry out such slaughter, and I wonder how small children, copying one another, can be so cruel.

There were rotting remains of a bridge over the small river that flowed into the pond; its remaining rib-like structure had been pushed up quite high by the ice. During one of his visits to Borki, my cousin Gienio Morski went across the beams, turned to us, girls in our early teens, and announced that we women were cowards, and that we dare not stand on the edge of the water as he was doing. I was infuriated by this insult. I gathered my courage and crossed the river on the beam. It always hurt me that in life women were discriminated against, that wherever they went they were not allowed to do this or that. I sometimes cried at night because I had not been born a boy. Perhaps that is why, in my obstinacy, I loved to roam the forests alone with my revolver, and why, pretending to be a tomboy, I sought male diversions. Every evening as soon as dusk arrived, a servant would come out of the house and ring a bell; we then had to return home. On one occasion I had gone to Rohotenka on horseback. During the ride back, the horse balked; it was lame, and I had to walk leading it by the reins. I returned home late only to discover that Tatuś had sent out farm hands with lanterns along different tracks to look for me. Tatuś was anxious by nature; neither did he like the sight of someone else suffering.

Tatuś was religious, but in his own way. Once, when he was still a youth, my devout aunt Salunia, his sister, took him to the arbour of lime trees to help him examine his conscience.[12] She started with the sin of pride. Tatuś told us how he asked her to stop the reading for he knew that he was not at all proud, whereas after reading a many-page-long analysis of pride he might have come to the conclusion that he had been sinful all the time. Tatuś forbade Salunia from giving him any further instruction in moral theology. He felt that after any such microscopic analysis of every involuntary thought he would lose all sense of proportion and, being so entangled, would never be able to go to confession properly.

Indeed, Tatuś could not bear narrow-minded or pedantic people who, according to the Belarusian phrase, 'like to pick husks off shit'. 'Myself, I can't prove that God exists', he said, 'but I feel the presence of God's law in the order of the universe'. He found long repetitive prayers like the rosary unbearable. He said that if some village woman had come to him with a request, for instance to give her some branches for firewood, and instead of making her request once she had kept on repeating it over and over again, he would have got so cross that he would have sent her away with nothing. He was of the opinion that, similarly, God would not bear being bored with long talk.

Meat was not served during Lent. Yet this period coincided precisely with the greatest slaughter of pigs before Easter, and the larder was full of prepared delicacies. Occasionally Tatuś would sneak there with a penknife to have a slice of ham. Whenever he spotted us he would whisper: 'Quiet, just don't say anything to Zosia [his wife].' Having been in a convent school for so many years, where it was knocked into our heads that breaking church commandments was a mortal sin, my soul was at a loss. I was rendered highly sensitized on this issue, for I could not believe that Tatuś, with his noble character and his exceptional sense of justice, could be condemned for such an act of greed so charmingly committed, while so many egoists and heartless people who stuck to the letter of church law and fasted pedantically were supposed to be better than he was. I have finally lived to see the Second Vatican Council end this Pharisaic preoccupation with what enters the stomach. It was high time too. How many people have been tormented over the ages with the enforcement of fasting! When my famished husband Michał was in a Soviet labour camp during the Second World War and on the edge of starvation, he declined a piece of lard offered him by a fellow prisoner (probably on a Friday or some other day of fasting).[13] Is it not scandalous that children have such principles hammered into them?

My father disapproved of swotting, and his heart always bled when he saw us leaving for school. He considered that the existence of books was enough; that anyone capable of studying at school could learn by himself from books. He cited himself as an example.[14] He was not an engineer, but he constructed and set in motion a starch-processing plant all by himself. He made all the calculations of the rotation of wheels and of the transmission belts himself. Once, out of curiosity, he asked an engineer acquaintance to go over his construction and to identify any possible faults. After examining the plant and checking all the calculations, the engineer established only one error: too much material had been used in the building of the walls, which could have been a few inches thinner. Such a minimal saving on the wall would have represented a small fraction of the fee Tatuś would have had to pay a qualified engineer for constructing the plant. And if the wall was made more durable, what harm was there in that? After Tatuś's death in 1938, cousin Leoś sometimes entered the plant when it was operating at full power, and watched how one steam engine powered the potato shredder, the rinsing equipment, the machine mixing the potato pulp in vast tanks and another extracting the starch. All this functioned as if by itself, as if moved from the afterlife by Tatuś's spirit. Leoś commented that he was impressed by how the brain of one man could bring to life inanimate machines and thus achieve wonders.[15]

Tatuś was a good example of an independent autodidact, an entrepreneur by God's grace – if one can say that. He would throw himself like a pike into the whirlpool of business; if one area of his activity began to show a deficit, he quickly thought of another. Among other such enterprises, he showed an interest in beekeeping. I remember well how he occupied himself personally with our first couple of hives. Sometimes the bees stung his neck really badly through the protective net; the numerous stings stuck in his neck looked like bristles on a hog's skin.[16] There was no end to all sorts of new ideas, to the extent that Mamusia had to restrain him. For instance, she had to remind him that he no longer had the youth to build a drying house for milk that was to be used in the production of chocolate, something he was encouraged to do by a Jewish businessman.

For a long time Tatuś intended to dictate to me all his life's reminiscences. I cannot forgive myself that I had not managed to do this, deterred as I was by the fact that Tatuś wanted to tell the story in verse, like Mickiewicz's *Pan Tadeusz*. Tatuś had an unparalleled gift for storytelling. Once when he was in bed, he recounted the tale of *Baba Yaga* the witch, conveying with his voice the pathetic menace of the story. His rendering of the tawny owl's voice was most convincing, as well as the other voices associated with the tale. Nobody else could ever tell a story like that. It is sad to think that the tape recorder had not yet been invented, and that the timbre of my father's wonderful voice is lost for posterity, whereas today the whole world is flooded with dishwater from anybody's mouth. The heart bleeds and the ears swell.

Sometimes we spoke about ghosts. Tatuś did not believe in them, although Uncle Leon did hold forth a little about spiritualism to the adults, and in secret from the children. Tatuś told us how he once returned to Borki, tired after a ball, and entered the drawing room; at the time he was unmarried and lived alone. Suddenly, in the light of the moon, he saw the figure of a very old lady sitting on a sofa, her face covered with a lace veil. She was swaying to and fro as if welcoming Tatuś. Tatuś froze dumbfounded and wanted to flee. But curiosity got the better of him, and he stepped forward. It emerged that it was a raspberry plant which was swaying outside, and was visible, in the moonlight, through the lace curtain. The shadow cast on the sofa created the illusion of a veiled woman. Tatuś used to say that if he had run away then out of fear, he would have been certain to the end of his days that he had seen a ghost.

Before the First World War, during the period of the tsars, there was a rumour that one of the old roadside cemeteries was haunted by a white apparition. One night, Tatuś happened to be passing by along that road, and indeed his horses started to rear. By the light of the moon he caught sight of a figure in white, of extraordinary height, moving among the graves. Peasants going nearby used to make a sign of the cross with piety, and avoided this cemetery at night. However, one daredevil later took a shot in the direction of the ghost. The ghost fell down and began to groan. It emerged that the 'ghost' was a peasant wrapped up in a sheet and walking on stilts. He put on this act during the night to frighten away uninvited guests from the cemetery where, with utmost composure, his companions were distilling moonshine. In such a way those breaking the law fear neither the night nor graveyards. So why should noble-minded people be cowards? Tales told by nannies to children do great harm; the children become afraid of the dark and are scarred for life. When we were naughty as young children, one of the servants frightened us with the story of the fiend *Biebies*, who wanders at night in empty rooms.[17] From then on, we always felt ill at ease in the dark. I sometimes ponder the fact that 'decent' people can be easily intimidated, whereas born thieves are not scared of the night; they neither fear the dark nor ghosts, and are not deterred from a chosen course of action by any risk of the consequences of their behaviour.

Tatuś also loved to tell us how many times he was able to escape from difficult situations by using his initiative. There were many stories, especially from the time of the First World War, that he wanted to dictate, but never managed to. On one occasion he reminisced how, as a youth doing military service, he took part in Russian army manoeuvres. There was a frost, and the idiotic commander ordered the soldiers to swim across or wade through a half-frozen river. Pneumonia was a certain outcome, and indeed within a few days half the army became seriously ill; many men died. But Tatuś glanced at some bushes nearby, spotted a small raft, jumped on it and pushed himself across with a stick. He landed on the other side with dry feet. He was punished for disobeying an order, but his action had saved his life.

In 1904 war broke out between Russia and Japan. None of the Poles had the slightest desire to risk their lives for the tsar, but little could be done since conscription was introduced in the Słonim area. Tatuś approached a high-ranking official in private and offered a bribe to be excluded from the call-up. During the period of tsarist rule one could do anything with a bribe. This dignitary demanded something like several tens of thousands of roubles; it was hopeless, because Tatuś would probably have had to sell Borki for this purpose. It was only then that someone suggested to Tatuś that he should give about 100 roubles to a lesser Russian functionary with a request for advice.[18] This official informed him that the call-up would cover only the rural districts and would not extend to the towns; he therefore advised Tatuś to go to live with his relatives in Wilno and to register there as a resident. And that is what Tatuś did. The high-ranking official, in the meantime, did not receive the big money he had been expecting and breathed vengeance. But there was nothing he could do as Tatuś was already outside his jurisdiction. This episode taught Tatuś an important lesson: whenever, from then on, he was to find himself in a similar predicament he would always approach the 'necks' of bureaucracy and avoid the 'heads'. He always did well out of this.

Whenever Tatuś had to deal with any legal matters, he never used the services of a lawyer, whether in connection with the liquidation of customary peasant rights (*serwituty*) or dealing with some theft in the forest. Relying on his own eloquence and the logical presentation of his evidence, he always won his cases. The estate was not burdened by any debts, except for some old outstanding payments still left over from the pre-1914 period when Tatuś's siblings had been paid off; the payments of these instalments had been fixed by the Land Bank for forty years. Tatuś's innate competence in running a business, which was particularly evident during his work in the Landowners' Association, was widely known. It was not surprising, therefore, that one day Senator Godlewski arrived in Borki to persuade Tatuś to stand as a parliamentary candidate for the Nowogródek constituency. This was the crowning moment of Tatuś's prestige and reputation in the district. The temptation was great, for the post carried a monthly salary of 1,000 złotys – no mean sum during the Great Depression. But Tatuś declined. He would have felt ill at ease wheeling and dealing behind the scenes in Parliament, which he compared to a jungle. Emeryk Czapski became the deputy instead.[19] Tatuś never strove to enter high society, and he was displeased that I felt the need to visit the philosophy professor Adam Żółtowski and his wife Janina (née Countess Puttkamer) at Bolcieniki.[20] Tatuś had no desire to be anybody's pawn: he preferred to be a pike in his own pond than a roach in somebody else's lake.

It was partly as a result of this absence of servility in his character and the respect he had for personal independence that Tatuś was opposed to the idea of my going to university. 'What will you get out of it?' he said. 'Your school friends with law degrees will end up as petty officials, always with some boss above them, terrorizing them. At most they'll earn 200 złotys per month. The official at the post office in Rohotna earns only 75 złotys per month. Occupy yourself with our bees and you will be independent of any potential bosses and you will do much better financially.' And that is what happened. After paying the girls who worked the centrifugal machines and my small sixteen-year-old assistant Fiodor, my monthly income from honey averaged about 200 złotys net. Normally, most of my profit was made during one week of sufficiently muggy weather when the buckwheat blossomed. During this week or two, I would earn 2,000 złotys from my honey. I used to sell it to the Pakulski Brothers in Warsaw and to Pomorski's sweet factory in Poznań.[21] The honey was transported to the railway station in lime casks, each containing 100 kg of the golden nectar. I charged one złoty and 80 groszy per kilo.[22] As for Fiodor, he proved to be a loyal and worthy boy during the sacking of the manor house in 1939. I then gave him, for safekeeping, my twelve volumes of Piłsudski's writings.

At first I was frightened of the bees, but eventually developed a great love for beekeeping. Some of hives stood not far behind the house, while the rest of my apiary was located in the Great Field. I travelled there in a two-wheel conveyance with Fiodor; attached at the rear was a box containing a smoker and other equipment. For working among the bees, I wore a linen garment of my own design; it covered me down to my feet and was done up at the front. During heat waves I wore it directly on my naked body. I also sprayed myself with water. Once, when I was trying to catch a swarm in a small tree, about forty bees got under my garment and stung me terribly. Sometimes

Figure 5. Irena at work as a beekeeper in Borki.

I had to spend several days lying at home with a swollen face and hands. Despite this I survived in my occupation for nine years in Poland and then another fifteen years in England. I became very proficient and I got great satisfaction observing bees flying with pollen, or noting the beautiful colours of the transparent rings of the thorax of the Italian bees I had propagated. I imported Italian queen bees for that purpose; they arrived in special boxes. To stand in the middle of a noisy and busy apiary in the spring was exhilarating. All around me life blossomed. In May I delighted in the first open catkins of willow and osier trees. Next came the blossom of maple trees. Our park had several old and tall bird cherry trees, the likes of which I have not seen since. One can come across small bird cherry bushes everywhere, but although they produce a wonderful scent, they have masses of coarse flowers. Draped on these old trees were twisted small branches with an ancient appearance as if they had been sculpted by a different hand; they were covered with flowers that seemed attached by neat lace embroidery. This was not just a sea of white flowers – these were hanging curtains of unusual delicacy. To behold life and spring in that setting, and to breathe the smell of fields full of blossoming buckwheat which the bees liked, or the scent of the lime trees in the park full of the fragrance of their flowers, was a joy difficult to describe.

6

Before the storm

Death of Irena's father – Running the estate without Tatuś – The farmer on the white charger – The German law student and a planned visit to Berlin – A trip to Italy

On 10 February 1938 we were hit by a great calamity: the death of my father. He died suddenly at night after a bath. Mamusia was not there – she had gone to Wilno to see a doctor because she was unwell with heart problems. Tatuś was meant to follow Mamusia to see the doctor about his heart because he also felt a certain uneasiness. None of the rest of the family was at home because my sisters and I were all in Warsaw. And that is where the news reached me. It is difficult to describe the tragedy that befell us. Nor do I want to tear at old wounds. On arriving home, I found the whole road leading to the house already covered with conifer needles,[1] and the whole family assembled. Uncle Leon was there with his wife, as were my cousins Kazio and Zygmunt and Tatuś's sisters. The locality was gripped by fear for the future. The peasants were so shaken that there was not a single case of theft, although the house had stood without a living soul inside. Thieves also feel the magnitude of someone's death. It was said that when Marshal Piłsudski died, not a single burglary took place in Warsaw; the criminal world too felt the solemnity of the moment.

Pan Józef Godlewski arrived by car, and offered his services if there was any need of help with running the affairs of the estate. Mamusia was totally heartbroken and she greeted Pan Godlewski with the face of Queen Niobe, completely shattered. But she also showed great fortitude because she immediately took all matters into her own hands. There was no need to accept Pan Godlewski's offer, since Mamusia had acted as Tatuś's secretary all her married life and was well acquainted with the business. Sokołowski, the governor of the province of Nowogródek, came by car, as well as the district governor. But at the funeral, several days later, it was mostly the family who were present. Cousin Leoś took many photographs of those present, all with sad faces. In the church, in his beautiful baritone voice, Zygmunt Protassewicz sang Tatuś's favourite hymn, Moniuszko's 'O, Władco świata Wiekuisty Boże' (O, Lord of the world, God Eternal).

The world of our childhood had collapsed irretrievably. Writing a letter to Hans Albert Reinkemeyer, with whom I had become friends thanks to Professor Lutosławski, I just could not bring myself to put on paper that Tatuś was no longer alive, so I did not even mention it. However, I somehow found it easier to write about it to Professor Lutosławski. Hans Albert was later shocked by the fact that I was able to write about matters which were trivial in comparison, without even mentioning my father's death. But it was not easy to write about it to Hans Albert who had lost his own father not long before. There are things one sometimes keeps to oneself. I was also concerned that Tatuś had died suddenly, and therefore without receiving the Last Rites. Later, in Palestine, I was to arrange for an entire convent of Carmelite Sisters to take Holy Communion for my father's soul. Tatuś's death had an impact in our district comparable to Piłsudski's in all Poland. Tatuś's body lay on a catafalque in our dining room; whole pilgrimages of peasants came to see the 'master' (Pan) for the last time, while local Jews wept as if he had been someone close. In the cemetery we planted fir trees around his grave; perhaps they will mark his resting place for posterity.

Tatuś had had a heart attack three years earlier near the ponds and had to be brought home on a cart. Perhaps if he had received proper treatment thereafter he might have lived longer. However, war broke out the year after his death and brought about the ruin of Borki and of his whole life's work. Would it have been worth it, then, to live a little longer? To perish at the hands of a murderer, or in Siberia, as was to happen to so many others? We were in despair, but God knows what He does. Tatuś was summoned by God while still in his prime; he was loved and respected. He left in dignity, and avoided, as others did not, the humiliation inflicted by the invaders.

As for the estate, considerable help came from Uncle Leon who stayed on for a time and found for us an honest administrator, Pan Jerzy Turzański. Pan Turzański who was shown the financial ropes of the Borki estate by Mamusia got down to his tasks conscientiously. However, these tasks exceeded his capabilities, for he came from a family of small landowners and had never managed a farm on such a large scale. He knew how to deal with the peasants, he understood people and he was worthy of trust. He wanted to sort out the mill in Wężowszczyzna, which Mamusia had received as part of the division of her parents' estate. He went there during harvest time and stayed far too long, having left the task of stacking the rye to the steward. The rye that year was dark green, as tall as a forest, and it swayed in the wind; in short, an excellent harvest was expected. This was possible because perennial lupin had been grown on this field for several years, and had then been ploughed into the soil. To use perennial rather than annual lupin was Tatuś's agricultural innovation which was even reported on the radio. The perennial lupin was mixed with oats or another cereal and was sown in springtime. After the cereal has been harvested, the lupin propagates itself; it is then ploughed in and by the second autumn the soil has been enriched, like nothing else, with nitrogen and humus. This method saves much labour, because sowing annual lupin would have required the field to be ploughed again the following spring, to be followed by a second sowing. All this extra effort was now unnecessary.

It had been some time now since Tatuś's death, yet passers-by were amazed by the rye sighing in the wind on the fertile expanse of the Great Field. And to think that this crop was all but ruined! The harvested rye had been stacked incorrectly and incompetently; the rain made it damp and the grain became mouldy and unsuitable for sale. It was with difficulty that the blackened grain could be used on our estate. Pan Turzański felt this deeply: it was not just the financial loss but also because his reputation as the manager of the estate had been compromised. I admired Mamusia's tact for she did not rebuke him for this with a single word. Perhaps she felt she was partly to blame for having sent him to deal with the mill near Lida during the summer; as a result the harvest in Borki had not been properly supervised. It is good that Tatuś did not see this, for he would have been distressed by such bungling of his favourite pursuit which was the enrichment of the fields with perennial lupin; in some sense he treated it as a scientific experiment in the fertilization of the soil.

Otherwise the management of the rest of the estate was excellent. The starch-processing plant had been reactivated by Tatuś a few years earlier and was working. The sawmill was also functioning. Cousin Polik helped with the sale of some of the forest to Jewish merchants; with this money we started to put up buildings for me on the Great Field. We used the watermill by the pond for our own needs. Tatuś had earlier sold his steam-powered mill which had ceased to be profitable. Fewer and fewer people brought grain for milling, while the cost of firing the steam engine was great. In addition, one had to pay a tax on the size of the diameter of the mill wheel, without any consideration as to how often the mill operated. Once Tatuś got really cross with the tax office for its intransigence and incompetence. He informed the tax office by letter that he had been forced by the office to sell his steam-powered mill, but that the tax office would not incur any loss because he had just found another great source of income. He explained that this came in the form of starlings which every evening sat on the reeds and deposited great amounts of fertilizer in the water; the plankton thus multiplied, and the fish found more free food. How the tax office in Słonim reacted to this submission of a new source of income, I do not know.

With Tatuś gone and no son to succeed him, the family was greatly troubled by the future of Borki. It was with this in mind that my aunts nearly persuaded me to marry Lech Górski. He had a degree in agronomy and had been pursuing his profession on Pani Wanda Roycewicz's farm. He fell out with her and was temporarily staying in Ladzinki with his herd of cattle. Lech's father also had big money for it was on his land that the town of Baranowicze was expanding.[2] The son liked farming; he was also modern and well read in English literature. He visited Borki on a beautiful white former racehorse which reminded me of the bright white charger in the film *The Thief of Baghdad*. However, although Lech was pleasant, he did not have Tatuś's good looks. His sisters were very ugly, and only his married brother was handsome. Furthermore, Lech committed an unforgivable faux pas. He called on us during the whole summer of 1938, and was full of praise for my sister Hania's singing. He constantly sat next to her by the piano and kept on telling me how fortunate I was to have such a sister. No sooner had Hania left for Warsaw than he immediately started to pay attention to me. I felt offended. Being a provincial farmer, he clearly did not consider Hania as suitable material for a wife, whereas he told me that I would have good-looking sons, of which he dreamt. Lech had a warm heart and the local parish priest Father Goj simply adored him and used to go for rides in his car. Also the seventy-year-old Pani Sidorowiczowa, in whose house he lived for a time, came to love him as if he was her only son. In short, Lech had many of the qualities to be Tatuś's ideal successor in Borki, but he was not my type. He was a little too pushy. In any case, I was unsuited to be a country housewife; I was constantly restless with a yearning for the wider world.

The same year (1938) I nearly went to Berlin. I was persuaded to go by my penfriend Hans Albert Reinkemeyer, who was a law student in Berlin. We first met sometime in the spring of 1937, when I was staying in Wilno with Aunt Salunia on Pohulanka Street. It so happened there was no one else in the house when I received a letter from Professor Lutosławski inviting me to meet him and a German guest who had just arrived from Berlin. The professor disappeared and I invited Hans Albert for lunch. I was taken aback by his intelligence and told him that one day he would become a great man. He admitted that he had always aspired to that, but he had not revealed it to anyone. His ambition was to become Germany's foreign minister. He had lost his father and his mother only had a small pension, but he was being helped in his academic career by a professor in Berlin who also believed in Hans Albert's potential.[3]

Hans Albert was shown around all the churches of Wilno by Tadeusz Stulgiński who happened to have arrived from Warsaw. Soon afterwards Professor Lutosławski came to Borki with Hans Albert and left him there for two weeks. Hans Albert was not good-looking; he was slim and had blonde hair, like Bolesław Piasecki. Hans Albert's complexion was somewhat grey in colour as if tinged with blue, and his teeth were greyish. But he was engaging. It was a strange thing, but once when we were sitting in my blue room, after we had finished talking, neither of us spoke. A complete silence descended, the sudden silence of a deep harmony of souls. Although he did not make a physical impression on me at all, I sensed what Professor Lutosławski would have described as a 'kinship of spirit'. Once when we were picking mushrooms he unexpectedly proposed to me. I answered that I only wished to remain friends. He responded: 'I agree, for the time being.' Later he persuaded me to come to Berlin for the winter of 1938–9, with my music, to delight the Germans with Polish singing and to meet his mother and sisters.

My travel papers were ready. I had also obtained permission to attend lectures at the University of Berlin as a 'guest listener' (*Gasthörer*). And then out of the blue my aunts in Wilno accused me of pursuing some old professors while neglecting Borki. Indeed, I had invited Professor Studnicki[4] and Hela's father, Judge Jamontt, to visit. If that was not enough, they also reprimanded me for planning to travel to Germany instead of saving Borki and marrying Górski. Pressured by my aunts, I cancelled my trip abroad and returned to Borki to face the possibility of marrying Lech. Eventually a time had to come to put an end to my youth and to start to live for Borki and the family. However, Uncle Leon was in Borki at that time and saved me from making such a personal sacrifice for the sake of the family estate. Just as Pan Lech was about to get the ring, I made off to Warsaw without telling him and vanished into thin air, like camphor. The sequence of events was broken – and was never resumed. Lech gave up trying. Indeed, early the following spring (in 1939) he married an heiress to a vast estate in the Poznań region. That estate was millions in debt, but he loved to be in the whirl of finance and was not put off by the debts. He was desperate to have a son, and he was eventually able to escape with his family to the United States where his sister was married to a Polish consul.

During the summer of 1938 my bees produced an exceptionally large amount of honey, worth something in the region of 3,000 złotys. I therefore bought myself a Persian lamb coat and decided to join a Catholic youth excursion to Italy scheduled for the spring of 1939. Somebody in Warsaw had unexpectedly suggested such a trip, although by leaving the country at that time I was going to miss the wedding of my cousin Halina Jamontt and Henryk Skrzyński, a friend from her university days. Henryk was related to Count Aleksander Skrzyński, the minister.[5] Halina had remained for me the ideal of an intelligent and modern woman. She completed her law studies at Warsaw University and later spent some time in Paris where she attended economics lectures. She had also worked for two years at the Polish Embassy in London under Count Edward Raczyński, the ambassador.

The district governor Wacław Iszora, whose administrative district was in Praga on the eastern bank of Warsaw, registered me as a resident, and immediately secured a passport for me. The family in Wilno were fearful, for there was talk of war. But Governor Iszora allayed any misgivings and reassured me that if war did come, all that would happen is that I would have to stay in Italy.

I set off with a large youth group to attend the international congress in Rome organized for Easter 1939. The leader of our party was a beautiful young brunette, the daughter of the former minister Karol Niezabytowski. The trip was unbelievably cheap, about 400 złotys. By comparison, Aunt Mania Żórawska had paid about 2,000 złotys for an adults' excursion, but that included entertainment, whereas we went on a cheap pilgrimage to the centre of Christianity. We were received by various Catholic organizations which provided guides in many towns; a nun showed us around the galleries and museums of Rome. I am so pleased that I was able to see Italy, for such an opportunity would never arise later. I was still young and had the resources of Borki.

I was deeply impressed just by crossing the Polish border, for I had not yet been to the west. The wonderful countryside of Czechoslovakia with its beautiful settlements made of stone and brick spoke of a material culture higher than Poland's.[6] We passed through Vienna at night. The Alps looked like something out of a fairy tale. There was a full moon, and on the mountain peaks we could see the eternally sleeping glaciers. Our train rushed at a dizzying speed through long tunnels, as if down towards some suicidal bottomless abyss, only then to soar upwards unexpectedly on its rails, as if on a swing or on the crest of a wave.

We stopped in Venice to see St Mark's Cathedral. In the evening, gondolas lifted us along the mysterious dark waters illuminated by the reflection of the city's lights. But I liked Florence most; it looked as if it had been lifted intact from the Middle Ages. Michelangelo's statues spoke of Phidias. I was overwhelmed by the city's galleries. With my restless eyes I tried to take in as many of the outstanding paintings as possible, but it was like looking through a kaleidoscope which eventually blurred my vision. There was an alabaster bust of Savonarola in our hotel; it generated an uneasy awareness of the city's past and provided an introduction to the soul of this mysterious place where Savonarola met his death at the stake. I will not conceal that I was sometimes influenced by figures such as Savonarola.[7] We admired the delightful hills surrounded with greenery and guarded by tall cypress trees. We visited the dwellings of the old hermits. Somebody even tempted spring by swimming in the Arno. The walls of the houses were covered with climbing wisterias on which swung heavy racemes of blossoming fragrant violet flowers. In Assisi we descended into the tiny house of St Francis where I bought a picture of the famous Holy Cross. Who would have thought that a fragment of this picture is still in my possession. I was to use it to wrap the bottle of water when I later baptized thirteen children in Siberia, all descendants of exiled Polish insurgents of 1863.

We journeyed further south, towards Naples. Some of our party went up to the summit of Vesuvius, while I chose the blue grotto on Capri. I have to admit that the ruins of Pompeii moved me greatly. Looking at antiquity with my own eyes, reading various notices on the walls – such as '*Cave Canem*' – was something unforgettable. In the museum in Naples we saw the plaster casts of human beings and dogs, contorted in agony as death consumed them.

We spent a week in Rome attending the world congress of Catholic youth. I seem to remember that we stayed in the convent of the Sisters of Nazareth. The sisters showed us around the museums. I never saw anything so incredible as the Greek alabaster sculptures in Rome. When sometime later I saw the Three Graces in a museum in London, I found them dreadful. I could not comprehend how a sculptor could preserve in stone such unattractive women deprived of all poetic shape. If he had entitled his composition 'Dancing Cooks' it might have been just possible to stomach. Returning to Rome's museums, my attention was drawn to what no one else seems to have written about: the bust of Cato with his wife. This married couple became a symbol for me of one spirit in one flesh. Every marriage should be such if it is to become the sacrament of the union of two people. In my mind, such spiritual beauty of a genuine marriage always stood in contrast with the loneliness of celibacy, which was contradictory and against nature. Whenever any nun or any priest tried to prove to me the superiority of celibacy over marriage, the harmony of souls I perceived in that sculpture doggedly convinced me that they were not right. I did not yet know much about life, but my instinct told me that the greatest fulfilment of mankind is achieved in the togetherness of two kindred souls.

The papers read at the congress and the discussions that ensued were full of profound things about religious instruction. It was a real pleasure, for the first time in my life, to hear English spoken so beautifully by a lady from India, who looked like an enchanting character from a fairy tale. Several African women were present, but most of the others were short, bespectacled and unattractive women from Belgium. In such company, the Indian looked like a queen. French was the working language of the congress. There was not a single representative from Germany; Hitler had prohibited any German participation in the first Easter celebration of the newly elected Pope Pius XII. I have to admit that in the papal gardens in Castel Gandolfo I was sorely tempted to pick the first orange I had ever seen growing on a tree. I envied the papal cows their luxurious accommodation adorned with blue tiles; the animals lived in hygienic conditions and had running water which flowed in pipes to their troughs. The firework display in the gardens of the Vatican, held during a reception for us, was most colourful and we ate delicious cakes while talking in company.

On the contrary, St Peter's Basilica made an unpleasant impression on me. Everyone knows that it was built by the extortion of tribute from the faithful, even using such methods as the sale of indulgences. For me, the basilica was therefore the symbol of the division of Western Christianity. Furthermore, living in Poland, which had neither a royal court nor ceremonial parades as in England, I was unpleasantly shocked by the 'pantomime' of papal ceremonial. My unpleasant impression was completed when, just as I was about to enter the basilica for Easter Mass, some Polish squire or other sporting a walrus-like moustache rushed out of the church, clearly morally shocked by what he had seen inside. He spun around as if in a trance during St Vitus's dance. Tearing at his moustache, he wailed: 'And this is supposed to be Christianity!!!' I then went in. Mass was said as it is today, with the priest facing the congregation, which terribly offended those not expecting it. Nor was there any evidence of quiet spiritual reflection near the altar. Everyone present, and I mean everyone, was standing on benches or chairs, and shouting 'Viva, Papa!' And above, over the heads of those present, floated the Pope on his litter, as if on a Persian flying carpet from *One Thousand and One Nights*, or as some new incarnation of Buddha. But I looked at Pius XII's ascetic face, into his blazing Savonarola-like eyes, and I understood how far he was spiritually from the profane parade around him. That is why, unlike the Polish squireen, I did not rush out of the vast colonnaded basilica. I remained, waiting for an end to the yelling of the Roman crowd. Only then could I rally my thoughts after the crush of so many contrasting impressions.

After visiting Padua we headed for home. I returned to Borki via Kraków where I called on the Lutosławskis. Mamusia, who had also once been to Florence and to other places in Italy with her father, read my postcards from Italy with great feeling, and relived vicariously the enthusiasm of her youth. Such were to be my last free travels.

Part Two

1939 to 1945

Introduction to Part Two

Hubert Zawadzki

Irena returned home from Italy just as the international situation was worsening, although she is unlikely to have then imagined that before the year was out her life in Borki as she knew it would come to an abrupt and violent end – and that the summer of 1939 would be her last in independent Poland.

To seasoned observers, however, it was clear that a 'Polish Crisis' was in the offing. Hitler was continuing on his path to overthrow the international order established at Versailles and was dreaming of conquering 'living space' for the German nation in the east, while Stalin was ready to fish in troubled waters. Poland had declined Hitler's double-edged offer to join the Anti-Comintern Pact against the USSR which would have turned Poland into a springboard for a German assault on the USSR. By mid-August, Poland had also refused to join a tentative British and French proposal for an eastern 'peace front' with the USSR, for among Stalin's conditions for joining such an initiative was the entry of Soviet troops into eastern Poland and the dissolution of the Polish-Romanian alliance. Both German and Soviet demands would have ended Poland's fragile and only recently won independence. Stuck between the devil and the deep blue sea, the Poles would have to rely on their own inferior forces – and on what they expected would be effective assistance from Britain, and especially France.

If he could not move against the USSR with Polish cooperation, Hitler would have to do so over Poland's corpse. To secure Poland's speedy defeat before the autumn rains and to prevent the USSR from siding with the Western Powers, Hitler set aside his anti-Bolshevism and decided to strike a deal with Stalin. The Soviets for their part had no wish to be drawn into a war with Germany at this stage and were willing to respond to German overtures. The result was the Nazi-Soviet Pact of 23 August whose secret clauses, revealed only in 1946 and denied by the USSR until 1989, provided for the joint division of east-central Europe and the partition of Poland. Borki was situated well within the envisaged Soviet zone. A formal treaty of alliance between Britain and Poland, signed on 25 August, momentarily unnerved Hitler but he did not really expect the West to fight for Poland. As August moved towards September, and as anti-Polish propaganda on the German radio acquired an increasingly virulent form, even in distant Borki, in Irena's words, 'one sensed the gathering of some subterranean disquiet'.

Early on 1 September the German war machine went into action. Despite offering stiff resistance, and without any Western help (the half-promised French general offensive in the west never materialized), the Poles stood little chance in this unequal struggle. Their fate was sealed when the Red Army crossed into eastern Poland on 17 September. Not wishing to appear as an aggressor, Stalin delayed his move as long as possible, until he could claim that the Polish state had collapsed. Many Poles, including the Polish authorities, initially assumed that the USSR would be neutral during the Polish-German war. How wrong they were.

Irena may have 'rebelled inwardly' when in late August a cousin had forecast 'the imminence of the final disaster: the entry of the Soviets', but that is what happened. On 18 September Red Army soldiers arrived in Borki. Irena describes how in her district, where ethnic Poles were in a minority and where there were no Polish troops, revolution arrived from the east on Soviet bayonets. And she does not conceal the social conflicts that erupted with the collapse of Polish authority in her locality, nor her own patronizing views at that time of the local Belarusian peasantry. Yet her account is not always consistent. On the one hand, she writes that 'it was the anger of the people that destroyed the existing order', and that in her district 'all the peasants went crazy'. On the other, she admits that Catholic villages did not take part in the general looting. Furthermore, in a letter of 1944 to Senator Godlewski she offered an even more nuanced picture: she asserted that even the Orthodox villages would not have succumbed to the temptation to rob were it not for notorious local thieves who instigated the attacks; and that in some places local peasants even protected the manors.[1] Indeed, it appears that the Soviets were welcomed mostly in areas where there already existed large groups of local communists who were able to draw crowds from among the poorest Orthodox Belarusians in the countryside and least well-off Jews in the towns. They were often joined by former convicts: those who had been in Polish jails for political reasons as well as common criminals. There was, not surprisingly, little support for the arriving Soviets in areas with a Polish majority and little violence in districts where interethnic relations had been good before the war. Nor did wealthier Belarusian peasants take part in robberies. And Irena would not have known that many of the robberies and killings in northeastern Poland during this period of anarchy were initiated and even planned by local communists, former members of the Communist Party of Western Belarus (KPZB) and their sympathizers.

Furthermore, Irena generalizes from what she saw as the relatively bloodless events in her own immediate district to state that the Soviets, 'not sullying their hands with blood [...] took over all the eastern borderlands (*całe Kresy*)', and gives the misleading impression that the Soviets did not meet any resistance in eastern Poland. It is a fact that most of what was left of the Polish Army was still engaged against the Germans and that Irena's province of Nowogródek had been almost denuded of Polish troops, while the Polish High Command ordered its forces not to fight the Soviets unless attacked. The general confusion was compounded by the behaviour of the Soviets who in some cases presented themselves as allies against the Germans, while in others they committed atrocities against Polish soldiers and civilians. Yet there was resistance to the Soviet entry on the part of some members of the Polish Frontier Defence Corps and by some regular military units, assisted by civilian volunteers, in or near towns, such as Wilno and Grodno, and in Polesie. Molotov, the Soviet Commissar for Foreign

Affairs, stated later that the Red Army lost 737 men killed and 1,862 wounded in the fighting against the Poles. Polish historians mention that the Soviets lost up to 3,000 killed and up to 7,000 wounded with about 100 Soviet tanks and armoured vehicles destroyed, while the Poles lost about 2,500 killed and 7,000 wounded. And this does not take into account the victims of the violence generated by Soviet-inspired diversionary units and by pro-communist insurgents, as well as by reprisals meted out against such groups and individuals by Polish units.[2]

After an intensive campaign of repression and intimidation, on 22 October 1939 the Soviet authorities forced most of the inhabitants of occupied eastern Poland to participate in a charade of an election intended to legitimize their authority and to pave the way for the incorporation of 'Western Belarus' and 'Western Ukraine' by the USSR which formally took place in November 1939. In 'Western Belarus' (which included the pre-war Polish provinces of Polesie, Nowogródek and most of Wilno and Białystok), support for the official list of candidates ranged between 90.67 per cent and 99.02 per cent of the votes cast![3] On 24 March 1940 'elections' took place to the Soviet of the Union, the Soviet of Nationalities and the Supreme Soviets of the constituent republics of the USSR. These elections were preceded not only by a vigorous propaganda campaign but by numerous arrests and, above all, by the first mass deportation organized in February 1940 in all of the recently annexed territories. The expected result was a population that had been cowed into submission. Needless to say, support for the designated candidates was almost unanimous, as reported by *Izvestia* five days later.[4]

All that Irena says in her account on the subject of the elections is that they 'were announced'. Nothing more. Yet in her deposition to the Polish government, dated 20 April 1943, which consists of answers to a questionnaire issued by the Polish Foreign Ministry to Polish citizens who had recently left the USSR and in which one question dealt with the elections, Irena could not avoid the subject and had no choice but to write as truthfully as possible. She chose to do so at some length, but only about the elections held in March 1940.[5] This account is included in Chapter 7, and confirms some of the known circumstances and details of that event. Why is the subject of the elections virtually omitted in Irena's 1968 text? Why did she not admit to her children how she had acted in the face of this most brazen violation of genuine democratic principles? One can only assume that Irena voted as she was told, but like so many others she must have felt deeply humiliated and in some ways tainted by the experience.[6]

On the other hand, Irena is not reticent in providing evidence of the growing disillusionment of the local peasants with Soviet rule. Working as a nurse among the local population in 1939–40, both in the Borki hospital and during home visits to the sick, Irena had an ideal opportunity to observe the changing mood of the district's inhabitants who were now deprived of most of their former property and herded into Soviet-style collective farms and into performing all kinds of public works. Indeed, even NKVD reports reflect the growing discontent and disillusionment with Soviet rule in 1940–1 of many Belarusian inhabitants of former northeastern Poland.[7] While Irena found this 'emotional change'[8] a highly gratifying development, she is frank enough to admit that by the turn of 1940–1 many of the peasants were awaiting 'liberation' by the Germans.

In her account and in her letter of 1944 to Senator Godlewski, Irena writes in positive terms about the Jews of her district, mentioning that many Jewish traders and merchants suffered as a result of Soviet policies, and highlighting instances of help offered by local Jews to her family during and after the period of lawlessness following the arrival of the Soviets. The latter point fits well with other evidence that the good relations which had existed historically between the landed gentry and local Jews in northeastern Poland survived into the period of the Soviet invasion.[9] Except for a mild rebuke of what she called the Jewish 'semi-intelligentsia' of the local small towns, there is no explicit criticism of those Jews who cooperated with the Soviet authorities: she even acknowledges that her family was saved by the Jewish communist activist who presided over the 'people's court' in Nowojelnia. She writes fondly of Dr Atlas and of some of the Jewish refugees from Warsaw whom she befriended in Borki. There is no hint in her account or letters of the anti-Jewish hatred which the Soviet occupation generated among many local Poles and Belarusians, who unfairly identified all Jews with the repressive Soviet regime and which was to explode in such violence in many areas with the arrival of the Germans in 1941.[10]

Some readers, perhaps more familiar with the history of Nazi atrocities than with the Soviet record of repression, may wonder why Irena's family escaped from Borki to Warsaw in German-occupied Poland in October 1939. In many ways the reasons were quite obvious. In the first instance, Irena's brother-in-law Jan Karczewski had come across the German-Soviet demarcation line to fetch his wife and their two small children, and to take them back to their home in Warsaw. It would have been surprising if they had left Irena's mother behind. After the sacking of Borki and the traumatic experience of their arrest and 'trial', the family could hardly expect anything but a bleak and uncertain future under Soviet rule. Branded as 'class enemies', they were under virtual house arrest among a population that included many hostile individuals collaborating with the Soviets. Not only had the family been dispossessed of their estate, they now faced penury when in October 1939 the Soviets nationalized all banks and seized all saving accounts of over 300 złotys. The problem of food supplies and, with the approach of winter, the problem of fuel must also have dwelt on their minds. Furthermore, Irena's wider family's tragic experiences in Russia following the Bolshevik Revolution (when two of Irena's uncles died) and the Bolshevik presence in Borki in 1920, set in the context of Poland's existential struggle against Bolshevik Russia at that time, had all contributed to a profoundly negative image of the Bolshevik state as a mortal enemy of Poland's cultural and religious values, an image particularly strong among the Polish and propertied population of the eastern borderlands. On the other hand, in Warsaw, the family would have a roof over their heads, and would benefit from a regular income from the guest house belonging to Irena's brother-in-law. The family had every reason to feel that they would be more secure and anonymous in a large Polish-speaking city.[11] And, bearing in mind the family's experiences in 1914–18, they might have expected at this early stage of the war that the German occupation would be more 'civilized'.

As for Irena, she remained in Borki and its neighbourhood during almost the entire period of Nazi-Soviet cooperation which lasted until 22 June 1941, during which period postal links existed between the Third Reich and the USSR. She was then able to correspond with her mother in Warsaw, although not all the exchanged letters and cards reached their destinations. Irena's mother remained deeply worried about Irena's plight in Borki and frequently, but unsuccessfully, encouraged her to come to Warsaw with the offer of accommodation and even the prospect of some medical work.[12] In 1939–40 Irena was also able to correspond with her relatives in Wilno during the period of Lithuania's perilous independence – after the USSR had handed over the Wilno district to Lithuania in October 1939.

But apart from strictly family news, Irena was cut off from reliable information about the outer world. The Soviet press reflected the spirit of the Nazi-Soviet Pact and during the so-called Phoney War directed its propaganda against Britain and France, the 'imperialist war-mongers'. Irena mentions some of the rumours circulating at the time, for instance that a Polish army was being formed in Lithuania (before it was annexed by the USSR in June 1940). There was no question of such an army being formed in late 1939 or early 1940. Most of the Polish soldiers (about 12,000) who had escaped to Lithuania and Latvia in September 1939 were interned by the local authorities; after the annexation of Lithuania and Latvia by the USSR, these men were transported to the Soviet interior. During the Soviet-Finnish winter war of 1939–40, there were also rumours among the Poles living under Soviet occupation that Polish troops had been sent from France to fight on the Finnish side.

Irena's morale clearly suffered after her move to Ladzinki in October 1940 and she 'feared a psychological breakdown'. Little wonder that she reacted so enthusiastically to the letter from Berlin in late 1940 from the mother of her German friend Hans Albert Reinkemeyer, and that she even entertained fanciful hopes that Hans Albert might arrive in Borki! But this, surely, could only be with the German Army. Indeed, Irena mentions the existence, already at the end of 1940, of 'widespread murmurings about the possibility of a German-Soviet war'. It is unlikely that she knew much about the nature of the Nazi regime in German-occupied Poland, and would have had no inkling of the horrors that the Nazi invasion would inflict on the population of her region after June 1941. At the same time, her (and her family's) memories of the German presence in the east in 1918 were those of a German Army very different from Hitler's Wehrmacht and SS.

Irena was deported to Siberia in June 1941 in what was to be the last of the four mass deportations to the Soviet interior of 'hostile and harmful elements' (in Soviet parlance) from the eastern provinces of pre-war Poland – and which was only interrupted by the German invasion. The total number of Polish citizens deported has been the subject of recent debate. The traditionally accepted figures, based largely on the findings of the wartime and post-war Polish governments-in-exile, suggested about one million people. Recently partially accessed NKVD files suggest under 400,000, although it is not clear what criteria the NKVD used. The issue will remain unresolved until all relevant NKVD archives are made available to independent scholars.[13]

Irena does not specify the route she took to Siberia, but it was most probably the same as that taken by Michał Giedroyć with his mother and sisters in 1940. In his autobiographical account *Crater's Edge*, Giedroyć describes his deportation as an eleven-year-old through Smolensk, then on a loop south of Moscow to Ufa, then through Kuibyshev, Chelabinsk, Kurgan and Omsk to Novosibirsk; this was the usual route.[14] It also needs to be emphasized that Irena was fortunate that she was a single person with no family or young children to care for, and that she was travelling to Siberia in the summer and did not experience the horrific first deportation in February 1940 when temperatures were well below zero.

Irena describes her conditions of work in *kolkhoz* 'Stalinets' in the Kansk district of Siberia. There were two main types of collective farm in the USSR: the state-owned farm (*sovkhoz*; pl. *sovkhozy*) where peasants provided hired labour; and a collective farm (*kolkhoz*; pl. *kolkhozy*) which was theoretically owned by all its members. However, the *kolkhozy* were controlled by the state, their labour force was strictly regimented and they had to deliver an assigned amount of produce to the state at set prices. Only after all the various taxes had been paid and all the contributions fulfilled did the members of the collective receive their shares calculated on the basis of so-called workdays (*truda-dyen*) that they had put in. A 'workday' represented the expected output of work per day; each job had a subjective measure of output.

In her draft deposition to the Polish government, Irena mentions that the so-called free deportees like herself were not subject to any physical violence by the NKVD. In that sense she was fortunate, for Polish women in Soviet prisons and labour camps were often subject to brutal interrogations, degrading and humiliating searches and even sexual exploitation. In their depositions to the Polish government, Polish women who left the USSR in 1942 were very reticent on the subject of sexuality, but there is ample evidence that even outside the Gulag system Polish women were exposed to sexual harassment on the part of their Soviet supervisors; some were forced to sell their bodies for food or jobs. The fear of rape was particularly noted by Polish women who found themselves deported to Soviet Central Asia.[15] Irena speaks obliquely about the 'demoralization' of the local population in Siberia and 'widespread perversions', an impression that also found an echo in other Polish women's depositions.

Both in her account of 1968–9, and especially in her letters of 1944, Irena asserts the cultural superiority of the Polish prisoners and deportees towards their communist oppressors, and reveals a great sympathy for ordinary Soviet citizens, fellow victims of Stalinist tyranny. In the latter case, it applied in particular to those who were descendants of Poles sent into exile during the tsarist period. Irena's perception of the cultural gulf between the Polish 'west' and the Soviet 'east' fits well with Katherine Jolluck's findings in *Exile and Identity*.[16]

Irena was most fortunate, to put it mildly, that her twenty-year 'sentence' of compulsory work in *kolkhoz* 'Stalinets' ended up lasting only two and a half months. The turning point in her Siberian story was her release from the *kolkhoz* on 15 September 1941 as a result of an agreement signed in London on 30 July 1941 by General Władysław Sikorski, the prime minister of the Polish government-in-exile and Polish commander-in-chief, and Ivan Mayski, the Soviet ambassador to the United Kingdom. This led to the restoration of diplomatic relations between Poland (as represented by the exiled government) and the USSR, and to the creation of a Polish Army in the USSR under the command of General Władysław Anders, one of pre-war Poland's most promising younger generals. Anders knew the 'East' well: he spoke fluent Russian and had distinguished himself while serving in the tsarist army during the First World War, and had also endured Soviet captivity from October 1939 until August 1941, including seven months in solitary confinement. The so-called Soviet 'amnesty' (the decree was issued on 12 August 1941) embraced all Polish prisoners of war (those who were still alive) and most other Polish detainees in the USSR, although not all of them were easily able to leave their places of detention. This dramatic change in Polish-Soviet relations was a consequence of the Nazi invasion of the USSR, and Churchill's pressure on two of Britain's allies to cooperate despite the recent Soviet treatment of the Poles. With the Germans advancing rapidly deep into Soviet territory in 1941, Stalin was willing to make this concession. Numerous local Soviet officials were baffled and incredulous, for such an amnesty for an entire national group had never been issued before, nor consent ever given for an army of a foreign power to be created on Soviet soil. Many labour camp commanders were reluctant to lose their Polish slave workers for fear of not fulfilling their production targets.[17] One example was Irena's aunt, Irena Valdi-Gołębiowska, who had been sentenced to fifteen years' hard labour in 1941 for refusing Soviet citizenship and for refusing to work as an artist for the Soviets; she was not released from her lumber camp in the Urals until five months after the amnesty.[18]

Tens of thousands of Polish civilians, including families and men of military age, began a spontaneous movement of migration from all parts of the USSR, especially from the inhospitable north, to the region where the Polish Army was being organized, initially at Buzuluk between the Volga and Ural rivers, 140 km from Kuibyshev to which all embassies, including the Polish Embassy, had been evacuated from Moscow in the face of the German threat. In early 1942, the Polish Army was moved to the Soviet Central Asian republics of Kazakhstan and Uzbekistan, which is where Irena and her companion Franciszka Bartoszewiczowa headed. The condition of many of these emaciated people was terrible; ironically more of them died during this 'voluntary' migration south in 1941–2 than during the compulsory deportations of 1940–1 to the Soviet interior. Where their conditions were tolerable, the Polish Embassy advised Polish civilians to stay put; needless to say, this advice often fell on deaf ears.[19] The flight eastwards, from the invading Germans, of ten or more million Soviet refugees, the removal of Soviet factories to the east and large-scale troop movements to the west generated confusion on the entire Soviet railway network in 1941–2, and only compounded the travel difficulties faced by the Poles.

After relocation to Soviet Central Asia, the different divisions and support units of the Polish Army were scattered over a wide area, mostly near towns along the railway network of the Central Asian republics. Communications between all these establishments was not easy: it was over 1,200 km by rail from the most easterly establishment in Otar to the most westerly in Kermine. General Anders's own HQ was in Yangi-Yul south of Tashkent, roughly in the centre of the vast region in which the Polish Army units were located.

The Polish Embassy was reopened in Kuibyshev (Samara) on the Volga on 15 October 1941. Under the embassy's jurisdiction was the *Delegatura* with twenty delegates' offices located across the USSR where there were major concentrations of Polish deportees; one of these offices was in Dzhambul (where Irena and her companion alighted after their long train journey from Kansk) where there was also a distribution point for goods sent from abroad (mostly from the United States) for the relief of the Poles. Under the delegates was a large network of approved volunteers (*mężowie zaufania*;

men/women of confidence, who numbered 351 by August 1942) who administered the relief at local level.[20]

General Anders's Army (which Irena joined as a women's auxiliary nurse on 11 February 1942) was evacuated from the USSR to Iran in two phases: the first in March 1942 and the second in August 1942. A total of about 140,000 people were evacuated, of whom 80,000 were troops and over 40,000 were civilians (including 13,000 children). The British government and the Polish military authorities (Generals Sikorski and Anders) were concerned whether the Red Army would survive the German onslaught (this was still long before Stalingrad) and also whether the Soviets would be capable of supplying the Polish forces; Soviet supplies were erratic and often inadequate. Initially, Sikorski had hoped that the Polish Army formed in the USSR would fight alongside the Red Army and enter Poland from the east. Scarred by her Soviet experiences, Irena vigorously condemns such ideas. Yet providing there was genuine Soviet goodwill, such a strategy made eminent sense; it assumed, of course, that Stalin was prepared to tolerate an independent Poland emerging after the war. Growing political difficulties soon made such a strategy unrealistic, and even Sikorski came to the conclusion that it might be necessary to evacuate the Polish Army from the USSR. Indeed, Stalin had already agreed in December 1941 to a limited evacuation.

The British were also anxious to obtain more troops for the Middle East. Supplied and equipped by the British, and after a period of recuperation, the Polish Army would strengthen the Allies' position in the Middle East against the two-pronged Axis assault: one from the north towards the Caucasus and the Caspian Sea oil fields, and the other from North Africa towards the Suez Canal (the menacing advance of Rommel's Afrika Korps was not checked until the second battle of El-Alamein in late October 1942). It is important also to note that already in August 1941 British and Soviet forces had entered Iran to overthrow the pro-German regime there, and had established zones of occupation in the south and the north of that country, respectively. Prior to the first evacuation, Anders ignored orders from London, and included civilians in the move to Iran – for which Irena praises Anders enthusiastically. By mid-1942, Polish-Soviet relations were deteriorating, and Anders successfully argued for a second evacuation. This time the Poles insisted on the evacuation of the Women's Army Auxiliary Services and of 'military families', to which the British and the Soviets (who attached strict conditions) eventually assented. Many Polish civilians were able to join the exodus by being classified as military 'dependants' by Anders's staff.[21]

Among the difficulties facing Anders's Army in the USSR was the status of Polish citizens who were not ethnic Poles. In January 1942 the Soviets issued an order that only ethnic Poles could be recruited by the Polish Army; Polish citizens of Jewish, Ukrainian or Belarusian ethnicity originally resident in eastern Poland were to be excluded. The Soviets insisted on treating them as Soviet citizens, although many succeeded in passing themselves off as ethnic Poles. Facing a variety of difficulties, only about 4,000 Polish Jews managed to join the Polish Army with about 2,000 accompanying civilians. Of the Jewish soldiers, about a half were to desert when the army reached Palestine; many of them then joined Jewish underground organizations fighting for a Jewish state in Palestine. Among those who left the Polish Army in Palestine was Menahem Begin who organized the Irgun terrorist movement against the British and eventually became the prime minister of Israel in 1977.[22] How much Irena would have known about the Polish government's pre-war support for the Zionist movement (in order to promote Jewish emigration from Poland to Palestine) one cannot tell. She certainly would not have known about the clandestine military assistance and training which the Polish government was providing in the late 1930s to Zionist paramilitary organizations in Palestine.[23]

Irena's harrowing account of illness and mortality among the Polish troops in Soviet Central Asia confirms that in some respects the deployment of the Polish Army to the south of the USSR was unfortunate. Indeed, it appears that Irena's worst experiences (when working among the sick and undernourished Polish soldiers in Central Asia) occurred ironically when the political situation had taken a turn for the better. The great extremes of temperatures in the south, the accompanying diseases and the often unsatisfactory living conditions took their toll on the already emaciated former deportees and prisoners. Altogether over 3,000 Polish soldiers and about 10,000 Polish civilians died in Uzbekistan, Kazakhstan and Kirgizia between February and August 1942, mostly from typhus, malaria or dysentery. Most soldiers (about 2,500) are buried in Uzbekistan. The expectations of the Polish commanders that the south would have a benign mild climate proved ill-founded, although the proximity to Iran proved an asset when it came to leaving the USSR. Despite these difficulties, the morale and discipline of the surviving soldiers were exceptional: the shared hardships of Soviet captivity, the pervading sense that Poland was indeed not lost and the revived hope for a better future created powerful bonds which were to last for many years. In Keith Sword's words: 'In many quarters there was a mystical sense of renaissance, of rebirth from the dead.'[24] In 1944–5 these same men, now forming the Polish Second Corps, were to fight with great distinction in Italy: at Monte Cassino, Bologna and Ancona.

Irena's view of those who were ill and who were unable to leave the USSR in 1942 is somewhat melodramatic, although understandable from her perspective. And that is how the individuals leaving the USSR would have felt for their unfortunate comrades. Quite a few of the hospitalized soldiers who were left behind, but yet who managed to recover from their illnesses, subsequently joined another Polish Army, this time commanded by the pro-Soviet Colonel Zygmunt Berling and formed under Soviet auspices. The so-called Berling Army fought alongside the Red Army in 1943–5; it suffered heavy losses (for example, at Lenino in October 1943), but those men who survived eventually returned to post-war Poland with their families.

The Berling Army was part of a Soviet plan to create subservient Polish institutions in the USSR. The political wing of this initiative was the so-called Association of Polish Patriots (*Związek Patriotów Polskich*; ZPP) founded in the USSR in March 1943 on the initiative of Polish communists, in opposition to the Polish government-in-exile in London. The chairman of its governing council was Wanda Wasilewska, the daughter of Piłsudski's close friend and eminent Polish socialist Leon Wasilewski. The ZPP purported to be an all-embracing democratic association of Poles who found themselves in the USSR during the war. While ultimately serving Soviet plans for a future communist-controlled Poland, the ZPP did organize Polish schools and orphanages in the USSR, and published Polish literature and textbooks. In 1945–6 it was to organize the 'repatriation' of Poles from the USSR; it was dissolved in 1946. In

1945 Wasilewska married Korniychuk, a Soviet deputy foreign minister, and settled permanently in Kiev. She was never to surrender her Soviet citizenship. Wasilewska features in some of Irena's reflections on the Polish Question during the war.

The second evacuation of the Polish Army from the USSR lasted twenty-two days, from 9 August to 1 September 1942, and involved twenty-six transports. The ships used were mostly converted tankers which were packed with people in horrific unsanitary conditions: the largest tankers took 4,000–5,000 people but only had six lavatories. The sea journey lasted about thirty-six hours. Irena's ship left the port of Krasnovodsk on 17 August 1942.[25] It also happened to be her birthday: she was thirty-two.

Judging from her notes and army records, Irena spent about a month in Iran and about a month in Iraq: she entered Iraq on 22 September 1942 and reached Palestine on 24 October 1942. In the meantime, the Polish civilians (numbering 41,000 and consisting mostly of women and children) who had left the USSR with Anders's Army in 1942 were moved to various parts of the British Empire: over 5,500 to India; over 13,000 to East Africa; over 4,000 to North and South Rhodesia (now Zambia and Zimbabwe); 550 orphans to South Africa; and over 800 children with their carers to New Zealand. Over 1,400 exiles went to Mexico. Most of the 4,500 exiles remaining in Iran were transferred to Lebanon at the end of 1945. Of course, all these exiles represented a small minority of the civilians originally deported into the Soviet interior from eastern Poland in 1940–1.[26]

Like other Poles in a similar position, Irena credits General Anders (whom she likened to Moses) with her liberation from 'the land of slavery', from 'the Soviet hell'. In her eulogy to Anders she acclaims the general's charismatic leadership, his 'real' understanding of Soviet Russia, his military valour and his courage in Soviet captivity, although she incorrectly states that Anders had been in a Soviet labour camp. General Anders had been badly wounded fighting the Germans in the defence of Lwów in September 1939 and was in a military hospital in Soviet-occupied Lwów until December 1939. He refused to collaborate with the Soviets and was then imprisoned in a dungeon until the end of February 1940 when he was unexpectedly transferred to the NKVD Lubyanka prison in Moscow. He still refused to collaborate and was placed in the more severe Butyrki prison, also in Moscow, where he remained in solitary confinement and received no medical treatment until the end of August 1940. He was sent back to the Lubyanka and remained there until 4 August 1941. On that day, still on crutches and in prison clothes, he was brought before Beria, the commissar for internal affairs in charge of the NKVD, to be informed that he was free and that the Polish and Soviet governments had agreed that he should command the Polish Army in the USSR. What a change of fortune![27]

Anders's Army, later transformed into the Polish Second Corps, was more than just a military formation. Under its auspices there blossomed a wide range of cultural activities: newspapers, textbooks, even new editions of works of literature and scholarship, as well as artistic productions. It also catered for the education of the men, women and children in its charge, such as the school for young Polish soldiers in Nazareth where Irena was to work for over a year. From 1942 onwards, the Polish Army in the Middle East directed many suitably qualified young people, mostly young women, to study at four of Beirut's institutions of higher learning. Most studied medicine, dentistry, engineering and pharmacology, but some also studied architecture, art and literary subjects. During the academic year 1946–7 there were over 250 such students in Beirut. Aware of the appalling losses among Poland's educated population at the hands of the Germans and of the Soviets, the Polish government-in-exile was anxious to create a large body of educated and professionally qualified people wherever there were educational opportunities in exile.[28]

Irena's world view in 1942–5 was clearly coloured by her negative Soviet experience, by the absence of reliable information about the wider war and by a failure to appreciate the vital role of the USSR in the struggle against Nazi Germany – with all its implications for Poland. Indeed, she admits how 'naive' she and other Poles in the Middle East were in assuming that an independent Poland would be restored after the war.

The outbreak of war in 1939 begins Part Two of Irena's story, marking a dramatic and decisive change in her life with consequences that she could never have imagined.

7

'The end of our world'

Our last summer – The Red Army arrives – Looting of the manor – A night in the forest – A people's court – The social order overthrown – Beginnings of Soviet rule – Irena's family escapes to Warsaw
This chapter includes extracts, shown in italics, from Irena's 1943 deposition to the Polish government.

'The Year 1939. O Year of Years!' ('*Rok 1939. O roku ów!*')[1]
Oh fateful year,
Oh wound that in my memory still bleeds,
What curse had sent you to our door
Engulfing us in Satan's maw,
In golden autumn with our world and gods …

And it was my fate to live to see the end of our world, the one that has gone; and, somehow or other, to strike roots in new ground … in a new world. Out of ashes and ruins a new life has begun to sprout, towards an unknown tomorrow. And I was cut in two, by what had irretrievably gone and by what had not yet arrived. Unlike Lot's wife, we must not look back in case we turn into an inert statute of Niobe made out of the salt of our tears, dried by the winds of destiny. New ploughs await new ploughmen, so in God's name let us go forward with love, faith and yearning; for what matters is to be with the young ones, and perhaps to live for another twenty years.[2]

Oh Wacio! Recollection has stirred the romantic strings in my soul and ushered forth deep feelings. My fingers run over the white keys of my typewriter; from it letters of ash have started to fall, filled with the melody of days gone by and over which hangs the great Babylonian inscription: MENE, TEKEL, PERES.[3]

We had a beautiful and dry summer in 1939; the first one I remember when the bees produced no honey. The peasants' fields were covered with a rippling ocean of fragrant buckwheat blossom. But the sun mercilessly dried up the heavy white flowers laden with nectar that seemed heavier than lead. The bees flew around lost, and landed less and less on these milky Persian carpets. Instead they collected nectar from the many lime trees in the park and this early honey was devoured by fast-breeding larvae.

My sister Jula came to Borki for the summer with her wonderful four-year-old Marysia, lively like quicksilver; baby Basia also came, wrapped in her swaddling clothes. Pan Turzański's nephew, Bolesław, a young freshly qualified lawyer, also arrived for his honeymoon with his wife; she was robust and ruddy, and as delightful as springtime. The groom beamed with happiness as he strolled with his loved one along the avenue of the old lime trees. His declarations of love scared away the nightingales and, in the evenings, the owls. My mother watched the loving couple with emotion. Perhaps it brought back memories of the charm of her own honeymoon. I also was affected by their true happiness and remembered with sadness how Mania Kozłowska and Kazio Protassewicz used to walk along the same avenue. But in Mania's case this avenue did not lead to her happiness, but to her grave.

My young sixteen-year-old cousin Dziutek Morski also came; he seemed all confused in his puppy-like admiration for me. My sister Hania, looking gaunt and pale on account of her emotional predicaments in love, called by once. Jula's husband Janek called briefly; he was attending military manoeuvres at the time, and looked beautiful in his uniform. He sat down at the piano and filled the park with Chopin's melodies. Everything overflowed with the spirit of youth, with happiness and with an undefinable calm ... before the storm. For one sensed the gathering of some subterranean disquiet; the German radio was barking with the fury of mad dogs, and emitting a vehement, virile and imperious lust. Despite this, a certain strange tranquillity settled on the still trees in the park and in the forest, which was covered with an early autumnal deluge of golden and red leaves.

I left for several days to visit our Protassewicz relatives living in Proście where the estate was bravely run by young Maurycy Protassewicz.[4] His regal sister Stacha (Stanisława) eclipsed everyone with her dignified charm. Their energetic mother set the overall pace of life in the house. I joined them in outings across the fields and to Nieśwież.[5] Yet I rebelled inwardly when their other sister Irena, full of wistfulness, forecast the imminence of the final disaster: the entry of the Soviets, the loss of their lands, as well as the death of Maurycy – which, alas, was to happen soon during the military operations in Pomerania.[6] Aunt Salunia Połubińska with her granddaughter Jola went to Mohylna (in Polesie) where Witek Kontkowski had built a small modern country residence for his wife Mila and the family. From there Salunia wrote letters to me which fully reflected her benign frame of mind. The radio announcement that the Soviets were crossing the border (on 17 September) was to reach Salunia in time, enabling them to escape back to Wilno by the last train.

The German attack on Poland on 1 September roused us from the sweet slumber of the golden Polish autumn. The radio broadcast dreadful news about the rout of the Polish armies and about German fighter aircraft even firing on young shepherd boys working in the fields. A summons from the Polish Red Cross managed to reach me with instructions to be prepared to respond to the next call-up. It never came. All of a sudden, Zygmuś (Zygmunt) Protassewicz arrived by car in Borki with his wife Jadwiga Smosarska with the intention of leaving her in Borki in our care. He himself, as a reserve officer, wanted to join the forces engaged in battle. I felt most uncomfortable that Mamusia did not want to receive Jadwiga. Mamusia argued that it would be better if Zygmunt left his wife in the care of his brother Kazio in Mołodeczno where he was the district governor. Mamusia's advice against staying in Borki probably saved their lives, for they continued by car to Wilno, and then on to Lithuania where Smosarska managed to obtain a special American visa on account of her artistic work. They were then able to fly to the United States.[7] While Zygmunt and Jadwiga went on their way, our barns and farm outbuildings filled with refugees from the Łomża area, whom we also fed.[8]

One day soon after (18 September), the first Soviet tanks approached the village of Borki. The first person to run up to them was Augustyn Borowik, our former forest-keeper, who asked the Soviet soldiers what they had brought for the people. 'It's your day' (*Vash dyen*), they replied, whereupon Borowik immediately ran to the manor.[9] He entered the kitchen packed with the fugitives from Łomża, and demanded to see 'the young ladies'. I came in and was struck dumb. I looked at Borowik's face, usually full of servility, and I now saw his eyes burning bright, a murderous venom coursing through them, borne out of a desire for riches, a desire that had been accumulating in his mind. My views on Judas are different today, but then I was reminded of the scene with Judas in the Garden of Olives. He jumped up to me, his hideously deformed face close to mine but not to kiss me, and shouted: 'You should be hanged, because you have an estate and wealth, and I don't.' He tried to grab me with his clammy hands. I replied: 'Alright (*kharasho*), but I'm getting my revolver first.' I rushed to my bedroom, pulled out my revolver from under the pillow and, agitated to the core, I began to approach the kitchen. I opened the door, but there was no sign of him. My hand holding the revolver fell.

This was a prelude to what would soon await us. Eventually tanks, or was it only soldiers, arrived in front of the manor house. We were ordered to surrender our weapons, which we did: two shotguns and my revolver. The second revolver was with Pan Turzański who had gone off somewhere in the neighbourhood. We barricaded the house, and I brought all gardening forks, axes and hoes indoors. If we were going to die, we would do so defending ourselves! There were still many men from Łomża in the house, some of whom had weapons, but they all behaved passively throughout, as if all this was happening without them being there.

Night was drawing in fast. In my youth I had read more than enough in *Fire and Sword* about massacres carried out by the rabble.[10] I now had to witness, in its full terror, the sight of a crowd of peasants,[11] armed with iron crowbars, gathering around our manor in the dead of night. After a time, a fifteen-year-old boy, Wacek, was sent to us as a 'mediator'. At the boy's baptism his mother had timidly asked the priest: 'Let him be named Pan Wacio' (she was unable to utter my father's first name without the addition of 'Pan'). And so this 'mediator' informed us that the peasants had no wish to kill us; they would let us leave quietly providing they could loot the manor house. While he was there, Wacek glanced at Janek Karczewski's boots (Janek had in the meantime arrived from Warsaw which was being bombed), and said: 'I like those boots.' Janek was ready to take them off, when I told him: 'Why those? Give him some other ones.' Wacek left the house with another pair.

Following this act of 'mediation', Mamusia quickly slipped out into the dark night. Jula, along with Janek and the two children, were invited to stay with the children's nanny, and they left for the nanny's cottage. I was terrified that they would be killed on the way. All the numerous men from Łomża were standing motionless in the dining room; they gradually dispersed themselves. As for myself, I dared not go to the village to ask for shelter. After my father's death, I was the one who had continued to live in the house, whereas both Jula and Hania had been living in Warsaw for many years. I felt that, after Augustyn's 'performance', all the odium towards the lords would focus on my person.

My young cousin Dziutek Morski was still with us. I told him to take some clothes or food because we had to escape to the forest; from there we would slip away to Słonim and beyond. I seized an umbrella in case we encountered dripping water from the trees in the forest, a piece of sheepskin to sit on and a pair of lovely white plaited shoes handmade in Warsaw. We slipped out into the park and quietly sneaked along the road, lined with horse chestnut trees, towards the grove. The mild September evening was so warm and quiet that, hiding behind the trees, I could hear the mature chestnut cases splitting loudly in the branches and the conkers falling to the ground. Nearby I could hear the footsteps of women streaming from Ladziny, a village 3 km west of Borki, carrying sacks to rob the manor. It was a very beautiful evening and the romantic setting reminiscent of Sienkiewicz's novels lent colour to all the dramatic moments of that night. I feel sorry for those who experienced the hell of German concentration camps, for over there were monstrosity and hideousness. My experiences under Soviet occupation may have had their ghastly episodes, but everything took place within the bosom of the natural world in all its beauty. There was danger, but there was also the beauty of the drama. My sense of poetry and of painting found an artistic and aesthetic nourishment. It was as if the wheel of history had turned back, and I had found myself, as a real actor or hero, dropped into a scene set in the great panorama created in Henryk Sienkiewicz's novels.

We groped around in the dark forest not knowing where to go. Perhaps we could spend the night in the cottage of the leaseholder of our brickworks? But I was afraid. And so we stayed in the forest till daybreak. Throughout the night we shivered in the damp as we kept our ears alert to any crunching sound on the litter of conifer needles, for a man or a wolf could have easily crept up on us. Exhausted after a sleepless night in the forest and with nothing to eat, we could go no further. In the end I sent Dziutek to reconnoitre a lonely cottage on the edge of the forest. The kindly peasant living there immediately sent someone to find out what had happened to my family. After about an hour, a wagon was sent for us by the father of our servant Gienia Tarasik; we were also invited to his house. We discovered that Mamusia and Jula and all her family had survived the night which they had spent in the cottage of the nanny, the wife of my assistant beekeeper Fiodor.

On the second day, Mamusia and I set out to the manor house. Apparently the attack on the house had been led by Augustyn Borowik and Adam Szeremiet who had once been imprisoned for stealing smoked meat.[12] We also discovered that the village's burly carpenter had entered the drawing room and had destroyed Tatuś's bust with an axe, exclaiming: 'The lords are finished!' (*Koniets panou* in Belarusian). Everything had been looted. Only the portraits still remained hanging on the walls. But where could we hide them? I regret I had not taken away the portrait of Bishop Protassewicz. But where to? Because of the legend associated with his person, I removed the portrait of

Klemens Minasowicz and gave it to the Tarasiks to keep in their loft. But was it later eaten by rats? I also learnt that before the looting of the house, Mamusia had thrown a bag of family silver under the porch on the side facing the bower of lime trees. The advice I gave, to give the silver to my servant Mania for safekeeping, proved unwise, for as she went through the village, she kept looking around. People noticed that she was carrying something. The redheaded leader of the village called the local vigilantes. They took away all the beautiful silver, leaving Mania with only a small spoon. Perhaps the silver and the spoon saved Mania from being physically violated? In what had been Tatuś's office, the floor lay strewn knee-deep with scattered documents and papers pulled from the filing cabinet. Again, it is a pity I did not take away something of importance. But again, where to?

After several days, during which we were able to get some rest among faithful peasants, the Soviet tanks and soldiers returned. The soldiers ordered us to go out onto the road and to walk to Iwież, 2 km away. I walked with Mamusia, Janek and Dziutek (Jula had been allowed to stay behind because of her small children) along some deeply dug trenches beyond the village. We were escorted by soldiers with guns pointed at us. There was a spot in my back where my nerves tingled, waiting for a bullet to hit me there. We prayed as we walked. We were kept overnight in Iwież, after which we were loaded onto wagons, our hands tied behind our backs. Mamusia was at my side or just behind me, and I heard her say to me: 'I feel like Marie Antoinette!' She too was able to feel the significance of the moment through the prism of history.

Following us on foot all this time was the old redhead from the village of Borki; I cannot remember his name. It was he who denounced us to the Soviets, saying that we had machine guns or gold hidden in the forest. He wanted to make sure that the Soviets finished us off. He still kept some village documents from the time of the tsars; he was also Orthodox. A faithful servant of the former emperors, he now transferred his loyalty to the Bolsheviks.

We arrived in Nowojelnia (a health resort set in a pine forest 13 km north of Borki) where we were locked up in a one-room cell. I normally feel totally exhausted after nights without adequate sleep, and I felt awful in the morning. A state forestry official was then carried in and placed on the floor. Fearing that the peasants were going to lynch him for having honestly guarded the forests in his care, he had tried to poison himself by drinking petrol. This proved not to be so easy, for he seemed to have only burnt his gullet and his stomach. He groaned and writhed in agony. Despite this, several peasants armed with sticks came all the way to the jail and rushed up to him. One of them was jumping like a devil over a soul that had fallen into his hands, shouting wildly and waving his stick over the head of this man who may have been dying. Despite the fact that I was also a prisoner, I could not bear this. I walked up and protested in the name of the Red Cross, and demanded that the sick man be taken to hospital. Some soldiers did carry him away, but whether he survived or not we never found out.

Throughout this time, our redhead kept an eye on us to make sure that we were condemned. However, at that point there arrived a young Jew wearing a red star, a former teacher in Nowojelnia (or perhaps Dworzec).[13] He announced to all and sundry that he considered us not guilty. There had been a law that said it was allowed to own a landed estate, so we had one. The soldiers of the Red Army had abolished this law, so we no longer had an estate. He certainly saved us, although the redhead was not pleased. In any case, we were allowed to go free. I spent the night at the house of the Salesian Fathers where a few priests still remained in the emptied premises. Mamusia was received hospitably by our former meat merchant, Lejzer. His beard was so dark and thick that on one occasion, when he was holding a black ram while driving his wagon, it was very difficult to distinguish him from the animal. In this period beards were not fashionable; only Jews wore them, which made them look strange in their anachronism.

We returned from Nowojelnia to Borki on foot, avoiding crossroads alongside which armed peasant guards were encamped. They were armed with rifles supplied by the Soviets and were rounding up all sorts of fugitives and handing them over to Soviet soldiers. We walked at night, observing from a distance the campfires of the peasant guards. There was singing and shouting, and the unmistakable smell of roasted pigs or geese, taken from the local manors. The members of these bands tore apart their food and chewed it to the bone. The sight of it all reminded me of the image of the devils' banquets on Łysa Góra (Bare Mountain).[14] All the peasantry had gone crazy, overcome by a madness of stealing everything they could in the area. Nevertheless, I should add that only Orthodox villages took part in the looting of Borki; nobody came from the Catholic villages. Although they were Belarusian in speech, the Catholics considered themselves to be Poles.[15]

The looters had a go at the priest's house in Rohotna where Jula had found shelter, but Pan Turzański was there; he came out with a stick and chased everybody away. Not everyone had such courage; others felt defenceless in this period when the peasants wielded power. Yes: 'It's Your Day'. These were important words for many peasants who had been chained to their work in the fields. They felt themselves to be free and almost the masters of the world. With this slogan the Soviets unleashed the basest instincts among the masses, and achieved what they intended. It was the anger of the people that destroyed the existing order. It was the anger of the people that led to the rounding up of policemen, civil servants and all state forestry officials. It was the anger of the people which made sure that those who collected taxes or who put thieves in prison were not spared. Now these thieves became ringleaders: they led the assault in the first wave, to be followed by the enraged masses. The Soviet soldiers had only arrived as 'liberators' of the poor working people from the oppression of the landowners and the capitalists.

Besides, the Soviet soldiers behaved themselves properly, for those must have been their orders. When we were still in Iwież, held under arrest in some cottage, a female Soviet soldier came in; she saw some religious pictures in the corner of the room and was about to slash them with her bayonet. Immediately, other Soviet soldiers told her to stop. Yet there was no protection against the local peasants who knew all the paths in the forests and the fields by heart, and who knew everybody who exercised authority and everybody who was wealthier than they were.

We returned to Borki from imprisonment in Nowojelnia. There was nothing left in the house; even the door knobs and the kitchen tiles had been torn off. Our kindly carpenter, Wasyl, came and repaired the stove in the annexe to the house so that we could cook something. Wasyl was a peasant who liked the good life. As a carpenter, he was able to fix anything; he always did well. He recounted to us how many hogs he used to sell annually, and how he had prospered under Polish rule. Besides, during the First World War he had been a prisoner of war in Germany and was able to observe the higher culture there; he saw things in a broader perspective and was immune to communist propaganda. He even said how well he had fared while working for a German farmer. He told the farmer that he did not want any pay; what he asked for was to be 'fattened like a pig'. And so he gorged himself on bacon fat. He even had a woman there. Wasyl liked a good meal, but he was also kind towards everybody. He had a long moustache which stuck out stylishly. It was also said that it was Wasyl who was secretly responsible for providing a hitherto childless married couple with a child, to provide comfort in their old age. In any case, now that we were treated almost like plague-stricken untouchables, it was Wasyl who, after Lejzer, first offered us a helping hand.

From then on, we lived in the annexe and somehow got food, probably from kindly women in the village. Janek and Dziutek went to dig potatoes of which we were allowed to keep 200 poods (3,276 kg) to survive the approaching winter.[16] We were also allocated one or two of our own cows. And so we just kept our bodies and souls together, sitting quietly in our couple of small rooms to the accompaniment of the sound of the pines being cut down in the grove. Mamusia's grand piano had already been removed and sent to Russia, so our only music was the noise of axes and the buzz of the peasants' voices as they hurried to carve out for themselves as much manorial land as possible. My seventy-five beehives had already been chopped up by the locals. As for Tatuś's much-prized carp farm, one of the most unpleasant moments after the arrival of the Bolsheviks was when the peasants emptied all the ponds simultaneously, and carried off tons of fish by the sackload. It was a warm autumn: the fish rotted, while the ponds, now deprived of water and all life, stood out like empty eye sockets. All around the stench of dead fish arose from the mud. *Sic transit gloria mundi …*

It was a strange existence. While we were mostly confined to the house, Jula's little daughter Marysia moved about quite freely among the peasants who gathered at various public meetings. Marysia even walked all by herself beyond the lake to spend time with Mikołajowa, the mother of her former nanny Luba, and to have something to eat there. Incidentally, Luba had taken our sewing machine on which Elza Melcer, an old spinster, and later Gienia Taraszczuk, had made dresses for us. Luba said that she would not return the machine to Jula; she would only hand it back if Mamusia turned up for it in person. Despite the war, Mamusia did not lose her sense of honour, refusing to ask that chit of a girl for the machine. The machine remained with Luba, and for the good, since Luba knew how to sew and probably made a living from it during and after the war.

In the meantime, news reached us of many tragic happenings elsewhere in the neighbourhood. We were relieved that we had got off relatively lightly. A young Jesuit in Skrundzie and his seventy-five-year-old organist had been hacked to death by some peasants.[17] The two old Mikulski ladies, the owners of large forests on their estate of Litwa, and the ones whom Abramek had once suggested to Polik as a good catch, were not only killed, but also hacked to pieces 'to stop them from regrowing'. Orthodox priests, like the one in the village of Horka, were assaulted and stripped to their underclothes; the following day, however, this priest's clothes and shoes were returned.

On the same day as the attack on Borki, the neighbouring Ladzinki (the home of the Sidorowicz family) was also a target for the looters. They broke in through the windows and removed everything they could carry. However, the next day, some of the looters, affected by pangs of conscience, returned a few trifles. One of our servants also gave me back a suitcase full of my dresses; these I would later sell in Russia. But she kept two of my fox furs. Some people brought back other items; and later this or that woman would bring us a piece of smoked pork fat or some bread. And so our peasants were not bad; it was only that they could not resist the temptation to plunder. Besides, as my daughter Helenka was to comment in 1967, the peasants had no jumble sales which are held in every town in England. And so, with the permission of the soldiers of the Red Army, the poor rushed to the only 'jumble sale' the war provided for them.[18]

All the Soviets now had to do in our district, from which the 'enemies of the people' had been swept away, was to organize a new authority based on different ideological premises. This was: everything for the good of the common people. And so all landed estates were divided and distributed among local peasants; nearby pine trees began to be cut down, one after another.[19] All railway travel was made free, so everybody made haste to take advantage of this sport. Local village committees, composed of peasants, were set up:

> However, each of the village committee chairmen ('predsedateli' in Russian), such as Sajczyk and his successor Tomczyk, as well as others who helped the Soviets were thieves with no scruples. In any case no one was employed by the Soviets who could not demonstrate his 'communist past', that is who had not been in prison; unfortunately, in most cases, they had been in prison for more prosaic reasons – ordinary theft. Lower-ranking officials and teachers were allowed to stay in their posts, but at every turn they were terrorized and forbidden to attend church. Honest folk were completely terrorized; no one was certain of his life or possessions; there were informers and spies everywhere, so people were frightened to speak Polish or go to church, or just to speak. People were even afraid of their own shadows.[20]

And elections were announced:

> The first elections [of 22 October 1939] took place among the recent echoes of the rumble of tanks and in an atmosphere of terror generated by renegades and the dregs of society. In February [1940], in temperatures of minus 30 degrees, settlers[21] were deported (wherever an infant died the corpse was thrown into the snow). A rumour was spread that after the second elections [to be held in March 1940], that is after the 'enemies of the people' had been exposed, a second deportation would take place. Printed lists with the names of carefully selected candidates were handed out. Voters could cross out names <u>but only behind a screen in the presence</u> of the militia. Everyone <u>had to</u> vote. Ballot-boxes were brought to the sick and the elderly. There was no way out. In any case, resistance would have been of no avail; the elections would have been carried, but much blood would have been spilt. And so all the Poles voted, even [Catholic] priests. Everyone voted because everyone <u>had to</u>, because everyone was defenceless.[22]

In the meantime, Jula's husband Janek made his way back secretly to German-occupied Warsaw, as did Pan Turzański. Janek discovered that his house had survived the bombing and the siege of the city. He therefore returned to Borki with a smuggler from Grodno who was going to lead us across the border to Warsaw. But I did not want to leave Borki; I would have fallen into a state of moral collapse if I had to ask my relatives in Warsaw to support me. Janek invited me to his house, but why should I burden him and the children with my person? The upshot was that one day the faithful Heljasz and another peasant loaded Mamusia, Janek, Jula, young Marysia and baby Basia onto wagons and set off for the railway station. I was terrified that some peasant band might murder them on the way. In case they had to come back, I kept their bedding and two cows, along with the potatoes in the cellar.[23] As for Dziutek, he made contact with some resistance organization in Słonim from where he was sent to Warsaw; there he joined Janek's family. It is strange, but when they were all living with me, I continually suffered from nervous diarrhoea. I lived in perpetual fear that the NKVD might arrive. But from the moment my family departed I slept as soundly as ever.

8

Under Soviet occupation (1939 to 1941)

Dr Atlas establishes a hospital – Working as a nurse – The winter of 1939–40 – Aunt Hela and Uncle Leon – Mojsze Helman's story – Jewish neighbours old and new – Peasants of Borki and beyond – Irena's inner freedom – The hospital is moved – Escape to Ladzinki – A letter from Berlin – The sad story of cousin Dziutek Morski – An ominous public meeting
This chapter includes extracts, shown in italics, from Irena's letters written in 1940 and 1944.

I was alone in the house, but not without moral sustenance. Fiodor had saved my bedside cupboard which contained twelve volumes of Piłsudski's writings which my cousin Leoś had bought for me just before the outbreak of war. Every evening I would lock my door with two bolts, and place an axe and a hoe by my bed. I would then feast eagerly on the Marshal's writings and, carried away by a vision of heroism and adventure, I would drift into deep sleep. No, Poland cannot perish if it has sons like that, and if the writings of such a son possess such a hidden force. I was proud of those writings. They gave me strength, inspiration and the greatest consolation which promoted healthy sleep. I read them every evening. Once again, the idea of the finger of God, of which Piłsudski was sometimes conscious, spoke to me more about His existence than any formal catechism. I dreamt of Emilia Plater, and about the possibility of a national insurrection in which I might be offered some part to play. I also thought about defending the faith, and spreading it in this deluge of barbarism. Altogether, this generated an internal moral strength which not only protected me from fear, but which also instilled such boundless happiness in my soul that I was surprised. How could I be happy sleeping all by myself with the knowledge that I might be killed at any moment? Yet that state of enthusiasm was a fact, and I understood the profundity of the Marshal's words when he said that serving an idea by itself creates such happiness that one no longer needs any rewards.

In the meantime, a Dr Atlas arrived in Borki.[1] He was twenty-six years of age and had finished his medical studies a few years earlier in Italy. He announced that, in the name of the Soviet authorities, he was going to organize a hospital in Borki manor. I showed him my certificate issued by the Polish Red Cross; with that, he allowed me, whether willingly or not, to work as a nurse, for there was no one else to assist him. I was now entitled to a monthly salary of 280 roubles, and I was also legally authorized to continue living in the house.[2] For a period I remained the only nurse, and Dr Atlas instructed the hospital orderly to wake him up during the night in case of an emergency rather than disturb me. In this way I had enough strength to look after the sick, who filled the whole house during the day, as well as to maintain my own health. I remained for many months in my state of happiness until Dr Atlas engaged two other people as nurses and introduced night shifts which exhausted my nerves and made me feel constantly drained and short of sleep. It is odd how my body cannot tolerate even one sleepless night.

During the early phase of his posting in Borki, Dr Atlas often travelled to Słonim to procure medicines from the Soviet authorities because the Polish pharmacies had been destroyed by Soviet soldiers. 'We don't need this; we've got everything' (*Nam ne nado; u nas i tak vsyo yest*), they said as they smashed a large bottle of iodine.[3] As a result, I was to sleep all alone in the house for a total of three weeks. My quarters were in the furthest room of the annexe, while Dr Atlas lived in the office in the main building. During those three weeks, I slept like a log. Occasionally, there would be a tap on the small window; I would put out my hand, and a peasant or a woman from the village would pass me a piece of smoked pig fat or some bread. Once, as dawn was approaching, I heard the distinct sound of footsteps as if someone was walking in a circle in the dining room, the room in which Tatuś's body had lain on a catafalque after his death. 'What can this be?' I thought to myself, for the entire house was locked. Had Dr Atlas returned a day early from Słonim? I began to feel rather uncomfortable, but I got out of bed (it was already getting light), and went into the dining room. There was no one there. I rushed around the entire house. There was no sign of a living soul; Dr Atlas had not come back. It then occurred to me that it might have been Tatuś's spirit walking about, to let me know that he was looking after me. One supposedly did not believe in ghosts, but I remain puzzled to this day as to what those footsteps were. If it was a ghost, it was clearly someone strangely benevolent, for at the time I did not feel frightened; on the contrary, I felt better in spirit and returned to bed. The following day I told the doctor about this, whereupon he also went through the entire house and even looked in the loft. We did not find any evidence of anyone else having been there.

The doctor pressed on with procuring what was necessary for the hospital. He purchased some linen cloth from the peasants and had some sheets made. He managed to secure some iron beds, and arranged a sickbay for women in the dining room and one for men in the former drawing room. A separate small room was reserved for expectant mothers. On one occasion, we had a woman in labour, groaning in agony as her husband stood beside her. Dr Atlas had never before attended a birth, so he had to read it up in a book. He briefly left the room to wash his hands. The woman then said that she always gave birth standing up, and her husband placed a linen rug underneath her. Before either the doctor or I could turn around, the baby fell out smoothly onto the rug. This was the first time for me too, but all the doctor had to do was to cut the umbilical cord and tie a knot. However, later on we had to deal with an unpleasant incident. A woman, who was a village 'midwife', was brought to us suffering from heavy bleeding. She said that she had heavy menstruation. Dr Atlas believed her, for after all she was supposed to be a midwife and knew about these matters. Because the haemorrhage was not easing, the doctor told me to give her an injection to slow the flow of blood. At that moment a paramedic from Horka, who also worked with us in Borki, ran in. Looking horrified, he asked the doctor to step aside for a word. 'What on earth have you done taking her word at face value? She's well known for performing abortions with a wire.' On this occasion she had tried this method on herself. The wire had been dirty and the injection to slow the flow of blood only enabled the faster spread of infection. Indeed, her temperature soared; she was then taken by car to Słonim. Because penicillin was not yet available, the poor woman died there, leaving behind four children and a husband. She had used her own 'weapon' on herself, while I, unwittingly, had assisted in her death by administering the injection. How important it is not just to have medical knowledge, but also an understanding of the psychology and mentality of the people you are treating.

The peasants were also superstitious. Once Mamusia had ordered some kohlrabi seeds, some of which she gave to one of the village girls. The swollen stems of the kohlrabi grew above ground level, unlike turnips with which the peasants were familiar. 'She's cast a spell!' and 'It's a bad omen!' cried out the old women of the village. Pilloried by them, the girl might have committed suicide out of despair, had Mamusia not intervened in all this commotion and explained that it was quite natural for those particular seeds to produce stems above the soil. There was also a woman who suffered from very bad headaches. She eventually came to Tatuś for some medication. He diagnosed an advanced state of anaemia, but he knew this woman to be so tight-fisted that she would rather sell an egg than eat one. And so Tatuś gave her something to see her off, and added that she must eat one egg a day, but only from a black hen. Because this bordered on some magical power, the woman began to eat eggs from a black hen and soon her anaemia, brought about by malnutrition, ended. Uncle Piotr Protassewicz was also well known for 'charming away' a bacterial infection of the skin (erysipelas). The women came to him, and he would recite some mysterious prayer while burning a wisp of flax under his hand. And it helped. But how?

I spent many interesting and pleasant moments while working in the Borki hospital, because I was able to meet a whole kaleidoscope of people whom I would not have otherwise come across. I also made visits in the area to administer injections, for example in Ladziny. One very old peasant I had dealings with told me that he wanted to live a little longer to see how the war would end. But I got a real fright when the wife of the redhead, who had tried to have me condemned earlier, fell ill with pneumonia. Remember, there was still no penicillin. The doctor sent me to give her an injection. In her cottage I boiled my own syringe which had survived the looting of the house. My hand trembled as I administered the injection because I could see the redhead observing me suspiciously. If his wife died, he would probably have accused me of murder; I therefore prayed inwardly for her recovery. I was lucky: the woman survived. Despite this, the redhead continued to shadow me everywhere like a bad spirit. At night I was frightened to go to the privy outside the house, for I could not be certain that someone with an axe was not lying in wait for me in the isolated little building on the edge of the park. I therefore emptied my chamber pot through the window. Because there was a frost (it was the winter of 1939–40), a large icy mound grew outside; the redhead even accused me of violating hygiene regulations! Whenever I went out anywhere, it was at an unexpected time and I always went armed with a hoe.

And where did my legs not carry me? I even crossed the fields and reached Izmajłowszczyzna where I managed to meet Aunt Kama. After her manor had been razed to the ground, she had found sanctuary with her servant Magdalena. It was spring 1940, and I can remember as clearly as today that I wore Hania's lovely summer dress: it was white with red dots. Frightened out of her wits, my aunt just stared at my calm countenance. On another occasion, a lady who lived a few kilometres away let me know that she had some important matter to discuss. I walked to her house to discover that they had not been looted; she therefore gave me 150 złotys or more which I was able to send, with some food supplies, to Aunt Hela Protassewicz in Lida.[4] It was also with emotion that I greeted Pani Grunerowa in the sickbay in Borki; she had travelled a considerable distance to find out what had happened to me.

There was an unusual amount of snow during the winter of 1940. It was so fine and deep that horses sank in it up to their middle; even wolves could not run across it. I used this opportunity to set off on my skis through all our forests to observe the extent of the devastation and to establish which trees had not been felled. I cannot remember ever experiencing such ecstasy of beauty as in the forest of Chadybowszczyzna, the one in which some years earlier I had had my encounter with the wolf. The forest was covered in snow, and in the clear light of the sun it glowed as if ablaze with diamonds; the white fields were iridescent with the colour of gold, and the shaded expanses with blue. It was a strange enchanted world of stalactites. The forest seemed lifeless and motionless, but in its full majesty of gold and with the diamond-like sparkles on the snow-laden branches it was alive, proud and inaccessible in its royal stateliness.

In the spring of 1940, I was able to visit Aunt Hela (wife of Uncle Leon) and learn what had happened to them since the arrival of the Soviets. Uncle Leon was a great democrat. When the Bolsheviks arrived in 1939 and when there were many attacks on manor houses, it was the peasants who formed a guard to protect him. Nonetheless he decided to flee to Wilno. He hid important legionary papers, took his poems and went. He threw the poems away in the snow when he noticed some Lithuanian border guards. For a time he languished in a Lithuanian prison, but somehow managed to get out. He and Aunt Hela then went to live with relatives, the Narbutts, in the nearby town of Lida. During the Soviet occupation, he earned a living by repairing watches. Aunt Hela went about in a headscarf pretending to be a servant, and cultivated a small vegetable garden. Leon wrote a few of his poems again from memory, but his beautiful translations of Pushkin and other poems were lost for good. Nervous exhaustion, a fondness for black coffee and cigarettes, which he smoked by the hundred every day, no doubt had all undermined his health. One day he called out 'Hela!', and collapsed dead.

Aunt Hela was a person of exceptional kindness and dedication. She was overcome with emotion and was deeply moved by the fact that I had travelled in such dangerous circumstances to find her. I learnt then about Uncle Leon's death and I visited his grave which was overgrown with weeds ('because he liked weeds', said Aunt Hela). She gave me Uncle Leon's notebook containing the fragments of his poems which he had tried to remember. By a strange coincidence, this notebook survived with me through Siberia, and I still have it with other mementos. Aunt Hela admitted to me: 'Only now have I reconciled myself with God's Will that our son Ziuk is dead. For how would I be able to protect him now? There in Heaven he is safe. I also wondered where I could hide Uncle Leon. But he's dead too, so nobody can arrest him now.'

As to religion, Aunt Hela had liberal views which was not surprising given her socialist past; but in Lida she experienced a psychic-religious conversion and attended church daily with a new-found focus. How strange are the workings of God. Here was our district overwhelmed by a sea of barbarians, all around us the destruction of the entire legacy of Christian culture, everywhere savagery and brutality; and yet at the same time there occurred, unobserved by anyone, the 'Mystery of the Transfiguration' in one soul. In the light of eternity, even Piłsudski had diminished in stature: 'You know', Aunt Hela remarked, 'on a few occasions I even detected a spontaneous expression of pride in him, but I did not want to mention it to Leon who worshipped Piłsudski unreservedly'. I was never to see Aunt Hela again; she died from typhus several years later.

One of our patients was an old blacksmith from Rohotna, by the name of Mojsze (Moyshe) Helman, who used to travel with his old wife to the hospital in Borki. I used to give him intravenous injections for some complaint or other. He related to me how Pani Wanda Roycewicz's manor house in Rohotna had been devastated and that her French books lay scattered in the peasants' cottages. In the park beyond her house stood a small baroque chapel containing the graves of the Wołłowicz family, including those of Pani Wanda's parents. The Soviets decided to raze the chapel to the ground; they persuaded some young Catholic peasants to climb onto its roof and knock down the cross and statues of angels. When news of this reached Mojsze, he simply shook with indignation. He harnessed his scrawny old nag and drove to the house of the former lady of the manor. Through an opening he descended into the crypt of the chapel; he removed his cap and uttered the words: 'I am sorry, great Lords, for disturbing you, but I wish to see if all is in order.' Robbers had been here too, but what was there to take? So Mojsze cast a glance at the bodies of the dead and noticed that the yellow boots of Pani Wanda's father, who had been buried forty years earlier, still looked as new as ever. He left the chapel, and with a massive stone covered the entrance to the tomb. He then collected all the broken marble angels and the cross, and transported them in full view past the office of the commune, before arranging them around a fenced cross that stood at the crossroads. A crowd of spectators gathered. With his hands on his hips and adopting a stance of self-importance, Mojsze looked proudly at the rabble, and then uttered a sentence which must have sounded strange coming from a Jew: 'Well! Who amongst us is the greater Catholic now?' Should Mojsze Helman not receive a posthumous Papal decoration for bravery?

Much later I was to write about these happenings to Pani Roycewicz. Before the Soviets reached our district in 1939, she had managed to escape with her horses to Wilno where she sold them. There, she met someone with whom she was able to go by air to the southern hemisphere – to Brazil. After the war, she wrote a long article about Mojsze and the devastated Wołłowicz chapel, which she published in the weekly *Wiadomości Literackie* (Literary News) in London. However, she chose not to mention me by name as the source of her information, referring to me merely as 'a neighbour who wrote to me'. I felt hurt, but clearly I meant nothing to her. On the other hand, I remember with gratitude her kindness to my mother when, after the war, she sent her a beautiful outfit and other items from across the seas, signing her letter 'always the same Wanda'. No doubt, she remembered fondly the days of her youth when Tatuś was in love with her. Sadly, in about 1966, Wanda Roycewicz died from a stroke. And so passed away the Sappho or the George Sand of our part of the world.

Returning to Mojsze, he was so kind that, while on a journey to Lida, he delivered money and food from me for Aunt Hela Protassewicz. She was moved by this, but decided to pass them on to Aunt Wera (Ewarysta) Przybytko, the youngest of Tatuś's sisters and a warm and convivial person, who was living in dreadful conditions in Siberia where she had been deported in 1940 with her daughters and grandchildren.[5] I was also able to send something to Aunt Wera, and I still have the letters she sent me from Siberia. Indeed, working in the hospital in Borki under Soviet rule I was able to save some of my earnings; I was in a position to send this money to my family in Warsaw using the services of Suczek, although he kept some of it for himself.[6] In that period, there was widespread smuggling across the new border. It even happened that individuals, who had probably stolen something from the manor in Borki, turned up at Jula's home in Warsaw with the utmost composure, as if nothing had happened.

How did I get on with Dr Atlas? Well, on no account would he travel alone with me in the carriage so as not to jeopardize his reputation among the Soviets. And when in May 1940 I organized prayers for peasant children in my room, he told me to stop. On another occasion, I gave my cow's calf to the hospital on credit; Dr Atlas ate the calf's liver without offering any of it to me or to the paramedic. Otherwise, he was unusually considerate and showed great loyalty in important matters. There was the case when a seriously ill woman asked for an Orthodox priest. I got in touch with the priest in Horka who, despite having been robbed by the peasants, showed courage in daring to come to a Soviet hospital to hear the sick woman's confession. Just as the confession was taking place, Dr Atlas appeared, and immediately withdrew, summoning me to his surgery. 'Miss Irena', he said, 'I did not see that', and continued: 'but in future, should anything like this arise, please let me know in advance, so that I will not be present in the hospital'. Fortunately, the ill woman later recovered. On another occasion he unexpectedly asked me, out of curiosity: 'Please tell me why you work with such enthusiasm among the peasants who robbed you and why you are helping to run a hospital for them in your own home?' I answered frankly: 'I've heard that a Polish army is being formed in Lithuania, and that it might come here; a Polish field hospital might be established here'. 'I did not hear that', Dr Atlas responded. And yet, had he been a real communist, he could have used my remark to my disadvantage. He himself admitted that he still believed in God, but that in the face of the Soviet deluge no son of his ever would. The unfortunate man probably never lived long enough to have a son, and probably perished later at the hands of the Germans who were to burn captured local Jews in Słonim.[7]

I therefore very much hope that old Mojsze and old Abramek managed to die a natural death.[8] However, a dreadful fate must have awaited the unfortunate young Helmans from Rohotna and their children; also Itka who had a small shop in Borki and who was unfaithful to her husband; and Lejzer with his family who had given hospitality to Mamusia after her release from jail. May their memory be honoured. Maybe in Abraham's bosom God has wiped away all their tears. Here in England I ordered a Holy Mass to be said for their souls. And I continue to regret that it was not given to me to do something in return for their kindness during the Soviet occupation.

During my life in the country, I had dealings only with simple, uneducated Jews. In our part of the world, the Jews went about their business dressed in gaberdines and wore long beards; their odd appearance was different from everybody else. As a result, people thought that to be such a Jew was in some sense shameful, even that the Jews seemed to belong to a lower order of society. As for the peasants, they were seen as the most inferior, almost as if it had been ordained by nature. The local Jews were tradesmen, pedlars and shopkeepers. They had their faults and virtues, but they constituted an indispensable element in society. In the absence of an ethnic Polish business class in our district, the Jews were the only people who could help if one wanted to sell part of a forest, or a calf, or fish or the skin of a killed fox. The local gentry and smallholders of petty noble descent considered trading to be dishonourable. Nor was there ever a German-speaking urban population in our part of the eastern borderlands. The peasants were mostly illiterate.[9] So the Jews filled the gap: they were that nerve that connected everybody in the realm of economic exchange. Every landed gentleman had his Jew, for he could not have coped without one. He was easy to deal with, he was always available. He knew which way the wind blew, he was able to conjure up anything you needed, however urgent, including money. He could always buy anything, absolutely anything. A Jew could lease a garden, and sometimes a whole landed estate. With his book on the Jews, Jędrzej Giertych tried to create a negative impression of that race.[10] But for me, his book only aroused admiration for that people, so resilient, gifted, enterprising and talented, capable of operating with vast sums, and yet, when necessary, able to live on herrings and potatoes, and to survive in the worst of conditions.

Much was said before the war about the Jews having become the masters of Polish culture, and that Poland in the end would contain a second Judea; that 60 per cent of all industry and trade was in their hands; that they were a cancer that would devour us. The ONR (the National-Radicals) conducted such anti-Jewish propaganda. Despite all this, I am glad that Poland did not expel its Jews, as had been done by the Spaniards who sullied themselves with such a cruel act.[11] While some might argue that there were too many Jews in Poland, it was hardly their fault that they had been persecuted everywhere, and that even the tsarist government, despite Russia's vast expanses, had forced them to live in the western borderlands of the Russian Empire.[12]

The conduct of local Jewish traders [in 1939] was excellent. In our district all such Jews, petty traders etc., with whom one had personal contact, showed themselves to be 100 per cent loyal to Poland (this was not the case with the semi-intelligentsia of the small towns). In any case, the Jewish merchants in Słonim and elsewhere were totally ruined with the arrival of the Bolsheviks; their goods were either sequestrated or else they were ordered to sell them at reduced prices with one Polish złoty declared equal to one Soviet rouble. Many Jews were deported and arrested. Tears and lament reigned in Słonim.[13]

It was only in Borki after the outbreak of the war that I personally encountered educated Jews. In addition to Dr Atlas, quite a number of Jews arrived from Warsaw, some of whom were employed by the doctor. They were cultured people and well read. Once I went for a walk with a group of them in the forest; they declaimed highly humorous poems, even making fun of themselves, like the poem that 'everywhere you can find a Rappaport'.[14] They were joined by another physician, Dr Gomuliński, and his wife, a dentist. What an admirable woman! She was tall and good-looking and very fond of literature. The persecution of Jews at the university prevented her from studying for a degree in Polish literature, which was what she had dreamt of doing.[15] She was obliged to go to Paris where she completed her dentistry studies. There she fell in love with a wonderful Frenchman and was so happy with him. However, her despotic father forced her to return to Poland and marry a doctor for practical reasons, providing he was Jewish. Her husband was a good man but physically weak, suffering from chronic catarrh. She complained to me that, had it not been for her father's old-fashioned views, she would now be living a full life in Paris instead of being an exile.[16] She was the only one in Borki who was not afraid of spending time with me or of showing me friendship. She was proud and charming, and unyielding in character. I observed this woman with admiration, and it was she who changed my views of the Jews. She was ultra-modern, and belonged to a veritable elite of spirit and body. Dr Atlas also engaged another refugee couple, the Pawłowskis, to help him. They were fairly primitive. The wife was self-assertive and unsophisticated, and worked, supposedly, as a nurse. What a contrast between her and another Jewish nurse who showed such interest in the doctor's equipment, enquired about its usage and clearly showed a determination to learn.

Of the long-established Jewish residents of Borki village, one couple springs to mind. The husband had a fondness for alcohol, which was not generally the case among ordinary Jews. The wife, poor thing, was constantly worried about her husband, and spent much of her time buying up eggs, which she mixed with flour to make macaroni, as if preparing supplies for some future famine or deportation. There was another Jew whose name, I think, was Zyg, who presaged the imminent end of the world. I disagreed with him, since it had been given to me to survive the upheaval of 1939. Evidently, he seemed to sense the end of the Jews – which is what came to pass.

As for our peasants, it has to be admitted that the Bolsheviks did wonders with them, although it may take time for them to acquire cultural refinement. In the battle for existence, it seems it is those who are capable of enduring physical labour and the cold who survive. Although they may lack sophistication, they are generally healthy and even-tempered – if one is to omit the mob hysteria shown in 1939.[17]

There were among the peasants individuals who stood out by their sterling qualities. I remember a young boy with pneumonia who lay in the sickbay in what had been our drawing room. It proved not to be a difficult illness, and his quick recovery was attributed by Dr Atlas to the exceptionally pleasant atmosphere generated at home by his loving parents. The parents and the children of that family were all handsome, healthy-looking and with a great innate intelligence. And I thought to myself: what a shame that such children will end up as common peasants. One wonders how much natural talent was wasted in this way. Perhaps the Bolsheviks later enabled them to get on in the world. At one time there was a girl, also I think from Ladziny, who used to come to work for us as a washerwoman. She had such a wonderful singing voice that Uncle Antoś used to say that, if he had the money, he would have paid for her musical training. She would have exceeded Callas, for her voice was not only wonderful, but pleasant and with a balanced timbre. Alas, the girl got married and that was the end of that. One has to admit it, but the Soviets did immediately spot great talent. That girl would have become an opera singer, without losing contact with her family and without being exposed to selling herself to various impresarios, which in the West is sometimes the only way to succeed as an artist.

One of our outpatients was a young peasant from Iwież who had cancer in his tonsils. What a naturally noble-minded character he possessed. He described his life in primitive words: 'I didn't steal and I never dragged myself through the courts.' His crystal clear soul expressed itself in such a way. He later died in his village and took up the place which was rightfully his since birth: in heaven. There was also a woman who came to the hospital from a village beyond the Great Field. Her entire head was covered with abscesses. Dr Atlas lanced them and squeezed out the pus. That woman also suffered like a saint. I almost felt a reverence for these wounds as if they were those of Job; wounds which Providence for its own higher reasons had inflicted precisely on her.

There was also the kindly Jan Zych who knew how much I used to enjoy horse riding. One beautiful and sunny winter day he turned up in a sleigh and took me for a ride. He and his wife did not initiate their young son in their anti-communist views, in case he might unguardedly blurt it out somewhere. Their good-looking boy was later promoted to be the director of a dairy in Grodno. I was to be informed about this after the war in a letter from the daughter of another Zych, the same daughter who was to bring our surviving family photo albums from Borki to my family in post-war Poland. I had at first given the albums to the wife of the blacksmith for safekeeping; after her death the albums were looked after by Wiera Borodziuk. On the day I carried the albums to the blacksmith's wife, I could not help feeling envy that the blacksmith's family had their own cottage while I was wandering around homeless. I then remembered the following verse from the Gospels: 'Foxes have holes, and birds of the air have nests; but the Son of Man has nowhere to lay His head.'[18]

Despite the external oppression of this period, I felt an inner freedom in my soul, and I knew that no one could take this spiritual freedom away from me. Christianity gave me this: it had shaped an inner fortress inaccessible to the temptations of the external foe. At that point, I understood the meaning of the idea that the enemy who can kill your body but cannot kill your spirit is not a threat, for there exist, in another dimension, higher indestructible eternal values. It can be said that my wartime experiences deepened my faith considerably: I survived, sustained by the Gospels. And it was not some wallowing in suffering, nor was it capitulation. On the contrary, I sensed a kind of spiritual barometric high point, a certain *élan vital* against the backdrop of total ruin and material decline. For I felt that Providence had charged me with some mission. I recollect with sentiment this phase of my life, this religious-patriotic romanticism of mine. Those were great and beautiful moments, and I regret a little that, here in England, I have somehow lowered my flight; that I have become more sober and pragmatic, and that my view of life is now rather more 'positivist'.[19] *C'est la vie.*

I ought to add that at one stage I became extremely popular among the peasants: in fact, it became something of a fashion in the villages around to invite me to weddings. It seemed improper to refuse such invitations, and furthermore, I did not feel any hatred towards the peasants. It was Tatuś who once taught me how to rise above events. He illustrated this with the example of a forestry worker who had once sold a few of our pine trees without permission, and whom Tatuś had scolded angrily. Soon afterwards, through the wall of the steward's office, I heard this worker vent his venomous feelings by cursing my father in the coarsest of terms for having caught him red-handed selling the timber. I went to my father and told him what I had heard; I then suggested that this thieving and malevolent man should be dismissed from our service. Tatuś heard me out, but then said that I was wrong. 'If I throw him out now', he explained, 'nobody is going to employ him in the middle of the year; he'll be without work, and he has all the makings of becoming a good bandit. I mustn't allow this to happen.' Tatuś continued: 'I'll put up with him until the spring, and then send him away when labourers usually end their contracts. And as for his cursing, remember the maxim: is the moon bothered when dogs bark at it? The peasants are like ignorant cattle; one cannot hold a grudge against them.' The lesson I learnt from this episode saved my soul from being corrupted, which would have happened had I boiled with hatred or with a desire to take revenge on the peasants for having deprived us of all our possessions, as was the case with many other landowners. I am glad that I was incapable of harbouring feelings of hatred or of personal grievance towards the looters.

What did puzzle me was how they were able, quite shamelessly and as if nothing had happened, to invite me to wedding celebrations in their homes in which they had put up the curtains from our drawing room. I also attended the wedding of Jadzia, the daughter of Adam, our coachman, to someone from the village of Iwież. The peasants who discreetly left food for me did not do so on a daily basis, while the food provided in the hospital was poor. As a result I often felt undernourished. I therefore enjoyed tucking into the smoked bacon fat at that wedding reception, despite the fact that the meat came from our pigs. It was not very pleasant to see another of Adam's daughters wearing my shoes while I was almost barefoot. But I felt most saddened when I saw the coachman's wife quite calmly stir the mixture for pancakes in the splendid porcelain tureen, decorated with roses, which had been one of Mamusia's wedding gifts. What mattered is that I kept my sense of humour.

In any case, within a year of the Soviet occupation of western Belarus, the peasants bitterly regretted the end of Poland. Once I overheard a conversation in the Borki hospital when one peasant told another that he would 'kiss the arses' of the former gentry if the latter came back. For what had happened? Having immediately distributed all the landed estates among the peasants for propaganda purposes, the Bolsheviks next imposed compulsory requisitioning on all agricultural produce, and then proceeded to take back all former manorial land, as well as all looted furniture, horses and cows. What was worse, they even seized the land the peasants had owned before the war. Collective farms were now created.[20] The poor naive peasants had fallen into a trap, but it was too late. Even on Sundays they were driven into the forest to cut trees, not for their own use, but for construction projects elsewhere.

> *By the end of 1940 [...] the peasants began to wait for the Germans as saviours. Only then did they come to appreciate Poland [...] At the turn of 1940/1 only a small number of individuals were content with the Bolsheviks: those who had made a career as officials, or those who from birth were types described by Lombroso, [...] who felt comfortable with the decay of moral principles brought about by the Bolsheviks. Many weak heads, who had allowed themselves to get entangled into cooperation with the Bolsheviks, [...] now felt like those who had sold their souls to the devil and now found there was no return. [...] Judging by the mood among the peasants then, I fear that many of the best people, just because of their hatred of the Bolsheviks, entered into cooperation with the Germans the moment they arrived.*[21]

A general depression overcame the locals. As a result, credence was given to the most unlikely rumours, for they raised people's spirits.

I have not yet described my scrapes with the NKVD. One evening, when I was already in bed, there was loud banging at my door: it was the Soviets, wanting to search my premises. I was in my nightdress. I let them in, but immediately returned to my bed. 'Hand over your weapons!' they demanded in Russian. 'I have none', I replied, 'go and look'. They looked everywhere, including a small shed nearby in which I had hung the now frameless portrait of *Hetman* Makowiecki. They then noticed a picture of Our Lady of Częstochowa hanging on a wall in my room; it was damaged but still intact. 'Take it down!' they ordered. In moments like this, an episode in the Gospels comes to mind, in which we are told by Jesus not to worry what to say when brought before the authorities, 'for the Holy Spirit will teach you in that very hour what you ought to say'.[22] I was in a trap, for if I refused the Soviets could have shot me on the spot; but to take the picture down was unacceptable, and I believed my hand would have withered away if I committed such a sacrilege. After a momentary prayer seeking God's guidance, I replied evasively: 'Let it hang there' (*Puskay povesit* in Russian). The soldiers turned around and left. Had I taken the picture down from fear, who knows if, having lost face in their eyes, I would not have also lost my virtue: I was alone in the presence of six strong, armed men. God saved me thus.

I was later summoned by an official letter to report to the NKVD offices in Słonim. I travelled there via Horka, just south of Borki, where I called on Pani Hejnowska, a teacher, with whom I left my clasp knife. In Słonim I visited Pani Lętowska and her children, as well as Regina Sielicka, a school friend; Regina was a tutor to the Lętowski boys, and was held in high esteem by the family for her upright character. An atmosphere of panic prevailed there, because Pan Lętowski and other men from the neighbourhood had already been arrested. They were all surprised that I was moving around the area in such a carefree manner. At the NKVD office I was asked only about weapons, and then allowed to go. I took the opportunity of being in Słonim to have my hair waved by a Jewish hairdresser. The perm was done so well that it lasted until I caught typhus in Russia; even afterwards my hair continued to have curls. I was surprised by the fine furniture in the hairdresser's home, since the local Jews usually lived in poverty. The old granny of the family praised her grandson: 'Oh, how clever he is; he's so small, but he was able to sort out some business away from home very cleverly...'.

My other visit to Pani Hejnowska in Horka coincided with the death of her very elderly husband who passed away quietly and peacefully. As in the case of my grandmother, it was a beautiful, aesthetic death of the blessed. Pani Hejnowska was forty years old when she married; her husband, an administrator on Pani Roycewiczowa's estate, was twenty-five years her senior. She married in order to look after him in his old age. Pani Hejnowska told me how sometimes, on purpose, she would leave a door slightly open, or fail to do something else, in order that her husband could point it out to her. This enabled the old man to feel that he was still in a small way the master of the house, although in fact he was totally dependent on her.

Pani Hejnowska had been a teacher in Rohotna; she was full of patriotic and religious enthusiasm, and was much loved in that Catholic village. It was hard for her to get used to working in Horka which was an Orthodox village. But even there she won such great respect that nobody robbed her when the Soviets arrived in September 1939; I looked with envy at her cosy and comfortable home, where she was as snug as a bug in a rug. Now she was ordered by the Bolsheviks to teach in Belarusian, which was hard work for the poor thing. But in no circumstances could she bring herself to teach atheism to the very children whom she had earlier taught about God. Fortunately, someone else was employed for that purpose; this person happened to be a Jewish teacher, and he relieved her of the task of teaching atheism. It was sad to see so many devoted teachers suffer when the Soviets overturned the educational principles they had been following hitherto. In that sense it was perhaps fortunate that Pani Hejnowska, who had health problems with her liver, did not live long; so ended her spiritual suffering.

I was also able to make a number of other visits further afield. One was to the Catholic priest in Wysock, a village about 15 km south of Borki. Guarded faithfully by both the Catholics and the Orthodox, he had survived the upheavals in 1939. He was known for his great idealism because he did not charge the peasants anything for administering the sacraments. He was an exception among the clergy, and the behaviour of the peasants demonstrated that they valued him highly. On another occasion I was driven to Zdzięcioł on some errand.[23] There I found the dean in a pessimistic frame of mind as to the fate of our region. The church was packed with worshippers. Subsequently a rumour was started that I had been seen there barefoot and that I had been crying in the church; this reached even Halina Skrzyńska in Radłów in Nazi-occupied Poland.

In the spring of 1940, Dr Atlas was informed that the Bolsheviks had decided to transfer the hospital to Kozłowszczyzna and to re-activate the Borki starch-processing plant to which new machinery would be brought from Minsk.[24] However, I did not want to move to Kozłowszczyzna where there was an NKVD post, and especially since I had resolved to stick it out in my own house. In mid-May Dr Atlas moved to the new location. Eventually all the Jews left for Kozłowszczyzna, with the exception of the Gomulińskis, for the wife had found work as a dentist in Rohotna. For a while there was also a dentist in Borki, a pleasant elderly woman who by some miracle had managed to escape from the Germans with her pedal-operated dental equipment, and who immediately and bravely got down to work.

The new director appointed by the Soviets to run the starch-processing plant was a Ukrainian who moved into the manor house with his wife. She later gave birth to quadruplets, while he made a lot of fuss about it with the authorities. He treated me in a friendly manner and engaged me as a clerk in his office. He told me that he liked Poles, for his mother (or was it his grandmother?) was Polish, but that he could not stand Jews. On the other hand, his management of the plant proved awful: the potatoes, which had been requisitioned from the peasants and which had been covered with straw and earth in a pit, rotted away. Even though the potatoes had not fully matured, he had issued instructions for the deliveries to take place in order to keep the starch production going.[25]

Be that as it may, once again my life seemed to shape itself conveniently, until the day when Soviet inspectors appeared. Because I had been a landowner, they instructed me to leave my office job and do manual work instead. Not only did I completely lack the physical strength to work in a potato field, but I had no intention of losing face with the peasants by degrading myself in such a way. And so, one day in October 1940, I escaped to Ladzinki, just beyond our lakes, to stay with Pani Sidorowicz. Before going, I was able to arrange for my wardrobe with mirror (it had been looted but someone returned it to me later) to be stored with Jan Zych. My bed was transported secretly by Pan Majewski who drove his wagon unnoticed out of Borki, taking advantage of the bustle of numerous peasant wagons bringing potatoes to the starch-processing plant. As for me, I picked up a few pots and escaped on foot along the ponds. The director was to hold a grudge against me for not selling him the wardrobe and other items.

And so, in the end, I was able to spend a whole eight months with the hospitable residents of Ladzinki. They included the seventy-year-old Pani Julia Sidorowicz, her brother Nowicki with his wife and his brother-in-law Pan Majewski who worked there as a steward. They had a cow and adequate supplies of food; I was therefore able to make up for all the lean months in Borki and to strengthen my body before my deportation to Siberia. I milked the cow and tried to help wherever possible in order to repay my hosts' kindness. But because my muscles were feeble, I found all physical work hard going, almost torturous.[26] But at last I was living with a family. The only unpleasant events were the visits of a certain peasant who was a functionary of the local village committee.[27] He kept an eye on me, and one day arrived with other officials to go through my possessions. One result of this was that they took away a couple of our best family photo albums which had Mamusia's annotations; I had unnecessarily brought them around to look at them.

More welcome visitors to Ladzinki were the family's relatives, the Gruners. The peasants had not robbed them, for there were no villages in the vicinity of their house. Unfortunately, Pan Gruner was arrested, but somehow survived and later became an army instructor with the Polish forces in the West. Pani Ada Gruner had a delightful seventeen-year-old daughter, Marysia, and a brave son. We all revelled in admiration at Marysia's flamboyant looks: her lovely mouth, beautiful complexion, long plaits reaching the ground and her tall figure. What a magnificent girl she was! Her deft hands were graceful, but they controlled a pair of the wildest horses with extraordinary firmness. Despite the presence of the Bolsheviks, she regularly travelled alone to Słonim to sell butter and vegetables. Together with her brother she worked the plough and tilled the soil. Marysia knew that she was very pretty and delighted in it. She lovingly brushed her wonderful long blonde hair. It was with focused attention and some emotion that we observed how she fell under the spell of her own beauty, for it was so becoming. How pleasant it is to be so young and so beautiful, I thought to myself with a shade of envy, and to have such steadfast good looks, for they were based on a healthy and strong physique. I was a little offended by the fact that Marysia used to emphasize that she was not an idealist, and that she was a freethinker in matters of religion. It was perhaps hardly surprising, since Pan Jan Gruner was descended from a family of Protestant Courlanders. He was a chartered engineer, a weapons expert; he also possessed some interesting specimens of African weaponry. It was with indignation that I listened to the Gruners's account of how, because of leather shortages, they now made soles for shoes out of their wonderful African drums and shields.

In the past we had often visited the Gruners at their cottage. The house was in a neglected state, rather reminiscent of a humble yeoman's dwelling. This may have been the result of the fact that Pan Jan was an urbanite who had moved to the country because of unemployment or laziness. Before the war, I had once met his brother, a young paediatrician, who had come to visit Pan Jan. I did not find the brother very agreeable, for he bragged how he was earning so many złotys for every letter of the alphabet that he wrote down on a medical prescription. He was later shot by the Germans. When I heard about his death I could not help thinking about what he had gained from all this money; would it not have been better if he had treated his patients in a more altruistic manner? It was unfortunate that in pre-war Poland priests and doctors lived off human misery and grew rich on it.

While performing an active social role in Borki, my morale had been high; but now, being dependent on others, I feared a psychological breakdown. Then, in late 1940, unexpectedly and across many frontiers, came a letter from Berlin from the mother of Hans Albert Reinkemeyer.[28] She informed me that Hans Albert was in France, that everything was going very well for him (*'es geht ihm ausgezeichnet'*) and that he had asked her to write to me since he was not able to do so himself, because he was anxious to learn if I had survived. So there was someone who was thinking of me, someone who might even show up where I was. I was therefore not totally alone. I replied to Hans Albert immediately:

We are living at the moment through an exceptionally significant and new period in history. And we do not yet know how it will end. In any case, many things will end irrevocably and new forms [of existence], still unknown to us, will blossom. War brutally changes life, it is a sudden reshuffling of cards from which there is no going back.

It is good that you have survived the war. And if, God willing, you happily live to see its end, you will see how you will return a different, more mature person.

Normal daily life is full of falsehood; people flounder in an illusion of pretence, in trifles, in conformity. War reveals naked reality in all its truth and reveals man such as he truly is.

Despite so many disasters and such tragedy, I personally have become enriched spiritually in this period and have experienced many beautiful and lofty moments.

I have come to know what it means to lose everything; what it means to feel the threat of death, of destitution, of hunger; to know what it is to be in prison; to know what changes people with whom one has lived in harmony into such rapacious hyenas; and to witness a raging mob driven by its most base instincts. I have come to base my ideals on stronger foundations and values, in faith in a new life which like a phoenix will rise from the ashes. I now rely totally on God. I have strengthened my character; I now find a neighbour in every human being who deserves our full love and whom one should always be able to forgive.[29]

Much later, after the war, I was to hear from Mamusia that Hans Albert had called on Jula in Warsaw, enquiring about me, and that he was subsequently sent to the Russian Front. That was the last news I was to receive of him. His mother's letter, fragments of which I still possess, boosted my morale and lifted me from my state of torpor. There were widespread murmurings about the possibility of a German-Soviet war, and I got down immediately to improving my knowledge of German. Within six months I had mastered the language to such an extent that I was able to write postcards to Mamusia in Warsaw in German; I conveyed to her a rosy description of our beautiful winter and how well I was doing in Ladzinki.

I wanted to reassure Mamusia about my own person. But I fear that these cards were probably read by Dziutek Morski who was then going hungry in Warsaw and he hastily set out to visit me.[30] I do not know whether he thought he would find food in Ladzinki, or whether he was hoping to bring me to Warsaw where Aunt Janka Górska (née Żórawska) had offered me the use of an apartment. Mamusia wrote to me about this. But poor Dziutek never made it. He must have perished somewhere in the forests near the border, especially since he might have been carrying some compromising underground publications, for he was in contact with the Polish Resistance. He was scared of returning to his mother in Poznań which had been annexed to the Third Reich in 1939, and chose what turned out to be the worse option of going across the border to Belarus. Julia Morska, his unfortunate mother, so kind and an angel of mercy to all around her, waited for years for her lost son's return. It was only this year (1968) that she sent me a sad poem which she had written about Dziutek, or rather about his unknown grave, covered in wild rose bushes, in some forgotten forest thicket. It seems that her maternal heart now sensed that he would not come back. I have located the letter from Aunt Julia Morska with the text of the poem which she reads out every year on All Souls' Day when she orders a Requiem Mass for the repose of the souls of her husband and of her son.[31]

'A Sad Anniversary. To My Lost Son' ('*Smutna rocznica. Zaginionemu synowi*')
I cannot understand, nor bear the thought
that you are gone,
that the woodland track to your nameless grave
is overgrown with bramble or with fern
and thorns protect your bloody head
and your dead eyes, my son,
my only son.

On All Souls' Day the graves are candle bright,
but yours is dark, unvisited:
My heart will shed a ruby light,
my eyes bedeck with crystal tears for flowers,
and there religiously I'll place
a rosary of longing pain-filled hours.

It is better to die oneself than to outlive one's own children. And yet Aunt Julia has pulled through, and now spends her time visiting all her relatives wherever there is any misfortune or illness, and, despite her venerable age, helps as much as she can.

It had been deeply inculcated in me never to miss Sunday Mass. Even in March 1941, despite lurking dangers and the deep mud caused by the melted snow, and wearing some kind of rubber boots, I waded on foot 3 km along flooded and slushy roads from Ladzinki to the church in Rohotna. When full spring had finally arrived, I set off with a bunch of enormous peonies, walked past the office of the local commune where the smashed angels which Mojsze Helman had collected were still lying, and brought the flowers to the church to adorn the altar. The frightened peasants only looked on; they were scared of going to church. Nothing immediately happened to me as a result of my flowery procession in front of the NKVD post in Rohotna. However, it soon became clear that the Bolsheviks were keen to arrest me. At a public meeting the peasants pleaded on my behalf, saying that I had not been an enemy of the people because I used to throw sweets to the children when driving in my carriage, and because I used to give medical assistance to the sick.[32] But the peasants' intervention only delayed the inevitable.

9

Siberia

Deportation – Trust in God's protection – Long journey to Krasnoyarsk – Life and work in kolkhoz 'Stalinets' – Hunger – Other Polish deportees – Stalin's 'amnesty' – Baptisms – Move to Kansk – The kindly Serafina Verobyova – Pride and conceit – Siberia's agriculture – Unwelcome proposal by the NKVD – Flight from Kansk
This chapter includes extracts, shown in italics, from Irena's draft of another deposition to the Polish government (1943).

The memorable night of 20 June 1941 arrived when a cart and an armed soldier appeared in front of the Sidorowiczes's house in Ladzinki. I was told: 'Get your things' (*Sobiray'sya* in Russian), and was given an hour to pack. My possessions were briefly inspected by a Jewish woman doctor with whom I was acquainted, and who was later to provide medical care to the peasants in the village. She noticed Tatuś's signet ring among my things, but pretended not to see it, and so allowed me to keep it. I then started to pack. I thought I would be taken no further than Słonim and, since it was June, I left behind my long fur. I took with me only my sheepskin and two suitcases of clothes. Pani Nowicka, Julia Sidorowicz's sister-in-law, then handed me a chamber pot. I also took an enema with me. But I left behind a marvellous painting of Our Lady which Pani Sidorowicz had given me earlier as a present. I was never again to see such a splendid painting. It was framed, and I was not sure whether to cut it out and bring it with me. To this day I regret not having taken it, for it might have survived my long wartime travels.

We travelled for 30 km through the great forest of Słonim. It was a beautiful June night. During our journey the Soviet soldier and I spoke about little else but God. He tried to persuade me that God did not exist because Soviet airmen had not encountered any angels above the clouds, while I tried to prove that God did exist. The conversation was conducted with great Soviet courtesy. At one point my chamber pot fell from the cart onto the road. Thinking, perhaps, that this was a cooking pot, the Soviet man stopped the cart, jumped off and picked up the pot for me.

When we arrived in Słonim, I realized that I had not been brought to the NKVD headquarters for further questioning. We had arrived at the railway station. Everything there was in a state of turmoil: lots of people, general weeping and wailing. It turned out that the Soviets had gathered together for transportation to Siberia all the remaining local Poles deemed 'unreliable' by the Soviet authorities: '*a most diverse collection of people: families of military men, policemen, civil servants, teachers; also shop-owners, wealthier peasants, the so-called kulaks, and others*'.[1] All the important people, the 'big fish', had already been deported in 1940.

And whom should I bump into at the station but the Gruners. They were sensible enough to bring with them their food supplies and even their agricultural implements, such as scythes and axes; they obviously knew that they were being sent to colonize the steppes of Siberia. In any case, they had plenty to take with them, including whole barrels of salted bacon fat. Accompanying us in the truck was also the family of Dr Tomaszewski of Grodno: his mother Helena, his wife Janka, his daughter Hela and one-year-old son Leszek. Everyone in the truck wept, while the Gruner women, sitting on their barrels, sobbed loudly. By contrast, I only had a single ham which was all that was left over from what had been eaten at the Sidorowiczes's in Ladzinki. The ham, incidentally, came from a pig which I had bought after selling the cow which I had brought with me from the hospital. The only other food I had with me was just a small bag of dry grain. I had given away the barley cereal I had to the teacher in Iwieź, and quite unnecessarily, for his family had ample supplies. Also at the station were some women from Słonim who ran along the platforms asking if anybody needed anything. I asked for a toothbrush and for some glycerine, which was immediately brought for me.

Eventually, all the railway trucks were loaded with their human cargo. '*There were hardly any men on board, but mostly women, children, and old people on the brink of death.*'[2] And so we set off into the unknown, following the familiar route taken in the past by our insurgent ancestors.[3] That there was now a war gave hope to our hearts.[4] A rumour was later to reach my cousin Halina Skrzyńska that I had been deported to Siberia on an open rail wagon. No such thing happened, but after I was taken away, a whole legend developed about me, with all sorts of distortions and tales being added. It was also fortunate that we were travelling in the summer. When deportations from our area took place in the winter of 1940, many people froze to death, and even many of the escorting soldiers lost their toes to frostbite.

We travelled for three weeks in sealed trucks. Often we would see railway trucks going in the opposite direction, laden with armaments and swarming with soldiers. The sight of Soviet troops made a dazzling impression as they sang beautiful war songs, such as '*Moskva moya*' (My Moscow) or delightful ones such as '*Rastsvetali yabloni i grushy*' (Apple and Pear Trees in Bloom). All were heading for the German front. Once a day the doors were opened to enable us, under escort, to collect some water; at the same time soldiers passed to us a bucket of thin soup, some herrings and some bread. I would jump out of the truck with Marysia Gruner to fetch the water. On one occasion, like a mermaid, she undid her long hair which then fell to her waist; even in wartime she had not lost her coquetry. I then noticed the figure of a soldier with most unusual features. He seemed to me like an allegorical version of an ancient Roman soldier; his face was that of an eternal warrior of human history.

I had very little with me, but I did not shed a single tear. Not for a moment did I allow myself to feel despair or doubt, feelings which I considered would have been a sin against Providence. That is what I had been taught at school, and this saved me from a breakdown. I became convinced that, with trust in God's Protection, one can survive the greatest pitfalls in life, especially in circumstances when the first signs of reckless doubt could bring about moral collapse, as happened to more than one person. Furthermore, I was going into a Godless country, and I could not allow myself to commit any grave sin, for who, in the absence of any priests, could then give me absolution? Not enough had been done to instil within us a degree of spiritual self-sufficiency, which Protestants possess. The theoretical knowledge that full contrition wipes away all sins did not provide the certainty that this was so in fact; for how could one verify that one's contrition was full?[5] This 'hygiene of thought' enabled me to come off well throughout all my time in the Russian hell; not only did I do so with composure (for that is the most difficult), but with a spiritual 'barometric high', and often with enthusiasm and good humour. And so, travelling alone to my doom, I was able to admire through the window the unknown countryside passing outside, while all those around me were in tears. I even remarked to my fellow travellers that we had been given a free excursion across the whole of Russia! Supporting myself with such a positive attitude to our reality, I was able to draw much spiritual satisfaction in conditions which otherwise seemed hopeless.

On a more prosaic level, the enema I had taken with me saved my life, for I was to suffer from constant constipation, largely as result of the monotonous salty food we were given during what proved to be a long journey. My chamber pot was used by everybody in the truck for the obvious purpose; it was emptied through an opening in the floor in a corner of the truck which we separated with a hanging blanket to offer a modicum of privacy.

Three weeks later we were unloaded at the station in Krasnoyarsk in eastern Siberia. Waiting for us were numerous carts drawn by skeletal horses. This sight had a disheartening effect on us, for the dogs we encountered also had sunken flanks and protruding ribs: all evidence of long-term hunger. Travelling on one lorry was a beautiful woman who could be heard arguing with the Soviets and telling them that she would complain to the Queen of Italy! The woman in question was the wife of General Skotnicki[6] who had been arrested by the Soviets in the castle of the Radziwiłłs where she had taken refuge. Indeed, the Radziwiłłs had been released from the USSR as a result of the intervention of the King of Italy.[7] Pani Maria Skotnicka was trying to persuade the NKVD officers that someone in high authority was also going to speak on her behalf. In the atmosphere of general depression surrounding us, Pani Skotnicka's nerve definitely had a positive effect and effectively restrained the official 'eagerness' of our guards. In fact, '*the NKVD did not subject us, so-called "free deportees", to any physical punishments, beatings, or anything of that kind; on the other hand they abused us with the most perfidious moral tortures, they ridiculed us, they ridiculed Poland and its government, and our religion*'.[8]

The Gruner family was sent to a prosperous state-owned farm ('Noshyno' in the Kansk region) where they fared well, being in good health and accustomed to physical work. Marysia, who had completed a course at an agricultural college, was employed in the scientific preparation of foodstuffs for pigs. While feeding the animals their grain, she would drop some into her boots, and so provided her family with some extra bread. I ended up worse off because our collective farm (*kolkhoz* 'Stalinets' in the Aban region, Kansk district) was only partly state-owned and was neglected. Most of the men had been taken to the front, and women were forced to work everywhere. And who from our group was fit for such work? In the end, granny Tomaszewska bravely took upon herself the task of cooking communal meals for us, which meant boiling potatoes. As a result, when her daughter-in-law Janka and I returned from the field, there was something hot for us to eat. I offered to share with our group the ham I had brought with me, while the Tomaszewski ladies had many packets of groats. *'The other Poles in Malakanka village, in which we were placed, were the wife of a schools inspector in Poland and her son, one "kulak" family, one farming family (here there were some men), the wife of a sweetshop owner, and a policeman's family.'*[9]

General Skotnicki's wife was also there, in the same dwelling as the Tomaszewski family and myself. She had brought with her a large number of enormous leather trunks which she arranged as a partition on the shared floor space, and thus gave herself and her beautiful young son a separate living area. Today I suspect that some of these travelling trunks might have belonged to the Radziwiłłs, and that they had been whisked away under the noses of the Bolsheviks who were removing everything from Nieśwież Castle. We were never to find out what most of the trunks contained. Pani Skotnicka was a beautiful salon lioness, and had changed husbands four times; one of her previous husbands had been Ślizień, a wealthy man from our parts. I, on the other hand, in my convent school ignorance, had no inside knowledge whatsoever of that side of life. I admired her astonishing complexion and her beautiful teeth; only Aunt Marzeńka's teeth possessed such marvellous whiteness. However, Pani Skotnicka's slightly greying hair suggested that she was over forty. I was to meet her some years later in Jerusalem when she was working for the Polish Red Cross; by then she had used peroxide on her hair and looked twenty years younger. She was elegantly dressed and so even more beautiful. She invited me to her residence in Tel Aviv and showed me her wardrobe full of the most fashionable dresses. But those are later times.

Idiotically, I worked hard on the *kolkhoz*, whereas Pani Skotnicka repeatedly bandaged one or other of her fingers as if they were injured; she would show them to the collective farm chairman (*predsedatyel*) and so avoided having to go out to weed cucumbers. In fact, she was the only one of us who intimidated the chairman with her self-confidence; he was helpless in the face of it. Whenever we feared that our possessions might be searched, she would hide her wonderful pearls and other jewellery in a saucepan containing preserved fruit, which stood on the window sill. My only precious item was my father's signet ring, which was safely concealed in a jar of ichthyol ointment.

The chairman was a typical Party dunderhead who made life difficult for the kolkhoz workers and who meanly rationed everything. [...] We were driven to work in the fields regardless of the weather, anybody's state of health, or the lack of footwear. We were to be paid in the new year (according to the number of 'workdays' done) out of the doubtful surplus of the kolkhoz.[10]

When harvest time arrived we were sent out to distant meadows. Raking hay the whole day was hard work. In the evenings a large cauldron of appetizing soup was prepared for us. But I never ate this food, for to my horror I realized that it was served in the place where all the boys and girls slept together in the hay. Fearing the sexual amorality of these people, I could well imagine what took place there at night. Summoning what was left of my strength and feeling hungry, with only a piece of dry bread on my person, I had to cover a couple of miles in order to return to our house for the night. During one of these solitary walks I was spotted by a bull grazing with a herd of cows; it raised its tail and started to charge in my direction. I was terrified, but noticing a small copse nearby, managed to climb on to one of the slender little trees just in time. The furious animal then began to circle the trees; I was in danger of having to spend a night in this desolate place. Eventually, I spotted a cart passing nearby and, because the bull had moved away, I rushed towards the vehicle and begged the driver to take me home.

I usually returned to the house in a state of total exhaustion. For the work I did I only received a few hundred grams of dark stale bread which contained impurities.[11] It was fortunate that the same portion of bread was also given to the Tomaszewskis's small children; and since they could not bear eating it, I was able to consume their share of this rock-like substance.

One could buy milk for children and old people at a lower price directly from a centrifuge, and for other adults only if they worked. [...] Families with menfolk fared better, especially if some of the men also possessed a trade such as carpentry, for they earned more. Sometimes one had to work several days to earn one 'workday'. We lived in constant fear that we might not get any bread the next day, but we did not suffer from starvation because we had all brought with us some food or some items of clothing from home; so for the time being we lived off our supplies from Poland.[12]

The Tomaszewski women had exhausted their supplies, what with their small children to care for. Pani Tomaszewska sold off all her beautiful possessions, including a chocolate-coloured outfit made in Warsaw. In fact, to provide better food for the children, she sold everything she had, which was not much, for she had brought with her only a couple of bundles, containing mostly nappies and children's clothes. Despite the poverty, her one-year-old son Leszek grew so exceptionally well that it was a pleasure to watch the plump toddler.[13] Whereas I had escaped to Ladzinki with only two small cases, there were other Poles who had brought with them suitcases full of things, which they were able to sell locally; and I have to admit that none of those people offered me at any time even a single piece of food. They did not ask if I needed anything, and I simply could not bring myself to say that I was the poorest among them, and that I had very little to eat.

I also remember the first time I stole. Sometimes, while weeding cucumbers, I managed to eat some juicy fruit in secret; but this was during work and, although forbidden, it was a rather natural thing to do. Later, it became a more difficult business. I was very much bent on stealing a head of cabbage from those that grew behind our house. We were to be paid only in the new year (1942) for our extra 'workdays', while it was difficult to survive forever on stale bread. My conscience was clear since, ultimately, the Soviets had deprived me of all my fortune. But what now mattered was not to be caught, for such a theft carried a one-year prison sentence.[14] One day I was sent out to weed the cabbages. I took with me a piece of string, cut a whole cabbage and attached it to the thread. I then walked back home, as if nothing in the world mattered, while dragging the cabbage behind me. In this way the cabbage arrived at our house unobserved. I devoured the whole thing with great appetite.

One source of food came from an unexpected quarter. On account of the war with Germany and in view of the eastward advance of the front, the Soviets organized the mass deportation to Siberia of the Volga Germans.[15] These deportees also appeared in our settlement. They had brought with them all their movable possessions, including sacks of grain and other items. They rushed to the Poles to buy up from them what they could in the way of clothes in exchange for smoked bacon fat or grain. One of the Volga Germans told me in private: 'He's already in Baku...' (meaning Hitler).[16]

> On the whole the Poles enjoyed a lot of respect and sympathy on the part of the local population (obviously this excluded Party members). Little wonder: we were their new companions in adversity, and new fellow victims of communist terror. Sometimes some of the locals would surreptitiously bring some bread or a litre of milk for the children. In any case, in many of the local families we were openly told that some of their ancestors, sometimes even the mother or father, had been Poles and Catholics (after all, this was Siberia!), and they in all sincerity confided in us about their miseries. We, on our part, felt a cultural superiority over our surroundings, we felt our worth and held in contempt the subversive evil inculcated in the souls of many locals by the authorities; but for the innocent part of the population we had great and genuine fellow feeling, all the more so since so much Polish blood ran in their veins, so much wasted blood.[17]

One day in September 1941 the chairman of the collective farm came to tell me that he had received official information that, on account of my landed past, I was to work on his collective farm for twenty years![18] This was tantamount to a death sentence, for I no longer had the strength to carry on like this without proper food. To fall into hopelessness and despair would have been a normal reaction to such news. But I immediately got a grip on myself, and I forbade myself to dwell any further on this subject. The reward for this came from Heaven: the following day, the same chairman approached me and said that ... I was free! Thanks to Stalin's agreement with Sikorski, all Poles detained in the USSR were included in a general amnesty![19] It just shows that one should not be worried even by distressing news, for the next day may bring unpredictable things. Not everyone got out of Russia as luckily as I did, but in my case the words of the poet proved to be true: 'Whoever places his life in the hands of His Lord ...' (*Kto się w opiekę odda Panu Swemu ...*).[20]

After the 'amnesty', we were able to find work for ourselves. The Poles therefore made an effort to help the local collective farm workers dig potatoes on the workers' own smallholdings.[21] In return we got a basket of potatoes which kept us fed. By chance I met some women who were making enquiries whether there was anyone capable of baptizing children. Polish insurgents from 1863–4 had been exiled to the district in which we now found ourselves. Here, they had married local women and had children; some children were even born out of wedlock. Well, the mothers of the great-grandchildren of these insurgents felt it right that their children should be baptized into the Catholic faith, in particular since the last local Orthodox church had been burnt down a long time ago, and there were no Orthodox priests anywhere. I was delighted with the prospect that unveiled itself: I saw this as the start of my mission to bring Christianity to Godless Russia.

I had with me a picture of Christ on the Cross, from Assisi, which had miraculously survived my journey to Siberia. I wrapped the picture around a small bottle of water in order to sanctify the water in some small way. I then baptized a total of thirteen children. One of the boys, a ten-year-old, was so frightened that he refused to come down off the stove for anything. His mother pulled him down by his leg and held him firmly so that he could not take to his heels. The husbands of these women were all in the army, and the women wanted to have their children baptized in secret from their husbands. I was deeply moved by these scenes of faith, a faith which was still smouldering among these people and was only waiting to burst again into flame. Today, after the Second Vatican Council, I probably would not have attached such weight to baptism where there were no conditions for Christian life. Instead, I would have been guided by cold reason, but at that time I was driven by enthusiasm to save the souls of those children through baptism; according to the doctrine of St Augustine those souls would otherwise have been sentenced to damnation. My thoughts on this are different now, but then I believed in such nonsense taught to us in the convent school. Such teaching is contrary to the facts of the Gospels, for as we know Christ specifically used the example of Jewish, and hence unbaptized, children as those who would enter the Kingdom of Heaven.[22]

After several weeks I moved to the small town of Aban, northeast of Kansk. There, together with a large number of other Poles, we all slept on the ground. At least we were far away from the *kolkhoz* where we would have had little hope of surviving the approaching winter in its large cold building. Food remained scarce. Again, I helped to gather in potatoes for which I received a basket of the crop. I remember looking with envy at a man baking a turnip in a fire. Walking along a road I noticed wagons carrying sugar beet. I stepped forward and asked the drivers if I could buy one; they told me no. But one kindly little man imperceptibly touched a beetroot which then fell on the ground. In this way I fulfilled my dream of eating that beetroot raw.

Those Poles who had their families with them, and who had been allocated accommodation in what were, relatively speaking, cosy huts, had decided to spend the winter on their collective farms. Marysia Gruner came to see me in Aban. She came empty-handed, so I had to share with her the last of the lard I kept in a box. She was so alarmed by our seemingly hopeless condition that she returned to her *sovkhoz* and decided to stay there with her family. After the war the Gruners were to go back directly from Siberia to Poland.

Eventually I decided to move further away, to Kansk. Some Pole I encountered told me that he also wanted to go there, so the two of us hitched a lift on a wagon going in that direction. On the outskirts of Aban we stopped and I went into a hut,

I think for some water. I was welcomed by a hospitable little woman. She showed me a photograph of her husband who had worked all his life at the post office. She told me how the poor man used to wake up much too early out of fear of being late for work (*chtoby ne opozdats*); they obviously did not have an alarm clock, and he was petrified of being punished for arriving late. It was a consolation to the widow that her late husband no longer had to worry about being late.[23] I saw horse-drawn carts full of young men going to the army at the front. They were all singing loudly and rejoicing that they were going to surrender (*yedut poddavatsya v plen*). Unfortunately, their sad fate was not to be so rosy, for those who surrendered in large numbers were placed by the Germans behind barbed wire where they were abandoned and starved to death.

The Pole, who had attached himself to me, told me much too firmly that, if necessary, he would throw all my belongings into the river so that we could travel lighter. Nothing was going to slow him down from reaching the Polish Army, news of whose formation had already started to reach us. In Kansk I found my way to the home of Serafina Verobyova, a woman of great kindness who had already taken in a group of Poles: Pani Dylowa and her son, as well as the young Pęski, a former medical student who now offered free medical assistance and advice to many of the deportees. The young medic succeeded in scaring away my fellow traveller whom he sensed to be a violent criminal; he was surprised how naive I had been in believing everything that the suspicious Pole had been telling me.

I probably spent a month with Serafina Verobyova at her home on 20a Pioneer Street, in Kansk. Serafina was in despair because her husband had been called up. She told me that her greatest wish was that he would return from the war alive, even if without legs and arms. In Kansk we witnessed the arrival of the harsh Siberian winter: Serafina made sure that her five children were always kept warm sleeping on the stove. She sold us her delicious sauerkraut which was kept frozen in a massive barrel in her lean-to. Pani Dylowa, for her part, had brought with her many of her husband's clothes; by selling them off gradually she was able to provide good and tasty food for her almost adolescent son. The boy had a beautiful voice and frequently sang songs such as '*Hej tam na górze*' (Heigh ho! Yonder on the Mountain); but he was lazy and his mother had to do everything for him. I once set off in minus forty degree frost to buy a pine tree for fuel. Together with Pani Dylowa's son I then tried to saw the tree into pieces, work which I found very hard indeed. In Kansk, I also sold my sister Hania's ball dress, which I had somehow managed to hang on to. With the money I went to the market where I bought some wheat flour and a piece of pork. Milk was sold in frozen blocks laid out on tables. The boiled flour seasoned with a morsel of the ham tasted wonderful. I dreamt of eating nothing else for the rest of my life.

In Kansk, I also met the likeable Pani Wojciech with her eighteen-year-old daughter Zosia who had just finished her secondary schooling in Poland; Zosia had dark eyes and curly hair. Pani Wojciech was very religious and wanted to set up some kind of lay religious society among us exiles. The daughter was rather reserved in manner but fully conscious of her youthful attractiveness. She showed me her photo albums in which she featured surrounded by her admirers from school. I once saw her strumming a guitar, while an elderly Russian ex-prisoner, his eyes fixed on her charming youthful self, hummed some beautiful gypsy songs. In Kansk, Zosia found a job as a cashier;

because of the prevailing local habit of keeping the small change, she was thus able, in the course of a month, to collect the equivalent of a second salary. Later on, apparently, Zosia entered a medical school in Beirut. With her mature personality and her ability to remain calm in different surroundings and circumstances, she probably reached great heights in her career, unless she got married too early.

I also remember an interesting scene when I went with Pani Dylowa to visit a Russian woman who wanted to buy Pani Dylowa's husband's undergarments for her own husband, a chartered engineer. Despite his good pay, the engineer did not have any proper European underwear. This tall, good-looking Russian woman was also later to parade herself wearing Pani Dylowa's colt skins; apparently she paid for these clothes not only with money but also with some jewellery left by her grandmother in tsarist times. Well, when we arrived at the Russian woman's home we witnessed a curious conversation between her husband, a handsome Georgian, and another dark-haired man who turned out to be a medical doctor. They were discussing how each one of them would react to the following scenario: in prison a new torture has been devised which involves giving to two prisoners a vomit-inducing potion and then binding them together face to face with their mouths touching. The doctor said that it would suffice to rinse one's mouth thoroughly with some potassium permanganate. His eyes flashing ominously, the Georgian responded that if anyone tried to attempt something like that on him, then that person would certainly not meet a natural end! Such were some of the interesting conversations – and how very appropriate for the times.

It then occurred to me that un-Christian revenge could be a natural reaction borne of pride, whereas so-called forgiveness may be linked with the absence of one's own self-respect. I too have within me such pride, for I would destroy any man who tried to approach me with dishonourable intentions. But would this be a grave sin? Without this trait I would not possess a sense of dignity as a woman. I claim no merit for the fact that throughout my life I managed to avoid dangerous pitfalls; it was the consequence of my own innate pride, whether good or bad, or perhaps even of my conceit. That is why I could never understand women who were venal; I felt contempt for them. Now, with the passage of so many years, I think about this differently; for the range of human characters represents a whole kaleidoscope, and every person reacts according to the specific constituent traits of his or her own character or temperament. In the past, influenced by my convent-induced moral code, I used to condemn all worldly deviations; today, I search more deeply and discover many surprises in human motives. And I sometimes ask myself: does puritanism kill what is most essential, that is the human heart in its natural manifestation? Who can untangle the complex puzzle of human feelings? That is why it is better not to judge others lest we are judged ourselves.

In Russia in 1941, I observed to my horror the demoralization of shepherd boys, and generally of the local inhabitants. This, combined with horrible sacrilegious cursing, created a pervading demonic atmosphere. Many other people also came into contact with widespread perversions; we can find traces of this in post-war memoirist literature. By the time I had crossed the Soviet border, all this, together with the perfidious questioning and interrogation by NKVD specialists, and the general moral quagmire in Siberia, had created within me a certain palpable sense of the presence of the 'devil' in Russia. In the past, the figure of the devil had been for me a scarecrow with little reality attached to it. But in Russia his presence could be felt. Today, in retrospect, I am not sure how to explain this reaction psychologically. Was such a personification of evil perhaps not a projection of the contrast, or rather the conflict, between 'my ideal world' and 'their world'? Perhaps there, in that abyss of human suffering, eternal fear and anxiety for every moment of life, the people could not live in any other way; perhaps they regarded their condition as natural, and those perversions as the only touchable physical pleasure available to them.[24]

During my stay in Kansk, a certain Cossack used to visit my landlady with his woman. He was tall, about forty years old, but his impressive good looks had been ruined (judging by his pasty complexion) by the dozen or so years spent in forced labour camps. He recounted stories about his happy childhood in the Ukraine where as a boy he had been a footman dressed as a Cossack in the service of Countess Sobańska. How handsome he must have looked then! And to think that he was to spend so much of his subsequent life in ghastly prison conditions. He had been recently released, and was now being sent to the front. In the name of what was he to fight? For his own oppressors? No! He was going to surrender. The poor fellow – a sadder fate probably awaited him. May God at least reward him in the next life for his life's defeat! No sooner had the poor man left when his so-called wife returned to her previous husband who had abandoned her earlier: they celebrated their second wedding with vodka! Of the shadow of the young Don Cossack there only remained sadness in my soul! I even gave him my address in Borki so that should he happen to be there he could leave news that he was still alive.

At one point I was approached by some *kolkhoz* to run their apiary, for which I would be paid 1,000 'workdays'.[25] But I did not want to leave again for the deep countryside. Furthermore, knowing very well the extent of thieving there, I was worried about being responsible for state-owned bees. All it would need was for someone to steal some honey; I would then be blamed and I would end up in a labour camp for goodness knows how many years. It is worth noting that many local peasants travelled to Kansk where they secretly sold grain stolen from collective farms; I even had to buy some of it to make some gruel. I was too naive to cope in a country governed by the law of the jungle, and I was too religious to be able to get fully involved in all sorts of embezzlement, even if my survival depended on it. In the long run, it would have been torture for me to vegetate at this level in a country where, without stealing, one could die from hunger. Incidentally, my husband once told me how he survived miraculously in a Soviet camp by being employed as a secretary in the camp hospital; he also told me how some bandits, fellow prisoners, came to like him and used to toss him some extra food.

Yet how prosperous had this country been under the last tsar! Each farmer had several horses and many cows. The most marvellous cucumbers grew on the rich black soil without the need of any manure or intensive cultivation. I observed this strange soil, this black earth; it was so black, in comparison to our Polish sandy soils, that it was difficult to believe that it was not coal dust. The people here had been well-off, and they remembered the good old days.[26] No wonder that when their land was taken away from them, the locals were not keen on working for the *kolkhoz*. The state requisitioned from the collective farms whatever it could, and paid the workers only in kind according to the number of annual 'workdays' they had earned! In some instances, up to half of the potatoes would be left frozen in the field because no one was bothered to dig them up in time. I arrived in Siberia in July; it was warm and everything was growing beautifully, but there was still ice at the bottom of the wells.

Siberian honey had a taste I had never encountered before; it was white in colour, buttery in texture and aromatic. I was able to taste it once on the edge of a spoon. Other Polish women with a good supply of clothes for sale bought the honey by the jugful; they preserved forest fruit by cooking them in honey. Unfortunately, I did not have the opportunity to taste these specialities; I only saw how others spread them on their sandwiches for work. There were many Polish girls who arrived here frail, but who grew robust like buxom hinds after working in the fields. Unfortunately, it was too late at my age of thirty to start building up muscles, which I had not had the opportunity of doing hitherto. I continued to be as thin as a rake because I had lost whatever body fat I had. My menstruation also completely ceased in Russia; it did not resume until after I had crossed the border into Palestine a year later.[27] The people, horses and dogs of the Siberian countryside hardly ever saw any bread flour. The state removed the best flour; all that was left for making bread were rather mouldy remnants. On the other hand, the town of Kansk was well supplied with all the best kinds of grain. All one had to do was to register in the town as a resident, and one would receive a ration book for bread. I therefore went to the town offices to register. The result was that I did receive a bread allowance for myself. However, a few days later, a written communication arrived requesting that I report to the local branch of the NKVD at 8 o'clock in the evening. Having registered in the town I had immediately come to the attention of the NKVD.

I set out there with trepidation; my female Polish acquaintances blessed me with the sign of the Holy Cross and prayed for my safe return. Far away on the edge of town I eventually found the prominent detached white building which housed the NKVD. There was frost all around: it was minus forty degrees which was normal there in December. In this frost and in the dusk I noticed a small boy of about ten years of age. He was standing by the building and weeping bitterly. 'Why are you crying?' I asked him. 'My father went inside here two months ago, and he still hasn't come out. I wait here every day; perhaps he'll come out …', was the boy's reply. It gave me the creeps as I contemplated what might lie ahead.

I rang the bell and was immediately taken to a room downstairs. I was then subjected to cross-examination by an interrogator well versed in firing the most unexpected questions. The interrogator had a face from the human underworld. I tried to keep control over my answers. Then, without any sound, a door opened. Out of a lift emerged an NKVD colonel. He was Jewish, aged about fifty, with slightly greying hair; he was elegantly and stylishly dressed, and perfumed. He seemed prince-like after the police methods of the interrogator. With a courteous gesture he invited me to join him in the lift; we went up to the second floor, to his office. This NKVD chief expressed an interest in the fact that after the 'amnesty' the Poles in Kansk now felt freer and had begun to organize themselves and to offer each other some help. He said that Stalin had come to an agreement with Sikorski, that we were now friends and that our common goal was our joint struggle against the German invaders. That is why it was extremely important to know, he continued, if all the Poles were in favour of cooperation with that common goal in mind. I was alone, he added, with nothing to lose and much to gain, providing I assisted him with getting information. I would be given a fur coat. I was overcome with fear. It was a situation identical to the one in Borki involving the picture of Our Lady! And this time too, I linked my thoughts to God, which provided me with immediate help.

I could not agree to his proposal, for that would have been treason. Even if I had said 'yes' in order to get away in one piece, and even if I had no intention of keeping my word, I would still have signed 'a pledge with the devil', just as Twardowski had done.[28] I would never have broken free from their clutches. To say 'no' would have meant certain death; the weeping boy outside was evidence of such an outcome. The room I was in was padded with layers of cotton wool or some other insulating and soundproofing material. There were several cupboards or rather doors through which my dead body could have been thrown into the bottom of some tunnel. I found the only solution to my predicament: I started pretending that I was an idiot. I muttered; I answered that I knew nothing (*Ya nichego ne znayu*); I prattled away. The colonel suddenly lost his temper, opened the door and threw me out into the frost like a dog. This time his phrase was not so polite: 'Get out!' (*Poshla von!*).

I returned home to find a group of anxious Poles awaiting me. I told them everything about the interrogation. The omens for the next day were not good. Accompanied by Pani Franciszka Bartoszewiczowa,[29] who had arrived here by some miracle with the aim of escaping to the Polish Army, I immediately collected my bags and set out on foot at night to the railway station. Without tickets, we jumped on the next train going south, where General Anders was forming his army. There was a woman with a child in her arms who jumped on the train as it was already moving. She was unable to get inside the goods truck and froze to death, together with her child, like a caryatid. At some station further down the line an axe was used to knock her frozen body off the outside of the truck; like a statue it fell into the snow on the railway line.

I wrapped myself up in my silk-covered eiderdown (which had been beautifully made for me for 5 złotys by some Orthodox nuns in Wilno), sat down and leant against the wall of the truck. At one point my eiderdown froze so fast to it that I had to make a really big effort to tear it free. Pani Bartoszewiczowa, in her turn, covered herself with some pieces of fur. On a dark December night in 1941, in the midst of such drama, we silently spent our first Christmas Eve in Russia. Instead of a wafer, we munched some dry rusks, a bag of which Pani Bartoszewiczowa had brought with her.[30] During the journey, someone jumped out of the truck and stole some pieces of coal from a heap by the railway track. We were therefore able to light a small iron stove that stood in the middle of the floor of the truck; we even tried to fry some frozen beetroots we had found. The Poles whom I had left behind in Kansk were also gradually to make their way south.

10

Joys and sorrows in Central Asia

**Dzhambul where dogs howled – Accepted as a nurse by the Polish Army –
Anti-typhus quarantine station at Chokpak – The epidemic spreads – Irena's
inner happiness – Nightmarish days – At death's door – Medical staff at
Kermine – Tragic conditions at Kenimekh – Evacuation from the USSR**

We continued our journey into the unknown, a journey that would eventually take
us to Tashkent.[1] Hunger and the cold remained our constant companions. At one
stage, a starving boy surreptitiously crept under the bench, made a hole in Pani
Bartoszewiczowa's bag and then helped himself to some of her rusks. Later these rusks
drew the attention of an unprepossessing fellow traveller. He claimed to be a doctor
and offered us work in the army. Not surprisingly, Pani Franciszka shared everything
she could with him, and even allowed him to sleep leaning against her back. He turned
out to be a fraud and the army later scared him away.

After some time, we arrived at a station where we could hear dogs howling. The
existence of dogs meant that there might be enough food around for us too. We left
the train and stepped directly onto the snow. The name of the station turned out to
be Dzhambul, in southern Kazakhstan. Pani Bartoszewiczowa had not been robbed
in 1939 and had with her many belongings, so we hired a porter; it proved to be her
misfortune because the porter ran off with a basket of the Mendoza family silver. We
spent the night in the open air. I only had a sheepskin and my eiderdown to keep me
warm, and I would have died from the cold had Pani Bartoszewiczowa not covered me
with one of her furs. In the morning I went reconnoitring. No one was willing to take
us in. By then I could barely stand; I felt I no longer had the strength to go any further.
Then, unexpectedly, a one-legged cobbler offered us a corner in his mud hut for the
night. We slept head to toe in a recess of the mud hut on some sort of bed made out of
sticks laid side by side.

Pani Franciszka dreamt of buying a goat which would enable us to live off the sale
of its milk. At length, she discovered a military restaurant for air force personnel on
an upper floor of some building. Every evening she turned up there with a pot and
was given some excellent soup to take away; sometimes a tasty dumpling or a scrap
of some meat could be found floating in the savoury liquid. How well they feed their
airmen, I thought, for on one occasion we also received a couple of doughnuts. I, for

my part, bought a bag of onions and fried two every day. As fuel we used bits of coal collected along the railway track by the cobbler's eighty-year-old common law wife. The cobbler, having lost one of his legs, was proud of the fact that, as an invalid, he was given precedence by everyone. He was about sixty-five years of age and continued to insist on his conjugal rights, something the old woman found difficult to bear. During the night we could hear her grunting.

Among the Poles arriving in Dzhambul, I met Pani Korycka with her husband and young son; she was a Tartar from Kopciowszczyzna, an estate that had once belonged to the Żórawskis. The poor boy died after my departure, but in Palestine God later blessed them with a daughter whom they christened Elżbieta. I think that afterwards they left for Argentina. Pani Korycka's sister worked in Palestine as a driver and later married despite the fact that she had been ill with tuberculosis. I was also enchanted by the Pawulski family. Their father was already in Palestine, I think. Pani Pawulska was good-looking, but her children were even more beautiful. Her young sons were so stunning that even they attracted attention, while the young daughter was simply a little goddess. They lived in poverty, receiving only some help from the field station of the Polish Embassy in the USSR that had been opened in Dzhambul. Despite this, the twelve-year-old beauty rolled her curls every evening and looked like the very picture of an angel. Later, the Pawulskis moved on, and all traces of this charming family were lost. If they survived the miserable life of the young soldiers (*junacy*) in their tents, the boys would probably have joined the Polish cadet school in Camp Barbara in Palestine.

The Dzhambul field station of the Polish Embassy handed out all sorts of clothing to the Poles. I still had some of my own clothes, so I felt it would be dishonest to receive anything from them; all the more so, since I could not yet get used to accepting something for free. I learnt that a Polish division was being formed nearby, but I was not accepted by them. Eventually, I discovered that the 8th Division was being organized in nearby Shakhti. I collected my things and took a train to the railway halt at Chokpak. I was able to leave my things at the halt because the Polish Army was already there.[2] I then set off with others on foot to Shakhti where we were all going to ask to be accepted by the army. I am still amazed by how miraculously I was able to cover 17 km on foot in snow and in a sharp frost, and that too after so many weeks of living mostly on onions and Pani Bartoszewiczowa's rusks. The people making that journey were in rags, and moved like a file of ghosts, stopping only occasionally for the call of nature. I ended that walk in a state of utter exhaustion, only to be told that the army had no need for women because, we were told, they would demoralize the troops. I therefore reached for my Polish Red Cross certificate. It made all the difference. I was immediately enrolled in the Polish Women's Army Auxiliary Service and given work in the hospital, especially since there were several recent cases of typhus. It was 11 February 1942.

In charge of the nurses was Commandante Julia Masłoniowa. Her room was prettily decorated with green blankets like in a knight's chamber. She herself was a beautiful woman; dressed in uniform and with a crown of pinned up hair on her head, she looked like the incarnation of a goddess of war. She issued an order that I should be given a couple of blankets, after which I was taken to an unheated room to have a nap on a bed made of plaited twigs. To get warmer I gathered some hay from somewhere out of which I improvised a mattress. A young nurse, who happened to be my immediate superior there, called by and reacted sharply at the sight of the 'rubbish' I had brought in. 'It would not look well', she continued with her melodious voice, 'if General Rakowski's adjutant made an inspection here'.[3] Indeed, I noticed a handsome officer nearby, sporting a finely trimmed short beard; the young nurse was clearly attracted to him. They all looked well fed and happy, and so found it difficult to show empathy with someone who had reached total exhaustion and who only dreamt of collapsing onto a pile of hay to warm her miserable bones. I also noticed that the blankets I had been given had not been disinfected after use, and here there was concern about typhus. I therefore turned for mediation to the charming young chaplain Captain Judycki who immediately arranged for my blankets to be changed.[4] The commandante was deeply offended that I had not come to her directly with this matter, but at that point I simply lacked the self-confidence to see her personally with a complaint. Right from the start I did not feel well at Shakhti. I was used to plug all the holes, so to speak, and I was immediately placed to work in the ward for the contagiously ill. At the same time, I had the impression that the well-fed company of mutual adoration wanted to keep a comfortable distance from the sick and to lord it over the hospital as if from Mount Olympus.

It was while I was in such a sad and wretched frame of mind that I was approached by a sergeant in the medical corps who asked me if I might be interested in taking up an independent position in the anti-typhus quarantine section in Chokpak. The medical officer there, Captain Kamil Niedziałowski, was looking for volunteers for that work. 'Why don't you go there?' said the sergeant, 'I also want to get out of here to breathe more freely; it will be totally different there, and you'll be able to work without anyone bossing you about.' I succumbed to the temptation although I was not entirely certain that I had the necessary qualifications. Dr Niedziałowski turned out to be a handsome and elegant man. He was pleased that I had reported to work in Chokpak and he reassured me as to my suitability for the job. And so began my wonderful period of work in Chokpak.

It would be difficult for anyone to believe that one can feel happiness amidst corpses, with illness and human misery all around. All of a sudden, I reached a 'spiritual peak' of fervour and idealism of the kind that had once animated me during my work in the hospital in Borki. I became radiant and lively. It helped that Dr Niedziałowski had an extremely chivalrous attitude to women and at work treated them like real ladies. His attitude helped me recover my sense of human dignity after so many months of being morally ill-treated in Russia. Eventually, I selected another Polish woman to be my auxiliary nurse. She was young and graceful, with a beautiful complexion, and she became immediately enchanted with the doctor, while he too was not entirely indifferent towards her. After a time, a qualified nurse arrived, so I suggested to the doctor that he should appoint her as the senior sister. However, he declined to remove me from the post I had received at the beginning.

I would also like to add that in Chokpak Father Judycki baptized a dozen Soviet children through my mediation. Local women begged the Orthodox chaplain in the Polish Army to baptize them, but he was frightened. Father Judycki courageously risked his own person and baptized all who asked him.

The sick lay side by side in barracks which had been designated as a hospital. At first the epidemic did not reach raging proportions, so Dr Niedziałowski and his colleague Dr Danek[5] were hopeful. The first person to die was a young boy who had an abscess on his hand. His hand was one enormous swelling, but without penicillin there was little we could do for him. And then the sick started to die like flies. The first victims were buried in coffins. Later there were not enough coffins; even if we had wanted to continue using them, there was no source of wood in the desert of Kazakhstan. And so the poor wretches were then thrown into common pits. Whenever one looked, one could see Father Judycki, in his high officer boots covered in DDT, bending over the sick who, with their remaining strength, were making their confession. One sick man expressed his regret that he had wasted so many of God's graces during his life. There were also a couple of more decent rooms where the ill lay on proper beds; those who were put there counted themselves lucky. There were two sick members of the Skirmunt family from near Lida in the hospital; the one in the better quarters survived.[6]

To cope with the growing epidemic, we were told to put up tents in the snow next to the railway line; the sick were placed there next to barely flickering stoves. When I set out with the doctor every morning to make a so-called medical round, we encountered nightmarish scenes: there were dead people in every tent. In the end we were counting about twenty-five deaths every day. I observed one beautiful, lifeless lad, and my heart ached to see someone in the flower of his youth die like a fly. On one occasion the doctor spotted a watch on the hand of one victim and commented: 'If only he had sold his watch, he would have been able to rent a room with some Kazakhs, and would have survived. He would have avoided the tuberculosis which he has caught in addition to typhus.'

One day, news burst upon us like a bombshell that some soldiers had got stuck in a snowdrift; the enthusiasm to rush out to save them gripped us all. On another occasion, two very recent volunteers, a mother and daughter, unexpectedly received an order to set up some tents in a snow storm. It was quite a sight to see the unfortunate mother, who was no longer young, and her daughter struggling with all the ropes while the wind blew their waterproof pelerines up above their heads. It was a miracle that the two volunteers survived; I was to meet both of them later in Scotland in the Polish military hospital in Taymouth Castle.

For their diarrhoea, the sick were treated only with bismuth and some powdered camphor; there was also something else which escapes my memory. Hospital orderlies took out the chamber pots. Late one evening I was still up meticulously sorting out the camphor portions when Dr Danek came up and told me to stop. 'Whatever you do won't help them anyway; we give it to them because one has to give them something', he explained. In one of the more decent barracks there lay a young, intelligent and handsome Jewish man; looking after him continuously, like a guardian angel, was his young wife. They looked like a couple of married students. The doctor started to lose his patience with the wife who enquired ceaselessly about what her sick husband should have to eat. Should she buy a chicken and boil it for her husband? When the young Jewish man recovered, Dr Danek remarked unequivocally that it was only because of the personal care of the wife. I observed with what deep feeling she sponged his whole body with diluted potassium permanganate – he had typhus – and fed him with spoonfuls of chicken broth. I was full of admiration for this woman, with her beautiful yet sad Niobe-like face. God had rewarded her solicitude. Later she herself fell ill, but not severely; she did not even lose consciousness. Eventually, she was moved to Vysokoe, a village southwest of Chokpak, where I was to meet her later. I really regret that I cannot remember the surname of this charming young couple who embodied for me the ideal of marriage. The emotional impact they made on me was similar to the one I had experienced earlier in Rome when looking at the bust of Cato and his wife. When one encounters couples who represent a veritable spiritual unity and possess such mutual devotion, one enters that greatest of mysteries, namely the natural human sacrament of Marriage.

My closest friend among the nurses in Chokpak was Bronka Kossakowska. A person of principle with a spotless character and a genuine concern for the soldiers, she was also full of girlish charm. Bronka and I worked with enthusiasm and for the cause. Dr Niedziałowski charged Bronka with responsibility for catering, and she made sure that the soldiers had the best food possible. Apart from our work, Bronka and I saw nothing of the outside world. There were three other nurses there who readily saw themselves with admirers from among the officers. Later they detached themselves from us and were persuaded by somebody to go to Guzar in southern Uzbekistan.[7] Bronka and I shared quarters, sleeping head to toe in one bed at the home of a Kazakh woman. Our landlady was pleasant and was to look after us when we both fell ill, ostensibly suffering from a cold. On the other side of the wall lived a little old man who played melancholy melodies on some instrument. I do not know where Bronka was sent after her typhus in Chokpak. It was only in Persia that our paths crossed again, by which time she had married a young airman. She then told me how Father Judycki had married them, and that she had now acquired the additional burden of worrying about her husband's fate and well-being.

We worked in exceptionally depressing, simply appalling conditions; but my inner fervour enabled me to rise above the tragic reality in which we found ourselves. It would be difficult to believe that this was in fact the period of my <u>greatest</u> inner happiness (in addition, of course, to that similar period in Borki). We returned from work exhausted, but in a little room all four of us nurses would eat together, accompanied by the doctors who treated us like society ladies. How pleasant were those communal meals, when as well as sharing our food we also shared the enthusiasm of altruistic work for the benefit of others! Never again in my time in the army was I to encounter such a good and pleasantly integrated team as then. This unity of purpose of people serving at the same post was more than just *ésprit de corps*.

At first, I caught a cold and bronchitis. This worried me because, having to work with a high temperature, I lost my vigour and enthusiasm. Incidentally, it is for those qualities that Father Judycki promised to recommend me after the war for a Cross for Valour (*Krzyż Walecznych*).[8] I told the doctor that somehow or other I was able to carry on with my work, but that I no longer had any strength or enthusiasm. Soon afterwards my temperature went up again. Dr Niedziałowski tried to comfort me by withholding the truth, saying that this was not typhus. But it turned out to be so. Indeed, two doctors suddenly fell ill as well as all the other nurses. So our entire team was sent to bed, and from somewhere other medical personnel arrived to replace us.

Those were nightmarish days. The sick doctors were removed to Vysokoe where conditions were better. Despite that, the woeful news soon reached us that Dr Niedziałowski had died.[9] And yet he had claimed that he could never again catch typhus because he had already suffered from it during the previous war. Nurse 'X', who continued to be in love with the doctor despite her own illness, reacted with indignation when I suggested that a flea must have bitten him. 'What do you mean, a flea! Dr Niedziałowski couldn't have any fleas. You're insulting his memory!' Her own illness proved not to be serious, and she was later able to make visits to the doctor's grave. At the same time, she took all the doctor's possessions, which she eventually began to sell off in order to survive. News of this reached the doctor's wife, a career nurse who summoned the police to Guzar, where Nurse 'X' had subsequently moved, and they recovered the doctor's property. Living in poverty, the unfortunate nurse later died there from dysentery. Later in Palestine, Dr Niedziałowski's wife was very anxious to meet me. I managed to avoid this, not wishing to be questioned about her late husband. In any case, not long afterwards she herself died.

Pani Franciszka Bartoszewiczowa followed me to Chokpak. She was accepted by the army to cook for the sick. During her medical inspection the doctor expressed surprise that her muscles were like those of a man. It was hardly surprising, for she used to work in the field with the farm labourers. I remember with affection how she fried potato pancakes and brought them to me when I could not bear the mess food provided for us; this continued to be thick rice served with a piece of camel meat. I had once seen skinned camels on a cart being delivered to the army; they looked like purple monsters. Ever since, and despite my hunger, I could never put this meat into my mouth.

It was good to have some kind people around during my illness. The medical NCO, the same one who had earlier suggested that I join the anti-typhus quarantine station, proved to be very kind-hearted. One of the medical staff told me about his life's tragedy, how he had fallen in love and had married a beautiful girl. He so admired her beauty that he spent all his pay on her clothes and appearance so that everybody would admire her at social gatherings. Eventually she was enticed away by a certain officer. Later, in Siberia, the two men happened to meet, and looked at each other in silence ...

In addition to typhus, I also caught a chest infection. Putrid pus streamed from my nose. The state of my health was hopeless. I looked with envy at other nurses who were only mildly ill and who almost made light of it. At one point I felt that I was weakening. With what was left of my strength I reached for a bottle of wine next to my bed which some officer, a friend of Zygmunt or Kazio Protassewicz, had given me. Drinking this wine may have saved me from death, because I was sure this was the crisis. After the wine I suddenly felt my heart beat more strongly. I felt that I was not yet dying. This also coincided with the arrival in Chokpak of Dr Weiss, who prescribed some tablets for my infected bronchi, and nurse Hanka, who immediately started to give me intravenous injections of glucose. Nurse Hanka worked with ease; she was always cheerful, and she played the mandolin, which created a pleasant atmosphere. She introduced a lively vivacity into what was an atmosphere of death and plague, perhaps because, not being burdened with Catholic puritanism (she was Jewish), she lived her sexuality to the full. She did not feel at all embarrassed when, for example, all of a sudden, she got into the bed of a certain handsome officer who was convalescing after typhus. He later used to visit her somewhere in Tel Aviv where she 'chose freedom', that is she ran away from the Polish Army into the bosom of 'her own people'. Once, while I happened to be walking past some tents, I noticed her sleeping outside, with total abandon, wearing some kind of a bikini. I therefore approached her and covered her with a sheet that was lying nearby in order to remove temptation from soldiers who had been sexually starved in Russia. Hanka was amoral, but she was pleasant and warm-hearted; it is due to her glucose injections that I may owe my own survival in Chokpak.

At that point someone issued an order that the longer-term ill would be transferred to better quarters at Vysokoe. Orderlies approached my bed and began to lift me up, whereupon I created a real scene. With what energy I had, I seized a knife and said that I would stab anyone who approached me. I knew that the frost outside was a dozen or so degrees below zero, that Vysokoe was about 17 km away and that I had inflamed bronchi. I was convinced that the hospital authorities wanted to take me there to get rid of me; or rather, considering me already at death's door, they were now going to sentence me to certain death. I told them that I had worked in Chokpak, that it was here at my post that I fell victim to typhus and that it was here that I wished to die, not anywhere else. My words had the desired effect: I was left alone. Several weeks later, when I had been cured of my bronchial inflammation, I announced that I was now willing to be moved to Vysokoe. To protect myself against the frost, I wrapped myself in my silk-covered eiderdown, the same one that had saved me in all my scrapes in Russia. I was placed in a cart (or was it a sleigh?) which then took me to Vysokoe, the same Vysokoe where our head doctor had died.

Not much later the sick Pani Bartoszewiczowa was brought there as well. She still had time to make her confession before she fell unconscious; in that state she died. Once she had expressed her opinion to me that weak people like me would die out, and that only the resilient and healthy like herself would survive. Unfortunately for her, the very opposite happened. Typhus is a disease of the blood, so my anaemia was an advantage in those circumstances, as too was my younger age. May God reward her for all the good she had rendered me! The poor thing was put inside a sack and buried in a common grave.[10]

My fever, accompanied by a temperature of forty degrees, raged for a month. After that, I suffered from constipation, and it was with difficulty that my enema managed to shift the residue in my intestines. Those were real tortures. I did not want to drink, and I was unable to eat the same thick rice with camel meat we continued to be served. At the same time, through the hospital window, I could see Kazakh women selling sour milk and unleavened flat cakes (*lepyoshki*). I would have given anything for just one mouthful of sour milk after all these weeks of fever! I had not a single penny because my 8th Division had left Russia in March – with it went my unissued pay. To make matters worse, right in front of me, I could see a nurse constantly rushing to a mildly ill woman doctor lying behind a screen and bringing to her either a hard-boiled egg or some other special delicacy. I then understood what it means to be abandoned and forgotten by everyone. Then, out of the blue, I was approached by the young Jewish woman, whose husband had recently recovered, and who now lent me several hundred roubles. I was now able to drink sour milk daily, and this gradually set me on my feet.[11]

Figure 6. Irena after typhus, Kazakhstan, 1942.

My full recovery still lay far ahead. Leaving Vysokoe by train I was still so weakened that I was unable to get off the wagon to fill my mess can with water; yet the summer heat stifled me with a barely controllable thirst. An unknown soldier took pity on me and brought me some water. My fellow nurses were so preoccupied with their flirting that they showed no interest at all in my plight, despite the fact that I had made sure that one of them was accepted for work by Dr Niedziałowski. I found this lack of gratitude hurtful. Evidently I must have looked so poorly and so unprepossessing that the living no longer accepted me in their company; but as it turned out it was I who survived. Perhaps it is good that they were so happy in their own group, for experiences worse than mine awaited them later.

To be separated from my division, where I was known, and to be left somewhere in the rear, possibly forever in Russia, was a cause of great despair. But at least I was able to attend a month-long medical course.[12] Eventually, on 1 August 1942, I was attached as a convalescent to the 7th Division stationed in Kenimekh in Uzbekistan, about 180 km northeast of Samarkand. I was still little more than a skeleton and almost without any hair, for my beautiful locks had been cut off. I wandered like a ghost in the desert, but because the army had sent me some money I visited the local market and gorged myself on delicious and wonderfully aromatic melons. I was advised to leave in deposit the remaining pay arrears, and indeed, later in Scotland, I was paid off with £99 in cash.

A source of spiritual consolation was the first Holy Mass I attended in Russia, this land clasped in Satan's embrace. It was celebrated in the desert of Uzbekistan by Bishop Józef Gawlina and it made an enormous impression on me.[13] He arrived by plane from Palestine and brought with him sackfuls of oranges. I remembered Bishop Gawlina from a parade in Warsaw where he had cut the impressive figure of a young dignitary.

I now noticed, with pain, that his hair had greyed. How mercilessly time brings down all youthful good looks.

I was put up in a concrete barrack with a group of other nurses. We slept on folded blankets on the floor. There were many graceful young girls there who worked in the hospital and who, despite our small food rations, looked healthy and had the energy to go out on dates. I find it difficult to remember their surnames now, or even their faces, but I have fixed in my memory the tall figure of Krystyna (Krysia) who married a very young doctor there. She led communal prayers and dominated those around with her personality. Her husband was charming, but he was shorter than his wife and had protruding teeth. She treated him like a son, and was inclined to keep him at arm's length and to patronize him. She possessed many social graces and *savoir faire*; she was always mixing with the high echelons of the military. She was terribly scandalized whenever any member of the Women's Army Auxiliary force wandered into one of the men's tents. Our commandante kept a close eye on the morals of her women charges.

Unfortunately Krystyna was to find her personal life deeply entangled later in Iraq. While running a recreation room for military personnel, she fell in love with a much older doctor and left her husband. I was to meet her later in Nazareth where she spent some time resting after a spell of heart trouble brought about by her experiences. She was a devout Catholic and a high-minded person, and went through internal tortures: she had met someone so well suited to her, her ideal so to speak, yet she was not free. Without saying anything, she once showed me a letter from this older doctor. The letter expressed great admiration and veiled sentiments for her; it was done in the style of a man of the world and of high quality who, as a connoisseur, an aesthete and a thinker, had appraised her accordingly. It was an exceptionally beautiful letter. Her husband was nice and very kind, but he was no eagle, and would have been incapable of writing such a letter. She then asked me for my opinion. I replied evasively, for I would have felt uncomfortable telling her that this was a devil's snare and a beautiful temptation, and that it was improper for her, as a married woman, to receive such a letter. In my simple-minded sense of morality, this was the temptation of the serpent in the Garden of Eden. A married woman is not free, and has no right to hear compliments from the lips of other men, especially since behind them lurks the call of someone's love, even if of the most sublime kind. Everyone felt sorry for the husband, for he was an exceptionally pleasant, helpful and idealistic man, and everyone was indignant with Krysia who had met someone whom she had chosen with full engagement of feeling. The result was that she moved away from her husband as well as from the other man, and suffered in loneliness the tragedy of this late encounter. However, in England, I think she decided to divorce her husband and went on to marry the doctor after all.

In Kenimekh I also worked with Estera Witkowska, a career nurse from Poland.[14] She worked with great dedication and lavished wise motherly care on the sick in her charge. She had a highly noble character; there was something in her of Esther from the Old Testament, or of some other female personage moving through Jewish history. That is why I did not forget her. When I was later transferred to Palestine, Estera did not accompany us to the Holy Land and remained in Iraq caring for the sick. From Palestine I sent her a letter in verse with a dedication. I was subsequently to meet her in Scotland where she worked in the general surgery unit of the military hospital in

Taymouth Castle. Because of her utterly unshakeable sense of duty she remained with the Polish Army, and it grieved her that so many Jews had deserted once they reached Palestine. One of those who did that was the chief doctor in Kenimekh, a hysterical type, who did not bring much enjoyment to Estera's life. She was always so absorbed with her work among the sick that she had no time for her private life and only got married much later in America, but too late to have the son she always dreamt of. We have remained in touch ever since. For the last twenty years she has had a well-paid job in a Jewish (Bundist) archive in America; she also sent us sundry parcels with clothes. Last year (1967) she even visited me in England from the United States.

I also worked in nearby Kermine where our superior initially was Pani Łaciszowa, a very pleasant person of principle. She lived to see a miracle: she stayed behind in Russia after our evacuation and managed to extricate her teenage son from a *kolkhoz*. Both of them subsequently emigrated to Canada. She was replaced by a new twenty-one-year old nurse who displayed despotic tendencies; she ignored the views of people whom she should have consulted and ruthlessly acted according to whim. At the same time the new nurse was a fanatical workaholic and, despite her typhus-swollen legs, untiringly carried out all sorts of inspections. I did not like her because one could not feel any kindness in her, only fanaticism and the ambition to get to the top.

In Kermine, I became fond of two charming girls who were mutual friends: the extremely tall Ula and the shorter Kazia. Ula probably sensed that her husband, a policeman, had perished,[15] for she tried to ensnare our young Jewish apothecary. Despite his good looks, this young man kept himself aloof from women. Later Ula got involved with some doctor whom she eventually married. She stayed for a time in Palestine before moving to England. Kazia was saddened that after her wedding Ula broke off her friendship with her. I remember how on one occasion they bathed together in a bathtub: they looked like shapely buxom goddesses. Kazia later worked as a nurse in the desert in Egypt where Dr Żyznowski was the chief doctor in a technical school for young soldiers.[16] The poor thing developed tuberculosis there and was sent to England for treatment. I corresponded with her by letter all the time, and I think I even sent parcels to her mother in Poland after the war. However, by then I had tiny children and so was afraid to meet her in case the infection spread to my little ones.

The chief medical officer in Kermine was Dr Krzywański, a very pleasant middle-aged gentleman who lost a daughter there, a casualty of his work with the typhus patients.[17] His wife and two other daughters were in Palestine; the daughters later married in England. The chief surgeon was Dr Kiełbiński who had an oddly shaped head. He lived with a charming and very young woman doctor whose very feminine good looks I admired, because I always liked Junoesque women. She worked with enormous grace. Once, later in Iraq, I was to witness how she calmly applied bandages soaked in a solution of potassium permanganate over the whole body of a young woman driver who had been pulled out from underneath a blazing vehicle. The driver was in terrible distress thinking that her face had been ruined. Sometime later I saw her with her face completely healed and without the slightest scar.

The doctors in Kermine were intent on dissecting all the corpses in that awful Uzbek heat; I was puzzled at first as to why they were doing this. The young Dr Cało, who was charged with most of the autopsies, was indefatigable in carrying out these tasks. He acquired incredible skill which proved to be of great help later during the fighting in Italy. He features in one of the photographs in Wańkowicz's book *Monte Cassino*: he appears with a surgical mask on his face during an operation, looking like a young Dr Kildare.

All the corpses around us and the mass mortality of the Poles in Uzbekistan had poisoned even the most resilient spirits. But then spring arrived, the spring of 1942. Its arrival made a great physical impact on us. Just think that the mere news that crocuses were blossoming in the mountains had the effect of setting us up on our feet. The sight, through the carriage windows, of red swathes of tulips flashing by along the railway line restored a yearning for life and for survival. No! Man cannot live only by the spirit, because he is an integral part of Nature, and that same blood pulses through his veins. Without greenery, without flowers, even man's spirit will decompose in its torpor. I observed somewhere a couple of small leaves opening up on a shrub and immediately felt that I would not die in this treeless desert of Uzbekistan; it was as if the shrub's green fingers drew me out of the horrible abyss of non-existence back to life, to spring! Oh, how one wanted despite everything to move beyond the disaster of our existence and live to see better times.

Yet, as spring turned to summer, the desert of Uzbekistan made an increasingly disheartening impression, as did the pitched tents of the 7th Division. In the opinion of the doctors, the soldiers had to be moved from there, or else they would expire from

Figure 7. Irena (standing 4th from left) with other members of the Polish Women's Auxiliary Service in Uzbekistan, 1942.

the heat since their small single tents provided no protection against the sun. And that is what happened. Those who had not been finished off by typhus in Chokpak now lay in pools of their own blood on the floors of the hospital barracks without any sheets: there they died like flies. I remember one soldier lamenting loudly: 'Mother! Why did you give birth to me!' With those words he died. Eventually, I began to work in those barracks although my strength had not yet been restored. I choked from the stench of bloody diarrhoea in which all the people there, without exception, ended their lives. The nights were the worst. Full of concern for the souls of the dying, I used to run time and again to find the priest whenever death seemed imminent. A pale merciless moon shone through the window and packs of jackals howled in the distance.

In one of the wards in Kenimekh the sick rose in revolt. They were dying from dysentery and pellagra, and it suddenly entered their heads that they were being treated incorrectly and were therefore being condemned to certain death. The mutiny was led by a handsome young man, Dąbrowski. My heart bled on hearing how desperate they all were to stay alive by staging their tragic revolt; it was so reminiscent of my own state of mind when I had typhus. The doctor in charge flew into a mad fury and with his screaming, silenced the revolt. Another doctor might have broken down alongside his patients had he allowed his feelings to move him to pity. I later discovered that the aforementioned Dąbrowski, who had fought so hard against death, finally passed away. However, the dull sloucher in the next bed survived, because his mother appeared; she probably fed him some fruit and thus saved his life from pellagra and dysentery. It was precisely the absence of mothers and wives, watching over the sick and running to the Uzbeks to exchange some last rag for a cup of sour milk or some fruit, which prevented so many from being saved.

What could have been done for these men in the army? The cause of their illness was overheating in the tents. Everybody had to live in those tents, and it was too late by the time the sick landed in the cooler barracks with concrete floors. Grapes were later purchased for them. But what good was that? The soldiers' damaged intestines could not digest the grape skins. I therefore squeezed the juice out of the grapes for them, but the liquid had more glucose than vitamins. Afterwards I ate the pips and the skins myself rather than throw them in the bin, but my stomach was fortunately healthy thanks precisely to the fact that I slept in a cool barrack for nurses. On one occasion, General Anders arrived to visit the sick in Kenimekh. I remember his conversation with Bratkowski who showed him a photograph of himself as a neat good-looking boy, and compared it to how he had now changed into a caricature of a man, as a result of pellagra. His entire skeleton was visible, his ribs in particular were protruding and his complexion was of a strange uneven colour. Taken as a whole he reminded me of one of those skinned camels; it was a sight difficult to forget.[18] On one occasion I was giving some juice to a soldier in my care who was lying on the grass; he had an aristocratic-sounding surname and was very good-looking. I asked the doctor whether there was any hope that he might survive. 'Yes', came the reply, 'providing he could be sent immediately to another climate'. Unfortunately, there was no such possibility for these soldiers. Although the first wave of Polish troops had left the USSR in March 1942 (against the orders sent from London by General Sikorski; he had no personal knowledge of Russia), General Anders only succeeded in getting the second wave out in August.[19]

The day came when we were informed that we would be leaving Russia. It is difficult now, after so many years, to realize fully what one felt at the thought that we had lived to see the miracle of getting out from this man-made hell. One felt all the more the tragic situation of those who were ill. I knew that feeling – remember my division had been evacuated in March while I had been left to my fate. Only by a miracle did I find myself now among the living. Sick men, sometimes dripping with blood-stained diarrhoea, used the last of what strength they had to march in rank during training (an idiotic thing to be doing in such conditions) in order somehow to get into the wagons with the healthy men and so to escape from Russia. Such men died on the way, but at least until the end they had hope in their hearts that they might survive. As for the bedridden sick, they could not be taken on the journey and were left behind to perish. One of those who had concealed the fact that he was suffering from typhus in March 1942 was my future husband; he managed to cross the Caspian Sea before becoming gravely ill, in Pahlevi, I think.[20] But he had reached freedom and there in Iran one could get fruit. In Iran he also found his mother who helped him financially.[21] As a soldier, he had hardly a penny to buy extra fruit, which the army did not provide.

We travelled by train to Krasnovodsk, a port in Soviet Turkmenistan on the Caspian Sea. For the journey we were given tins of food which I later swapped for wine. For a tin of beef I would get a mess tin full of wine. The wine gave me the strength and power to drag my feet somehow from place to place as we were hurried along at the station in order to board our ship. These transactions were illegal, so they were conducted out of sight in the side streets of Krasnovodsk. Many scandalous things occurred, such as the instruction issued by our authorities that we should surrender all our roubles, on pain of punishment. This money was then meticulously handed over to the Russians. When everybody had done that, it transpired that our train did not take us all the way to the port, and that we had to pay ourselves to complete the journey either by tram or by some local train. Many Polish civilians abandoned all their possessions in order somehow to make the great effort to cover those 7 km to the port on foot. We in the army only had knapsacks and some other kit, but we could hardly throw them away. The people in my group were very lucky that someone on the train, a civilian I think, was sufficiently wise to keep some roubles; he saved us all by paying for our tickets. How many Polish civilian families lost everything, casting away furs and other costly items which in some cases they had carried with them across the whole of Russia? It would be worth investigating who was responsible for issuing this draconian order which deprived us of our remaining roubles.[22] This order sent more than one exhausted Pole to the grave along that final stretch from the railhead to the port. The route was littered with piles of items which the Russians then set about plundering. Witnessing these human jackals at work was my last spectacle in the land of the Soviets.

11

From Persia to the Holy Land

A taste of paradise – Under canvas in Khanaqin – Crossing the Jordan – School for young soldiers in Nazareth – Difficulties with fellow nurses – Finding congenial company – Wlastimil and Ada Hofman – Spiritual consolation – Travels in Palestine – Kibbutzim and the Jews of Palestine – Cousin Jadzia Przybytko – In praise of General Anders

Persia! We crossed the Caspian Sea by ship and landed in Pahlevi.[1] We were then transferred to motor coaches. These travelled at dizzy speeds down the narrow hairpin bends on mountain roads which terrified us out of our wits. We entered a green land overflowing with melons. Oh, the sight of that tropical greenery and the possibility of buying delicious juicy watermelons and other fruit from local Persians whenever we broke our journey – this was a taste of paradise. Unfortunately, many people, mostly children, died from exhaustion in Pahlevi. But I was spared the sight of these final victims who, on the threshold of paradise, failed to attain their freedom in this world. I was with the army and with those civilians who managed to remain tolerably well on their feet. I remember the taste of the first flatbread, the first egg and the first onion; and I remember the juicy softness of the fruit. Army food was awful, for it consisted mostly of thick boiled rice with fat mutton, impossible to swallow in the heat. If the rice had been offered in the form of a watery soup without the fat, it might have been somehow edible. Many people, exhausted by their recent illnesses, now fell ill due to this fatty gruel. This was one of the scandalous features of the nourishment of our army.[2] The only way to survive was by exchanging dry rations for fruit with the Persians, even though it was against army regulations. Besides, some people had managed to squirrel away money from somewhere. The poor soldiers were the worst off, for their pay was meagre. I did not smoke, so I was easily able to sell my cigarette rations and buy something to eat. But this too was illegal.

This prosaic aspect of life was only of superficial concern to me; I kept going physically by eating a piece of fruit from time to time. My inner soul was longing for a new beginning in what seemed like a strange new incarnation. At last I would be able to get to know the East: to observe palms full of sweet dates and to observe how real people of the East lived.

In due course, we headed for Iraq. At one point we set up our tents in the desert. With the yellow sand as backdrop, our squat soldiery lacked grace in comparison with the troops of Sikhs serving in the British Indian Army. The Sikh soldiers were slim, beautiful and smart, like roe-deer of the desert. Their green turbans added glamour to their appearance. I did not imagine that eastern peoples could be so good-looking, and our soldiers so unsightly by comparison. Each one of our soldiers, once he had recovered his physique through ample food, became somehow stocky and shapeless. We lived for a time in a certain oasis. There were palms around in addition to a few buildings. There was even a small river flowing through the land. On one occasion, I went for a walk along its bank and came upon an extraordinary sight: a Sikh was washing his long hair in the water, and then hurled himself, Ophelia-like, into its current. My modesty overcame my curiosity; I moved on and did not gaze any longer at that enchanting spectacle.

Eventually we set up camp for a longer period in Khanaqin, just inside Iraq, where we were to await our turn to depart for Palestine. We slept side by side in a tent for members of the Women's Auxiliary Service. We ate out of the same pot as ordinary soldiers, for Lieutenant Zieliński informed us that since we did not have officer rank he could not admit us to the officers' mess. The officers, in the meantime, lived comfortably in their own well-furnished tents where they had camp beds, waterproof canvas washbasins and other luxuries. It was only later that Pani Żylińska, the head of the Polish Red Cross, forced through the decision that all nurses were to receive NCO ranks. Later, in England, each one of us was at least a lieutenant. Back in the desert, however, the officers readily set about engaging in all sorts of flirting, reducing the women to the lowest social status rather than raising them.

Despite this, I did not lose my sense of humour. I composed a revue for the 23rd Infantry Regiment of my 7th Infantry Division which was performed by a campfire in Khanaqin. Woven into this parody were satirical remarks about friends, female and male, such as 'the faithful husband who loves constantly' (Heller), or 'Sophie who loves' (Wojcicka), or 'someone with a geisha's eyes' and so on. I wrote a little jibe about everyone. And everyone there roared with laughter.

However, there followed an unpleasant episode. At one point the doctor in charge of the sickbay in this transit camp made an appeal for nurses to volunteer to help with the sick. I was still unsteady on my feet, I still had no hair on my head, but in order to earn my keep, so to speak, I turned up with several other naive nurses. I said that I would gladly help on condition that it would not prevent my departure to Palestine with my unit. The commanding officer agreed, and I began my nightmarish work. By chance I fell victim to a ruthless career nurse who, seeing that I looked poorly, decided that it would be easier for me to work at night. Perhaps other nurses were able to manage the occasional nap during their night shifts, but in my concern that no one should die without receiving the sacraments I had not a moment of peace. I continually found hopeless cases and urgently sought out the chaplain who had to crawl out of his bed in order to give the Last Rites and hear confessions. It was here that one person suffering from malaria philosophized that he was a non-believer. This obstinate freethinker from Warsaw added greatly to my anxieties. I prayed for him, and eventually he agreed to make his confession. After three such nights in a row I felt

I would not last long, for at the same time it was absolutely impossible to sleep during the day in our communal tent: the flies bit mercilessly and my fellow nurses very happily flirted, laughed and chattered. In the meantime, a large contingent of military nurses arrived from Palestine; they were well fed, in excellent form and were surrounded by a swarm of male admirers. Naturally they all ate in the officers' mess – where else!

Then the order arrived for our 7th Division to depart. Seeing that so many rested medical personnel had poured in from Palestine, I rushed without any qualms to the senior doctor with the request to be relieved from my temporary duties, according to our earlier agreement, since my division was to leave in a few days' time. 'Out of the question!' my temporary superior declared categorically, to my horror. What to do? Despite my three sleepless nights, I summoned my remaining strength and resolved to rebel against this obvious violation of the promise made by my superior. Without permission I jumped into a motor car going to Quizil Ribat where General Anders's headquarters were situated and where General Szarecki, chief of medical services, had his office.[3] General Szarecki's adjutant refused to admit me, but due to a happy coincidence I was spotted by Commandante Żylińska who was in charge of all the nurses of the Polish Red Cross.[4] I reported to her that I had undertaken the extra work on the understanding that I would not to be separated from my division once it received orders to move. I reported further that I had not yet fully recovered from my time in Russia, that I had completely ceased to menstruate as a result of my general exhaustion, and so on. As luck would have it, Pani Żylińska happened to be a friend of the Stabrowski family (that is the family of the mother of Kazio and Zygmunt Protassewicz). She asked me if I was related to them, then picked up the telephone and spoke to somebody. On replacing the receiver, she informed me that I was to leave the day after next for Palestine with my division. I had been saved.

But I very nearly again lost this opportunity through my idiotic loyalty and concern for my nurse friends. It suddenly occurred to me that Pani Hala Gutowa might not know that we were leaving the next day. I set out in some vehicle to see her. Her husband did not show any interest in whether I had the means of getting back to my quarters. It was only by a miracle that I caught a lift and was able to return just in time for my unit's departure.

Our route took us into the heart of Iraq.[5] How many different memories flashed back from the tales of *One Thousand and One Nights*! We crossed the Tigris and journeyed through places not far from the legendary Garden of Eden of Adam and Eve. In the desert I collected strange stones of volcanic origin; in places they rendered the desert almost black. I regretted that we only stopped fleetingly in Baghdad itself. I devoured with a greedy eye the delightful secluded nooks and crannies of Baghdad's leafy suburbs, and the narrow streets full of motley crowds wearing turbans and strange garments. I admired the ornate weapons of the Kurds and their wild appearance. Beautiful to behold was the Persian Guard in Baghdad with their green uniforms and turbans, which I saw just as they were crossing the river on horseback.

Our crossing of the Jordan made a great impression on me. There were small details too, like seeing hens which I had not seen for such a long time, or the first smart prams in which well-fed and coddled Jewish infants were happily wailing – such a contrast to the primitive conditions in Russia and Persia. To suddenly inhale moist sea air and to see the first clouds in the sky over Palestine was something unbelievably soothing after a period of well over six months spent in the desert, without clouds, under an eternally scorching sun breathing oven-dry air. It is strange, but no sooner had we crossed into Palestine then my menstruation returned. There's little to say, but climate does perform miracles. Our entire army could have been saved if even six months earlier our units had been sent here, simply to recover after Russia; as it is, thousands of soldiers had been left behind pointlessly in graves in that inhuman land.[6]

I experienced profound emotion on entering Palestine, that Promised Land. Someone who is not a Christian or a Jew will never feel that inner jolt on crossing into that land. As always, I recorded my impressions in verse, writing hastily on my lap in the lorry. Naturally, the first person with whom I shared my enthusiasm was Estera, and to her I immediately sent a letter in verse, for it was she who was particularly in my thoughts at those moments.

At first, we were taken through Tel Aviv to Rehovot where there was a transit camp.[7] The presence of pregnant women auxiliaries, who had been brought there from every quarter, made one blush in shame for them. There I also met two of our nurses from Iraq. One was the pleasant Marysia who bragged that she had 'an allowance'. The father-to-be was an officer. My friend Halina Heller predicted that it would end badly, saying: 'Of course he won't marry her'. And that is what happened. This Marysia had a sweet personality and had been duped by a charming rogue's deliberately misleading promises. Personally, I avoided men like the plague, especially officers. I was repelled by their behaviour to the extent that I only decided to marry Michał because he was not an officer. Of course, one must not generalize, for there were many men of integrity among the officer class who either remained faithful to their absent wives or approached women with the honourable intention of marrying one. However, unfortunately, it often happens that individuals who behave in a shocking way are more noticeable and tarnish the reputation of the majority.[8]

After my arrival in Palestine, I asked Dr Wit Tarnawski, the chief medical officer of all the young soldier schools, if I could work in Nazareth, out of sentiment for my school in Wilno.[9] He readily agreed, and in this way I was to spend over a year in this delightful although rugged and mountainous corner of Palestine. The conditions in the school for young soldiers in Nazareth were primitive, but they were better than among the tents of Barbara, the Polish Young Soldiers Cadet School.[10] However, they were much worse than in Ain-Karem (near Jerusalem) where the school for girls was under the authority of the Polish civilian authorities and not of the military, and where living conditions were closer to normal. The staff there enjoyed civilized standards, and rooms were not so cramped. Even in Nazareth, teachers immediately received the rank of sergeant and a monthly supplement of £5. Furthermore, many of the ladies had husbands with them, so they were entitled to a 'family' supplement. Initially, chaplains and doctors also had the rank of sergeant before their status was raised to officer rank, in line with British practice.[11] However, other members of the army health service continued to be treated badly, which contributed to the fact that the teachers looked down on them with contempt. I obtained the rank of corporal. The pay was £6 a month, which was very little, bearing in mind I had neither a husband nor lovers with money, and that I had been stripped of all my most necessary items after my time in

Russia. In addition, the interpreter lost my watch (a present from my brother-in-law Janek Karczewski) after it had been repaired; we looked but could not find it in the grass. I therefore had to scrape together money for a new one.

At first I felt very uncomfortable in Nazareth. I felt greatly offended by the lack of moral restraint which I encountered when I shared living quarters with some of the staff from the sanitary department there. I was not yet married, and so I was all the more shocked by the 'earthy' approach to life of some of the women auxiliaries who took themselves off to hotels in Tiberias. They remarked that if one can afford love, then one can afford to pay for a hotel, and they looked on me with contempt for denying myself 'life's opportunities' which brought with them rewards in the form of gold necklaces and the like. Knowing life better now, I would simply not have paid so much attention to these goings-on which poisoned the atmosphere at the time, and, feeling less scandalized, I would have had stood a better chance of experiencing my own great religious moments undisturbed.

Perhaps I was odd, but I preferred to spend my time reading French books in the library of the Salesian Fathers, or to spend my last penny on travelling and seeing something interesting, or even, for the lack of company, to roam around by myself among the rugged mountains in search of beautiful views and unknown flowers, rather than to sit constantly in the company of uninteresting colleagues and listen to their confidences which filled me with revulsion. To share communal living quarters was a torment, all the more so since after work numerous military men of different kinds would come and visit; they would sit on the beds and chat in a friendly way. I felt

Figure 8. Irena (2nd row from top, 3rd from left) with staff and boys at the school for Polish young soldiers in Nazareth, 1943.

embarrassed. Of course nobody come to see me, so I covered my head with a sheet and went to sleep straightaway. This clearly infuriated some of my colleagues: on one occasion one of them started to pelt me with oranges, while another, the wife of some NCO, threw away a precious stone I had picked up in the Persian desert. Yes, there were various trips around Palestine which the occasional person would join, but I did not meet anyone who would set about exploring Palestine alone and independently as I did. After some time, at my request, I was able to move to a small bedroom nearby shared by Pani Antonina (Tosia) Schwetz and another lady who worked in a recreation room. I was finally able to breathe freely, away from the coarse behaviour and the total lack of manners of some of my colleagues in the communal quarters.

Pani Schwetz was the wife of a forestry inspector from the foothills of the Carpathians and used to visit Dr Tarnawski in Kosów. Dr Tarnawski had once been engaged to Aunt Hela Protassewicz's niece, so I immediately found myself able to engage in interesting drawing-room conversation in pleasant company; instead of criticism, I encountered approval of my conduct and of my sightseeing. Pani Schwetz had a wonderful eleven-year-old daughter Alusia, who was later painted by Hofman, and an urchin of a son by the name of Marek. She was therefore tied down by these children and unable to go anywhere. She was forty years old, but looked very young: she had a dignified face, with a beautiful complexion. In the past, she had played Chopin beautifully. In general, and there was no denying it, she was a lady among what were in most cases women of social pretensions. Before the war she had entertained in a grand manner at her home. Her husband did not return from Russian exile; apparently he froze to death somewhere on the way. Pani Tosia was employed in the office of our school; her son was with her, while Alusia was somewhere else at a school for young girl soldiers, although she was able to visit her family often.

It was only when I started sharing quarters with Pani Tosia that I felt at home in Nazareth; there I began to feel happy. At night each one of us slept under a mosquito net suspended from the ceiling. The young soldiers, aged seven to about ten, slept in a single large dormitory. Before being appointed as a nurse in the sickbay, my first job in Nazareth was as a hygienist: I made sure that the boys washed themselves, and sometimes I even scrubbed their dirty ears. With the doctor we inspected the boys' bodies, in particular their skin, and even the smallest pimple had to be rubbed with gentian violet, to protect the boys from skin diseases which were so common in the hot climate. The school's commanding officer was Lieutenant Bułyha, subsequently appointed to captain; he was a very decent man, but he stuck to the letter of the law. The post of bursar and administrator was held by the delightful Captain Przybylski, known as 'daddy' (*tatuńcio*), who took a fatherly approach to all problems. He later organized trips to the health baths in Tiberias. In those days I did not yet suffer from rheumatism, so I did not take advantage of those facilities, but I gladly visited the town nevertheless.

It was in Tiberias that I met the painter Wlastimil Hofman and his wife Ada.[12] He lived in the Franciscan monastery there and spent his time painting. Later Dr Jan Freundlich, the medical officer in Nazareth, invited them so that Hofman could paint the valley of Nazareth. Dr Freundlich took care of Pan Hofman's health; Hofman started to have bouts of fainting which were connected with over-work, for he spent whole days painting in the sun, without any breaks.

By the time the Hofmans had moved to Nazareth, I was already working in the sickbay; this consisted of receiving boys for all sorts of treatment during break-time between lessons. If there were not too many people in the sickbay, I was free the rest of the time. Wlastimil Hofman painted on the balcony of the sickbay, so I was able to delight in observing his subtle technique and the ease with which he painted without having to make any corrections. I became friends with the Hofmans, and I helped him find all sorts of unusual models for his paintings.[13] We succeeded in persuading Father Cross, a French Salesian, to pose for Hofman. Father Cross was the only Salesian left with us from his establishment after the building was handed over for the use of our school. Father Cross's splendid bearded figure served as a model for a picture of St Joseph. He was a deeply pious priest whose missionary work was exclusively among the Arabs for whom he always said a separate Holy Mass in the lower tier of the church, and whom he addressed in Arabic. He was a man of inner concentration, dedicated without reserve to his mission. Hofman also used a young Polish cleric as a model for Christ in his painting entitled: 'Birds of the Air Have Nests, but the Son of Man has Nowhere to Lay his Head'. But while working on the painting, Hofman suddenly declared that what emerged in the picture was not Christ but Jan Hus.[14] Another of Hofman's models was the hunchback organist from Malta who would have made a good Quasimodo.

Hofman and his wife represented the ideal of marriage in their spiritual unity, in their joint work and their shared goals. Hofman's mother was Polish and his father Czech. He told me how once, lying in bed, he ventured to reveal his secret to his father: 'I feel myself a Pole …' The father replied: 'Good that it's not a German.' That is how Hofman's confession ended. He was converted to Polishness by the art world of Kraków with which he totally fell in love. Even in his old age, he professed himself an unworthy pupil of the great master Malczewski.[15] Hofman's great inner humility was a characteristic rarely to be found in a genius. Because of his gentle character he would have perished in the real world were it not for his wife whom he had met in Prague during an exhibition in that city. She was an admirer of his work and spent the rest of her life assisting him in all practical matters; without this care he would not have survived. I once mentioned that it was a pity they had no children. He replied that artists should not have children, since all the artists' children he ever knew went off the rails. An artist is so absorbed in his work, he continued, that he is unsuited to bring anybody up, unless it involves an adult and in the field of art.

Pani Ada Hofman always spoke enthusiastically about the various liberation movements in the Czech lands. Having been brought up in an atmosphere of reactionary Catholicism, I did not always feel comfortable with the Hofmans's broad interpretation of Christianity, and feared being infected with what I then might have regarded as some banned heresy. It is only now, after the Second Vatican Council, that I have come to appreciate how much I benefited from listening to their narratives. It is these narratives which, among other influences, enabled me to perform an inner reshuffling of cards, and helped me to free myself from the Catholic Church's excessive tendency to harangue. I was able to move towards a broader attitude in matters of religion; an attitude that was not only tolerant but also federal in principle: equal with equal in the eternal march towards what for us human beings remains the unattainable full divine truth. I am astonished by the overbearing self-assurance of the Catholic Church of those days that it possessed all there is to know of divine matters. Yet, in his letters St Paul writes most clearly that 'now we see indistinctly, as if through a looking-glass, and only in the eternal Kingdom we shall see everything: face to face'.[16]

Today, in 1969, after familiarizing myself more closely with the history of the Czech lands, I have played a part in the publication of an article by Paul de Vooght, calling for the rehabilitation of Hus.[17] The wrong inflicted on Hus has always given me pain, and I am pleased that I have contributed, albeit minutely, to the revival of this subject in the press. To a certain degree, it was a spiritual recompense on my part to the Hofmans. I informed them of this article and received a lovely letter from the aged Hofman expressing his delight with this, since, as he put it, Hus had been fighting 'precisely for those ideals which are especially threatened today'.[18] Evidently Hofman referred here to communism.

Still in Palestine, Hofman used my profile for a beautiful painting, entitled 'The Transfiguration', with Mount Tabor in the background shrouded in hail clouds. Unfortunately I put off its purchase for the lack of ready money, and was pre-empted in this by Dr Freundlich.[19] Hofman also painted Polish soldiers and so recorded the presence of the Polish Army in the Middle East. But hardly anyone bought these paintings, for who was concerned with art in times of war? Still, Hofman was able to earn enough money for the paints and canvases he needed. Only Dr Freundlich (who came from Kraków) spent all the money he could buying up Hofman's best work; he believed that the war would come to an end and that art would again acquire a commercial value. The paintings Dr Freundlich had bought for a song travelled later with him to Poland.

Hofman took the rest of his work with him when he too returned to Poland. Indeed, he was to be condemned by many of the exiled Poles for returning. But where else was the artist supposed to go with his artistic output but to his fatherland to which to bequeath his legacy? Governments and politics are ephemeral, but one's country remains one's country. As a result of this timeless view of politics, Hofman faced some harassment and was frowned upon in senior military circles. It was perhaps partly because of this that he lived modestly in a secluded spot, and that it was not possible to use his presence in Palestine to further the national cause.[20]

Among my best friends in the Middle East were Kazimierz (Kazik) and Halina Heller. We first met in Kenimekh (in Uzbekistan), and strengthened our bonds of friendship in Persia.[21] I remember how in Kenimekh a certain nurse stole my handkerchiefs; I recognized them drying on a line but felt too embarrassed to make a big deal out of it. It was then that Halina Heller approached me and presented me with a couple of her own hankies. Halina's only son died in Russia; the boy had shown great feeling for the beauty in flowers and would certainly have become a gifted painter. I encouraged them to have more children. They continued to have no confidence in the future, but eventually, in Palestine, they did have a son, Julek, who is at the moment studying at an art academy in London. Later, in England, they had another son, Adaś. Both Hellers were remarkably kind-hearted. I remember seeing Halina, with an expression of great solicitude, leaning over a woman teacher who had fainted. Later, when I was already in Scotland, I was surprised to receive an enormous crate of oranges which Pan Kazik sent me all the way from Palestine. After arriving in Palestine, Halina (who had been a teacher before the war) found employment in the school for girls in Ain-Karem. She recovered her good looks once she had been nourished back to good health; she dressed well and had beautiful curly hair.

In Palestine I also met Julia Masłoniowa, my beautiful commanding officer from Chokpak. She was astonished to see me among the living. It is perhaps because she thought I was dead that my Polish Red Cross certificate and my school leaving certificate had got lost somewhere among her things; I had left these documents with her in Shakhti. Julia Masłoniowa was now the director of the school in Ain-Karem and was looking for teachers, so I was delighted to recommend Halina Heller and Hala Gutowa. Thanks to this both of them were able to spend many years in civilized conditions working in the school near Jerusalem, to which they were often able to travel. Also, as teachers they immediately received the rank of sergeant and a supplementary allowance of £5 per month, while their husbands received good salaries too. One can therefore say that fortune had smiled on them. The two ladies lived quietly in a small detached house where I once visited them. They used to buy each other gold bracelets as presents on their names' days. And whom should I also encounter but Melchior Wańkowicz who was then in Palestine as a war correspondent. I visited him in Tel Aviv where he cooked a goulash for me on a primus stove.[22]

One eminent guest in Nazareth was Bishop Gawlina who visited our school. On that occasion I had the honour of witnessing him admit into the bosom of the church thirteen Orthodox boys whom I had persuaded to convert to Catholicism.[23] There was one Jewish boy who had been greatly impressed by the services held in the wonderful basilica at our monastery; he wept openly when the bishop decided it would be unwise to baptize him on the grounds that he was under age and that he was going to stay behind in Palestine with his aunt. The doors of this beautiful basilica were opened wide, and the bishop spoke wonderfully while gazing into the distance at the valley of Emek Israel (Jezreel) where King David had once fought wars. The bishop referred to those biblical times and to our own fate dictated by the fortunes of war. Everything that he said, which was enveloped with the beautiful artistry of his innate oratorical talent, made a great impression on the listeners. Also in the crowd was our military interpreter, a Jew, who spoke to me after the sermon in the following way: 'Your bishop's words were like honey' (perhaps he had Samson's honey in mind). After Bishop Bandurski, Bishop Gawlina remained in my memory like a spiritual pearl, truly a joy to one's eyes and ears.

Many people in this period of wartime calamity experienced a religious renaissance. Unfortunately, the war had an altogether different effect on others. I was greatly shocked when at one of our outposts, a certain senior nurse, 'living' apparently with her doctor, said openly that she was going to Palestine where she intended to 'live her life to the full' (sexually) for all time. Axel Munthe described in *The Story of San Michele* how in times of plague some people fall on their knees while others throw themselves into each other's arms in a sexual frenzy.[24] It was also said on the quiet that the Soviets had deported prostitutes from Lwów and that they too had joined the army. In any case, here and there morals evidently began to falter, to the extent that at one meeting Bishop Gawlina devoted an entire speech to the great and beautiful role played during the insurrections of the nineteenth century by patriotic Polish women of standing.[25] The bishop appealed directly to the assembled women auxiliaries not to lower that high standard set by the heroines of the previous century. I was profoundly moved by Gawlina's beautiful appeal, and I was therefore all the more shocked by the malicious and mocking giggles that could be heard, here and there, coming from some of the auxiliaries. It may have been unfortunate that I had lived most of my life in the narrow confines of my family, and before that in a convent school. Perhaps it was also that I myself had been living a deeply religious life since the arrival of the Bolsheviks in Borki. Furthermore, after the loss of my homeland and, what I feared, of my family, I sought consolation all the more in Palestine in my communion with God.

I also dreamt of seeing more of Palestine; I was sometimes able to do so by catching lifts, but this was not always possible. I was also deprived of an opportunity to travel to Lebanon. I visited Halina Heller in Jerusalem only once because I could not afford the fare there and I did not want to ask her to lend me a pound. However, I did visit the magnificent basilica on Mount Tabor, as well as Tiberias, Capernaum, the environs of Jerusalem, Haifa and Tel Aviv. I swam in the Dead Sea and participated in the celebrations in Bethlehem on Christmas Eve 1943. I was disappointed with the holy sites, because I had expected to find them in their original biblical state, only to discover that numerous and various temples had been built everywhere, sometimes with the least tasteful internal design: for example, on the site of the Holy Sepulchre in Jerusalem or in the Church of the Annunciation in Nazareth. The only object which made a great impression on me in the latter church in Nazareth was a small circle with the inscription: 'Verbum caro hic factum est' (Here the Word became flesh). The whole interior of the Church of the Holy Sepulchre, with its hanging lamps and the various Orthodox or Coptic pieces of stucco, grated on my feelings, while the sight of the clergy of the different denominations competing greedily for the possession of these sites created an unpleasant impression of human pettiness in the presence of the sacredness of these places. However, only someone who has been to Palestine can feel the patina of the bygone times of the Old and New Testaments. The indescribable landscape and climate, the Arab population, the donkeys and the primitive conditions all contributed to the whole picture.

One day I set off alone to a fortified Jewish kibbutz in the hills not far from Nazareth. The Jews received me very hospitably and treated me to a simple meal which all the workers ate together in a common hall. I was surprised to find numerous Polish books in the library, while the watchman who showed me around originated from Poland. I was therefore able to speak Polish with many people there. The crèche was nice and modern, although run on communist lines, since parents only came to visit their children who remained the common property of the kibbutz. As far as I can remember, what shocked me a little was that couples in the kibbutz cohabited without any legal endorsement. Later I visited a second model agricultural kibbutz near Tiberias. There I encountered numerous reminders, unpleasant for me, of the Russian model, such as the absence of religion in social life. Despite this, there remained in my memory the pleasant side of the hospitality of these people towards us Poles. I felt overwhelmed with admiration for their courageous pioneering life.

Near Rehovot I also visited a modern school of agriculture and animal husbandry. I was particularly interested in their apiary of fifty hives; I therefore borrowed a protective face net to have a closer look at how beekeeping was run there. The hives were of the Dadant-Blatt type.[26] The honey from the orange blossom tasted delicious. Because of the war, the farm was somewhat underpopulated and I think the school was not functioning. From the depths of my memory I seem to recollect that the excellent breeding bees there were Dutch.

Haifa is beautifully located. I visited places with ancient relics associated with Elijah in a delightful corner on a nearby mountain slope, Mount Carmel. I missed my bus back to Nazareth and thus had the dilemma of where to spend the night. Unsure of what to do, I went to the municipal police. At the entrance to the police station I was unpleasantly struck by the sly face and the dark, cruel and brisk eyes of the duty officer. Something smelt of the NKVD, and I began to feel uneasy. Nevertheless, I was politely given the address of the local YMCA where I spent the night. That same evening I had to make a quick exit from a cobbler's shop where I wanted to have my shoes repaired. The cobbler met me by pointing, with his hand, to pictures of the leaders in the Kremlin. He fixed his eyes on me and asked: 'Well, Stalin, good?' (*Nu, Stalin, kharasho?*). I was in a Polish uniform, so I quickly stepped out of there. It was improper to listen and, being in their country, I felt unable to respond. I had the impression that much of Palestine was undermined by Soviet propaganda, probably via emigrants from Russia. Who knows, the Soviets might have established a permanent foothold there, had they not started openly to persecute the Jews in Russia, and had they not supported the Arabs by supplying arms before the last Israeli-Egyptian war of 1967.

I hope that the Jews in Israel today (1969) have quickly cured themselves of their pro-Soviet sympathies which so filled me with fear in 1943. Yet how better informed they all were about everything than we deeply naive Poles! On one occasion, at an assembly point for departures for personnel going on short spells of leave, of which I once took advantage, I encountered hostility towards me, in my Polish uniform, on the part of a Jewish woman in an English uniform: 'You think that you'll return to Poland; it won't be you, it'll be Wasilewska.'[27] I was offended, but within a few years what she had told me so vehemently turned out to be the brutal truth. She was somehow better informed than our leaders who, certain that they would return to Poland, were organizing quick courses for future provincial and district governors in the country. Yet despite the pre-war anti-Jewish outbursts in Poland, the Jews who had come from Poland to Palestine were very fond of us Poles and showed us much kindness. Nothing moved me as much as their love of Polish books and of Polish films. All Polish films were available to our forces; they were lent to us by local Jews. And so, Jadzia Smosarska reigned permanently there on their screens, and I was able to remind myself of her looks.

With reference to the communist Wanda Wasilewska, it was my cousin Jadzia Przybytko who, during her long enforced stay in Petropavlovsk in Kazakhstan, was drawn into the Soviet-sponsored 'Association of Polish Patriots', led by Wasilewska. Jadzia had the qualities of a social do-gooder; she was full of enthusiasm and energy. She had inherited populist leanings from her father, Emil, who was known for his strong pro-peasant sentiments. During the First World War he sold grain from his estate to the peasants at rock bottom prices; to charge any more he considered profiteering. I could not have joined an organization such as Wasilewska's 'Association of Polish Patriots'. For me this would have been tantamount to treason. Being eight years older than Jadzia was, my patriotism had developed under the influence of the traditions of the insurrections of the nineteenth century and of Piłsudski's Legions. Jadzia, on the contrary, was still without any fully formed political ideas, for after her father's death there was no one at home who spoke about politics. With her broadminded and populist soul, it was therefore easier for her to believe Wasilewska's propaganda.[28] Even so, it has to be said that with her energy Jadzia did a lot of good, precisely because she belonged to this association. She was able to rescue Polish youngsters from Russia, and then worked on 'repatriating' the Poles from Wilno. For the last twenty years Jadzia has been the director of a nursing college in Warsaw, and has even travelled abroad on official business. And so Jadzia Przybytko entered the new (post-1945) Polish reality, whereas the Poland I knew had gone forever.

Before ending the account of my stay in Palestine, I must say a few words about General Anders. Everyone adored him as the saviour who had led us out of the Soviet hell. Anders was compared to Moses who had led his people from the land of slavery across the Red Sea to the Promised Land. He also succeeded in smuggling out countless number of civilians by listing them as soldiers' families, despite difficulties raised by the Soviet side and by the Polish government in London. General Anders had a real knowledge of Russia, while General Sikorski's government was drawing up, on orders issued by idiots in London, unrealistic plans for General Anders's soldiers: having suffered the torture of Soviet labour camps and of interrogations, they were now expected to hold feelings of idealistic affection for their erstwhile oppressors and to fight shoulder to shoulder with them against the Germans.

What an attractive personality Anders was; we could see his excellent physical prowess even after so many months spent in Soviet captivity. He demonstrated this not only in his superb dancing, for instance performing the mazurka, but also in his acrobatic, almost Cossack-like exploits on horseback when he jumped on and off and across galloping horses while accompanying the Shah on tiger hunts. In this period Anders was slim and looked very young; he had an engaging personality bathed in an aura of bravery. His military reviews made a profound impression when he fixed his dark eyes deeply on every soldier to whom he was speaking. He inspired confidence in everybody, and kindled faith in the struggle for a free Poland. He was a true leader, and no one was able to deny him that quality, not even his greatest enemies. He showed great concern for organizing schools for young soldiers, so that even the youngest lads could be prepared for future military service; he secured their status and their right to leave Russia with the army.

On several occasions during my stay in Palestine I attended commemorative assemblies organized in the schools for the young soldiers. What a standard, and with what spirit they sang! For example: '*Wrócimy znów … gdzie miasto Lwów*' (We'll Return Again … to the Town of Lwów), or '*Warszawa, dokąd przyjdą chłopcy malowani, chłopcy w Warszawie zakochani*' (Warsaw to Which Resplendent Soldiers Will Come, Lads in Love with Warsaw) or '*Serce w plecaku*' (With My Heart in My Knapsack).[29] Feliks Konarski (aka Ref-Ren) immortalized our wanderings, which were worthy of

Aeneas, in his songs '*Piosenki z plecaka Helenki*' (Songs from Helenka's Knapsack); Helenka was his wife.[30] Renata Bogdańska, daughter of a Greek Catholic priest and later Anders's second wife, led a colourful life with a wandering troupe of actors who performed Ref-Ren's plays.[31] Ref-Ren's crowning achievement was the song '*Czerwone maki na Monte Cassino*' (Red Poppies on Monte Cassino) which, gripped by an inner fervour, he composed during the night before the Poles finally stormed the monastery of Monte Cassino. Particularly moving is the photograph showing this young group, standing at the foot of Monte Cassino, and rendering this song for the first time, and with panache, on the day of victory.[32]

War is blood, tears and pain; but war can also possess an outward appearance of poetic beauty which wipes away many a tear with its song, a song that follows the army like a comet's tail, a song that enraptures and elates the spirit. I experienced many tragic moments during my work as a military nurse, but I do not regret it, since the very memory, the very feeling that one had worn a military uniform and had taken an active part in this our Polish military 'Aeneid', fills one with pride. My life was not wasted, and there were great and sublime moments. It is something which those who have not worn a uniform in wartime are incapable of understanding. Green was our uniform; we were 'green' in our heads, 'green' in our hearts and this innocence of life was still able to intoxicate us. Such a feeling overcomes a keen swimmer when he throws himself into the deep and when he delights in the element of the sea. I was young, I felt brave and so, in spite of everything, I was romantically happy in this unique adventure, which was the part of my life spent in Anders's Army in the Middle East.[33]

12

From Egypt to Scotland

**Two trips to Egypt – Unintended smuggling – Stiletto dagger episode in
El-Qassasin – Unexpected journey to England – Military hospital at Taymouth
Castle – Meeting Michał Zawadzki – Marriage**

I had several opportunities to go to Egypt. The first occurred sometime in 1943. There
was a young soldier in our school in Nazareth who had lost an eye after being hit by
an arrow fired from a friend's bow. It became necessary for him to be fitted with an
artificial eye. Dr Freundlich asked whether any of the nurses spoke French so that
the boy could be taken to the English hospital in Cairo. It emerged that only I had
reasonable knowledge of the language, so I reported to the doctor. I was a little scared
as to whether I would be able to find this hospital in Cairo, but off we set. Before we
left, numerous individuals, especially the well-paid teachers, gave me a lot of money to
buy gold chains and other objects in Cairo's gold bazaar. The doctor instructed me to
buy the largest possible number of chamois skins, since in Egypt they were a third of
the price in Nazareth.

Somehow I was able to find the home of the Polish Red Cross in Cairo, where
I stayed, and the hospital where I took the young soldier.[1] Having some free time to
myself, I managed, for £5, to go on a trip on the Nile to Luxor and Thebes where I spent
two days and where I visited the magnificent Egyptian temples. In the gold bazaar
I bought everything I was asked to get, as well as a pile of skins for the doctor which
I placed inside a leather suitcase I had bought for myself. I also remembered that Uncle
Koczan had brought a stiletto in a bamboo sheath from Kharbin (in Manchuria) where
he had worked building railways before the First World War. I found an Arab shop
where in secret, for £1, I purchased two stiletto daggers, one in a leather sheath and the
other adorned with an antelope horn.[2]

However, the doctor had not warned me that it was forbidden to bring anything
across the border between Egypt and Palestine. On my return journey, just
beyond or just before the Suez Canal, the train was stopped and the English police
approached to check if anyone was engaged in smuggling. In the adjoining carriage
a large number of shoes were removed from a large suitcase belonging to an English
officer who was then arrested. I panicked. What was I to do? I told the young soldier
to say, if asked, that the suitcase was his, while I went to the door of the carriage.

I noticed a Polish military policeman among the British. I turned to him: 'Excuse me, sir. What am I to do? I've got this and this in my suitcase purchased for the staff in Nazareth.' He told me that he would inform the other policemen that he would search my carriage, and that everything would be fine. On my return to Nazareth I learned that I could have got two years in prison for this smuggling, to which I had been exposed by the doctor who then made a tidy sum from the sale of the skins. Furthermore, instead of expressing their gratitude, everybody began to complain to me that for one teacher I had purchased a prettier gold chain than for the others; there were other similar cases of disgruntlement. In addition, the captain in charge of the school took offence and was furious that I refused to sell him one of my daggers. In the end I had created enemies for myself by risking my life for them. As for myself, I had bought only two skins which I sold for a handsome price in Nazareth.

My knowledge of French also came in useful during my second trip to Egypt in 1944 when I was seconded to another school for young Polish soldiers near Heliopolis.[3] I was able to accompany a group from the school who had been invited by the aunt of King Farouk to a reception in her villa. Farouk's aunt was a very beautiful young woman; she spent all her time talking in exquisite French with the wife of one of the Polish diplomats present there. An eastern waiter wearing a red fez brought in an enormous splendid silver tray full of delicacies and placed it on the table where I was sitting with the young soldiers. The villa was a wonderful building with all the sumptuousness of the East.

I was scarcely back in Nazareth from Heliopolis when in March 1944 all nurses of military age received the order to go to the front line in Italy where the Polish Second Corps was about to go into action.[4] I therefore set off back to Egypt, to El-Qassasin, near Ismailiya, which was the last staging post for Polish units leaving Egypt. However, since there continued to be a lack of transportation, we women auxiliaries had the misfortune of having to spend six months in tents in that desolate area of Egypt. One day our commanding officer ordered me to do guard duty at night near the tents. I was not given any weapon. Arabs used to creep up to our encampment and steal blankets; apparently a couple of white women had also been abducted. I was afraid, so I took with me one of the stiletto daggers from Cairo, the one I had used once before to drive away a pack of dogs that had encircled me near Nazareth. The following day, I needlessly boasted to somebody about being armed while on guard duty. I was denounced to the commanding officer who took my name for disciplining and, as a punishment, crossed me off the list of those going to Italy. Instead, she added my name to the list of those to be sent to England. I then wrote a mischievous poem about her, but to England I had to go. Little could I have imagined at the time the long-term effect the episode with the stiletto dagger would have on my life.

None of the women auxiliaries wanted to go to England, because all the Polish men there had already made a beeline for Scottish and English women, and had neglected their own fellow countrywomen. Also, there were no Arabs there who would work as cleaners and scrub floors, which is what we had to do at first in England.[5] These menial chores ended when I was transferred to the Corps of Nurses and appointed ward sister at Taymouth Castle in Perthshire.[6]

We finally left Egypt for England on the *Britannic*. During the sea journey we remained in constant fear of being torpedoed by German submarines. It is on that ship that I first came into contact with Anglicanism which roused my admiration. There was an English woman onboard who wrote up a wonderful poem which I copied down in my dictionary, but which unfortunately I have since lost. The poem spoke of how wide was the sea, how high the sky, but how all that was surpassed by the Saviour's Love.[7] There was no attempt in that poem to frighten us with hell, as had been the case in Wilno at the Sisters of Nazareth. The only unpleasant encounter on board was an awkward conversation I had with a senior British officer who did not conceal the fact that he was a committed communist. We arrived in Liverpool in August 1944. The weather was beautiful, but after so many years in different deserts we shivered in the cold and the damp.

On arriving in Scotland we nurses were billeted in Bolfracks House, not far from Taymouth Castle. Work at the hospital was very demanding. I struggled to summon up what was left of my strength for I found night shifts and the making of over a dozen beds exhausting. Because penicillin was not yet widely available, the stench of infection in the large halls of the castle was appalling. Fortunately, I was eventually transferred to work in the barracks near the river where the air was fresh and where there was a view of the woods beyond. I remember one handsome forty-year-old chartered engineer with a beautiful complexion who was suffering from high blood pressure. A month later he was no longer on the ward.

Most painful and tragic to witness was the arrival of transports from Italy carrying young lads without legs or hands.[8] One was blind and missing a hand; he had only vestiges of fingers on the other in between which his nurse was just able to insert a cigarette. I admired this nurse who managed to persuade the young man that he was only temporarily bandaged; she so engrossed him in casual conversation that the poor thing came to believe that his bandages would be removed any day and that he would see. I don't know what happened to him later. Another was an impressive giant of a man from the Polish mountains, a highlander with a fine distinguished face but whose legs had been amputated just below his hips. He stood bravely on his metre-long artificial legs when receiving Holy Communion. What a sight! Beauty embedded in such tragedy. Another twenty-year-old handsome lad, brown-haired, with both legs missing, told me that if he was unable to walk with artificial legs then he would commit suicide. In contrast, another one who had lost his arms below the elbow boasted that he would be held in esteem in Poland, and that his carer would even wheel him to brothels; he was full of good humour, and like the highlander had not succumbed to a nervous breakdown. Yet another, by the name of Jasio, had been clearing mines at Monte Cassino; although his eyesight was saved, both his arms had been ripped off below the elbow. He walked around, he ran around, he was young and lively, but he bemoaned painfully his fate and would stretch out the stumps of his arms to me with the words: 'Little sister, little sister!'(*Siostrzyczko, siostrzyczko!*). Sometime later, after leaving the hospital, I heard that he had attempted to drown himself in the nearby river. What has happened to all these lads now?

They were all operated on by Dr Redler, who was Jewish.[9] He sometimes carried out five operations a day, inserting, for example, bones from legs or ribs into holes in skulls.

None of his patients died; he had a magic touch. Deaths occurred only in the general medical ward, which is where Estera Witkowska worked after her transfer from the Middle East.

Another patient was the young Lieutenant Gabriel Gabrielewski of the 10th Dragoons who had lost a leg: he was beautiful and was adored by my assistant matron. Incidentally, she turned out to be an imposter because she had taken the surname of a fictitious husband; she eventually left for communist Poland. Lieutenant Gabrielewski was Orthodox and used to ask me if I was related to the Orthodox Protassewiczes of Wilno. There was in fact a certain Mikołaj Protassewicz from Aleja Róż (Rose Avenue) in Wilno who was Orthodox, and who even used to visit Mila Protassewicz in Rohotenka.[10] Today, Gabrielewski is the mainstay of the 10th Dragoons Association in London. Despite his artificial leg he is doing well for himself, for he has a good brain. He regularly sends me copies of the regimental publication '*Dragoni naprzód!*' (Dragoons Forward!) which contain numerous moving letters from former dragoons.

It was in this hospital full of wounded men that my private life was to change forever. I met Michał Zawadzki for the first time by accident, while on duty on the third floor of the castle. Several new patients walked in. One of them attracted my attention by his cultured and distinguished appearance, although he was only a dragoon with recognition of his education (*dragon z cenzusem*).[11] Michał had been an anti-tank gunner and had been wounded at the battle of Falaise Gap in Normandy in August

Figure 9. Irena and Michał Zawadzki on their wedding day at the Polish military hospital in Taymouth Castle, Scotland, 28 January 1945.

1944.[12] It turned out that he was a distant relative (on his father's side) of Aunt Salunia Połubińska. After seven meetings we got married in the hospital chapel on 28 January 1945. Michał had lost all his possessions in France, together with his watch, whereas I was a well-paid second lieutenant. I therefore purchased our wedding rings for a pound each, and an officer's uniform for myself for £16. We were both in uniform at our wedding. The marriage ceremony was conducted by Father Marian Kluszczyński, the Polish Army Catholic chaplain at the hospital, and the witnesses were my superior Adela Jaźwińska, and my friend and fellow nurse Wanda Lisowska.[13]

P.S. And so I have to thank my commanding officer in El-Qassasin for having sent me to Scotland. There I found a husband, and I now have fourteen grandchildren in England.[14]

Part Three

1945 to 2016

Epilogue: Exile and resettlement in Britain

Hubert Zawadzki

Early married life – The 'betrayal' of Poland – Birth of son – Life in Eastwood and the Duchess of Atholl – Reconnecting with scattered relatives and friends – Parcels to Poland – What happened in Borki (1941–5) – To return to Poland or not? – Morpeth camp – Birth of daughter – St Mawgan camp – American plans thwarted – Birth of second son – Michał's illness – Springhill camp – Birth of second daughter – Children's education – Revived contacts with Poland and with Borki – Return of wartime demons – Striking roots in England

Who knows whether in an alternative pre-war existence Michał would have been the husband of Irena's dreams. Certainly war and their Soviet experiences had changed her – and him. What is clear is that the emotions they felt in 1944 went beyond those of a couple embarking on married life together in 'normal' times. With his similar social background (he came from a landed family in Polesie, not all that far south of Irena's home district), Michał must have been for Irena a link to her lost world. And there was certainly no 'normal' beginning to their married life. Immediately after the wedding ceremony Michał returned to the sickbay and Irena resumed her duties as ward sister. It was a month later that Michał was released from hospital and granted four weeks' leave. He was then able to join Irena in nearby Bolfracks House where the Polish military nurses were billeted. On 3 March Irena obtained ten days' leave, and it was only then that the newly-weds were able to get away for nine days. They spent four days in London where they met Irena's cousin, squadron leader Apoloniusz (Polik) Protassewicz, who was based at Polish Air Force HQ at 1, Princes Row, SW1. On 9 March they returned to Edinburgh and continued to St Andrews where they spent a brief honeymoon.

Both Irena and Michał were still in uniform and under orders, and there was still a war on. Irena returned to Taymouth Castle while Michał discovered that he had been seconded by the Polish Ministry of Defence to attend a one-year course at the Polish School of Foreign Trade and Port Administration in London. The Polish government in London was training personnel to assist with the reconstruction and administration of post-war Poland. Yet the prospects of the legitimate Polish government returning to a 'free' Poland had long ago vanished. The government, led by the veteran socialist

Arciszewski, was still formally recognized by the Western Allies, but to all intents and purposes it was no longer relevant in the settlement of Poland's future. By February 1945 the Red Army was already in control of all of pre-war Poland, and the Soviet-backed 'Polish Committee of National Liberation' (PKWN), composed of Stalin's communist stooges and other fellow travellers, was establishing its authority in 'liberated' Poland with the help of the Soviet NKVD. In January 1945 the USSR had unilaterally recognized the PKWN as the Polish Provisional Government. The decisions taken by the Big Three (Stalin, Roosevelt and Churchill) at the Yalta Conference in February were a shock to the exiled Poles, and were condemned by them as an abject betrayal by their Western Allies. Without having any say in the matter, Poland was to be 'moved' further west on the map of Europe: the eastern provinces of pre-war Poland, about two-fifths of the country and representing most of Stalin's gains in the Nazi-Soviet partition of Poland in 1939, were to revert to the USSR. For Irena this meant there could be no return to her home in Borki. At the same time, the new Poland was to obtain substantial but still unspecified territories from Germany in the west and north. Stalin agreed that the Provisional Government in Warsaw would be broadened with the inclusion of democratic leaders from Poland itself and from among the Poles abroad; this government would then hold early and free democratic elections. Hoping that the Yalta agreement would permit a degree of political freedom in the new Poland, Mikołajczyk, the leader of the Polish Peasant Party and former prime minister in the Polish government in London, decided to return home. But would the Soviets allow free elections to take place in Poland – and would they respect the results?

Fully aware of the exiled Poles' objections to Yalta and probably feeling pessimistic about Stalin's real intentions, Churchill made a singular statement in the House of Commons during the Yalta debate on 27 February 1945, a statement that would eventually enable Irena and Michał to stay in Britain:

> In any event, His Majesty's Government will never forget the debt they owe to the Polish troops who have served them so valiantly, and for those who have fought under our command. I earnestly hope that it may be possible to offer them the citizenship and freedom of the British Empire, if they so desire. I am not able to make a statement on that subject today because all matters affecting citizenship require to be discussed between this country and the Dominions, and that takes time. But as far as we are concerned, we should think it an honour to have such faithful and valiant warriors dwelling among us as if they were men of our own blood.[1]

Despite the alarm expressed by the Foreign Office and various Whitehall mandarins with what became known as Churchill's 'pledge', the British Cabinet agreed to his proposal; however, it was emphasized that the combatant Poles were to be considered a 'special case' and that the concessions granted to them were a question of honour.

In the meantime, events in Poland left little doubt that the Soviets were determined to maintain their grip on the country: the structures of the wartime Polish Underground State, probably the most impressive resistance organization in all of occupied Europe, were ruthlessly destroyed, while the remaining armed units of the non-communist

Polish underground were hounded by the Soviet security forces and their Polish communist allies. The Soviets justified their actions by arguing that the rear of the Red Army, as it battled its way to Berlin, had to be secure. Furthermore, the PKWN had already in July 1944 granted the Red Army jurisdiction in 'liberated' Poland, and in September 1944 had signed an agreement with the Soviets to 'repatriate' (a euphemism for what amounted to ethnic cleansing) to the new Poland much of the Polish population of the lost eastern territories.[2]

Various publications in English and Polish from this period, found in Irena's and Michał's papers, indicate how closely they tried to follow these developments and how troubled they must have been by it all. Just to mention six titles in English: *Will Stalin dictate an Eastern Munich?* by William Henry Chamberlin (reprinted from The American Mercury, 1944); *Polish-Soviet Relations in the Light of International Law* by B. Montanus (New York, 1944); *Britain's Obligation to Poland* by John McKee, BA (Cantab), published in Glasgow; *Downward Path* by Stanisław Stroński (London, 1945); *Poland and Great Britain before and after the Crimea Conference: Documents* (London, 1945); *The Truth about the Liberty of Poland* by F.C. Anstruther. Some of the publications, bearing on the front cover a stamped message in large red letters: THERE MUST NOT BE A NEW PARTITION OF POLAND, were supplied by Senator Józef Godlewski, the old family friend and neighbour from the Słonim region who appears on several occasions in Irena's account, not least in connection with the episode of the duel that never was. Godlewski had managed to escape to Britain with his family. In 1942 he founded the 'Association of Northeastern Poland' to campaign in defence of Poland's rights to those lands. Irena had contacted him soon after arriving in Britain. 'I'm very glad you've survived the Bolshevik hell', he replied on 28 September 1944, and asked for information about Irena's family and her experiences under the Soviets.

While the inhabitants of Britain joyfully celebrated the end of the war in Europe, most Polish servicemen in the West felt that their country, which had fought from the very first day of the war and which had suffered so much, had been 'sold' to the Soviets. Subsequent developments brought further distress. On 21 June 1945, in the Kremlin, Stalin concluded a conference establishing the new 'Polish Provisional Government of National Unity' which now included Mikołajczyk and five other non-communists, but which remained dominated by the communists and their allies. On the same day, in a show trial held in Moscow, sixteen military and civilian leaders of the non-communist Polish Underground State, who had been treacherously kidnapped by the Soviets, were convicted, and in most cases imprisoned, for belonging to 'illegal organizations'. The next blow came two weeks later when, on 5 July 1945, Britain and the United States withdrew their recognition of the Polish government-in-exile in London and recognized the Provisional Government in Warsaw. On 7 July Irena's cousin Zygmunt Protassewicz wrote from New York: 'Our longing for our homeland and for our loved ones is great and is growing stronger all the time, especially when such sad news is arriving from the European Continent, and the attitude of our Allies is so evasive, opportunistic and betrays a feeling of their own weakness.' And Irena's good friend Halina Heller wrote from Palestine about 'the disaster of our dearest dreams'.[3]

At the Potsdam conference in July–August 1945 the United States and Great Britain reluctantly agreed for German territory east of the Oder-Neisse line (with

Stettin/Szczecin) to be administered by Poland until a final peace conference. Yet the simultaneous decision to expel the remaining German population from those lands, into which settlers from central Poland and the 'repatriated' Poles from the east were already pouring, only confirmed that the Soviets and the new government in Warsaw intended to make these territorial changes permanent.

While Poland's fate was being decided by the Great Powers, there was nothing else for Irena and Michał to do but to follow the line of duty. Michał's departure for London, where he arrived on 15 March, also meant long periods of separation. It was not easy to get back to Scotland to see Irena, bearing in mind that the train journey took twelve hours in each direction. Michał's diary records the visits he was able to make to see his wife during 1945: four days over Easter (Easter Day was on 1 April 1945), followed by monthly weekends (some longer than others) in May, June, at the turn of September and October, in November, and then a longer spell over Christmas (22–31 December). Irena and Michał not only faced an uncertain future but also an immediate concern: the future of their child, for Irena was pregnant and expecting to give birth in February 1946. She had been on maternity leave since 1 November and it was urgent that a suitable home be found for her. Irena was enchanted by the heather-covered mountains of the region and was keen to stay there, but no local landlord was willing to have a mother with a newborn baby. Shortly after Christmas of 1945, Michał, who spoke English, went further afield in search of accommodation. In Perth he learnt that the Duchess of Atholl, a friend of the Poles, had offered her residence in Eastwood near Dunkeld as a rest home for Polish officers. Irena was a second lieutenant and could therefore qualify. Michał's visit to Eastwood proved successful, and on Saturday 29 December both he and Irena travelled there to finalize arrangements for her to move in after her confinement.

While Michał had to return to London, Irena moved to Edinburgh to the Home of Mother and Child (*Dom Matki i Dziecka*), run by the Polish Red Cross. On 21 February 1946 she gave birth to a son (me) at Edinburgh's Western General Hospital. It is highly unlikely that Michał was able to visit her that day or even soon after, for he had earlier asked her to inform him of the forthcoming birth by telegram. He also discouraged her at the same time from returning to the Home of Mother and Child, and urged her to go to Eastwood as soon as possible.[4] But before that could be contemplated, there was drama at the hospital. To Irena's horror she found her newborn son with other babies, fresh after a bath, on a trolley parked in a corridor near some doors which were open to the snow and frost outside. By the next day I had developed pneumonia, and within a few days it seemed I might not survive. Following a nurse's advice, Irena baptized me herself and gave me the name Wacław (Wacio) in memory of her father (my second name, Hubert, was added later). I was saved by an injection of penicillin administered by Dr Zdzisław Małkiewicz, a paediatrician at the Polish School of Medicine in Edinburgh, who happened to be on duty. One of Irena's Polish friends at the hospital also had a newborn child who was ill, but the next duty doctor did not give the child such an injection. The little boy died. His distraught mother was never to get over her tragic loss.[5] On a happier note, at the Home of Mother and Child where Irena was transferred afterwards, she was able to provide milk for a newborn girl (Gogulanka) 'who', in the words of the home's administrator, 'owes you her life!'[6]

In April Irena and I moved to Eastwood which was to be our home for the next two years. Eastwood House is today a self-catering holiday let and is described as 'a beautifully restored Victorian villa sitting in a stunning location on the banks of the River Tay'.[7] Indeed, the setting was beautiful, with a belt of dense woodland covering a steep bank behind the house and with rolling hills beyond. From the point of view of family life the arrangement had a serious drawback: Michał could visit Irena at Eastwood but, as he was soon to discover, he could not live there. On 21 March 1946, a month after my birth, he successfully passed his final examination at the School of Foreign Trade and Port Administration. But where could he apply all this knowledge? He was still in the Polish Army, whose status remained uncertain; nominally it still owed allegiance to an exiled president and government no longer recognized by the host country. At least he was able to return to Scotland where on 1 April he was appointed education and welfare officer, and later storekeeper and caretaker, at a convalescent home for disabled Polish ex-servicemen at Auchmore House in Killin, at the western end of Loch Tay. It was a job that would last until the end of September 1947 when the home was closed. Unfortunately, not only was Killin 60 km away from Eastwood, not an easy journey up the Tay valley at the best of times, but Michał's post was residential. He was able to obtain leave occasionally to visit his family in Eastwood, but the long periods of continued separation had an unsettling effect on the married couple who were still unable to live together in what they could call their own home. Michał felt the separation very strongly and asked Irena to write at least every third day.[8] Yet there seems to be no denying that motherhood and the location of Eastwood had brought great joy to Irena, as her friend Halina Heller commented: 'Your last letter is you, Irenka, again "in your poetic phase". Nature and the countryside, bees which you love, and your little wonderful Wacio in a pram next to you have released in you feelings of contentment with life.'[9] A year later Mila Kontkowska commented in a similar vein: 'I get the impression from your letter that you lead an idyllic life: quiet, tranquillity, countryside, a healthy babe and a husband every week.'[10]

In the meantime, the continued existence of the Polish Armed Forces in the West (numbering some 250,000 with the largest contingent, the Second Corps, in Italy) was now a political embarrassment to the new Labour government in its relations with the USSR and the authorities in Warsaw, and a burden on the British Exchequer. For the Poles, however, their sense of betrayal was only further deepened when they were excluded from the great Victory Parade held in London on 8 June 1946. If offence could be added to injury, it happened that day. The Duchess of Atholl could only lament in her diary: 'Victory Day – v. sad that Poles were not represented.'[11] The Labour government had rejected Churchill's suggestion to create out of the Poles a 'British Foreign Legion' and was encouraging Polish servicemen to return home, claiming it had received assurances from Warsaw as to their safety on arrival in Poland. Less than half of the servicemen eventually opted to return. For the rest, and especially those who had only recently experienced Soviet captivity and whose homes in the east were now in the USSR, such assurances meant little as they awaited the free elections promised at Yalta. On the other hand, they had the reassurance, following Churchill's 'pledge', that no Pole would be repatriated against his or her will.

Fearful of an electoral defeat in early free and fair elections (such as that suffered by the communists in Hungary in November 1945), the Polish communists sought means to delay an election and in January 1946 resorted to a referendum which might give them some legitimacy. The referendum included three questions: on abolishing the Senate; on the government's economic policies; and on the new western border. The communists called for 'yes' answers to all three questions; Mikołajczyk's Peasant Party, still the largest party in Poland, called for 'no' on the issue of the Senate. The communists claimed 68 per cent of the electorate had voted three times 'yes', whereas the true figure (it was to be one of the most guarded secrets of the Polish communist regime) was only 27 per cent. Shocked by the limited support among the population, the communists gave themselves a whole year to intimidate and terrorize their opponents before inviting the country's inhabitants to the polls. The elections held in Poland on 19 January 1947 were blatantly rigged, with the communists and their allies claiming an overwhelming victory (80 per cent of the votes) over Mikołajczyk's Peasant Party.[12] British and US protests at this violation of the Yalta agreement had no effect.

It was already clear by 1946 that other solutions had to be found for those Polish servicemen who still refused to return to the new Soviet-dominated Poland. In the circumstances, the British authorities had little choice but to bring to Britain all the remaining Polish forces on the European continent and the Middle East (now numbering 137,000), and later also the soldiers' dependants scattered in the Middle East and in camps in East Africa and India. In September 1946, the British government announced the creation of the so-called Polish Resettlement Corps, a non-combatant unit of the British Army, with the objective of preparing those men and women for settlement and employment as civilians in the United Kingdom. The Corps was eventually joined by 114,000 Polish soldiers; it was to function for two years and was commanded by General Stanisław Kopański, who was more amenable to the British than General Anders. The Corps also included Polish sailors, while the British Air Ministry made separate arrangements for members of the Polish Air Force. The Polish Resettlement Act of March 1947, which reorganized the financing of the welfare provisions for the Poles in British care, was to complete the arrangements. On 17 September 1946 Michał was formally released from Polish military service and the following day enlisted with the Polish Resettlement Corps. As for Irena, she was released from the Corps of Nurses on 1 May 1946 and was demobilized on 1 October 1947.[13]

Eastwood offered Irena sanctuary, but life there was not without anxieties. First of all, she was undernourished: she was breastfeeding me, yet the portions of food served elegantly at the communal table were inadequate for her needs. She felt too embarrassed and shy to ask for larger helpings. Instead she would purchase additional bread in nearby Dunkeld which she ate with water, until it occurred to the staff to let her have extra milk. She also picked edible bracket fungus off a fallen pine tree which she then salted. In general, Irena was distressed by the waste of food at Eastwood. She cited the case of the resident cook, who had several children by Polish soldiers and who was ordered to throw away the leftovers of a gateau to the chickens rather than be allowed to take the food home to her children.[14] Irena was delighted by the interest shown in the Poles by the duchess who was well known for her public condemnation of the use of forced labour in the USSR in the early 1930s, for her support of the

Republican cause during the Spanish Civil War and for her opposition to Appeasement (she resigned her parliamentary seat in 1938 as a protest). As the Second World War progressed, the duchess had become increasingly critical of the Soviet treatment of the Poles and in November 1944 assumed the chairmanship of the British League for European Freedom which campaigned against Soviet control of the countries of eastern Europe. Nonetheless, when Irena started talking at the table about her Siberian tribulations, the duchess looked daggers at her and silenced her.[15] One suspects that on that occasion the duchess simply had no wish to discuss distressing subjects at mealtimes, for her commitment to the Polish cause was considerable. Indeed, it is quite likely that Irena was one of her sources about conditions in the USSR. In her part-autobiography the duchess recorded how she had informed one of her MP friends (Eleanor Rathbone) about 'what I had learned from Poles in Perthshire, who had been among the thousands deported to forced labour from Eastern Poland early in the war and whom the Soviet government had released under the Treaty it signed with the Polish government in exile when the Germans attacked Russia'.[16]

There were positive aspects of life at Eastwood. Irena's intellectual curiosity led her to the large library in the house. Although her English was still very basic, she was able to work her way through Aldous Huxley's illustrated biography of Darwin. 'I then understood', she was to write later, 'that evolution was a fact, whereas at my convent school belief in evolution had been condemned as a grave sin'.[17] At Eastwood Irena was also able to meet other Polish officers and to receive visitors: relatives and friends who were in the Polish armed forces and who were also stranded in Britain. One such visitor (in August 1946) was Witek Kontkowski, husband of Irena's cousin Mila, who had spent virtually the whole war as a prisoner of war in Germany. Once at the table when bread rolls were served, he took two while everyone else took only one. Irena quietly remarked that this was not a proper thing to do, to which Witek replied (also in Polish): 'I take no pity on the English.' At this moment the duchess's brother-in-law, Lord James Murray, who had mastered the Polish language during his long and strong association with the Polish forces stationed in Scotland since 1940, turned to Witek and in excellent Polish started telling him about his hunting trips to Poland before the war. Irena's heart sank as she feared this incident might lead to her dismissal from Eastwood. As it was, Lord James Murray was more than well disposed towards the Poles and nothing more was made of the matter.[18]

Another familiar face was Werner Amberg who, after imprisonment in the USSR, had served as an officer in General Anders's Second Corps and was in a quandary as what to do next. He was betrothed to Irena's cousin Jadzia Przybytko, who had recently returned to the new Poland from her Siberian exile and had thrown in her lot with the new regime there. Both Werner and Jadzia hoped to be reunited, but Werner was not prepared to risk returning to Poland, while Jadzia cherished the hope that he would join her there. They were never to meet again. Their personal tragedy was one of many caused by the political-ideological divide that had descended on Europe in the aftermath of the war.[19]

A more cheerful visitor was Commander Kamiński who enjoyed fishing in a nearby lake. On one occasion, his young Polish wife prepared a pike in jelly for the guests who were delighted with this gastronomic novelty, for freshwater fish was not eaten at Eastwood. The commander also presented Irena with a skinned eel which she marinated and ate in slices over several days. Also a guest at Eastwood was Lieutenant-Colonel Zbigniew Belina-Prażmowski, a Knight of Malta, who lived with his English wife in Glasgow. Irena remembered well his comment on Poland's westward shift on the map of Europe: 'Stalin's stroke of genius! There's coal there [in the ex-German lands], while there's only poverty in the [lost] eastern provinces.'[20] How this remark was received by Irena is not recorded. Belina-Prażmowski was something of a philatelist and persuaded Irena to send him interesting stamps, which helps to explain why so many of the foreign letters preserved from that time by Irena unfortunately have had their stamps removed.

Irena also made friends with several Scottish women. Mrs Theodosia de Lingen, whose daughter was the head surgeon in Edinburgh, was a kindred religious soul with a shared love of nature. Another close religious friend was Mrs Dorothy Ellaby who signed a Christmas card to me as 'Auntie Ellaby'. Kindly and efficient, Dorothy had provided invaluable help to the duchess's husband in the running of a hospital in Blair Castle during the First World War and in looking after child evacuees from Glasgow during the Second. Both Theodosia and Dorothy were to write warm letters to Irena long after she had left Eastwood. Another friend was Margaret Fairlie, a woman with clerical Catholic contacts, who kept bees.

Although far away in Scotland, Irena was not burdened with cooking or running a household; she was thus able to devote much time to corresponding with her many relatives, friends and former neighbours. Cousin Zygmunt Protassewicz (in the United States since October 1939) had been able to furnish her with information in early 1944 about the family in occupied Poland, but he had no news after the Warsaw Uprising and shared Irena's concern for her mother and sisters. No sooner had the war ended than Irena's surviving relatives in Poland, most of them dispersed across the country as a result of Warsaw's destruction and the boundary changes, began to seek each other out, sometimes through appeals on the radio. By the end of 1945 a family network by letter had been restored. Irena continued to write to addresses which no longer existed, but all that was needed was for just one letter to be forwarded to reach the addressee; in this case her aunt Jadzia Jamontt who now found herself in Katowice in Upper Silesia.[21] The family bush telegraph soon spread the news that Irena was alive, in Scotland, and married.

Particularly moving are the first letters Irena received from her family in Poland in early 1946. Although Irena's mother (who had made over a dozen enquiries through the Red Cross during the war) had received an unofficial report in 1943 via the Red Cross that Irena was then in Palestine, to have it confirmed that her eldest daughter was safe in Britain and married was true joy: 'Thanks to Almighty God that I have found you and that your lot has been settled.'[22] Yet she clearly still had no idea that Irena was in the army, for she asked 'why did you move to the north from a place with such a beautiful climate?',[23] as if Irena had any choice in the matter.

Irena's mother, her two sisters Jula and Hania, Jula's children, and cousin Stefan Protassewicz had lost everything in Warsaw and eventually found somewhere to live in the seaside resort of Sopot, which had escaped extensive damage during the Red Army's advance on neighbouring Gdynia and Gdańsk in March 1945. During the course of

1946 Irena received twenty letters and postcards from her mother, who gave her brief accounts of the wartime fates of relatives and friends; in some cases the accounts had to be cryptic, as in the case of Kazio Protassewicz who had been sent to the Gulag in 1945 ('as for Kazio – he's gone far away').[24] Her mother was an exceptionally good source of information, for as she wrote to Irena in March 1946, 'I correspond with many members of the family and acquaintances, because as displaced wanderers we should all keep in touch, and it is my only pleasure in our present circumstances'.[25] Yet it remained frustrating that letters took a long time and did not always arrive in the right chronological order: for example, Irena's letter to her mother of 15 May 1946 did not arrive in Sopot until 10 August, whereas a letter of 16 June arrived several days before the one of 15 May. On one occasion in late April 1946 Irena's mother was able to send a letter to Irena via a person travelling to Britain; she was then able to write in greater detail about the family losses during the war ('nothing but sadness') and suggested that Irena and her family should join cousin Zygmunt in America.[26]

There were also letters from her sisters, her aunts and other close relatives. Her sister Hania still could not quite believe that Irena had survived: 'To see your handwriting makes a big impression, for in my mind you are a mystical figure. There were stories that you were seen dead near Borki etc. Because of that you'll live long…'.[27] Sister Jula's first letter started: 'I am so happy that you're alive…'.[28] Her cousin Mila Kontkowska, who had not seen her own husband since 1939, wrote: 'You have won the lottery, and really it's so fortunate that you got married after the war'.[29] Irena's seventy-nine-year-old aunt Marynia Świackiewicz (now resettled from Wilno in Katowice) expressed a sad nostalgia for their lost world:

> To be sure, you were well known in our country for your generosity, kind-heartedness and diligence, and still today I have before my eyes the image of you as you were when I last saw you in Borki. From very early in the morning you are in your beekeeping outfit, or in your gardening clothes, and then you hurry with a bag to the villages to bring medical help to peasants, who are grateful to you. You were the pride of the family, a position you inherited from your father and my most beloved late brother. Yes, my dearest Ireneczka, everything collapsed under our feet; there remain only sorrow, pain and a boundless longing for everyone and everything!!![30]

Irena also received information from her cousin Halina Skrzyńska who had secretly left Poland across the Soviet zone of Germany (at one stage disguised as an American soldier) to join her husband Henryk, recently released after three and a half years spent in Nazi concentration camps, in the British zone.

Irena was thirsty for news and asked after everyone, as if trying to pick up pieces of her former life that had been shattered in 1939. She learnt of the deaths of her brother-in-law Janek Karczewski (in Auschwitz), of her mother's sister Janka Górska, of Marzeńka Protassewicz (Uncle Antoni's widow), of her much-loved cousin Leoś Protassewicz, of Aunt Mila Zbroja's husband Zygmunt (in Katyn) and of her good friend Hela Jamontt who had perished in the Warsaw Uprising and whose body still lay under rubble in the ruins of the city in April 1946.[31] She learnt of her sister Jula's second marriage and of her sister Hania's unlucky double widowhood and her role during the Warsaw Uprising when she sang in cellars and shelters to the resistance fighters.[32] Irena learnt that her elegant aunt Jadwiga Jamontt's apartment in Wilcza Street in Warsaw, where Irena had been a frequent guest, was no more and that Jadwiga was now in Katowice; that Aunt Kama (widow of Uncle Piotr Protassewicz of Rohotenka) with her widowed daughter Mila Zbroja and two granddaughters had settled in Zabrze (pre-war Hindenburg) in Upper Silesia where Mila was able to land a good job in industry; that Aunt Salunia Połubińska and her daughter Mila Kontkowska and grandchildren had been 'repatriated' from Wilno and were now virtually destitute in Kraków; that Uncle Wilhelm's widow and her cousin Kazio's wife and children had also left Wilno and were in a resettlement camp in northern Poland; and that her cousin Halina Kostrowicka and her children had returned from their Siberian exile. Halina Kostrowicka wrote a long moving letter from Szczecin in August 1946 about her 'getting out from [the Soviet] paradise' and about her 'compulsory health cure in the east'. With Irena's recent marriage in mind, she also added: 'I'm glad that you've ceased to be an impregnable fortress…'.[33]

Some of Irena's pre-war neighbours near Borki had also survived the war and had been 'repatriated' to the new Poland; among them was Julia Sidorowicz of Ladzinki whose family had offered Irena shelter before her deportation in 1941. She also resumed contact with the Hofmans who in June 1946 had returned from Palestine to their home in Kraków, as well as with Professor Lutosławski who with his family had spent the war in Kraków and who had resumed lecturing at the reopened university there. The eccentricity of the eighty-seven-year-old philosopher, who had once proposed marriage to Irena to be his wife in their next reincarnated life, had not abated. He continued to sign his letters as 'Your father' or simply 'Father', as if he still considered himself to be Irena's spiritual mentor; he even asked my mother for a photograph of my palm, or at least a drawing of the lines on my hand, so that he could establish 'a competent verdict about his [my] probable destiny'.[34] Halina Skrzyńska shared her amusement with Irena about Lutosławski's request: 'At the same time, you will land him in the hands of the U.B. [Polish communist secret police], since they will think that this is an aerial photograph for espionage …'.[35] Irena even enquired about her one-time suitors. Her mother informed her that Tadeusz Stulgiński, the sculptor, was alive, but that a different fate had probably awaited Hans Albert Reinkemeyer, the student from Berlin, who had visited Irena's mother in Warsaw in 1943: 'Albert didn't say much then. He asked after you, but because he was heading for the [eastern] front he did not have much time for his visit. He probably perished. He believed in his country's victory, but miscalculated.'[36]

Indeed, Eastwood became almost like a nerve centre for the flow of information across divided Europe and even across continents. Some information was urgently needed: Irena's cousin Mila Kontkowska, dispossessed and working at night as a telephone operator, was at her wits end as to how to feed and provide for her mother (Salunia), her two children and an elderly family servant, all cramped now in two rooms in Kraków. Since 1944 Mila had had no contact with her husband Witek, then a prisoner in Germany and now, in 1945, with the Polish Second Corps in Italy. At the same time Witek had no idea about his family's whereabouts. Mila was desperate: 'Have pity on me; help me to make contact with Witek! [...] Perhaps he's gone further south [Italy]; tell him to try and help us materially, if he possibly can.'[37] For Mila, Irena's letters were 'the only glimmer of hope'.[38] Irena made enquiries and was able to report that Witek was alive in Britain; she became a conduit for Mila's letters to him, letters which urged him to return to his family. Irena informed her own mother about the whereabouts of her mother's sisters Irena Valdi-Gołębiowska and Mania Żórawska, both still stranded in the Middle East. She wrote to Poland about her cousin Polik Protassewicz who, on account of his military position, had to be discreet in his contact with relatives there. Indeed, in all the correspondence of this period Polik was referred to as a female 'Pola' or 'Apolonja' to mislead the communist censors. Irena was able to pass messages from her cousin by marriage Zbigniew Kątkowski, who was a junior officer in the Second Corps in Italy and unable to write directly to Poland, to his mother.[39] Correspondence between the British zone of occupation in Germany and Poland was still unreliable and letters took many weeks. So Irena served as a link between Halina Skrzyńska in Lübeck and her mother Jadwiga Jamontt in Katowice. The Hellers, still in Palestine until 1947, were also in touch with Irena and enquired about the prospects for life in Britain. Halina Kostrowicka still had no idea about what had happened to her husband Daniel, but had heard rumours (false as it turned out) that he had been seen in Tehran in 1945, and asked Irena to investigate. Likewise, Jerzy Turzański, the last pre-war administrator of the Borki estate, asked Irena via her mother to find out the whereabouts of his nephew, the one who had spent his all too brief honeymoon in Borki in 1939.[40] Irena was able to provide a detailed account to Fela Hernas (née Bartoszewicz) in Poland about the death from typhus of her mother Franciszka Bartoszewiczowa, Irena's good companion during her time in Siberia and Soviet Central Asia. Fela had been waiting for her mother's return in vain, but found consolation in the fact that 'although she died in a foreign land, you, a close friend, were with her'.[41] In July 1947 Irena was even contacted by her old neighbour Wanda Roycewicz who had made a dramatic escape on horseback from Rohotna to Wilno in 1939, and had then succeeded in getting as far as Brazil. Wanda asked Irena for news of her old home, of her neighbours in the east, of the local Jews and of her family chapel.[42]

What was also remarkable, bearing in mind that Irena had a young child to look after and that Dunkeld was a small town with limited resources, was her ability to purchase items that were in short supply, or which were non-existent in Poland, and to send parcels to her nearest and dearest there. Judging by notes in her diary and the acknowledgements she received, Irena must have sent scores of parcels – and in some cases continued to do so for many years into the 1960s and beyond. She would put me in a pram and set off on foot for Dunkeld to conduct her business. It is highly probable that she also made trips to Perth for that purpose. Items sent included clothes and underwear for adults and children, shoes, sandals and material for suits; heels for shoes, sewing machine needles and thread; and medicines. Food ranged from raisins, tea, cocoa and sardines to orange juice and cod liver oil. There were some cosmetics, especially for her sister Hania who had resumed her artistic career (performances on stage, for Polish Radio, and later teaching at the Musical Academy in Gdańsk). Michał occasionally sent cigarettes to his mother-in-law who was very grateful although she regretted that she could not be of practical help to Michał and Irena as a good mother-in-law should be. Even Irena, who abhorred smoking, occasionally sent cigarettes to her nearly octogenarian aunt Marynia Świackiewicz who, like her late brother Wacław, was a regular smoker. Parcels valued at over £5 required export licences from the Board of Trade.

In 1946–8 Irena collaborated closely with Polik Protassewicz who, having been despatched by the Air Ministry to teach Russian to RAF personnel in different parts of the country, was not able to send parcels directly to Poland under his own name. Instead he sent them as if from Irena. His long list of items included old parachutes which could be turned into dresses, and leather which was particularly expensive in Poland. Irena's sister Hania admitted frankly in August 1946: 'It was you who clothed Mama, for she went around without the most necessary items'; and again in February 1947: 'Your parcels are a godsend, and have clothed us.' Sister Jula, with her characteristic down-to-earth attitude, praised Irena's generosity but also warned her not to allow herself to be exploited. Irena despatched clothes parcels to Germany to Halina Skrzyńska (who reimbursed her in pounds sterling) and who in November 1946 wrote poetically to Irena: 'You are so dear and such a family person, like that lime tree growing in front of the porch in Borki – with deep family roots – bringing together and embracing with its boughs the scattered surviving members of the wider family from the borderlands!'[43] In April 1947 Halina Skrzyńska thanked Irena for her 'heart of gold which you have inherited from dear Uncle Wacio and your mother in a Borki symbiosis' and for her cheerful letters: 'There are always touches of humour in your epistles, at times apostolic ...'.[44] Irena even sent parcels to several former villagers from Borki and its neighbourhood who had opted for 'repatriation' to the new Poland.

By the end of 1947 Irena had also learnt much about what had happened in Borki after the arrival there of the Germans in 1941. This information, some of which does not feature in her account written from memory twenty years later, came from individuals who had been in or near Borki during the period of the German occupation. The first rudimentary news that the manor house had survived reached Irena in late 1946 from her mother who had received the first of several letters from Borki (now in the USSR) from Wiera Borodziuk, who had been a servant at the manor house. This was followed in 1947 by very informative letters from Poland: from a former resident of Borki who identified herself only as Hela; from Ala Witbekowa, wife of a fisherman in Borki who had probably been employed on Wacław's carp farm; and from Irena's cousin Kamilla (Mila) Zbroja of Rohotenka who had fled to Wilno in 1939 but who returned to the area during the German occupation, and only survived 'through simply extraordinary good luck and the intuition of a hunted animal', as she put it.[45] Very detailed accounts also reached Irena in 1947 from Ninka Stabrowska (distantly related to Irena by marriage) who had also returned to the region after 1941. Ninka joined the Polish Home Army in the Słonim area; in 1946 she left for the new Poland, only to move on to the British zone of Germany to be reunited with her husband Tolik, an officer in the Polish Army stationed there. From Germany she was able to write freely of what had happened in the east. All these witness accounts make a coherent and complementary story, as follows.

Soon after the Germans had driven the Soviets from the territory of pre-war eastern Poland, Ryszard Protassewicz (probably a distant cousin of Irena's; it has not been possible to establish the precise relationship) arrived from Wilno, recovered much of the livestock and tools pillaged in 1939 and set about restoring the former Borki estate as a functioning economic unit, hoping to secure its future for Irena's family.[46] Impressed by his industry, the Germans even supplied him with cattle and horses. Pan Majewski, who had helped Irena escape from Borki to Ladzinki in 1940, became the Borki storekeeper, while Ala Witbekowa's husband was put in charge of breeding fish. Even a new orchard was established and was looked after by Fiodor, Irena's former beekeeping assistant. Of course, all farms of the region were obliged to supply the Germans with food stuffs; as a result they were later to become targets for Soviet partisans.[47] At the same time Ryszard Protassewicz was a member of the Polish Home Army and was secretly supplying its local unit in the forest. Tragedy struck at the end of 1943: Ryszard was betrayed to the Germans by several of his own people. Both he and Majewski, together with a large number of youngsters from Rohotna who considered themselves Polish and had joined the Home Army, were burnt alive in a barn in Zdzięcioł. Local people buried their remains in a common grave; an annual Mass for their souls was said for several years afterwards. With Ryszard gone, the Borki estate could only decline. Soviet partisans became active in the area: they burnt down Rohotenka, the farm in Ladzinki, the building raised by Irena before the war in Wielkie Pole (the Great Field), and the Borki barns and stables. The Borki manor survived because it was fortified and defended by the Germans. The starchworks, a solid stone building, also avoided destruction. With the approach of the Red Army in 1944, the Germans quickly left. Nearby towns suffered terribly as the front swept westwards: the centres of Słonim and Baranowicze went up in flames, and Lida was totally destroyed.

Irena asked for news of people she had known, including local Jews. It appears that her former assistant Fiodor was eventually conscripted by the Germans but escaped to the partisans (whether Polish or Soviet is not known), only to be recaptured and shot in Słonim. Irena's servant Mania was still unmarried and lived in poor conditions but attended church regularly. There was no sign of Father Goj, the parish priest in Rohotna, since his arrest by the Soviets in 1939. The Jewish dentist Gomuliński and his wife, who had so impressed Irena in 1939–40, had joined the partisans. There was no reliable news of Dr Atlas. Both Lejzer, the Jewish butcher who had given shelter to Irena and her mother in 1939, as well as Mojsze, who had so bravely collected the statues of the vandalized chapel in Rohotna, had perished, together with thousands of other local Jews, in the ghetto in Słonim. In that context it must have been of some consolation for Irena to hear in 1949 from her aunt Salunia Połubińska (who obtained this information from Mila Zbroja) that old Abramek 'had died peacefully before the arrival of terrible times'.[48] Irena's father had been very fond of Abramek and before the First World War had helped him out during the collection of funds to defend Dreyfus.

Irena must have been particularly touched by Ala Witbekowa's letters in which she wrote how she, Pan Gebel and Pan Majewski had grieved bitterly when Irena had been deported in 1941, and that her youngest daughter, who had died in 1943, had been buried in Rohotna near Irena's father's grave. Ala had planted flowers near his grave, and 'had watered them with tears because the poor master lies alone, far away from all his closest family'. Ala also added, with disarming naivety and nostalgia, that she and her husband, who had been resettled in the far west of the new Poland, prayed to God that Irena might yet return to Borki, and that her husband could work for her there breeding fish.[49] But none of that was to be. Since 1939 and by 1946 most of Irena's relatives and close friends had either been killed, deported, 'repatriated' or had fled the area which was now back again in Stalin's totalitarian grip. Gone too were all the familiar local Jews who had been an integral element of society there. More sober was Ninka Stabrowska's assessment that Ryszard Protassewicz's and her project of reviving Borki was the mere 'dreams of a decapitated head'. She recorded how many Belarusians begged her and other Poles not to leave, seeing in them almost a guarantee that Poland would return to their parts. But Ninka saw the larger picture and tentatively put all these developments in a wide historical perspective: 'In general we had to move out, and perhaps for good, like our people in the Kiev and Minsk provinces had to leave after the previous war. What do you think about this since you moved among people with a totally different view of the world? I'm very curious.'[50] Irena must have been pleased to know that her old home and the parish church in Rohotna (soon to be closed by the Soviet authorities) had survived the horrific cataclysm that had befallen the land of her ancestors. But she must have been under no illusions by then that her lost world could ever return. Mila Zbroja's account of destroyed towns, burnt manor houses, of others in a state of ruin, of woods cut down and of abandoned fields was hardly encouraging: 'A picture of misery and despair. Time does its own. Desolation and ruin staring out of every corner.'[51]

Although both Irena and Michał had the right to remain in Britain, this had clearly not been their wartime dream. They were also no doubt well aware of the immediate post-war hostility to the continuing Polish presence in Scotland among some Scottish trade unionists and members of the Labour Party, as well as some militant Protestants.[52] Furthermore, the prospect of manual work which faced the majority of the now stateless members of the Polish Resettlement Corps did not appeal to Michał with his qualifications and proficiency for languages. Yet to return to a Soviet-controlled Poland was not an attractive proposition. It was an issue that bothered them for several years: where to go, and what to do? Already in late 1945 cousin Zygmunt Protassewicz had planted the idea in their minds that they could join him in America: 'It would be good if we could all gather in one place and keep together. I am convinced that, more than in any other country, it is in the United States where it is, and will continue to be, easiest to arrange a new existence and attain a higher standard of living.'[53] Irena's mother, aware of and worried by Irena's and Michał's forced separation, encouraged them throughout much of 1946 to accept Zygmunt's invitation. Then in October 1946 she mentioned for the first time the idea of Irena and Michał returning to Poland, and continued in that vein into 1947. She was longing to see her eldest daughter, a sentiment that was poignantly felt with the approach of Christmas: 'What a pity we can't gather round the same Christmas tree.'[54] Not least was her concern that Irena was suffering in the terribly harsh British winter of 1946–7, especially since she had been informed that British homes had no proper heating, only open fireplaces![55] In April 1947 Irena's sister Hania also asked if they might return.

Other voices from Poland were even more emphatic. Jadzia Przybytko, committed to the new realities there, wrote from Warsaw:

I'm interested to know when you're going to return to the homeland, for I have no doubt that you will return. Truly, it is a waste of every person of worth who is not here, for there is so much to do, and I think that you over there do not understand this, and have no idea at all about our present reality. You know, Irenka, I would so much like to receive a detailed letter from you, for I'm unable to understand you. […] I'm very interested to hear about your life, but I feel for you, because I think that nostalgia must be tormenting you.[56]

Professor Lutosławski made the case even more forcefully:

You ask whether it is better to stay in Scotland or to emigrate? What does that mean? After all, Scotland is already emigration. At the moment it is better for Poles to return home, even their duty. Those who emigrate find that their national consciousness fades away. […] What keeps you in Scotland? Today all Poles are needed in Poland. Even in prison they can do more for Poland than if they remain abroad. But not everyone by any means is in danger of imprisonment.[57]

Nevertheless, in a previous letter Lutosławski said his son Tadeusz was in England and was doing well (apparently as a stockbroker), without attaching any criticism to his conduct.[58] By 1950 Tadeusz Lutosławski was in the Bahamas![59] Adela Grunowa, a former neighbour from the east, described her new life near Szczecin in brave and positive terms; she spoke of her beekeeping, and expressed regret that Irena had not returned.[60]

Some displaced people were returning to Poland from the West, including members of Michał's own closest family: his sister Wisia (Jadwiga) Strawińska, who had been in the Home Army and ended up in a German prisoner-of-war camp after the Warsaw Uprising, as well as his widowed mother who, after Siberian exile, had spent the rest of the war working as a school teacher in a Polish camp in Valivade in British India. Irena's cousin Witek Kontkowski agonized for many months about whether to return: 'Mila's letters sadden me so much that I feel helpless here, and yet I would not like to share Kazik's fate on returning to the homeland [Kazimierz Protassewicz had been sent to the Gulag in 1945]. I am totally at a loss.'[61] Or again:

Since returning from you a month ago I have been in a state of terrible moral indecisiveness. I conclude from Mila's letters and those from my sister that they expect me to return, whereas reason and considerations of state tell me not to. In view of my age I have no guarantee of employment here or of earning more [than what I receive now], so if I stay while continuing to help the family I shall be really pressed for money. My nerves can't cope any more with the separation. So what to do? If at least I could be certain that I could get them over here. Really, Ireneczka, I'm no longer able to think logically.[62]

In December 1946 Witek finally took the decision to go 'into the great unknown', and felt better for it.[63] He left Britain in March 1947 to rejoin his family in Kraków, after seven and a half years' forced absence. Zofia Turska, Irena's fellow nurse from their time together in the USSR and now living in a camp in Herefordshire, also opted for Poland after much soul-searching:

> What plans do you have for the future? Stay here, look for work somewhere abroad, or return to our homeland? […] [H]ere at the moment this is a subject constantly debated and talked about, for people themselves do not know what to do. Personally I have decided to return to Poland to be finally together with my family and to end this lonely wandering around the world; but I don't know what the family there will write about my decision.[64]

But there were other voices too. Irena's close friend and a former member of the medical staff at Taymouth Castle, Wanda (born Lisowska) and her husband Mirek Lekis, a junior Polish officer, seriously considered going to Argentina or Brazil and wondered if Irena and Michał would come as well; at other times they proposed that they should all join forces and take over a farm somewhere in Britain. The latter idea even reached Polik Protassewicz who expressed an interest and tried to dampen Michał's early enthusiasm for America. At the same time, the Hellers, who had decided to head from Palestine to England, hoped to arrange their lives there together with Irena. Ninka and Tolik Stabrowski, both now in a resettlement camp in Shropshire, were committed to Argentina and praised conditions there, not least the Argentinian government's favourable attitude to Polish immigrants. 'We have the impression', added Ninka, 'that it will take time for order to be restored in Europe. It's better therefore, without a doubt, to settle where there is no threat of a storm, for we have already gone through so much.'[65] The Skrzyńskis too, although stranded in the British zone of Germany, contemplated a future life somewhere outside Europe, where they feared war would come again soon, and even suggested humorously that together with Irena they could set up a *kolkhoz* in Argentina or Canada, with an orchard, a nursery for children and bees for pollination.[66]

Michał was unhappy living so far away from Irena. It was also clear that his post in the convalescent home would end in September 1947. Without a job he would have to rely on the limited pay offered to members of the Polish Resettlement Corps and face the prospect of menial work with a resulting loss of status. Most Poles then in Britain, even those with higher education, had to enter the British labour market at a low level, unless they were doctors and pharmacists whose qualifications were recognized, or graduates from British universities. And where could Michał and Irena live as a family? His thoughts began to turn towards the possibility of returning to Poland. But Irena had hoped that the warmly disposed Professor Studnicki, who had been to Borki before the war and was now in London and engaged in research in Chatham House, would be able to find suitable employment for Michał. In view of Michał's knowledge and personal experience of Russia, Studnicki suggested work for the British government as monitor and translator of the Soviet press. In December 1947 he even invited Michał to London to meet a contact, a British officer. The officer failed to turn up and did not reply to Studnicki's letters.

In the meantime, Witek Kontkowski, who had returned to his family in Poland, visited Irena's mother in Sopot in May 1947 and was able to give a first-hand account of life in Eastwood.[67] Irena's sister Jula reported that after talking to Witek it was difficult to establish where life would be better. Irena's mother's assessment was calm and realistic: 'One can live anywhere; one has only to get used to post-war conditions. The young will arrange their lives; for us of the older generation it is somewhat harder.'[68] Her mother's subsequent postcards carried mixed messages: she hinted at Irena returning to Poland, but also admitted that she and the family in Sopot were very dependent on parcels from abroad. In September 1947, she wrote: 'On the whole we have been clothed and shod by Polik, Zygmunt and you, because here you can only just earn enough to feed yourself, whereas everyone has relatives somewhere over the seas and it is only because of their kindness that people don't walk around in rags.'[69] She added in the same card that her sister Irena Valdi-Gołębiowska had made the right decision not to return. Jula too sent mixed messages: she invited Irena to come and live with her, yet at the same time informed her that Aunt Mania Żórawska strongly regretted returning to Poland from Iran.

And then, towards mid-October 1947, Jula received a letter from Irena and Michał asking whether they could find a roof over their heads in Sopot. There was great excitement in Sopot, as the whole family there gathered to discuss the matter. Replying immediately, Irena's mother suggested they could join her and Hania, adding: 'It's surely better to return here than to go over the sea.' She reassured Michał that with his commercial maritime qualification and knowledge of languages he was bound to find decent work in nearby Gdynia or Gdańsk, and that in due course they should be in a position to obtain new and better accommodation: 'The main thing is to settle and, as they say, to strike roots, and after that life will sort itself out.' She advised them what to bring and ended her missive: 'I enclose kisses to all three of you – perhaps we'll see each other soon!'[70] Jula too encouraged them to come as soon as possible for the autumn was mild. She added that if Dr Darski was in Gdynia or Gdańsk he would surely find a job for Michał.[71] Dr Darski had been one of Michał's lecturers at the School of Foreign Trade and appears to have returned to Poland. Even Irena's aunt Mania Żórawska, who had reconciled herself to life in Poland after the delights of wartime Iran, now spoke cautiously about their return, reminding Irena that she had two useful professions (beekeeping and nursing).[72] Michał's mother, now settled in Wrocław (formerly Breslau) after her return from India, was delighted that Michał and his family were going to return, while Michał's aunt Zofia Wyszyńska, who had survived the Nazi concentration camp for women in Ravensbrück, added encouraging words to the same letter: 'My dears, you are doing the right thing. Return. For those like Mynio [Michał] there will be work in the coastal region and elsewhere in the homeland, and in posts abroad where educated people are needed. At the moment I have contacts with [officials dealing with] Romania.'[73] Mila Kontkowska and her mother Salunia Połubińska, on the contrary, expressed alarm at this turn of events and strongly discouraged Irena and Michał from returning to Poland in favour of joining Zygmunt in America where they would be 'further away from this rottenness!'[74] Indeed, Mila's and Salunia's letters of 1946 and 1947 frequently contained, in a more or less cryptic and ironic form, negative references to deteriorating living conditions in Poland and the creeping Sovietization.

What emerges is that Irena and Michał were not of the same mind on this issue. A few weeks later Irena wrote to her mother that their plans had changed and that they were likely to join Wanda Roycewicz in Brazil. Yet Michał was still set on returning. Irena's mother did her best to encourage him in a separate letter of 11 November: 'I consider it the most natural thing to do to return to your own people.' They could stay in Jula's flat at 4, Chopin Street. And would they come before or after Christmas? She ended with a characteristic ironic touch: 'In general we all have déclassé hands [coarsened through hard physical work], but what can we do?' A day later Jula fired off a strong message: she urged Irena not to be swayed by Mila Kontkowska's negative view of life in Poland, nor to go to Brazil where Wanda Roycewicz lived alone and understandably sought company. She appealed: 'Irenka! Surely <u>the advice of your closest [relatives] is the most sincere and the best</u>. Nowhere on earth can you find paradise, but it's easier to live among those close to you than amongst strangers, especially since over here you will have a roof over your head and work, something you will not get there.' She gave useful advice as to what to bring with them, and described the many (undeniable) advantages of where she lived in Sopot. She concluded: 'I wait impatiently for a letter from Irena, for she has recently caused us concern by suddenly going back on her decision, and without offering any reasons. I hope that <u>she won't now lose</u> her resolve and that she will <u>prepare for her return</u>.'[75] In early December Jula was still hopeful, but remained puzzled by Irena's reluctance. Her daughters were so happy expecting to meet their cousin Wacio, and now they were sad, she wrote. 'Irenka! Tell us absolutely frankly why you don't want to return, and why at the same time you are upsetting Michał who wants to be among his own people and who wrote that he feels ill at ease there [in Britain]. [...] But perhaps we might spend Christmas Eve together; we have enough fuel, coal and wood, to last us until the spring.'[76]

Sometime in December 1947 or early 1948 Irena wrote to Sopot that they would definitely not return to Poland, and that after five months without work Michał had found a new job (which Irena did not specify) which would permit the family to live together. The disappointment in Sopot was as great as the sense of puzzlement. Irena's mother continued to ask for reasons, which were not forthcoming. What did finally end the idea of returning to Poland? Was it news that sister Jula was expecting her third child which would make living with her difficult if not impossible? Was it unpleasant news of rows between Jula and Hania over where their mother should live, over their widely different lifestyles, and over valuables inherited from dead aunts? Was it the prospect of material difficulties in Poland? Was it the offer of work for Michał as a stores and accommodation officer at the Polish resettlement camp near Morpeth in Northumberland? Or was it politics, a subject not even hinted at in the correspondence from Sopot?

How would Michał have been treated by the authorities in Poland? True, he had not been an officer, but he had been a rising civil servant in pre-war 'reactionary-bourgeois' Poland, and his class background stood against him. Would the communists have agreed for him to hold a responsible post in one of Poland's ports where contact with foreigners and spies (real and imagined) would be possible? Yet in a normal course of events there would have been much to do in Poland whose ports had been terribly damaged during the war. But it was not the Poland Michał and Irena had dreamt of. And during the course of 1947 the news from Poland got worse and worse: the rigged election was followed by a brutal campaign against Mikołajczyk's Peasant Party, the only remaining independent political party in the country, and by a general policy of repression. In fear of his life, Mikołajczyk fled Poland on 21 October. The communists next set about turning the Peasant Party into an obedient adjunct of their own power structure. Polish parliamentary life had become a parody. The Soviet grip on Poland was tightening: in July, under Soviet pressure, the Warsaw government withdrew its application to participate in the Marshall Plan, while Poland's armed forces remained controlled at all senior levels of command by the Red Army. All this was taking place in the context of a darkening international situation. Bitter disagreements between the Western Powers and the USSR over the future of Germany, the announcement of the Truman Doctrine (March 1947) and the creation of the Cominform in Moscow (September 1947) only confirmed that the Cold War had set in for good.

News, comments and advice from relatives and friends in Britain were also discouraging. Sometime in autumn 1947 Polik reported that one Polish Air Force colonel who had returned to Poland had been arrested, while another could not find work and was asking for parcels. Polik's letter of 21 October (written at the RAF station in Pershore) to Michał on the subject of Poland was hard-hitting:

> I neither encourage nor discourage anyone from going to Poland, because some gain by it and others lose, and there is no prescription for either outcome which anyone can predict. I see that Irenka wants to put you too much under her thumb. In my opinion, the decision whether to return or not should not be swayed by others' views; there should only be sober calculation. [...] But in my opinion you will not get a good post there until you join the [Communist] Party; on the other hand you will earn enough to feed yourselves better than here, but you won't have enough for clothes. But that's not so important because just knowing that you're in Poland will compensate for those shortages. What is at stake is your personal security.[77]

Wanda Lekis was surprised by Irena's earlier decision to return to Poland. She and her husband were set on South America for 'there is no sense in sitting on this island where our husbands can only find manual work'.[78] At that time they had no intention of going to Poland where pay was low and it was difficult to survive. Wanda quoted a friend of theirs, who had a British degree and good English, and who had returned and obtained a good position in the admiralty. He was fortunate, but when his wife came to give birth he was unable to pay the hospital or buy a pram for the child; he was obliged to ask his parents, who were both in Britain, for help. Ninka Stabrowska, preparing for Argentina, was surprised and ironically blunt:

> I have heard about your plans and desire to return to the homeland. I admire your courage, especially now after Mikołajczyk's escape; also, you have left it rather late to decide. Clearly you are looking for new moral sufferings and shocks. Polik told me you are afraid of becoming déclassée. My dear, surely there is no danger of mature people becoming déclassés, whatever profession they follow. A child can be so affected, but it will be up to you to prevent it.[79]

As for Professor Studnicki, he considered that staying in Britain should only be temporary, that another war (this time with the USSR) would come and suggested emigration to the United States, Canada or Argentina.[80] All this was grist to Irena's mill. Her memories of the USSR still tormented her; ultimately, she could not bear the thought of returning to the Soviet world. What clinched the issue was her concern for the future of her son in a Sovietized Poland. She told Michał (as she related to me many years later): 'I don't want Wacio to serve in the Bolshevik army.' And that was that. And of course she could not openly say this to her puzzled mother and sisters in Poland.

Irena had also written for advice to Dr Jan Freundlich with whom she had worked in Palestine and who was now in England in a resettlement camp in Norfolk, before eventually returning to his wife and family in Poland. His thoughtful and highly perceptive reply of 31 January 1948 arrived after Irena's (and Michał's) final decision had been taken, but it merits quoting at length for it puts the whole issue of emigration in a broader context with implications for life in old age and for Polish children born in Britain:

> And now the most important matter: the question of whether to return to the homeland. Do not consult or listen to anyone, because neither your family, nor friends, nor I, literally no one is in a position to offer you an objective reply and wise counsel in a matter which only you and your husband can decide. Not only reason but also intuition, I think, will dictate what you should do! The most I can do in reply to some of the points you make in your reasoning is to offer a few thoughts of my own – not taken from any propaganda scribblings of one side or the other – which may help you to make an easier decision. I do not believe that the political situation will change during the next five to seven years, and who knows, perhaps even longer; but in any case the present division of the world cannot last sixteen years (which you mentioned). If someone is here with a family he has to decide for himself what he prefers: a hard-earned but secure livelihood in an atmosphere of freedom (although somewhat restricted by a planned economy and progressing socialism) and complete personal security, with the possibility of an improved quality of life after many years of residence and naturalization; or, possibly an easier livelihood [in Poland] but in conditions of moral and political suffocation. In the first case, the grown-ups will also not feel happy here because, despite everything, they will have to contend with an alien society which will never regard them as its own, and will never give them the feelings that can only come when one is on one's own native soil, when one can see its familiar landscape and hear one's mother tongue spoken all around. But our children who are brought up and educated here will have almost all the opportunities of assimilating with [British] society, and not to yearn [for Poland] but to feel happy. The children might not feel any difference between themselves and English children around them (although the latter take longer to develop mentally than ours), but we the grown-ups will find it very hard here when it comes to being ill and with the approach of death. Children in Poland are being torn away in many ways from their families, tradition, religion, their native soil and non-materialistic Christian ethics. Here, on the other hand, and this must be stated candidly, our children are

in danger of complete assimilation or, in other words, the loss of their [Polish] national consciousness; unless – like Conrad – they are to suffer from divided feelings, an inferiority complex or guilt, and unhappiness. Perhaps this is not in line with our propaganda (which is correct from the national point of view), but parents who decide to stay in England, or anywhere abroad, should ask themselves what they want for their children: to be unhappy Poles or reasonably happy Englishmen and women?[81]

What impact Dr Freundlich's message had on Irena and Michał is difficult to tell. At any rate, Poland was not to be. Michał started his job in Morpeth on 20 February 1948 and was joined by Irena in early March 1948. At last they were able to live together. On 30 April Irena wrote (in English) to her Scottish friend Theodosia de Lingen: 'I got accustomed to the new place and I am happy in my little home with my family. I do some gardening and shall have in the May one beehive to get honey for children. Hier is much colder than in Eastwood and the spring is rather late, but now all round is green and fresh.'[82] But conditions in the Polish resettlement camp on Morpeth Common, located three miles from the town of Morpeth, were primitive and Michał's pay very modest. The ex-British Army camp had fifty pitched-roof dormitory huts and a number of Nissen huts. The 300 Polish servicemen with families who arrived there in 1946–7 found the huts unfurnished, except for straw mattresses. The huts had no internal walls and housed several families together; there was no running water, heating or cooking facilities. For several years the residents had to rely on communal washrooms, lavatories and a bath house, and had to eat their meals together in a mess hall.[83] On receiving what must have been Irena's frank description of her new conditions, her mother could only offer sympathy: 'poor Michaś has to carry water – you seem to have primitive rural conditions there, like in Belarus'. She added, reflecting a continental suspicion of English cooking: 'and have you got accustomed to the cooking which, it's apparently reported, is not that tasty for Slavonic palates?'[84] Michał's mother also expressed mild concern: 'That English cuisine surely isn't always to your liking.'[85] But Irena still kept her mother in the dark as to what sort of institution Morpeth Common was and what was the nature of Michał's work there.

Irena had a miscarriage in 1947 and lost twins, but was now pregnant again. When her time arrived she returned to Scotland, to Broxburn in West Lothian where there was a Polish maternity unit. During this period, I stayed with my father and attended the camp's nursery. In the autumn of 1948, Irena gave birth to a daughter, Helen. How long Irena and the newborn Helen remained in Broxburn is not recorded. But the family's stay in Morpeth Common proved short. In the spring of 1949 Michał was posted to the other end of England, to another Polish camp, in St Mawgan in Cornwall. There is no record of how Irena, Michał and their two small children made that long journey down the length of England, but what is known is that Irena's beehive was not left behind. The single beehive was a far cry from her large apiary in Borki, but she was determined to revive her beekeeping to supplement the family's modest income, and was to acquire further hives in Cornwall. Soon after arriving at St Mawgan, she again wrote to Theodosia de Lingen: 'We arrived safetely with children and bees in a delightful sunny place, not very far from the sea, 6 miles from Newquay, english riviera. We have well furnished 3 rooms (and small hall) near wood where I keep my bees. Good food. My husband is the Accomondation officer (as before) in the polish camp St. Magwan.'[86] One suspects that, in view of the cramped living quarters in Morpeth and his enlarged family, Michał was transferred by the National Assistance Board, which administered the Polish camps, to St Mawgan where accommodation was clearly much better. And it was in the St Mawgan camp that I was to start attending a Polish school located near the runway of the RAF airfield – with splendid views from my classroom window of Gloster Meteors taxiing before take-off. The residents of the camp had to rely on prepared food brought by lorry: breakfast included large vats of hot milk with cornflakes already inside, soggy rather than crisp!

Although Poland had been ruled out, Irena and Michał had still not decided whether to stay permanently in Britain. The idea of emigrating to America re-emerged and was encouraged by cousin Zygmunt who, with his wife Jadwiga Smosarska, had become US citizens in 1947, and who was therefore in a strong position to issue an invitation. In June 1948 Zygmunt informed Michał that the US Congress had just agreed to allow 200,000 displaced persons from Europe to enter the United States over the following two years. Two-fifths of such places were to be reserved for people from the Baltic States and from what had been eastern Poland (regions annexed by the USSR); Polish ex-servicemen with relatives in the United States could be considered also as a special case.[87] Irena and Michał accepted his offer, and in October Zygmunt informed them that he would send an affidavit, a condition required by the US immigration authorities, vouchsafing for the new arrivals and promising them shelter and upkeep until they had found employment. Zygmunt reassured Michał that job prospects in the United States were expected to improve.[88] In December Jadwiga wrote to Irena and Michał to congratulate them on the birth of their daughter; she added that an acquaintance who had recently returned from Poland spoke of 'terrible things':

> With every day the situation becomes more tragic. Those who have recently returned to the homeland find that after a month they want to get out, but unfortunately the iron doors have been slammed shut and there is no escape. Those returning have their passports taken away; and we hear with increasing frequency about the arrests of relatives and friends. God was clearly protecting you when you decided not to return.[89]

Irena, no doubt, could only agree with the last sentence. Indeed, at roughly the same time Mila Kontkowska wrote to Irena that (in the new repressive climate in Poland) she feared that their correspondence would soon have to end, and that 'those who have recently returned from where you are are in a bad way and cannot get any work.'[90] By the time the year was out the communists had achieved the monopoly of power in Poland. Czechoslovakia had also fallen to a communist coup, and the Berlin Blockade was in full swing.

In the meantime Polik was also applying to join Zygmunt in America. He had no written English and so a commission in the RAF, which he toyed with at one point, was out of the question. When his secondment to the RAF as a Russian language teacher came to an end in 1948, he registered as a resident in a Polish hostel near Ludford

Magna in Lincolnshire, but moved around the country earning a living doing a variety of jobs from fruit picking near Pershore to work in a factory in Irthlingborough in Northamptonshire. Of the latter he wrote: 'It's a factory producing Witabix [Weetabix], those strange biscuits which the English eat with milk for breakfast.'[91] The US Embassy advised Polik to apply to be included in the quota of 18,000 Polish ex-servicemen who were to be allowed into the United States. Polik asked Michał to translate his curriculum vitae for him.[92] Things moved quickly after that. Polik left Southampton on 31 January 1951 on the *Queen Mary* and arrived in New York seven days later. He joined Zygmunt in Connecticut and got a job in the factory that employed Zygmunt, eventually becoming a control supervisor.[93]

Yet Irena's and Michał's planned departure for the New World was not to be. Michał's medical examination, required by the US authorities, revealed a tumour in his right lung. Instead of America, Michał had to face the prospect of major surgery which took place in November 1949 at the Truro Infirmary. Michał spent four and a half hours in the operating theatre, but a heart attack during the operation stopped proceedings. The surgeon decided not to risk the patient's life and divided the operation into two sessions: the second was to take place within a year. Writing afterwards from the hospital, Michał tried to reassure Irena that because one rib had already been removed the second session would be easier and post-operative recovery less painful.[94] And this was not the only concern on Irena's mind; she was expecting her third child. The baby boy, named Michael, was born in the spring of 1950. When Michał telephoned the maternity ward for news he was informed by the nurse at the other end of the line that the newborn baby weighed well over 11 pounds. Michał jokingly remarked: 'It must be an elephant!' To which came the reply: 'No, sir! It's a baby!'

Life in St Mawgan had its consolations, notably the milder weather and even the odd trip to the beach at Newquay. On hearing of their new location, Irena's mother immediately consulted a small German encyclopaedia she had picked up in Sopot and was pleased to read that the entry under Cornwall included the phrase 'ein mildes Klima'.[95] Hearing more from Irena, she commented: 'I am glad that you too have some sun and more delightful surroundings', but also asked (and did so quite often in her letters) whether Irena had time for any enjoyable intellectual pursuits to relieve her nerves after the daily treadmill of housework and childcare.[96] Michał spent much of whatever free time he had on serious academic reading and on preparing for his University of Cambridge Proficiency in English exam. There also arrived an unexpected piece of news from the Far East. Michał's distant uncle Czesław von Wolf, an eccentric character by all accounts, and his wife had left Poland before the war and had settled on a plantation in the Philippines. They survived the war but were killed by bandits in 1950. They had no children; Michał was Czesław's only relative in the West whom the Philippine authorities could contact with a view to settling the von Wolf inheritance. It proved to be a complicated matter and it took three years before any funds reached Michał, who was fortunate to have secured the services of Dr Karol Poznański, an eminent international lawyer and former Polish Consul-General in Britain. The small sums that were gradually released over a number of years (after costs and taxes in Manila) were no great fortune, but they were of considerable help to the needy young family. The ingenious methods that Michał was to deploy to pass on their share of the inheritance to his relatives in Poland make a separate engaging story. In the meantime, in Cornwall, Irena continued to send parcels to her family in Poland.

It was not until February 1951 that Michał had his second operation, this time in the thoracic unit at Frenchay Hospital in Bristol where his right lung was removed. The operation gave Michał another twelve years of life before he was to succumb to cancer of the liver. The timing of the operation in Bristol was awkward, for it coincided with the closure of the camp at St Mawgan. The family was to be moved to yet another Polish camp, Springhill Lodges near Moreton-in-Marsh in Gloucestershire. On the eve of his operation, writing from the hospital, Michał tried to reassure Irena:

> I don't know Springhill, but wherever we happen to be will be better than Russia. Moreton-on-the Marsh has about 2,000 inhabitants and lies about 25 miles northwest (more to the north) from Oxford (over 90,000 people and an intellectual centre) ... Springhill is also not far from Fairford and Cirencester, so, my dear, you could meet up with Pani Hellerowa; perhaps she could visit us one day.[97]

Michał was still in hospital when, on 2 March 1951, Irena and her three children, with a coachload of other transferred residents, set off on the long road journey to Springhill. They were followed at some point by four of Irena's beehives, the limit set by the warden at Springhill; the remaining hives (number not known) had to be disposed of.

The Polish hostel at Springhill Lodges owed its name to two abandoned stone lodges situated at what had been the main entrance gate to the privately owned Springhill estate, deep in the Cotswolds at the crossroads of the A44 (Moreton to Broadway road) and the B4081 (Chipping Campden to Snowshill road). The camp was located in a bowl-shaped dip surrounded by extensive areas of woodland and some rolling fields, with a quarry nearby, and within sight of Broadway Tower. Built during the war to house Italian and later German prisoners of war, it was adapted in 1947 to its new post-war role as a settlement for Polish ex-servicemen and civilians with their families who by 1958 numbered 800.[98]

The initial accommodation provided for Irena and the children was cramped and quite unsuitable, and it was only after Michał's arrival that the family was allocated a larger but still primitive dwelling, namely half of a corrugated metal Nissen hut. Irena's mother, who had received a photograph of the family in front of the hut, was quite horrified, and asked: 'Will you move out of this "Diogenes' barrel" in which one can probably freeze in the winter?'[99] On the other hand, Mila Kontkowska, now reduced to being a factory worker and beset by all sorts of difficulties of life in Stalinist Poland, commented ironically: 'Your life seems to us almost a poetic fairy tale! You reside like a queen in your little house among shrubs and beehives, at the head of your small but constantly growing young family. With your husband you have your own "home" – you plan sensibly for the future, live according to a set budget; naturally this appears to you ordinary and normal!'[100] The family's quarters were indeed upgraded to a more spacious red-brick barrack after the birth of Irena's fourth child, Anna, in the spring of 1952. Although the camp had some family quarters with separate cooking facilities, Irena's barrack had no running water and the family had to rely on communal lavatories and washrooms, and communal eating facilities. At the age of not quite nine years old,

Figure 10. Irena with husband Michał and three of their children (left to right: Wacio/ Hubert, Anna and Helen) in front of their Nissen hut in the Polish resettlement camp in Springhill, Gloucestershire, c. 1953.

I remember helping to carry water and coal to the house. Springhill camp was not without entertainment or cultural life. Indeed, the facilities included: two choirs and two orchestras; a large hall which served as a theatre and cinema; a reading room which soon acquired a television; organized sport events; a hospital with a resident doctor (Dr Roman Żyznowski); and for a while (before being moved to the nearby Polish hostel in Northwick Park) an infants' school. There was also a church. Probably the most authoritative figure was the resident parish priest Father Józef Gołąb, who had survived five years in Buchenwald and Dachau concentration camps, and who now ministered to the religious needs of the camp's predominantly Catholic inhabitants. Any local English outsider who happened to enter the camp on the feast day of Corpus Christi and witnessed the mass procession of the camp's residents, in their Sunday best and lustily singing hymns, making their way from one outdoor altar to another, which adorned the camp that day, might rightly feel that they had been transported to a foreign land.

The camp offered a sanctuary to its large group of exiles, but those who were able-bodied had to contribute to their board and lodging, and therefore sought work outside the camp, mostly menial and often involving a long commute. From October 1951 until March 1953 Michał worked as a labourer and checker for the Ministry of Defence at No.1 Engineer Stores Depot (1 ESD) in Long Marston, 10 km south of Stratford-on-Avon. Between 1953 and 1955 he was employed by a private engineering firm Messrs Dowty Ltd in Ashchurch near Tewkesbury, a leading British manufacturer of aircraft equipment; factory work there involved night shifts. In February 1955 he was reappointed at 1 ESD as a checker, later becoming storeman II and I, and then stores foreman. Sometime in 1955, in circumstances unknown, he suffered a serious injury to one of his legs but recovered well.

In many ways Michał led a double life: a manual worker or foreman on weekdays; a dedicated scholar by correspondence in his spare time at home. In 1955 he secured an MA at the Polish School of Political and Social Sciences, and in 1960 an MA in philosophy at the Polish University Abroad, both émigré institutions based in London. His early death in 1963 prevented him from completing a doctoral dissertation in the philosophy of history under his mentor Professor Marian Kukiel. Known among the exiled Polish community in the Midlands as a good public speaker, Michał was sometimes invited to address Polish gatherings on important national anniversaries. The business of the Philippine inheritance also occasionally took him to London. In August 1954 Michał accompanied a large contingent of his former comrades-in-arms of the Polish First Armoured Division to Normandy, headed by their former commander General Maczek, to commemorate the tenth anniversary of the Battle of Falaise. During the stopover in Paris, Michał was able to visit Maciej Grabowski, his mother's cousin and a former major in Polish military intelligence, who had run a Polish underground network in Lille during the war, had been decorated and given a pension by the French government, and now lived in Paris with his French-Polish wife.

Polish was spoken at home and throughout the camp, but Michał and Irena were anxious that we children should develop our knowledge of the language and of Polish culture once we had started attending English primary schools and our family had moved out of Springhill. In the mid- and late 1950s Helen and I, the two eldest children, undertook a Polish correspondence course run by Polish exiles in London, while the grandmothers in Poland also sent Polish books to their grandchildren in England. Michał and Irena subscribed to the leading Polish émigré publications, regularly received books from the Polish library in London and considered themselves very much Polish patriots. They made regular financial contributions to the treasury of the Polish government-in-exile in London, but stopped doing so when the exiled leadership split in 1954. By the mid-1950s Michał had become more than reconciled to living in England. In a letter to Irena's cousins in Australia he gave a positive account of life in Britain despite the discomforts and inconveniences of camp life, concluding:

> I thank God that He has deigned to preserve me, my wife and children in this land of porridge, jam, greyhound racing and noble-minded lords in tweeds. I have no intention of becoming a British patriot, nor does anyone expect it of me. But if it were possible I would clasp to my heart beautiful Gloucestershire, soot-covered London and even ugly Birmingham. [...] One can live here and there is one thing I value above all: total freedom of speech, of thought and freedom for our national-cultural activities – within the law.[101]

Absorbed with childcare, Irena did not find it easy to leave the camp, except for organized shopping trips to Evesham or when taking us children to hospital: my brother Michael had an eye operation in 1954 and I had my tonsils removed in 1955.

But in autumn 1953 both she and Michał were able to take a break and travel to London where they visited Michał's relatives: the writer Franciszek Wysłouch (a former major in the Polish Second Corps) and his wife Basia, as well Michał's Woyczyński cousins. There was also personal contact with Halina Heller whom Irena, accompanied by my sister Helen and me, visited in the Polish camp near Fairford in September 1955; Halina Heller had invited me to spend some time with her family after my tonsillectomy. Afterwards Halina Heller brought me back to Springhill and was able to enjoy a few days with our family, as she wrote afterwards:

> I thank you very much for your very warm hospitality; I felt wonderful in the bosom of your family. Although I saw Pan Michał briefly in passing, nevertheless he turned my attention away from the petty concerns of hostel life. In your company we spoke about everything frankly and in plain language, and how pleasant that was! Here [in Fairford] I have to mind almost every word, for the atmosphere in our hostel is often as unpleasant as teargas, and in our kindergarten it is even worse. With you I felt a better person, even a little imbued with lofty feelings – because I have known Irka a long time and well, while Pan Michał could not be anything else but her husband, a friend and admirer of learning.[102]

Another visitor in 1955 was Irena's aunt, the singer and painter Irena Valdi-Gołębiowska (née Żórawska), who had come to England from Beirut in 1948 and eventually settled in Leeds. They had not seen each other since before the war. Irena was now able to learn something about her aunt's wartime saga. Both Aunt Irena (known as 'Tantesse' among the younger members of the family in England) and her sister Aunt Mania had been deported in 1940 from Wilno to the Urals (Tantesse for refusing to accept Soviet citizenship) where they worked as slave labourers in a lumber camp. They left the USSR with Anders's Army in 1942 and spent the next four years in Iran. Using her stage name 'Valdi', Tantesse gave musical performances there, even at the court of the Shah, and with her sister enjoyed a lively social life in the Iranian capital. It also emerged that the ever youthful Tantesse had 'rejuvenated' herself during the war by fourteen years. Indeed, although she was born in 1891, her surviving Polish passport, issued in Tehran in July 1944, puts her date of birth as 27 July 1905. She was clearly able to fool or bewitch Witold Okoński, the Polish chargé d'affaires in Tehran.

Despite the Cold War, contact continued to be maintained with the family in Poland. Some relatives, fearing for their jobs, were now reluctant to write, but the grandmothers proved unstoppable, as Irena's mother declared defiantly for any censor to read: 'I consider that one could not take exception if a mother communicates with her children about personal matters. I would have much to tell you and to recall if we could meet face to face, but unfortunately it's not feasible by letter.'[103] Nor did she have any compunction in sending Irena old family photographs (which arrived as a rule) as well as news of Wiera Borodziuk in (Soviet) Borki. Parcels continued to be sent east, although on a more modest scale, as well as medicines when needed. Irena's advice was even sought on various personal matters; in this context Irena succeeded in persuading her sister Jula to let her daughter Marysia (and Irena's god-daughter) to continue with her further education.[104] There were also echoes, expressed by Jula, of earlier hopes that Irena might yet return to Poland.[105]

In October 1956 our family of six moved out of Springhill to a brand new council house in Lower Quinton in south Warwickshire, near Michał's job at 1 ESD Long Marston. News of this impending move cheered Michał's mother who expressed delight that Irena would finally have 'civilized facilities'.[106] And Irena's mother wrote: 'I'm glad that at last you have comfortable accommodation and do not have to carry water, as had been the case and had been so strenuous with such a large number of children!'[107] So ended eight years of nomadic life in resettlement camps in England. Indeed, the house in Quinton was to be Irena's home for the next thirty-eight years, longer than the total of twenty-six years spent in Borki. In 1959 Michał and Irena became British citizens, a condition required by his employers if Michał was to secure promotion within the British civil service. Incidentally, before taking this step Michał sought and obtained permission from the exiled Polish government in London. Irena's bees were also moved to Quinton where a local farmer, William Stanley, allowed her to keep her dozen hives in his orchard on the northern slopes of nearby Meon Hill. Irena's was not the only Polish family in Quinton; soon others arrived and for many years even our immediate neighbours were Polish. Furthermore, several hundred Polish ex-servicemen, without families, were housed next to, and were employed at 1 ESD at Long Marston. The Polish camp there had a resident Roman Catholic chaplain, Father Franciszek Winczowski, whose Sunday services our family attended regularly.

Life in exile was not easy, but Irena faced everything with fortitude and a certain equanimity; when serious difficulties arose there was always consolation and support to be sought in God.[108] By all accounts Irena was happy in her marriage and with her family. It was the grannies in Poland who suffered most from the separation and the inability to meet their British-born grandchildren. 'My heart longs for you terribly', wrote Michał's mother to Irena in November 1948, 'I would give several years of my life (although I do not dispose of many) to see you all finally, to embrace you and to get to know you.'[109] The sadness was no less intense four months later: 'I suffer terribly that I cannot be with you and to see your little ones, and that they in turn may never get to know their granny – for who knows how long the present separation will last!'[110] In March 1954 she lamented: 'My very loved ones! Time flies and we are no closer to each other. I long for you immeasurably!'[111] And then in 1956 there appeared a promising light on the political horizon. In a series of dramatic events in Warsaw that October, which included the personal appearance in the Polish capital of Khrushchev and most of the Soviet leadership, Władysław Gomułka (who had suffered under the Stalinist regime) was appointed the new Polish communist leader. The changes he introduced marked a radical break with the Stalinist past and opened the road to a milder form of communist rule. With the beginning of a political thaw in Poland, travel to the West became more of a possibility, and this injected hope in Michał's mother's heart. In the summer of 1957 her dream finally came true: she was able to visit her son and meet our family. Irena's mother was to be less fortunate. In June 1951 she wrote: 'I often look at your photographs and am sad that I cannot see you.'[112] That July she asked: 'How are my little grandchildren known to me only from photographs?'[113] Her interest in the lives and the bilingual education of her British-born grandchildren remained unabated, but her failing eyesight and declining health made any thought of foreign travel unrealistic. She died in Sopot in March 1957, not having seen Irena since October 1939 and never having seen Irena's children.

Our education was bilingual but not evenly so, and in some cases was to proceed in a zig-zag fashion. Children of infant and lower junior age living in Springhill were bussed to a Polish-language primary school in the nearby camp at Northwick Park where they were expected to acquire a sufficient knowledge of English in order to be transferred at the age of seven to an English primary school. At the age of seven, and still only possessing a rudimentary knowledge of English, my sister Helen and I were in due course moved to the Roman Catholic primary school in Chipping Campden. Neither of us remember any special English-language provision offered at the school and both have rather negative memories of its discipline: I was once punished with blows of a ruler to my hand for not learning the nine times table. On the contrary we loved the school lunches, and discovered the English delicacies gravy and custard! What horrified Irena was the school's anti-Protestant sectarian ethos.

Exposure to the English world remained limited. Outside school there was almost no contact with local English boys and girls. The Polish children from Springhill were delivered by bus to the school in the morning and returned to the camp straight after lessons. Springhill was an island of Polishness; the camp was not only isolated physically but all social and cultural life was conducted in Polish, and of course only Polish was spoken at home. Adventurous children had some scope to explore the neighbouring countryside and some youngsters accompanied their mothers on organized shopping trips by bus to Evesham. Michał and Irena viewed the learning of Polish as paramount and assumed their children would pick up English at school. Neither Helen nor I remember having any English children's books at home in the camp, but for me there was one powerful incentive to read English in the form of the weekly boys' comic the *Eagle*. Helen's English benefited similarly by reading *Bounty*, *Judy* and *Girl*.

On moving to Lower Quinton, Irena's four children attended the local village school whose head teacher Mr Styler and other staff proved welcoming and supportive. There we made our first English friends at whose homes we were able to watch television for the first time. Our English also improved, although with mixed results. Whereas Michael and I failed the eleven-plus exam, Helen and her younger sister Anna were successful and attended the Stratford Grammar School for Girls, completing their GCE A Levels in 1967 and 1970, respectively. To avoid what they considered would be an inferior education at a secondary modern school, Michał and Irena sent their boys to a Polish boarding grammar school run by the Marian Fathers in Fawley Court near Henley-on-Thames. The school fees were to eat up what was still left of the Philippine inheritance.

Divine Mercy College (DMC, or 'Dracula's Murder Chamber' in the parlance of some of its wittier pupils) was not the best place for integration let alone assimilation into English society. Its pupils came not only from Polish families living in Britain but also from Germany. There was even one boy of mixed Polish-Iranian parentage from Iran. Some of the older boys had been born in the Middle East, Africa and other places of their parents' wartime exile. Most of the staff were highly qualified teachers from pre-war Poland who taught in English (with strong foreign accents), except for

Polish literature and history, and religious instruction. The school's ethos was strongly Polish and Catholic. Irena's cousin Halina Skrzyńska in Australia was delighted that I would acquire 'a Polish soul'.[114] Yet there were also cultural counter-attractions at the school: weekly English-language films and television, and the lure of 1950s and 1960s pop music which was listened to on transistor radios which several of the pupils possessed.

Michael and I did well in our GCE O Level exams (DMC only taught to that level) and we were admitted to the sixth form at King Edward VI School in Stratford (I in 1962 and Michael in 1966). With our father's death in 1963 Irena found herself having to oversee singlehandedly the latter phases of our education. But her knowledge of the English educational system remained vague at the best of times, so we had to forge our own way. I was encouraged by my new school to apply to read history at Oxford and was offered a place at Keble College; Helen went to study psychology with zoology in Reading; Michael went to the School of Architecture in Oxford; and Anna embarked on a nursing career. We all obtained full grants from the Warwickshire Educational Committee; Irena's fears that she would not be able to cope financially were also allayed by some assistance from the Civil Service Benevolent Fund. She also tried to make savings by making clothes for her children, growing fruit and vegetables and keeping chickens, and tried to bolster the family budget by selling honey produced by her bees. Lola Szafran (Estera Witkowska), Irena's Jewish friend from their wartime nursing days who visited Irena in Quinton in 1967, also sent some high-quality women's and girls' clothes from America.

As the Stalinist period in Poland receded into the past after 1956, our family's links with Poland intensified. Before his death, Michał and Irena were able to widen their reading to include several periodicals from Poland, sent by relatives. There were also further visits to Lower Quinton from Poland. Michał's aunt Zofia Wyszyńska (his mother's sister) called in 1961; she had come to England that year to join her son Wacław Zabłocki in Salisbury. In 1963 Zofia, a survivor of Ravensbrück, was invited by Sue Ryder to take up residence at the Sue Ryder Home for concentration camp survivors in Cavendish in Suffolk and where she worked as an interpreter and translator. Michał's cousin Stefan Zawadzki also visited Quinton in 1961; Janina Lutosławska (the philosopher's daughter) came in 1964; and Michał's mother came for the second time in 1966. Irena's cousin Mila Kontkowska (in Kraków since 1945), who had been so scathing of the communist regime in the 1940s, now even suggested that I might come to study at a Polish university, an idea that had apparently 'shocked' my father.[115] On the other hand, and despite his failing health, Michał seemed willing to entertain the idea of accepting his cousin Stefan's invitation to visit him in Poland. But Stefan's last letter on this subject (of 30 January 1963) never reached Michał who died on 13 February.

Shortly after Michał's death, his family in Poland invited Irena's eldest children to visit. And so Irena accepted the offer of the Lekis family (close friends from Irena's Scottish days) to take me and Helen with them in the summer of 1963 on a car journey to Poland. For us two teenagers it was our first trip behind the Iron Curtain; we were very warmly received by relatives on both sides of the family. Mila Kontkowska was delighted with our visit, and encouraged me to develop my link with Poland, 'this point of contact on the frontier of East and West'.[116] The following year, my two younger siblings, Michael and Anna, also made their first journey to Poland, although they spent most of the time at separate holiday camps in the south of the country. In 1967, after taking my final examinations in Oxford, I embarked on a longer tour of Poland, and by visiting even more of my scattered relatives was able to revive the family network within the country.[117] I even called on the painter Wlastimil Hofman, now living in the mountains of Silesia.

Indeed, the improved post-1956 atmosphere in Poland even encouraged Irena's American cousin Zygmunt Protassewicz and his actress wife Jadwiga Smosarska to visit Poland in 1958. Smosarska was not entirely happy in America and remained nostalgic for the country where two decades earlier she had shone on the cinema screens. She was fêted everywhere, and from then on she and Zygmunt were to make annual trips to Poland. In October 1970, as American citizens, they retired for good to Warsaw, the city they had fled in 1939. Now well-off as a former director of an American factory, the generous Zygmunt ('our family's Onassis' in Irena's words)[118] proved to be a godsend to many a struggling relative in People's Poland, and took an active role as a representative of those American Poles who contributed financially to the maintenance of the centre for the blind in Laski, west of Warsaw; he also joined a campaign to restore the old Powązki cemetery in Warsaw. Zygmunt's brother Polik also made several visits to Poland with his American wife.

Irena herself was never to visit post-war Poland, despite frequent invitations. She was apprehensive about coming face to face with her relatives after so many years, while her poor health and limited funds ruled out any foreign travel. This applied even when her sister Hania came to live in Paris in the period 1968–72 (as wife of the commercial attaché at the Polish Embassy there), and even though the Polish communist authorities had raised no objection to Hania meeting Irena. At the same time, in 1966 Irena went out of her way to arrange for a Lancashire firm to copy Hania's Polish Radio tape recordings onto vinyl records.

The new post-Stalinist political climate also enabled Irena's family in Poland to resume contact with Borki in 1956, after an almost ten-year break. Irena's sister Jula Prange (living in Sopot) was to correspond with Wiera Borodziuk (who had survived the war in Borki) until 1975 and it was through Jula that Irena was able to exchange letters and photographs with Wiera and Wiera's son Jan (Irena's godson). Wiera supplied news of the old manor house (which served again as a hospital in the 1970s), of people in Borki village who had been close to the family, and about life in the locality. By 1956 travel from Poland to Soviet Belarus to visit relatives had also been eased and it was possible for one former villager from Borki who now lived in Poland to travel to Borki; this particular individual was able to bring back to Jula two surviving Protassewicz family photo albums that had been left in the village for safekeeping. Many of these photographs were eventually to reach Irena. On learning of Irena's husband's death in 1963, Wiera wrote in a moving letter of condolence to Irena: 'Do not be sad and do not cry. God brings sadness but will also console you in your loss. You were deported and God freed you from bondage. You never thought then that you would survive; in the same way you will now get over your sadness.'[119]

Another link with Borki was through Staś Skorochod, the son of the family's former coachman Adam. Staś had opted for the new Poland after the war and happened to settle in Gdańsk where he did well financially running a car maintenance enterprise. He became friends with Jula and her family and even did some electrical repair work in her home. He occasionally visited his parents back in Borki, and it was through him, in 1959, that Jula was able to provide a notarial declaration on the strength of which Adam Skorochod was granted a monthly Soviet pension of 200 roubles for his long work as the Protassewicz family coachman. Altogether Jula was to make five such declarations to help the family's former employees in Borki. Irena was kept abreast of all these developments, and no doubt found consolation from Wiera's statement that Irena's family was 'well remembered' and from Staś Skorochod's verbal account on returning from Borki in 1959 that 'everyone fondly remembers Tatuś [Irena's father], because life there is sad and people are poorer'.[120]

Despite the enlivened links with Poland, Irena's fears of the Soviet world lingered on. This did not apply to Russian culture nor the Russian language: she read Tolstoy, Paustovsky and other Russian writers in the original and greatly enjoyed the songs of Aleksandr Vertinsky on records. But the Soviets were a different matter. She was already apprehensive in 1967 (when I was twenty-one) that, despite my British passport, I might be detained during my visit to Poland and be forced to do military service. She was positively alarmed about my plan in the spring of 1968 to join a British Commonwealth student party on an official cultural exchange visit to the USSR. The visit was a success and nothing untoward happened but I had to make a real effort to allay her fears. Irena was likewise horrified when in the summer of 1969 Helen joined an overland student trip to the USSR. But Irena's anxieties reached their greatest heights when, as a postgraduate student at Wolfson College in Oxford, I was offered a Polish government scholarship (sponsored by the British Council) to spend a whole academic year (1969–70) in Poland to undertake research for my doctoral dissertation on Adam Czartoryski. Short visits to relatives were one thing, but for her eldest son to be exposed for such a long period to the possible wicked machinations of communist officialdom was another. Her demons returned, and in her darkest moments she almost equated People's Poland with the USSR. She pressured me to abandon my plan and even sent me a Radio Free Europe article about Poles still languishing in the Soviet Gulag in 1967, on which she wrote in pencil: 'Read this before you decide to go to Poland for as long as nine months.'[121] This fear, coinciding with the completion of her memoirs in which she relived her wartime experiences and with the painful prospect of all her children leaving the family nest, may have contributed to Irena's breakdown in the summer of 1969. She spent several weeks that autumn in the Central Hospital near Warwick where she was treated for severe depression; mercifully, she gradually recovered and returned to her normal self. She also came to terms with my absence in Poland, and even encouraged me before my return home to visit Stulgiński, the sculptor, in his studio in Kraków, as well as some of her pre-war school friends. However, it was clear by then that Irena would find it hard to live alone, which is why Helen, on graduating in 1970, accepted a teaching post in Stratford and returned to Quinton for several years.

What lightened Irena's heart and gave joy to her spirit in the 1960s was the liberating message of the Second Vatican Council. Feeling herself no longer inhibited by any church restrictions on her conscience, she threw herself headlong into the great theological debates of the time. She embraced the reformist spirit in the Catholic Church, and in her correspondence (some of it quite trenchant and even strident) with various clergymen, Catholic newspapers (in England and Poland) and interested relatives, she applauded the liberal theologian Hans Küng, called for an end to clerical celibacy and for the liberalization of the church's laws on divorce, endorsed the cause of conciliar authority within the church, bemoaned what she considered as the church's disastrous alliance with the State under Emperor Constantine, and called for a return to the primitive church of the early Christians.[122] She went even further: she spoke approvingly of Einstein's 'cosmic religious feeling'[123] and suggested that the Christian message should take into account all the achievements of modern science.

Irena remained strongly critical of traditional Polish Catholicism, and her 'radical' religious turn, drawing on her deep-seated scepticism, was certainly profoundly influenced by her exposure in England to Western religious and philosophical thought, as she admitted frankly: 'The realism of English thought was a revelation for me. Perhaps the high standard of my husband's historical realism also made me fastidious in my choice of religious reading.' She continued: 'compared to Protestant thought, most Roman Catholic writing is now for me indigestible and anachronistic'.[124] One Polish priest in England decided to terminate his correspondence with Irena with the words: 'Discussion with you is very difficult because your criteria are drawn to a large degree from materialistic or at least deistic English writers. Please do not be surprised if it will not be soon before I write to you again.'[125] Irena was also able to refine her views in the extensive theological correspondence she maintained in the late 1960s (until the intervention of the Polish security services brought it to an end) with a liberal-minded Jesuit in Poland. Yet for all her radicalism, when her youngest daughter Anna asked her why she still went to Mass and followed church rules, Irena replied: 'Just in case' (*Na wszelki wypadek*).

Although Borki was deeply engraved in her heart, Irena came to love Britain, with its peace and quiet, its security, its tolerance, its National Health Service, its mobile libraries, its jumble sales and its freethinking philosophers and liberal theologians. And she did recognize the opportunities her children now had in the West: 'I mourn the loss of Borki, but is it not better for my children that fate had catapulted me into the wider world? It's better.'[126] One part of her quietly regretted that her children were becoming gradually anglicized, but the last thing she would have wanted for them is to be stuck in some inward-looking Polish 'ghetto', and she was always genuinely glad to see her children's non-Polish friends. Indeed, some years later she accepted as inevitable that her descendants would be 'totally absorbed into English society. It is the law of nature that a surrounding society absorbs …'. And she cited three examples of this 'law' in operation in Poland where individuals of non-Polish or partly non-Polish origin had become fully assimilated into Polish culture: the half-French Chopin; the poet and geographer Wincenty Pol (Pohl); and the artist Artur Grottger.[127]

Irena had survived the storms that had torn apart the Europe of her childhood and early adulthood, and had found sanctuary 'in England's hospitable land'.[128] During her life she had encountered some good luck; she had been helped by some kind people. Her strong religious faith had given her a sense of purpose and had done much to dispel any feelings of despair. She was quietly proud of her work as a military nurse.

Her wartime experiences had a profound impact: there was a greater spirituality; a consciousness that material possessions are ultimately of little value; that food should not be taken for granted and should be respected; that people should be judged for their personal qualities not their wealth or status. Her encounters with diverse ethnic groups and peoples, and with individuals of diverse social and cultural backgrounds, broadened her horizons. Indeed her hardships had mellowed rather than embittered her. Of course she could not remain unaffected by all the human suffering she had witnessed but would go on to face her husband's illness with a deep religious stoicism:

> During my life with Michał, during our first moments of romantic elation while we were engaged, my feelings deepened and I bound my soul with him. It is strange, but it was precisely through suffering, through suffering caused by his hopeless and long but heroic battle with his tumour, that this occurred. His death strengthened my bond with him most firmly. What was unimportant had gone, such as his silly bouts of impatience and irritation resulting from nervous exhaustion brought about by his illness. I looked rather at his youth, and at his splendid manly personage, which was wasting away then so tragically. What is essential has survived: his intellectual ability, inherited by the children; his breeding, which has also passed on to his descendants; and the qualities of his personality, cleansed spiritually by suffering, a suffering through which he linked his submission to the Will of God and in his prayers for us. There are things one cannot forget, which are and which will be consolidated in some new existence; there are things which defy destruction, either through death or separation. There exists some form of continuity which lasts. That is why I cannot imagine ever marrying again. There are things which are unrepeatable, even if they were not always easy the first time.[129]

The Borki manor house and remnants of its park survived the Second World War, and feature in Grzegorz Rąkowski's illustrated guide to historical buildings in Belarus.[130] Alas, when Helen and I visited Borki in 1997 we found the house abandoned and in a state of semi-ruin. During the winter of 2009–10 the house was dismantled and its once proud timber beams were used as fuel to heat the Borki starch factory. Wacław Protassewicz's creation, the starch-processing plant, had consumed his former house. Had Irena lived to hear this, she would have probably shed a quiet tear, but would then have said: '*Tout passe, hélas …*'. Perhaps the Four Gospels, which were buried in the foundations of the house many centuries ago, have not been disturbed.

The End

Postscript: Tying up some loose ends

Hubert Zawadzki

To the very end of her life Irena remained interested in her wider family, in the lives of her friends, of neighbours old and new, and of other individuals whom she had met during her eventful life. This applied also to those who had disappeared during the war or whose fate was unknown. In some cases, it took years if not decades to discover the truth of someone's wartime story or tragic end. It was only in 1959, for instance, that she learnt some details of Tadeusz Stulgiński's harrowing experiences at the hands of the Gestapo and in various Nazi concentration camps (Auschwitz, Sachsenhausen and Buchenwald).[1] In September 1967 Stulgiński sent Irena a catalogue of an exhibition, which included his work, held in Kraków in 1965 in memory of Polish artists killed or imprisoned by the Nazis. His handwritten dedication reads: 'In memory of our puppy years – pleasantly remembered moments in Borki.' Then there is the dramatic case of Daniel Kostrowicki (husband of her cousin Hala Przybytko) who, it was feared, may have committed suicide after his brush with the NKVD in Wilno – to the distress of his devout widow. It was only in September 1992 that an authoritative and very different story appeared in a Polish émigré newspaper in London, as follows. Using the pseudonyms 'Danek' and 'Zygmunt', Daniel remained an active member of the Polish Home Army (AK) in Wilno. In July 1942, when the whole of pre-war Poland was under German occupation, he took on an extra mission of guiding a light goods vehicle carrying cheddite and other explosive material from the AK in Warsaw to a safe place near Wilno. On his way to the meeting he and his comrade were attacked in Wilno by the Lithuanian police near the Green Bridge (Zielony Most) over the river Wilja. Exchanging fire, he managed to escape into Zygmuntowska Street where, to his misfortune, he ran into a long column of German army vehicles. He was shot while trying to reach the river. According to an unconfirmed report by a witness (a 'Pan S' of the underground authorities in Wilno), Daniel's body was taken to a mortuary by the Germans who then discovered that he was not quite dead, despite the eleven bullets that had hit him. He was then taken to a fort in Kaunas, after which all trace of him disappeared. Daniel was decorated posthumously with the highest Polish military order, the Virtuti Militari, on the recommendation of Colonel Aleksander Krzyżanowski ('Wilk'), the AK commander in Wilno province.[2] Irena immediately sent a copy of the article to Daniel Kostrowicki's son in Poland and passed on the news to Halina Skrzyńska in Australia for further dissemination among the family.[3]

Irena also speculated occasionally about the fates of Father Jan Goj, the parish priest in Rohotna, of Dr Yehezkel Atlas with whom she had tended the sick in Borki hospital, of Captain Kazimierz de Latour who had contacted her from his prisoner-of-war camp in Germany, and of her pre-war German friend Hans Albert Reinkemeyer. She was never to discover what had happened to them. Recent research, however, has yielded considerable knowledge about these four so very different individuals whose paths had crossed with Irena's.

Father Goj was arrested by the Soviets on 27 October 1939 for allegedly 'preaching against the communist ideology'. He was jailed in Słonim, then Baranowicze and then Minsk, from where he was moved in 1941 to an unknown labour camp. Details of his death are not known, but it probably occurred around 1951. According to a report of 24 August 1941, sent to Archbishop Jałbrzykowski of Wilno by the dean Father Cyrajski, Father Goj impressed his fellow prisoners with his calm and serene response to prison conditions, by his prayer, and by his constant encouragement to the prisoners to submit to the will of God.[4]

As for Dr Atlas, when the Germans arrived in western Belarus in June 1941, he was working in Kozłowszczyzna (16 km west of Borki) to where the hospital in Borki had been moved in the spring of 1940. The main Jewish ghetto established by the Nazis in this region was located in Słonim, while smaller 'satellite' ghettos were created in nearby townships, including Kozłowszczyzna and Dereczyn. In June–July 1942 the inhabitants of these ghettos were put to death. About 700 to 800 Jews were killed in Kozłowszczyzna, including Dr Atlas's parents and his seventeen-year-old sister Celina. Dr Atlas was spared because the Germans obviously still needed his medical skills. The effect of all this on Dr Atlas was shattering and set him on the road of resistance and revenge. He escaped and helped to organize a partisan unit, armed by the Soviets, which eventually numbered about 300 men, of whom a third were Jews. Dr Atlas told those joining him: 'Every additional day in your life is not yours but belongs to your murdered families. You must avenge them.' On 10 August 1942 the unit captured the German garrison in Dereczyn; the partisans killed seventeen Germans and two Lithuanians, and executed forty-four others over the Jewish mass grave. Dr Atlas took part in other daring exploits before being killed in action on 5 December 1942.[5]

Captain de Latour had taken part in the 1939 campaign as an anti-aircraft artillery officer. He then spent five and a half years in German captivity, and was freed from Oflag Lübeck only on 2 May 1945. It appears that in November 1945, instead of making his way to General Maczek's Polish armoured division which was occupying the German port of Wilhelmshaven or to General Anders's Second Corps in Italy, de Latour joined the remnants of a Polish nationalist unit (the 'Świętokrzyska' Brigade) which had been fighting the Germans and the Soviets, and which had made its tortuous way from Poland through Czechoslovakia to Germany. The brigade was dissolved by the Americans and most of its members enlisted with the so-called Labour Service Guard Companies attached to the US Army in Germany. These companies performed guard duties at American depots and other installations; some guarded convicted German war criminals, while others were employed in establishing American war cemeteries in Germany, Belgium and France. It seems that de Latour served as an officer in these companies for several years.[6] The next record of him is from 1950, when he left Germany for Australia, arriving in Fremantle on 31 December.[7] Irena had wrongly assumed that he returned to Poland soon after the war. In her account, she recalls receiving a letter from de Latour just days after her engagement to Michał. Her response, dated 9 March 1946, tells of her marriage and motherhood. It did not reach de Latour in Lübeck and was returned unopened. It appears that de Latour died in Australia in 1962.

Irena's family also assumed that Hans Albert Reinkemeyer had died on the Eastern Front. But it turns out that nothing could be further from the truth. During the war Hans Albert had indeed served as a captain in German Army Intelligence on the Eastern Front – but he survived the war. During the early post-war years, he worked as a lawyer in the law court in Celle (Lower Saxony), and in 1950 joined the foreign service of the newly created Federal Republic of Germany. After the establishment of diplomatic relations between West Germany and the USSR in 1955, he spent some time in the West German Embassy in Moscow; the same year he authored a published study on Soviet claims to a twelve-mile belt of territorial waters in the Baltic.[8] September and October 1955 were spent in New York as a member of the West German observer team at the United Nations. In 1959–60 he was a Fellow at Harvard where he and his wife Ola became friends with Dr Zbigniew Brzeziński, although, according to Dr Brzeziński, Hans Albert never revealed to him that he spoke Polish or that he had been to Poland before the war. On returning to Bonn, Hans Albert was appointed head of the Soviet section in the West German foreign ministry. He died relatively young, in April 1964, but his pre-war ambition to hold a senior position in Germany's diplomatic service had been largely fulfilled; he did not become foreign minister but at least it was in the service of a new democratic Germany.[9]

As for Irena's friends and colleagues who had died in Soviet Central Asia in 1942, she would have been pleased to learn that it finally became possible, in 1999, for the new democratic Polish government to begin the systematic tidying up of the Polish cemeteries in Kazakhstan and Uzbekistan, and the erection of memorials there. The cemeteries at Chokpak and Lugovaya Station were the first for which full details were obtained. The state of the Polish cemeteries in the Russian Federation and in Turkmenistan was still unknown at the beginning of the twenty-first century. Most of the military dead were buried in individual marked graves, although Uzbekistan is the only state of the former USSR where plaques with the inscription 'To the memory of Polish Friends' have survived. In 2002 a memorial was erected in the centre of Tashkent in memory of all Poles who had died in Uzbekistan. Polish military graves in Kirgizia have not survived.[10]

Irena died on 12 April 1994 in the Ellen Badger Memorial Hospital in Shipston-on-Stour, Warwickshire, and is buried in the Polish section of the cemetery in the village of Blockley, Gloucestershire.

Notes

Prologue

1   On Metropolitan Jonasz Protasowicz (d. 1577) and Bishop Walerian Protasowicz (c. 1505–79), see *Polski Słownik Biograficzny* (hereafter *PSB*), xxviii (Kraków: Polska Akad. Umiejętności, 1985), 523–4 and 517–21, respectively. In Polish, the family's surname has been spelt in a variety of ways: Protasowicz/Protassowicz/Protasewicz/Protaszewicz. In pre-1914 Russian documents, the family name features as: Протасовичъ/Протассовичъ. In Belarusian, it is written: Пратасевіч/Pratasievič and in Lithuanian: Protasevičius.

2   On other members of the family in this period, see *PSB*, 521–3; Seweryn Uruski, *Herbarz szlachty polskiej*, xiv (Warsaw: Gebethner & Wolff, 1917), 362–4; Kasper Niesiecki, *Herbarz polski*, 10 vols (Leipzig: Breitkopf & Haertel, 1839–45; repr. 1979), vii, 503–4. Documentation on the family's early history can be found in the Russian State Historical Archive [Russkiy Gosudarstvennyy Istoricheskiy Arkhiv (RGIA)] in St Petersburg: RGIA, f. 1343, op. 27, no. 6878, k. 83–6.

3   According to the Polish census of 1931, the district of Słonim (in which Borki was situated) had 126,510 inhabitants of whom 87 per cent lived in the countryside. The census recorded the percentage of the three main religious denominations as follows: Orthodox 70.2 per cent; Roman Catholic 18.8 per cent; Jewish 9.7 per cent; and the three principal mother tongues as: Belarusian 49.3 per cent; Polish 41.3 per cent; and Yiddish 7.3 per cent. There is a considerable overlap between Belarusian and Polish (both are Slavonic languages), and it is more than likely that the percentage of native Polish speakers was exaggerated by the census enumerators.

4   The population of Wilno was to grow from 154,000 in 1897 to 195,000 in 1931, after a serious dip during the wars of 1914–20. In 1900 neither Polish speakers nor Yiddish speakers nor Russians formed a majority ethnic group in the city, while Lithuanian speakers represented a tiny minority. The balance changed after the exodus of much of the Russian population in 1915 when the Germans occupied the city. A German census of 1916 recorded Poles as 54 per cent and Jews as 41 per cent of the population. According to the Polish census of 1931, the city's main religious denominations were: Roman Catholic 64.6 per cent; Jewish 28.2 per cent; and Orthodox 4.7 per cent. The city's three principal mother tongues were recorded as: Polish 65.9 per cent; Yiddish and Hebrew 28 per cent; and Russian 3.8 per cent. Lithuanian was under 1 per cent.

5   On this complicated subject, see Timothy Snyder, *The Reconstruction of Nations: Poland, Ukraine, Lithuania, Belarus, 1569–1999* (New Haven: Yale University Press, 2003), 52–72; and Theodore R. Weeks, *Vilnius between Nations, 1795–2000* (De Kalb: NIU Press, 2015), 111–23.

6 In the early 1900s Lutosławski collaborated with the leaders of the Polish National Democratic Party, although eventually they found little time for his romantic messianism. Roman Dmowski, the nationalist leader, remarked that Lutosławski 'lacked intellectual equilibrium'. See *PSB*, xviii (1973), 153–6.

7 IP: Lutosławski to Irena, 11 September 1935.

8 IP: Lutosławski to Irena, 26 September 1938.

9 Roberta Johnson, *Gender and Nation in the Spanish Modernist Novel* (Nashville: Vanderbilt University Press, 2003), 132.

10 See entry on Studnicki in *PSB*, xlv (2007–8), 124–34.

11 All of Wańkowicz's works were republished in sixteen volumes between 2009 and 2011 by the Warsaw publishing house Prószyński Media.

12 Mikołaj Kunicki, *Between the Brown and the Red: Nationalism, Catholicism and Communism in Twentieth-Century Poland. The Politics of Bolesław Piasecki* (Athens: Ohio University Press, 2012).

13 Unlike Rosa Luxemburg's and Felix Dzierżyński's (Dzerzhinsky's) 'internationalist' Social Democratic Party of the Kingdom of Poland and Lithuania which opposed Polish independence, Piłsudski's wing of the Polish Socialist Party supported the cause of an independent socialist Poland.

14 In a military demonstration on 12 May 1926, Marshal Piłsudski toppled the centre-right government of Wincenty Witos. Piłsudski's coup, welcomed initially by all the parties of the Left and by wide sections of the population, including many Jewish organizations, was carried out in the name of *Sanacja*, a term used in the sense of restoring 'health' to the body politic. Mass protests occurred only in the nationalist-dominated province of Poznań. Piłsudski's regime stood for the primacy of the state above what he considered was the debilitating factionalism of party politics, and became increasingly authoritarian after 1930. The coup had specific Polish causes, but it provides another example of the vulnerability of parliamentary institutions across much of continental Europe in the interwar period. See Jerzy Lukowski and Hubert Zawadzki, *A Concise History of Poland*, 2nd edn (Cambridge: Cambridge University Press, 2006), 238–51.

1 Wars and reconstruction (1914 to 1925)

1 The Zieliński family were Irena's near neighbours in Goose Lane, Lower Quinton in Warwickshire. *Polesia czar* (written in 1929) was a popular tango in pre-war Poland.

2 An aerated soft drink containing phosphoric acid, soda water and flavouring.

3 Irena is imprecise here. She probably has the Bolshevik coup in mind (the so-called October Revolution) which generated a long brutal civil war in Russia, rather than the February Revolution which toppled the tsar.

4 Wężowszczyzna was the home of the Żórawski family, situated about 40 km west of Lida.

5 Aunt Janka Żórawska married *inżynier* (engineer) Jan Górski and lived in Warsaw where her husband ran a department in the Ministry of Communication. According to Irena, he was shot by the Germans during a street round-up during the Second World War. However, Irena's mother reported that Jan Górski died in Auschwitz. IP: Zofia Protassewicz to Irena, 22 April 1946.

6 Irena probably has in mind Bolesław Wojtowicz (Woytowicz) (1899–1980), who was a pianist and composer of three symphonies. Before the Second World War, he taught

piano and music theory at the Warsaw Conservatoire. Konstanty Heintze (1889–1932) taught piano at the Warsaw Conservatoire and later moved to the Chopin Higher School of Music attached to the Musical Society of Warsaw.

7   Hania's stage name was Anna Borey.

8   Druskienniki (Druskininkai in Lithuanian) is today the largest and best-known health spa in Lithuania, situated in an attractive wooded location on the banks of the river Niemen. The spa was first opened in 1837. It was devastated during the First World War, and was not reopened until 1922.

9   Irena's parents were married there in 1909. After the Russian Revolution of 1905, the tsarist ban on the building of new Roman Catholic churches in Russia's western governorates was lifted.

10 Emilia Plater (1806–31) came from an old Polish-Lithuanian family of Livonian origin. She fought as a volunteer in Samogitia (Żmudź/Żemaitija) during the Polish Insurrection of 1831, having raised a partisan unit of 280 infantrymen, 60 horsemen and several hundred peasants armed with scythes. With the arrival of regular Polish forces in Lithuania, she was appointed commander of a company. With the collapse of the Insurrection she refused to withdraw to East Prussia and face Prussian internment. She died in hiding on 23 December 1831. She was immortalized by Mickiewicz in his poem 'Death of the Colonel' (*Śmierć pułkownika*), and is considered a national hero in Poland, Lithuania and Belarus.

11 This was probably part of the extensive programme of humanitarian relief aid across Europe organized by Herbert Hoover (1874–1964) who had been appointed the director of the American Relief Administration in 1918. He visited Poland in 1919 and much of his work was directed towards Poland, especially its impoverished eastern borderlands. A fundraising dinner in New York in 1920 alone raised one million dollars. In 1922, a monument was erected in his honour in Warsaw.

12 In 1936, Kazio Protassewicz was appointed governor of Mołodeczno district (in northeast Poland) which lay directly on the Soviet border. With the arrival of the Soviets in September 1939, Kazio and his family escaped to Wilno where he went into hiding. He continued to evade capture by the NKVD and then by the Germans who arrived in Wilno in June 1941. During the German occupation, Kazio was deeply involved in the Polish Resistance movement in the city. When the Red Army returned to Wilno in July 1944, it claimed the city for the Soviet Union and set about destroying the local structures of the Polish Underground State, despite the fact that the Polish Home Army had helped in the liberation of the city. Kazio was arrested by the NKVD and was sentenced to fifteen years' hard labour in the Gulag. He died from illness and exhaustion in August 1946 in a labour camp in Velsk, south of Arkhangelsk.

13 The writer Melchior Wańkowicz visited Borki on several occasions in the interwar period and described the house in lyrical terms in one of his published essays: 'let us not mince words – a marvel of a manor: old, built of larch, its walls bulging with a superstructure above and with annexes, set in a confusion of ancient trees. Some clever local carpenter had imitated Mansart and Lepantre or the work of Fontana – Marshal Bieliński's residence, no longer in existence and known to us only from etchings.' Melchior Wańkowicz, *Tędy i owędy* (Warsaw: Iskry, 1961), 147.

14 Eustachy was released from Russian service in 1857. He served in the Smolensk Regiment of Lancers in 1853–7, under the command of Grand Duke Nicholas Alexandrovich, but did not see action during the Crimean War. RGIA, f. 1343, op. 36, no. 20281, k. 18–20.

15 Eustachy and Apolonia were engaged on Christmas Day 1856 and probably married
    in the early 1860s.
16 This was a traditionally important source of income for gentry estates in this part of
    Europe.
17 Hajkowce was an estate of 200 hectares (494 acres), near Wężowszczyzna.
18 Although committed to the principle of equality among themselves, the nobility of
    the old Polish-Lithuanian Commonwealth prized elective titles, such as *cześnik*. These
    titles carried prestige in the local community and had become largely honorific by the
    eighteenth century.
19 Jan Klemens Minasowicz (1797–1854) was a painter, art teacher, art dealer. In 1840–2
    he taught drawing to the poet Cyprian Norwid (1821–83). Irena's mother was related
    to the Minasowiczes through her grandmother Praxeda Thugutt (née Minasowicz,
    sister of Klemens).
20 Apparently Klemens even took the head with him when he set off on his foreign
    travels in 1829. He returned with the head in 1835. The increasingly deranged
    Minasowicz collected old buns from the bakeries of Warsaw, as well as printed death
    notices which he removed from walls of churches and cemeteries. A wealthy man
    who was generous to local beggars, he refused to spend any money at all on his own
    creature comforts, even on essential medicines for himself. See https://whu.org.
    pl/2016/01/06/o-malarzu-ktory-z-milosci-zyskal-glowe/ (accessed 3 March 2018).
21 Midsummer Eve. Kupała was a local Slavonic deity associated with the rites of spring,
    involving young people jumping over a fire and sending reeds down rivers.
22 The Yatwings (*Jaćwingowie* in Polish) were known as Sudovians in medieval
    chronicles. An old pagan Baltic tribe, they inhabited a large area where modern
    Poland, Lithuania and Belarus meet. They were finally wiped out in the Middle Ages
    by the Poles and the Teutonic Knights.
23 During the existence of serfdom, the *serwituty* entitled peasants to use manorial
    meadows, woods and streams for grazing, gleaning and fishing. These customary
    rights were gradually abolished by the end of the nineteenth century in Austrian
    Galicia and in the Congress Kingdom of Poland, following the land reforms there
    in 1848 and 1864, respectively. However, these rights survived in some places in the
    northeastern borderlands of Poland into the interwar period when their gradual
    abolition took place. In return the peasants received some land from the manor. The
    serwituty were an important source of livelihood for the peasants, and their abolition
    was not always an easy matter. Their existence was considered an obstacle to the
    modernization of agriculture.
24 *Desyatin* is a Russian unit of measuring land, equalled about 1.1 hectares.
25 *Bigos* is a Polish hunters' dish; ingredients include sauerkraut, cabbage, smoked bacon
    and other fatty meats.
26 Dęblin (in Lublin province) has been the home of the Polish Airforce Academy
    since 1927.
27 The Wołłowiczes were an old historic family of Rus origin and substantial landowners,
    especially near Minsk; they played a prominent and distinguished role in the public
    life of the former Grand Duchy of Lithuania. In 1798 Antoni Wołłowicz was granted
    the title of 'Count' by the King of Prussia; the title was recognized by the Congress
    Kingdom of Poland in 1824 and in the Russian Empire in 1844.
28 Maria Rodziewiczówna (1863–1944) was a novelist, born into a landed family. In
    1881 she settled on the estate of Hruszowo in Polesie which she had inherited from
    her uncle, and where she became a close neighbour and friend of the Zawadzkis of

Derewna, the family of Irena's future husband Michał Zawadzki. Rodziewiczówna's ideals were best expressed in her novel *Dewajtis* (1889): 'Dewajtis' was the name of an ancient oak tree growing on her estate. Her *Lato leśnych ludzi* (Summer of the Forest Folk) (1920) conveys the beauty of the natural world.

2 Education, home and the stirrings of love

1 The social prejudices revealed here are worthy of note. The pupils at the Słonim *gimnazjum* were children of local burghers and shopkeepers.

2 The secondary school for girls run by the Sisters of the Most Holy Family of Nazareth was founded in 1915 by Mother Superior Waleria (Anna Czarnocka). She was succeeded in 1921 by Anna Łyszczyńska. In the same year, the school moved to a building in the district of Góra Bouffałowa, west of the city centre, on Sierakowski Street with the entrance on Piaskowa Street. The school was closed down by the Soviet authorities in 1940, and the building was burnt down by the Germans in July 1944. Adam Mickiewicz Street is today Gedimino Prospekt; Piaskowa Street is Valanciaus Street.

3 Kamilla (Mila) Protassewicz (1909–90) was the daughter of Piotr and Kama Protassewicz. She came second in a Miss Polonia competition in 1926, and married Zygmunt Zbroja (1904–40) in 1935. Her husband Zygmunt perished in Katyn.

4 Today, this is Odminių Street, just off Gedimino Prospekt.

5 *Faworki* is a great delicacy of the region, also known as *chrusty* (dried twigs), a deep-fried pastry sprinkled with vanilla sugar.

6 Witold (Wicio) Pilecki (1901–48) was Irena's second cousin, through the Żórawskis.

7 *Armia Krajowa* (AK) was a conspiratorial military organization operating during the Second World War in occupied Poland. It was a constituent part of the wartime Polish Armed Forces owing allegiance to the Polish government-in-exile. In April 1944 the AK had about 300,000 members. The AK was formally dissolved in January 1945, but its ex-members continued to be persecuted and harassed by the Polish communist regime until 1956.

8 Irena's remarks here about her cousin are brief and imprecise. Captain (*Rotmistrz*) Witold Pilecki served with the 13th regiment of Wilno Lancers during the 1939 campaign. He then joined the Polish Resistance. With the consent of his superiors, he deliberately allowed himself to be picked up by the Germans in a round-up in Warsaw in September 1940 with the aim of being sent to Auschwitz (Oświęcim) in order to learn more about conditions in the Nazi concentration camp. At that stage most of the inmates of KL Auschwitz were Polish political prisoners. His first report from Auschwitz reached Warsaw in November 1940, and then the Polish government in London in March 1941. His subsequent reports included details of Jewish transports which started arriving at Auschwitz in March 1942. In Auschwitz he also established a resistance network among the prisoners, an achievement that was recognized in the West in the 1970s with the publication of Józef Garliński's *Fighting Auschwitz* (London: Julian Friedmann, 1975) and M. R. D. Foot's *Six Faces of Courage* (London: Eyre Methuen, 1978). Witold succeeded in escaping from Auschwitz in April 1943 while being transferred to another camp. He took part in the Warsaw Uprising in 1944, and was subsequently a prisoner of war in Germany. After the collapse of the Third Reich, he made his way to General Anders's Second

Corps in Italy. With a small group of dedicated resistance activists, he was authorized by General Anders to return to Poland in 1945 to collect intelligence on the nature of Soviet control of the country. Arrested by the Polish communists in May 1947, he was tortured, condemned to death in March 1948 and executed on 25 May 1948. It was only after 1989 that it became possible to recognize his courage and achievement publicly in Poland. In September 1990 the Polish Supreme Court declared Witold Pilecki not guilty, and exposed the injustice of the 1948 verdict. In July 2006 Witold was posthumously awarded the Order of the White Eagle, Poland's highest decoration, by President Kaczyński. See the IPN website on Pilecki: http://www.pilecki.ipn.gov.pl/rp/biogram/7081,dok.html (accessed 28 April 2015).

9   Bandurski was an auxiliary bishop in Wilno in the 1920s. The Jesuit Piotr Skarga (1536–1612) was a preacher, theologian and writer active in promoting the Counter-Reformation; the first rector of the new University of Wilno (1579–84); and preacher at the court of King Sigismund III Vasa, from 1588.

10 '*Nikt nie więzi, nie zmusza, / Gdzie się woła Hulaj Dusza*'.

11 Today this is Basanavičiaus Street. The house was demolished c. 1960 to make room for a crossroads.

12 Prince Mieczysław Połubiński (1863–1919) was the owner of an estate at Perki in Wilno province; attended the Institute of Agriculture and Forestry at Puławy (1884–7); he also worked in the Land Bank in Wilno (1901–15). The Połubińskis were an old and eminent Lithuanian-Ruthenian princely (*knyaz*) family descended from the Gedymin dynasty.

13 Gedymin (Gediminas in Lithuanian) (c. 1275–1341) was Grand Duke of Lithuania (1315–41). Irena's attachment to Wilno seems contradictory in view of her negative views about town life; clearly Wilno was an exception.

14 Today the building houses the Russian Drama Theatre. Juliusz Osterwa (1885–1947) was an outstanding actor and innovative theatre director in interwar Poland. He founded the experimental theatre group 'Reduta' (Redoubt) in 1919, and was the artistic director of 'Teatr Rozmaitości' (Variety Theatre) in Warsaw in 1923–4. In 1925 he moved his 'Reduta' team to Wilno. He returned to Warsaw in 1931. Between 1932 and 1935 he was director of the Słowacki Theatre in Kraków.

15 The ultimate do-gooder Dr Tomasz Judym is a major character in Stefan Żeromski's novel about the misery of life for the urban poor of Warsaw and Paris: *Ludzie bezdomni* (Homeless People) (1900). Werther: the tragic hero of Goethe's short novel *Die Leiden des jungen Werthers* (The Sorrows of Young Werther) (1774).

16 Today the Lithuanian National Drama Theatre on Gedimino Avenue.

17 'I have completed a monument more lasting than brass'. Horace's *Odes*, III, xxx, 1.

18 Antoni Gołubiew (1907–79) was a historian, writer and Roman Catholic publicist. He studied history, Polish literature and mathematics at Wilno University. After the Second World War he lived in Kraków where he served on the editorial board of the leading independent Catholic paper *Tygodnik Powszechny*. He is best known for his four-volume historical epic *Bolesław Chrobry* (Bolesław the Brave) (Warsaw: PAX, 1956) about the first king of Poland, crowned in 1025.

19 Matthew 15:11.

20 This meant that no butter, eggs nor sugar could be eaten.

21 Jan Goj (1898–c. 1950) was ordained in 1931. In May 1937 he was transferred to Rohotna, an old and extensive parish with nearly 3,000 faithful, including the residents of Borki. See also the Epilogue.

22 Extract from Canto Five of the poem *Beniowski* by Juliusz Słowacki (1809–49), one of the great Polish poets of the Romantic period. The full extract in Polish: '*Widzę, że nie jest On tylko robaków / Bogiem i tego stworzenia, co pełza. / On lubi huczny lot olbrzymich ptaków, / A rozhukanych koni On nie kiełza …*'.

23 'Beware of the scribes, who … devour widows' houses': Mark 12:40.

24 Karl Kautsky's *Der Ursprung des Christentums* was published in 1909. Of course, although a Marxist but a hostile critic of Lenin and the Bolshevik Revolution, Kautsky would not have wanted to be thought a 'communist'.

25 Wacław Brzeziński (1878–1955) was the leading baritone in the Warsaw Opera in 1901–25; also known as the 'Polish Battistini'. He was tutor to Irena's cousin Zygmunt Protassewicz and his wife Jadwiga Smosarska.

26 The wife of Piotr Protassewicz (of Rohotenka) was Kama, born Morska. Gienio and Dziutek Morski were the sons of Kama's brother Antoni Morski.

27 Although she was roughly Irena's age, Halina Jamontt (b. 1911) belonged to the next generation: she was the granddaughter of Irena's father's elder sister Marynia Świackiewicz.

28 But he was not forgotten; see the Epilogue.

3 All not quiet in the distant provinces

1 Stanisław Szurlej (1878–1965) was a doctor of law, barrister and colonel in the Polish Army. He acquired fame and the nickname 'golden mouth' (*złotousty*) in interwar Poland for his oratory and his defence role in many prominent court cases, including that of the peasant leader and former prime minister Wincenty Witos at the so-called Brześć trial of opposition politicians in 1931–2. During the Second World War, Szurlej served with the Polish armed forces in the West as a senior military procurator. He settled in London after the war. Irena met him in Zakopane during the winter of 1936–7.

2 Judge Janusz Jamontt (1878–1951) was the author of *Zagadnienia kryminologiczne w mitologii greckiej* [Criminological Problems in Greek Mythology] (Warsaw: Druk. Policyjna, 1924), and co-author (with E. S. Rappaport and Raphael Lemkin) of *Kodeks Karny z 1932 r. Komentarz* [Commentary on the Polish Penal Code of 1932] (Warsaw: P. Pyz, 1932).

3 Matthew, 7:1; Luke, 24:34.

4 This occurred during the Polish-Bolshevik war; normal law and order had not yet been effectively restored in Irena's region.

5 Irena apparently told her daughter Helen that the grater had in fact been used on another part of the male anatomy, as the woman in question had had enough!

6 Widely used in peasant homes in the east of Europe, these stoves provided heat for the entire cottage and were large enough for a person to lie on, with suitable bedding of course.

7 On people settling personal grudges through denunciations to the Soviet authorities in 1939, see: Jan T. Gross, *Revolution from Abroad: The Soviet Conquest of Poland's Western Ukraine and Western Belorussia* (Princeton and Oxford: Princeton University Press, expanded edn, 2002), 117–22.

8 After the Second World War, Borki was again in the Soviet Union; following the border changes agreed at the Allied Conference at Yalta in February 1945, Poland lost her pre-war eastern territories.

9   Following Irena's death in 1994, I exchanged letters with Wiera's daughter, Vanda
    Feliksovna Sanyuk, who was still living in Borki. My sister Helen and I visited Vanda
    and her sister Yadwiga during our trip there in 1997.

10 Irena attended the first aid course in 1933. IP: certificate issued by the Warsaw
    Section of the Polish Red Cross, 10 April 1933. According to her Polish Army Records
    (MOD), Irena obtained a very good grade on completing the course.

11 This was probably Dr Władysław Ostaszewski, referred to as 'our little doctor', and
    who had just died, by Irena's aunt Mania Żórawska in a letter to Halina Skrzyńska,
    14 January 1966 (IP).

12 Although duelling was illegal in pre-war Poland, the law was sometimes ignored.

13 Reference to Władysław Boziewicz's *Polski kodeks honorowy*. First published in 1919,
    it had seven further editions by 1939. Part II of the Code deals with duelling.

14 According to Senator Józef Godlewski in his *Na przełomie epok* (London: Polska
    Fundacja Kulturalna, 1978), 286, this 'Mr K' was Pan Mieczysław Kutkowski,
    Jeśman's cousin and the director of the Słonim Commercial Bank. The affair of the
    funds of the Słonim branch of the Landowners' Association and of the duel that
    never was is described in a colourful way by Senator Godlewski in his memoirs.
    According to the senator, the affair was resolved by Irena's father agreeing to pay
    the underwritten sum (Godlewski says it was 5,000 złotys), and by Jeśman agreeing
    to pay Irena's father back in instalments. Godlewski, *Na przełomie epok*, 294–6; see
    359–62 for Godlewski's account of the correspondence in the Polish press about the
    affair.

15 This probably refers to the Warsaw daily *Kurjer Poranny* (Morning Courier) in which
    Wańkowicz published other articles about Wacław Protassewicz and Borki. This
    humorous piece, entitled 'Pojedynek Protasewicza z Jeśmanem' (Protasewicz's Duel
    with Jeśman), was reprinted after the war in Poland in a collection of short stories and
    articles in Wańkowicz, *Tędy i owędy*, 145–50.

16 Józef Godlewski-Gozdawa (1892–1968) was the owner of an estate in Synkowicze in
    Słonim district. He was very active in public life and served as a Senator representing
    the Nowogródek Province (1938).

17 During or after the Second World War, Wańkowicz met Zygmunt in a café in the
    United States; he asked Zygmunt if it was he who had wanted to shoot him! IP: Irena
    to Halina Skrzyńska, 18 July 1991.

18 The Minsk region of Belarus went to Soviet Russia in 1921.

19 This article was reprinted simultaneously by Wańkowicz in *Kurjer Poranny*, 20 March
    1938, 3, 6 and in *Słowo*, 20 March 1938, 9–10 following Wacław Protassewicz's death
    in February 1938.

20 It is not clear when Wańkowicz said this to Irena: in Borki before the war, or during
    the war in Palestine (Irena visited Wańkowicz in Tel Aviv), or in London after the war.
    Wańkowicz was probably referring to his 1934 *Szczenięce lata*. Jan Chryzostom Pasek
    (c. 1636–1701) was a swashbuckling gentleman from Mazovia who participated in
    Poland's wars with Sweden, Transylvania and Muscovy in the 1650s and 1660s. His
    memoirs (first published in 1838) cover the period 1656–88 and are a vivid source
    of information about Polish society and the wars of that period. This great classic of
    Polish memoir literature appeared in an English translation by Catherine S. Leach in
    1980: *Memoirs of the Polish Baroque* (Berkeley: University of California Press).

21 It is not clear which of Wańkowicz's books Irena has in mind. In his letter of 15 July
    1948 (IP), Senator Godlewski thanked Irena for her 'short and apposite' statement in
    his conflict with Wańkowicz, 'that cur' (*ten kundel*).

22 Literary reference to Mickiewicz's *Pan Tadeusz or the Last Foray in Lithuania* in which there is an account of a *zajazd* (foray): an armed policing raid organized by aggrieved members of the *szlachta* in the old Polish-Lithuanian Commonwealth to enforce a court decision on their obdurate fellow citizens.

23 Lala Kutkowska was in Warsaw in 1940 and later joined the Polish Home Army. She survived the war and later lived in Lubuskie province, part of the ex-German lands acquired by Poland in 1945. Clearly Irena had forgotten, when writing her account, that she had had news of Lala during and after the war. Michał Giedroyć (in conversation in May 2008) described Lala Kutkowska as 'one of the greatest eccentrics of the eastern borderlands'; in his memoirs, he refers to her as 'a rather frightening amazon'. Michał Giedroyć, *Crater's Edge: A Family's Epic Journey through Wartime Russia* (London: Bene Factum, 2010), 36.

24 It is not clear whether this incident occurred under Russian rule before the First World War or under Polish rule in the interwar period.

25 Horpyna was a physically intimidating witch in Sienkiewicz's swashbuckling novel *With Fire and Sword*. It is Horpyna's physical presence to which Irena alludes here.

26 On her visiting card in the 1930s, Wanda Roycewicz styled herself as 'Wanda de Roycewicz née Comtesse Wołłowicz'.

27 The Province of Polesie lay directly south of the Province of Nowogródek.

28 Henryk Roycewicz (Rojcewicz) (1898–1990), a major in the Polish Army, won the silver medal in equestrian team eventing at the Berlin Olympics of 1936.

29 Józef Wittlin (1896–1976) was a poet and writer associated with the 'Skamander' group of poets. He spent the Second World War in France and then in the United States, and co-founded the PEN-Club Writers-in-exile. His anti-war novel *Sól ziemi* (Salt of the Earth) (1936) was supposed to be the first part of a longer *Powieść o cierpliwym piechurze* (Novel about the Patient Foot-soldier); the manuscript of the second part was lost during the war. *Sól ziemi* appeared in English translation in New York in 1941. According to his notes, Wittlin and his wife stayed in Rohotna and Borki in 1931. I am grateful to Dr Nina Terlecka-Taylor for this reference.

30 Sergiusz Piasecki (1901–64), a man of Polish-Belarusian ancestry, had a very colourful past. He had fought against the Bolsheviks in 1918–21, and became a Polish spy as well as a smuggler. After the war, in Poland, he was sentenced to fifteen years' imprisonment for armed robbery. In prison he started writing his first novel, *Kochanek Wielkiej Niedźwiedzicy* (Ursa Major's Lover). This came to the attention of Melchior Wańkowicz who was visiting prisons and collecting material for a series of articles. The novel, about the life of smugglers on the Polish-Soviet border, was published in 1937 and became a major literary success. Sergiusz Piasecki was pardoned by President Mościcki in the same year and released. He wrote his next novel, *Bogom nocy równi* (Equal to the Gods of the Night) (1938), about espionage in Soviet Russia, while staying as Wanda Roycewicz's guest at Rohotna. He died in London. Irena's father's reaction to Piasecki's criminal past was interesting, as Irena related many years later: 'He [Sergiusz Piasecki] was once brought to Borki by Wanda Roycewiczowa; after the visit my father, with a sneering expression, firmly shut the lock at the bottom of our door.' IP: Irena to Franciszek Wysłouch, 4 January 1973.

31 Eliza Orzeszkowa, born Pawłowska (1841–1910), was a young lady and later mistress of a manor in the Grodno governorate who through self-education became one of Poland's most progressive and uncompromising advocates of social, racial and gender equality; a campaigner against ignorance and backwardness, and against the selfishness of the upper classes.

32 Abramek was a local Jewish dealer. On Abramek's friendly relations with Irena's father, see Chapter 5.

33 According to his death certificate signed by Dr Thilo in KL Auschwitz, Janek Karczewski died on 26 December 1943 (copy of certificate in possession of his granddaughter Kasia Pereira).

4 Warsaw: Relatives, love and a brush with dangerous politics

1 Leon Protassewicz fought as a second lieutenant in the First Brigade of Piłsudski's Legions against tsarist Russia in 1914–16. By 1915 the Legions were 25,000 strong.

2 Faustyn Czerwijowski (1873–1944) was a member of the Polish Socialist Party in 1904–6. In 1907 he co-founded the Public Library of the City of Warsaw, and was its director from 1912 to 1937. A plaque in his honour was unveiled in 1957 outside the library, which is located on Koszykowa Street in central Warsaw. Author of a series of books on librarianship, he also co-founded the National Association of Polish Librarians and was its president in 1924–6.

3 Their marriage (although with a slightly different version of the exchange between the two) features in Grażyna Kubica's *Siostry Malinowskiego czyli kobiety nowoczesne na początku XX wieku* (Kraków: Wydawnictwo Literackie, 2006), 129. Hela was in love at that time with the writer, playwright and artist Stanisław Ignacy Witkiewicz ('Witkacy') (1885–1939), and had been engaged to him in 1912–13. Kubica writes that, in marrying Leon, Hela 'had, so to speak, sacrificed herself on the altar of the fatherland (a truly patriotic idea)'. Because of her personal association and surviving correspondence with Witkacy, an eminent figure in Polish literature, a number of articles have been written in Poland about Hela. On the other hand, there is very little in Kubica's book about Hela's later life.

4 For his military service in 1919–21, Zygmunt was decorated twice with the Cross of Valour, and with the highest Polish military order, the Virtuti Militari. The latter he received personally from Marshal Piłsudski. Zygmunt completed his MSc in Construction Engineering (*Magister Inżynier Budownictwa Lądowego*) at the Warsaw Polytechnical Institute in April 1930. Krynica-Zdrój (located in the Beskid Mountains near the border with Slovakia) was the largest spa town in pre-war Poland, and probably the most fashionable. Zygmunt had a strong interest in music and dreamt of being an opera singer. In 1930 he even went to Milan for auditions. There he met the Polish tenor and actor Jan Kiepura (1902–66) who was appearing in Massenet's *Manon* at La Scala. Kiepura was looking for ways to invest his substantial earnings, and Zygmunt encouraged him to build a luxury hotel in Krynica. Kiepura put Zygmunt in charge of the project which was completed in record time within three years: Hotel 'Patria' was opened on Christmas Eve 1933. With the onset of the Great Depression, Zygmunt had wisely decided to abandon his singing ambitions. Zygmunt and Jadwiga Smosarska were married in February 1935 and lived in Warsaw until the German invasion in 1939. IP: Zygmunt's account of his professional life and of his war service, written for Irena in the 1970s. Zygmunt's life story also appeared (starting on 15 January 1989) in four instalments in the Warsaw Catholic weekly *Za i przeciw*.

5 Irena is incorrect here. According to his daughter Halina Skrzyńska, Maciej Jamontt died from tuberculosis in the prison hospital in Minsk in November 1940. She had

obtained this information from another Wilno lawyer who was imprisoned with Maciej Jamontt but who had survived the ordeal (telephone conversation with HZ, May 2007).

6 It is difficult to establish what Irena meant here. Although Adolf Skwarczewski (1900–91) was born in Russian Turkmenistan and may have spent his childhood there, his surname is of Polish provenance and his first name is definitely 'Western'. Furthermore, according to Dr Jan Tarczyński, a historian of motor transport, who met Skwarczewski in 1982, Skwarczewski spoke fluent Polish without any traces of Russian influence. Dr Tarczyński's letter to HZ, 2 September 2013. As for the Orthodox wedding, this may have been a practical solution if Skwarczewski's wife was Catholic and a divorcee.

7 If the sum is correct, then it probably represented either his commission on the cars sold in the summer months or his annual income. An eminent figure in the history of Polish motorization, Skwarczewski was not the representative of Ford but of Buick, Chevrolet and Cadillac. His main income was from the import of buses and lorries, and his firm's annual turnover in the 1930s amounted to ten million złotys.

8 Kazimierz de Latour (1905–62), the son of General Stefan de Latour, graduated from the Corps of Cadets in Modlin (1926) and the Officers Artillery School in Toruń (1926–8). He specialized in anti-aircraft artillery and was promoted to Captain in March 1938.

9 It is important not to confuse judge Janusz Jamontt with the barrister Maciej Jamontt (1881–1940), nor Hela Jamontt (1914–44, daughter of Janusz Jamontt) with Irena's cousin Halina Jamontt (1911–2011, daughter of Maciej Jamontt, later Skrzyńska). Janusz Jamontt's wife was Róża (née de Latour).

10 'IPS', pronounced '*eeps*' in Polish, stood for *Instytut Propagandy Sztuki* (Institute for the Propaganda of Art). Despite its sinister-sounding name, the institute was founded in 1930 as a rival to the conservative *Zachęta* (Association for the Encouragement of Fine Arts). It was located in a purpose-built building at 13 Królewska (Royal) Street on the south side of the Saxon Gardens in Warsaw. A promoter of modern Polish art, one of its pavilions was turned into a café which was much prized and patronized by the city's painters and poets. IPS was closed down by the Germans in 1939 and the building was demolished after 1945.

11 For de Latour's fate after 1945, see the Epilogue.

12 They appeared together sometime in the mid-1930s. Irena kept the original press cuttings (IP).

13 Tadeusz Kotarbiński (1886–1981) was Professor of Philosophy at the University of Warsaw, Rector of the University of Łódź (1945–9) and President of the Polish Academy of Sciences (PAN) in 1957–62. He was the creator of 'Reism', a materialist philosophical concept.

14 Irena had either forgotten or had never fully understood the nature of Piasecki's nationalist ideology which included a strong religious element. His ideal was 'an authoritarian Catholic-fascist-nationalist state which would establish moral values and promote corporatist social progress'. Kunicki, *Between the Brown and the Red*, xi; see also 4–40. In this context it is worth noting that there were strong religious undertones in East European variations of fascism.

15 Piasecki's first wife Halina Piasecka, née Kopeć (1914–44) was killed during the Warsaw Uprising.

16 Hela Jamontt (pseudonym 'Hela Warzycka') served in the Resistance, first in a nationalist unit led by Piasecki, and then in the mainstream Home Army (AK) as a liaison officer with the rank of sergeant. Energetic and highly motivated, she

was instrumental in the creation and then the running of an extensive welfare organization (within the Polish Underground State) providing assistance to Poles imprisoned by the Germans. She was killed on 21 August 1944 during fighting on Miodowa Street in central Warsaw while carrying a report to a commander of an AK unit. See her entry in *PSB*, x (1962-64), 404. Also: www.1944.pl/historia/powstańcze-biogramy/Helena_Jamontt (accessed 15 April 2015).

17 Wojciech Wasiutyński (1910–94) was a lawyer, Catholic-nationalist writer and publisher. He was a member of the ONR but in 1939 rejoined the mainstream National Democrats.

18 Emeryk Hutten-Czapski (1897–1979) was an active agriculturalist and philanthropist, and chairman of the Landowners' Association in Słonim (1925–31). He was elected to the *Sejm* (Parliament) (1930 and 1935) on behalf of the pro-government party and sat on numerous parliamentary commissions.

19 General Kordian Józef Zamorski (1890–1983) left the army in 1935 to become head of State Police. He escaped from internment in Romania (1939), and reached Palestine where from November 1940 to July 1942 he was in charge of the supply centre of the Carpathian Rifle Brigade. Later, he was acting commander of Polish Forces in the Middle East. He died in London.

20 Bronisław Wilhelm Pieracki (1895–1934), Minister of the Interior from June 1932, was shot in Warsaw on 15 June 1934 by a Ukrainian nationalist. His death provided the Polish government with the pretext to establish an internment camp in Bereza Kartuska. After Pieracki's death, the police detained 600 members of the ONR.

21 Zygmunt Łoziński (1870–1932) was the Roman Catholic Bishop of Minsk (1917) and was imprisoned in Moscow by the Bolsheviks (1920–1). He was Bishop of Pińsk in 1925–32. His beatification process was started in 1957.

22 Marynia Połaniecka was a character in Sienkiewicz's *Rodzina Połanieckich* (The Połaniecki Family) (1895) set in the late nineteenth century. The difficult love story between Stanisław Połaniecki and the beautiful Marynia who eventually becomes his wife is one of the central themes of the novel.

5 Wacław Protassewicz: The last squire of Borki

1 In fact, Zofia was Wacław Protassewicz's first cousin once removed. Zofia's father Stanisław Żórawski and Wacław Protassewicz were first cousins.

2 On Ninka Stabrowska during and after the Second World War, see the Epilogue.

3 Wilhelm's company, based at Bachat Station, Tomsk governorate, had been engaged in the construction of the Kolchugino railway. Bachat lies on the Novosibirsk-Novokuznetsk railway line, about 300 km east of Novosibirsk. Wilhelm was in Tomsk two weeks before the Bolsheviks launched their coup in Petrograd. IP: Wilhelm to Wacław and Zofia Protassewicz, 11 October 1917 (OS). The date of Wilhelm's death in a Bolshevik prison was later established by a Polish court as 10 April 1921.

4 Zatrocze belonged to the Counts Tyszkiewicz.

5 Did Irena have the Mikulskis in mind here? Irena's mother's aunt Joanna Żórawska (1840–1939) had married Stefan Mikulski (1832–93); they had three sons and four daughters. Elsewhere, in her notes, Irena did write that the wife of one of these Mikulski sons (Aleksander) was 'rather parsimonious by nature' (IP).

6 Of interwar Poland's major cities, Poznań had the smallest Jewish population.

7   Polik served with the Polish Bomber Squadron 300 based at RAF Cammeringham, Lincolnshire. From May 1942 the squadron flew Wellingtons; in 1943 it was converted to Lancasters and in March 1944 was moved to RAF Faldingworth, also in Lincolnshire. The rank of major in the Polish Air Force was the equivalent of squadron leader in the RAF.

8   It is unclear whether all of Jan Zych's experiences with the Bolsheviks occurred in 1939, or whether the earlier episode had occurred in 1920.

9   In his account of this incident, Senator Godlewski (*Na przełomie epok* [London: Polska Fundacja Kulturalna, 1978], 289–90) wrote that Wacław Protassewicz went to Warsaw to represent the landowners of Słonim district at a meeting of the Landowners' Association, and that he came upon a left-wing demonstration on Aleje Jerozolimskie (Jerusalem Avenue), the main east-west axis of the modern city.

10 It is worth noting that Jews still represented over a half of Słonim's population before the Second World War: 8,600 (53%) out of the town's total population of 16,300 (1931 census).

11 That is on Judgement Day. In other words, not in this life!

12 In the Roman Catholic tradition, this is done by a penitent in preparation for confession.

13 Irena's future husband Michał Zawadzki, a Polish civil servant, was arrested by the Soviets sometime in late 1939 while attempting to cross the border between Soviet-occupied Poland and Hungary in order to join the Polish Army being formed in France. He was convicted for this 'crime' as well as for acting against the USSR by boycotting the so-called elections organized by the Soviets on 22 October 1939. After being held in prison in Stanisławów and Odessa, he was sent to a labour camp. HIA, file 9887, Wołyń/Kowel: Michał Zawadzki's deposition to the Polish Government, 3 April 1943.

14 It ought to be mentioned that Wacław had attended a Russian secondary school in Minsk.

15 The starch works was still standing in 1997. By the entrance, there was a double metal gate painted in blue with two large red stars, and a sign in Russian: 'БОРКОВСКИЙ КРАХМАЛЬНЫЙ ЗАВОД' (Borki Starch Factory).

16 According to Melchior Wańkowicz, Wacław was apparently widely renowned for using bees to treat rheumatism, a service he provided free of charge. Wacław would place a single bee under the eiderdown of a person suffering from rheumatism. The bee would then sting the 'patient'. The next day two bees were used, three on the third day, and so on – until fourteen bees had stung the 'patient' on the fourteenth day. The process would then be reversed. After twenty-eight days the rheumatic 'patient' was allegedly able to whizz around happily on the dance floor! The otherwise witty Wańkowicz does not imply that such recovery came about through sheer relief on the part of the 'patient' that the treatment had ended. Wańkowicz mentions the bee treatment in two of his sketches which were reprinted in his *Zupa na gwoździu* (Warsaw: PAX, 1967), 51, 135–7. The second sketch is in fact entitled 'Bees under the eiderdown' (*Pszczoły pod kołdrą*).

17 *Biebies* is pronounced 'bee-yeh-bee-yes'. In Slavonic folklore, *biesy* (singular: *bies*) were fiends, demons, evil spirits. After the acceptance of Christianity, the *bies* became identified with the devil. Note Dostoevsky's novel Бэсы (Besy), translated into English as *Devils* or *Demons*.

18 Just before the First World War the rate of exchange was one pound sterling = 9½ Russian roubles. 100 roubles was £10 11s. 2d. (£10.55) – pre-1914 value of course!

19 Emeryk Hutten-Czapski was elected deputy to the *Sejm* in 1930 and 1935.
20 Adam Żółtowski (1881–1958) was a German-educated philosopher with a doctorate on the Polish philosopher Cieszkowski from the University of Munich. He lost his post at the University of Poznań in 1933 for criticizing the government's treatment of the political opposition; his political sympathies were with the National Democrats. He then moved permanently to his wife's estate in Bolcieniki, 44 km north of Lida. He lived in London after the Second World War.
21 The Pakulski Brothers dealt in colonial goods and wines, and produced mead, beer and tinned food. Pomorski specialized in the production of the delicious fudge known as *Krówki*, and of a wide variety of luxury sweets.
22 In 1939, 1 kg of standard state monopoly sugar cost one złoty.

6 Before the storm

1 Probably a local tradition associated with mourning.
2 Baranowicze, 40 km southeast of Borki, had a population of 23,000 in 1939; it was an important railway junction and was the chief town of the district of the same name.
3 Hans Albert spoke and wrote good Polish (which he was studying in Berlin) and was soon to learn Russian.
4 On Władysław Studnicki, see the Prologue. Incidentally, Irena helped to arrange a meeting between Reinkemeyer and Studnicki during the former's visit to Poland. Reinkemeyer's verdict was that Studnicki was too dogmatic in his 'political system'. IP: Reinkemeyer to Irena, n.d.
5 Henryk Skrzyński (1913–2008) was first cousin once removed to Count Aleksander Skrzyński (1882–1931), Austro-Hungarian and then Polish diplomat, Polish Minister of Foreign Affairs (1922–3, 1924–6) and Prime Minister (1925–6).
6 Easter Day in 1939 fell on 9 April. Irena probably made this journey to Rome after the Germans had entered Prague on 15 March and had established the so-called Protectorate of Bohemia-Moravia.
7 Girolamo Savonarola was a fifteenth-century religious reformer who preached against immorality and corruption in Florence.

Introduction to Part Two

1 On examples of villagers defending local manors, see Marek Wierzbicki, *Polacy i Białorusini w zaborze sowieckim. Stosunki polsko-białoruskie na ziemiach północno-wschodnich II Rzeczypospolitej pod okupacją sowiecką 1939–1941* (Warsaw: Volumen, 2000), 97–8, 110–14. Another example is the case of Derewna in Polesie, an estate owned by the family of Irena's future husband, where the lady of the manor Zofia Zawadzka (born Woyczyńska) was a social activist who had done much to provide cultural and welfare facilities for the local villagers. There the Zawadzki family was protected until the arrival of Soviet troops by local Belarusian lads led by nineteen-year-old Wańka. These events were witnessed by Zofia's nephew Jerzy Szyrmer, as related in his *Zebrane kartki z moich wspomnień* (Warsaw: Neriton, 2011), 49–50.
2 On the dramatic and complex events in northeastern Poland after the Soviet invasion on 17 September 1939, see Karol Liszewski, *Wojna polsko-sowiecka 1939r.*

(London: Polska Fundacja Kulturalna, 1986); Zbigniew S. Siemaszko, *W sowieckim osaczeniu 1939–1943* (London: PFK, 1991), 22–5; Keith Sword, ed., *The Soviet Takeover of the Polish Eastern Provinces, 1939–41* (London: Studies in Russia and East Europe, Macmillan in association with SSEES, 1991), 1–43 *et passim*; Gross, *Revolution*, 17–70; Wierzbicki, *Polacy i Białorusini*, 35–211; Marek Wierzbicki, *Polacy i Żydzi w zaborze sowieckim. Stosunki polsko-żydowskie na ziemiach północno-wschodnich II RP pod okupacją sowiecką 1939–1941*, 2nd edn (Warsaw: Fronda, 2006), 37–82. Wierzbicki used Polish, Jewish and Soviet sources, including NKVD reports, in his two works. Also Zachar Szybieka, *Historia Białorusi 1795–2000* (Lublin: Instytut Europy Środkowo-Wschodniej, 2002), 324.

3 For a rigorous analysis of the October 1939 'elections', see Gross, *Revolution*, 71–108. Also Wierzbicki, *Polacy i Białorusini*, 264–76.

4 On the March 1940 'elections', see Gross, *Revolution*, 108–12.

5 Irena's deposition to the Polish government is one of about 20,000 such testimonies by former deportees and prisoners in the USSR that are preserved in the archives of the Hoover Institution on War, Revolution and Peace, Stanford University, California.

6 Cf. Gross, *Revolution*, 113

7 Wierzbicki, *Polacy i Białorusini*, 317–23; Antony Polonsky, *The Jews in Poland and Russia* (Oxford & Portland, OR: The Littman Library of Jewish Civilization, 2012), 3:407.

8 A phrase Irena used in some rough notes she made (in 1943–4) about events she had witnessed in Borki and its vicinity in 1939–41 (IP). In a draft of a letter to an unnamed person in 1944 or 1945, Irena speaks of 'that psychological moment' in the changed attitudes among the peasants (IP).

9 For examples of Jewish help to Polish landowners in 1939, see Wierzbicki, *Polacy i Białorusini*, 114; Wierzbicki, *Polacy i Żydzi*, 133–4, 226.

10 Wierzbicki, *Polacy i Żydzi*, 189–220; Polonsky, *The Jews*, 3:399–412, 419–25.

11 Cf. 'Here [in Warsaw] things are expensive but one is able to lose oneself in a crowd and to sleep peacefully.' IP: Irena's mother to Irena, 13 June 1940.

12 'Everyone is slowly gathering here [in Warsaw]; you are the only one stuck there [in Borki]; we feel sorry for you as you observe everything slowly going to ruin and that you have no one to talk to.' IP: Irena's mother to Irena, 14 May 1940. Again, on 5 June 1940: 'I feel sorry for you that you live alone like a sheep among wolves.' And on 14 August 1940: 'Try to come here, for it's a pity to waste your youth in a spiritual desert.' In her last surviving card to Irena from this period (of 27 October 1940), Zofia seemed to accept her daughter's decision to stay: 'I am glad that you have found peace and inner contentment....'

13 The long-established figures are: first deportation, in February 1940: over 220,000 people; the second, in April 1940: about 320,000 people; the third, in June–July 1940: nearly 240,000 people; the fourth, in June 1941: about 300,000 people. These figures do not include Polish soldiers taken prisoner by the Soviets in 1939 nor the 150,000 young men from the eastern provinces conscripted into the Red Army in 1940. Keith Sword, *Deportation and Exile: Poles in the Soviet Union, 1939–48* (London: Studies in Russia and East Europe, Macmillan in association with SSEES, 1996), 15–27; Siemaszko, *W sowieckim osaczeniu*, 83–100; Gross, *Revolution*, 187–224. A discussion of the figures can be found in Katherine R. Jolluck, *Exile and Identity: Polish Women in the Soviet Union during World War II* (Pittsburgh: Pittsburgh University Press, 2002), 9–16; and in Polonsky, *The Jews*, 3:381–4. Timothy Snyder favours the lower estimates in *Bloodlands: Europe between*

Hitler and Stalin (London: Bodley Head, 2010), 128–30, 141. If one adds the numbers that left the USSR with General Anders (c. 140,000) and the number of Polish citizens (deportees from 1940–1) 'repatriated' to the new Poland from the Soviet interior in 1945–8 (c. 259,000), one already has a total of just under 400,000. And this excludes the countless thousands of Polish deportees who had died in the USSR, thousands who were kept by the NKVD in prisons and labour camps and who were also excluded from the post-war 'repatriation' programme, as well as Polish citizens of Lithuanian, Belarusian and Ukrainian ethnicity who were also excluded. Sword, *Deportation*, 184–96.

14 Giedroyć, *Crater's Edge*, 46–51.
15 Jolluck, *Exile and Identity*, 145–8, 161–75, 234–42. Cf. Anne Applebaum, *Gulag: A History of the Soviet Camps* (London: Allen Lane, 2003), 169, 185, 284–96 *et passim*.
16 Jolluck, *Exile and Identity*, 245–78.
17 Sword, *Deportation*, 28–42.
18 IP: Irena Valdi-Gołębiowska, 'Curriculum vitae'.
19 Sword, *Deportation*, 42–5; Siemaszko, *W sowieckim osaczeniu*, 171–4.
20 The working of this system is described in Sword, *Deportation*, 88–112.
21 Sword, *Deportation*, 60–87. Władysław Anders, *Bez ostatniego roździału. Wspomnienia z lat 1939–1946*, 6th edn (London: Gryf Publications, 1981), 122–5.
22 On the complex story of the Jews in Anders's Army, see Polonsky, *The Jews*, 3:526–32.
23 On this assistance and more broadly on pre-war Polish policy on Jewish emigration, see Timothy Snyder, *Black Earth: The Holocaust as History and Warning* (London: Bodley Head, 2015), 58–76.
24 Sword, *Deportation*, 59.
25 IP: Irena's diary.
26 See Witold Sienkiewicz and Grzegorz Hryciuk, eds, *Wysiedlenia, wypędzenia i ucieczki 1939–1959. Atlas ziem Polski* (Warsaw: Demart, 2008), 52–61; Sword, *Deportation*, 84–6.
27 Anders, *Bez ostatniego roździału*, 21–54. Zbigniew S. Siemaszko, *Generał Anders w latach 1892–1942* (London & Warsaw: LTW, 2012), 127–54, 170–95.
28 For a recent extensive and illustrated account of the saga of Anders's Army, see Norman Davies, *Trail of Hope: The Anders Army. An Odyssey across Three Continents* (Oxford: Osprey Publishing, 2015); for a brief account of Irena's wartime story and life in Britain after the war, see 557, 592–3.

7 'The end of our world'

1 The title is a literary allusion to 'The Year 1812' (O year of years!; *O roku ów!*), Book Eleven, in Mickiewicz's *Pan Tadeusz*.
2 Irena was to live for another twenty-six years.
3 The inscription signifies the end of civilization, of everything. The Bible interprets this as follows: 'MENE, God has numbered the days of your kingdom and brought it to an end; TEKEL, you have been weighed in the balances and found wanting; PERES, your kingdom is divided and given to the Medes and Persians' (Daniel 5:26–28).
4 Proście is situated just over 50 km east of Borki. There had been an important and long Protassewicz presence in that area, which included the main Protassewicz estate at nearby Ostrówek (which had belonged to Bazyli Olechnowicz Protasowicz in the

early sixteenth century). Irena and Maurycy (and his sisters) were probably eighth cousins. As of 2013, the ruined Protassewicz chapel in Proście was still standing.

5 Nieśwież is a historic town on the river Usza with a population of 7,500 in 1939; it was the seat of the Princes Radziwiłł. Nieśwież Castle was built in 1583 with additions made over the subsequent two centuries. The castle still stands and remains a major cultural and tourist attraction in Belarus today.

6 Maurycy Protassewicz must have been killed in action early in September 1939 while defending Pomerania (the so-called Polish Corridor) against the invading Germans.

7 Irena is imprecise here. Zygmunt and Jadwiga continued their journey (possibly by air) to Sweden, Norway and Denmark, and sailed from Copenhagen on the *SS Scanyork*, arriving in New York on 13 November 1939. Smosarska obtained her US visa in Kaunas on 2 October 1939: New York, Passenger Lists 1820–1957 https://www.ancestry.co.uk/search/categories/40/?name=_smosarska&name_x=s_1 (accessed 25 April 2018). There are different accounts of where and how Jadwiga Smosarska obtained her US visa. The matter is discussed in Małgorzata Hendrykowska, *Smosarska* (Poznań: Uniwersytet im. Adama Mickiewicza, 2007), 182–4. The book does not mention the episode in Borki.

8 Łomża is a town 200 km due west of Borki near the German border in East Prussia.

9 In a much earlier account, Irena wrote that when news of the approach of the Soviets reached Borki village, Augustyn Borowik, a notorious thief, tried to rally the villagers to loot the manor house. At first the peasants just laughed at him – 'a fool' (*durak*), they said. It is then that Borowik stopped one of the Soviet tanks on the Słonim-Nowojelnia road and asked for permission to rob the 'lords'. First Borowik and his companions looted the farm buildings on the Great Field. The peasants then seized the grain kept in the barns; they lowered the water in the fish ponds and took away as many carp as they could. (IP: Irena's draft letter to Senator Godlewski, written from Taymouth Castle, [probably late 1944]).

10 Henryk Sienkiewicz's novel *Ogniem i mieczem* (With Fire and Sword) (1883–4) is set in the Ukrainian provinces of the Polish-Lithuanian Commonwealth during the Cossack rebellion of 1648.

11 In her deposition to the Polish government dated 20 April 1943 (original in HIA: file 8032, Now/Słonim), Irena states that some of the looters (*rabusie*) came from as far as Obelkowicze, a village 7 km away. In her draft letter to Godlewski [1944], Irena refers to Obelkowicze as 'a village known for its thieves' (IP).

12 In her 1943 deposition to the Polish government, Irena states that Szeremiet was also an arsonist. In her draft letter to Godlewski [1944], Irena wrote: 'Szeremiet from Iwień village, a notorious thief, had spent time in prison for setting fire to his village' (IP).

13 Probably a local pro-communist activist.

14 Probably a reference to Łysa Góra, the highest peak in the Holy Cross Mountains (Góry Świętokrzyskie) in central Poland. Considered to be a sacred mountain in pagan times, it features prominently in a local legend about witches' sabbaths. In the eleventh century a Benedictine monastery (of the Holy Cross) was founded on the site of the pagan temple.

15 In her draft letter to Godlewski [1944], Irena also made the point that villages with a predominantly Roman Catholic population, such as Rohotna, did not participate in the looting of the manor. Likewise, villagers from Puzewicze did not loot Rohotenka, the nearby home of Irena's aunt Kama Protassewicz, nor did they permit others to do so. And then she added: 'Besides, even Orthodox villages would not have engaged in looting were it not for the lead given by notorious thieves...' (IP). Elsewhere Irena

cites an episode when (in 1940 or 1941) a large group of youngsters in Rohotna, having had a little to drink, began to sing the Polish national anthem at an evening party organized by the Bolsheviks: IP: Irena's draft letter to unnamed person [1944 or 1945].

16 Russian measure: 1 pood = 36 lbs/16.38 kg.

17 In her 1943 deposition (HIA) Irena wrote: 'The peasant robbers showed respect towards Catholic priests ... with the exception of the parish priest in Skrundzie who was killed while his seventy-year old organist was hacked to death. On the whole there were not many murders in the area. The Soviets killed the lady owner (who was pregnant) of the estate in Urbanowszczyzna, and some farmers, while peasant robbers hacked to death the Mikulski ladies.' Skrundzie lies about 30 km west of Borki.

18 In some rough notes (c. 1944) Irena wrote that communism as an organized cell or as an ideology did not exist in Rohotna commune before 1939; that the peasants welcomed the Bolsheviks because they had promised to give them gentry-owned land; and that many peasants clapped approvingly at public meetings for their own safety and to appease 'the terrifying power' represented by the Soviets. (IP).

19 In her draft letter to Godlewski [1944], Irena mentioned that the Soviets also abolished taxes.

20 Text in italics from HIA: Irena's deposition, 20 April 1943. That criminals were often employed in the new Soviet administration is confirmed by Gross, *Revolution*, 56–61. Gross was able to use Irena's deposition in writing his book: see 59, 117, 324.

21 This refers to about 9,000 Polish military veterans and their families who had been rewarded for their military service with plots of land in the eastern provinces in the 1920s. Their numbers were later augmented by civilian settlers. Most of these settlers were deported into the Soviet interior in February 1940.

22 Text in italics and underlined in the original: HIA: Irena's deposition, 20 April 1943.

23 It is difficult to establish when exactly Irena's family left Borki, but it was probably in the second half of October. The border between the German and Soviet zones of Poland remained open in both directions until 22 October 1939; nor was it hermetically sealed after that. A postcard sent to Irena in Borki by her mother from Białystok, and probably posted by someone well after their departure (IP: postmark 28 November 1939), briefly describes their journey and expresses the hope that with the help of Divine Providence the next stage (to Warsaw) will be successful. Białystok was on the Soviet side of, and near to, the Nazi-Soviet demarcation line.

8 Under Soviet occupation (1939 to 1941)

1 Dr Yehezkel (Jechezkiel) Atlas had fled east, with his parents and his younger sister Celina, from his native Łódź in the face of the German invasion of Poland. He must have arrived in Borki in mid-November 1939.

2 According to her army records (MOD), Irena began working as a nurse in Borki on 19 November 1939. Her salary would have been comparable to the average annual wage of industrial workers in the USSR, which according to Soviet sources amounted to 3,447 roubles in 1938.

3 The much-rehearsed propaganda phrases '*u nas vsyo yest*' (we have everything) and '*u nas etogo mnogo*' (we have plenty of this) were frequently used by Red Army soldiers in eastern Poland in 1939. Gross, *Revolution*, 28.

4 This must have happened before December 1939. The Polish złoty remained in use in the Soviet-occupied zone until it was withdrawn on 21 December 1939; all bank deposits of over 300 złotys had already been seized by the Soviet authorities. Although the pre-1939 rate was 1 złoty = 12 roubles, the Soviets imposed parity between the two currencies.

5 Ewarysta (born Protassewicz) Przybytko (1885–1945) was the wife of Emil Przybytko (1883–1929) of Chodziłonie. Although Ewarysta died in Petropavlovsk in northern Kazakhstan, her three children Halina (Kostrowicka), Jadwiga and Janusz, and her grandchildren survived the war in Siberia and were able to return to Poland in 1946.

6 Aleksander Suczek was probably a smuggler who operated across the Nazi-Soviet demarcation line. He is mentioned in Irena's mother's card of 22 August 1940 sent from Warsaw (IP).

7 For Dr Atlas's eventual fate, see the Epilogue. Irena also successfully persuaded Dr Atlas to spare the ancient lime trees near the manor house from being cut down for firewood. IP: Irena to Maryla Wiśniewska, 19 April 1973.

8 Abramek did in fact die peacefully; see the Epilogue.

9 Whether this was the case in Borki village is impossible to tell, but the Polish 1931 census suggests a different picture: illiteracy among the rural inhabitants (aged ten and above) of Słonim district was 34.2 per cent (36.4 per cent for men and 63.6 per cent for women). Perhaps we are dealing here with Irena's distorted perception of the local peasantry? Perhaps she only had women in mind? By way of contrast, in 1931, in the rural areas of Poznań province, illiteracy was 9.1 per cent and in Upper Silesia, 1.5 per cent.

10 Jędrzej Giertych (1903–92) was an ultimate Polish nationalist, and his political vision was of a Poland inhabited by nationalist and traditionalist Catholics. He was a prisoner of war in Germany (1939–45). In London after the war, he worked as a labourer and then a teacher, but remained active politically and as a writer. He was expelled by the exiled National Party (SN) for his extremism and anti-Semitism.

11 However the Polish government in the 1930s did encourage Jewish emigration from Poland. The reference here is to the expulsion of the Jews from Spain in 1492 by King Ferdinand and Queen Isabella.

12 Reference to the so-called Pale of Jewish Settlement to which the Jews of the Russian Empire were confined by tsarist laws. The Pale was created out of the lands of the former Polish-Lithuanian Commonwealth which had come under Russian rule in the eighteenth century, and was extended as far as the Black Sea. By 1897 about five million Jews lived in the Pale; the Pale ended with the Russian Revolution in 1917.

13 Text in italics: Irena's draft letter to Godlewski [1944] (IP). Indeed, while numerous Jews (not only communist sympathizers but also many professionals) found employment in the new Soviet administration, others (merchants, men of property and those labelled 'bourgeois') faced ruin and repression. Jewish cultural and religious institutions were either abolished or Sovietized, while all main Jewish political parties thought it prudent to stop their activities. Even among some Jewish refugees from the German zone there was such disillusionment with Soviet rule by 1940 that many opted to return to the German zone; for that they were deported to the Soviet interior. Polonsky, *The Jews*, 3:384–99; Sword, *The Soviet Takeover*, 57–70.

14 'Rappaport' was a widely encountered Jewish surname. The point being made here was that influential Jews could be found in all walks of life.

15 Nationalist anti-Semitic disturbances, and demands for separate 'ghetto benches' for Jewish students, increasingly took place in many of Poland's institutions of higher learning after 1935. Despite the opposition of many professors (especially in Warsaw, Wilno and Poznań) 'ghetto benches' became common practice in most Polish universities and polytechnical institutes from the autumn of 1937. Many Jewish students stood through lectures rather than submit to this indignity.

16 She could not know at the time, of course, that after the fall of France in 1940 many of France's Jews were to be deported by the Nazis, with the collusion of the French Vichy regime, to the extermination camps in the east.

17 Irena's remarks here and elsewhere about the Belarusian-speaking peasants in her district would certainly not have applied to the literate and enterprising Polish-speaking peasants of western Poland.

18 Matthew 8.20; Luke 9.58.

19 Polish Positivism (*pozytywizm*) is a reference to the political, social and literary movement started in Warsaw after 1864, and inspired by the French philosopher Auguste Comte. Positivism stressed the need for a constructive and empirical patriotism which focused on the modernization of the economy and on improving social and cultural conditions of the nation, as opposed to a romantic approach to life with an emphasis on the armed struggle for independence.

20 Soviet-style collectivization began to be introduced in the ex-Polish territories in April 1940 but was not completed by the time of the German invasion in June 1941. Peasants who were affected were only allowed to keep small allotments near their dwellings.

21 Text in italics: Irena's draft letter to Godlewski [1944] (IP).

22 Luke 12.12.

23 Zdzięcioł was a small township of 3,700 inhabitants, about 15 km northwest of Borki.

24 Kozłowszczyzna was situated 15 km west of Borki. In 1928 it had a population of 467 and possessed a Roman Catholic church, a turpentine and pitch factory, and mills.

25 No doubt he had to fulfil the quota prescribed by the 'Plan', the foundation of the Soviet planned economy. Cf. Irena's remark: 'or the totally idiotic Soviet economic management in Słonim about which one could fill entire columns in a humorous publication'. IP: Irena's draft letter to an unnamed person [1944 or 1945]. On the damaging impact of Soviet economic policies in the newly annexed lands, see Sword, *The Soviet Takeover*, 86–101.

26 During her stay in Ladzinki, Irena was sometimes ordered by the local Soviet authorities to report with a spade to repair roads. Two such orders, one from June 1940 and one from June 1941, have survived in her papers.

27 By then these committees were controlled by the Soviet authorities.

28 Frau Reinkemeyer's letter is dated 5 August 1940 (IP).

29 IP: extract from Irena's draft letter to Reinkemeyer [late 1940].

30 Dziutek left Warsaw sometime in April 1940. IP: Zofia Protassewicz to Irena, 29 May 1940.

31 All Souls' Day (1 November) is celebrated widely in Poland and among Polish Roman Catholic communities around the world. Families gather in their hundreds around the graves of their dead relatives, and place lights and flowers on the graves. Cemeteries become like blazing cities at night. Julia's poem is therefore particularly poignant.

32 At an earlier village meeting, probably in 1940, Irena heard the following words in her defence: 'She submitted to Soviet authority and she's working. Let her live [here].' IP: Irena's draft letter to her mother, 27 March [1940].

9 Siberia

1 Text in italics: extract from Irena's draft deposition [1943] (IP).

2 Text in italics: extract from Irena's draft deposition [1943] (IP). Irena calculated that her train consisted of seventy trucks. According to Soviet instructions of December 1939, the trains carrying these deportees were to consist of fifty-five trucks, including one for the guards and one for the sick (Sienkiewicz and Hryciuk, *Wysiedlenia*, 42). Each truck was supposed to carry twenty-five people, including children, with their possessions. In practice many of such trucks contained between forty and sixty people. The cattle truck in which the eleven-year-old Michał Giedroyć travelled to Siberia in April 1940 had about forty persons, mainly women, some old men and quite a few children: *Crater's Edge*, 44.

3 Irena had in mind those Polish patriots who had been exiled to Siberia after each unsuccessful Polish uprising against the tsars in the nineteenth century, except that in those days the prisoners had to go on foot.

4 Within a day or so of Irena's departure, Germany attacked the Soviet Union; 'Operation Barbarossa' started on 22 June 1941. Irena was fortunate that her train was not attacked by German aircraft. There were substantial casualties when five transports with Polish deportees from western Belarus were attacked from the air.

5 Irena refers here to the sacrament of confession in the Catholic Church. If the priest is satisfied that contrition is genuine he offers an absolution to the penitent. In circumstances where there is no priest, the church does recognize that a genuine personal act of contrition is sufficient to make one's peace with God.

6 General Stanisław Grzmot-Skotnicki (1894–1939), a distinguished cavalry officer, was commander of the Operational Group 'Czersk' during the fighting in Polish Pomerania between 1 and 5 September 1939. He died on 19 September from wounds received during the Battle of the Bzura river.

7 This would have happened during the period of the Nazi-Soviet Pact. On leaving the USSR, Prince Albrecht Radziwiłł and his mother Princess Bichette Radziwiłł, the last châtelaine of Nieśwież, were allowed to travel to Rome via German-occupied Warsaw. It does help to have friends in high places. Michał Giedroyć (conversation in Oxford, May 2007) described Bichette Radziwiłł (née Branicka) as 'an outrageous person' who used to gatecrash receptions in the Vatican; when papal guards tried to stop her, she would announce that she was the Pope's mistress!

8 Text in italics: extract from Irena's draft deposition [1943] (IP).

9 Text in italics: extract from Irena's draft deposition [1943] (IP).

10 Text in italics: extract from Irena's draft deposition [1943] (IP).

11 In her draft deposition [1943] Irena wrote: 'We received a handout of 40 decagrammes of dark stale bread which contained impurities' (IP). On rations for working deportees and their 'pay', see Jolluck, *Exile and Identity*, 63–4.

12 Text in italics: extract from Irena's draft deposition [1943] (IP).

13 The Tomaszewski ladies and Leszek survived their ordeal in Siberia, ending up in England after the war. Irena happened to meet them sometime in the mid-1950s in Fawley Court, then a Polish school run by the Marian Fathers, near Henley-on-Thames.

14 Apart from being in a labour camp for a year as a 'common criminal', Irena would also have been excluded from the provisions of the 'amnesty'; this happened to starving individuals who had stolen bread. Sword, *Deportation*, 53. She would therefore have

been prohibited from joining the Polish Army or leaving the USSR in 1942. Her subsequent fate would have been dramatically different.

15 They were the descendants of immigrant German peasant farmers who had settled on the lower Volga near Saratov in the second half of the eighteenth and in the early part of the nineteenth centuries. This policy had been initiated by Empress Catherine II in 1762. After 1917 the Volga Germans were the first Soviet ethnic minority to receive local autonomy; the Volga German Autonomous Soviet Socialist Republic (ASSR) lasted from 1924 to 1941. With the German invasion of the USSR, the Volga Germans (numbering 650,000 to 700,000) were deported to the east, and the Volga German ASSR was dissolved.

16 If uttered in 1941, this would have been a wild rumour, an indication nonetheless of the impact of Operation Barbarossa. Even in 1942, despite their big push towards the Caucasus, the German invaders were never to reach Baku (in Azerbaijan).

17 Text in italics: extract from Irena's draft deposition [1943] (IP). On the willingness of descendants of earlier Polish exiles to confide with the new Polish deportees, see Jolluck, *Exile and Identity*, 138–9.

18 Most deportees from eastern Poland were not told by the Soviets why they were being deported. Many, like Irena, were only told of their 'sentence' after arriving at their place of exile or labour camp.

19 Irena was released from her *kolkhoz* on 15 September 1941, a month after the amnesty had been issued.

20 A well-known religious hymn written in 1579 by Jan Kochanowski, considered to be the most outstanding of Poland's Renaissance poets.

21 Workers on collective farms were allowed to keep a small allotment to grow some produce for themselves. These were often the most productive bits of land in the whole agricultural sector of the USSR.

22 Christ's words: 'Truly, I say to you, unless you turn and become like children, you will never enter the kingdom of heaven. Whoever humbles himself like this child, he is the greatest in the kingdom of heaven' (Matthew 18.3–4). Traditional Christian teaching used to identify limbo (near the region of hell) as the abode for the souls of unbaptized infants, and of those righteous people who lived before the coming of Christ.

23 A telling comment on the harsh work discipline in the USSR in this period.

24 It is unclear what Irena means by 'perversions'. In her mind at the time, and in light of her strict convent upbringing, it may have been promiscuity or homosexuality. These views were to become less moralistic later in life.

25 This represented, roughly speaking, a three-year contract. Such offers were unusual for Siberia. Such a contract would also have prevented Irena from joining the Polish Army in 1942.

26 It is important to bear in mind that Muscovite serfdom had not been extended to Siberia; there were few gentry landowners there and land was plentiful.

27 Polish women who had been deported by the Soviets refrained from mentioning this aspect of their difficulties in their depositions to the Polish government, although it must have affected many women suffering from near-starvation; see Jolluck, *Exile and Identity*, 176–7.

28 Pan Twardowski is a character in Polish folklore, allegedly based on a nobleman who lived in Kraków in the sixteenth century, who signed a Faustian pact with the devil in exchange for magical powers. Many Poles were subject to NKVD pressure to become agents or informers; some agreed to secure their freedom but without intending to honour such agreements imposed under duress. It is difficult to establish how many

Poles were detained for refusing to cooperate with the NKVD. Sword, *Deportation*, 48; Siemaszko, *W sowieckim osaczeniu*, 131–3. Women were sometimes terrorized to become informers by threats that they would be moved away from their children or that some of their loved ones would be shot. Jolluck, *Exile and Identity*, 112–13.

29 On the Bartoszewicz family, see Chapter 3.

30 In Polish Catholic homes, a specially produced unconsecrated wafer is shared by all those present before the start of the evening meal on Christmas Eve. It is an essential feature in the celebration of Christmas.

10 Joys and sorrows in Central Asia

1 Irena and Franciszka Bartoszewiczowa travelled west from Kansk to Novosibirsk along the Trans-Siberian railway, and then south via Semipalatinsk and Alma Ata to Dzhambul (south Kazakhstan), a journey of over 3,000 km.

2 Chokpak is over 50 km west of Dzhambul; it was the headquarters of the Polish 8th Division.

3 General Bronisław Rakowski (1895–1950) was in command of the Polish 8th Division in the USSR in 1941–2. He commanded the 2nd Armoured Division in Italy in 1944–7.

4 Father Wiktor Judycki (1905–55) was a military chaplain from Grodno. After internment in Lithuania (1939–40), he was in Soviet captivity (1940–1). With the formation of the Polish Army in the USSR he returned to his post as an army chaplain. He was subsequently appointed chaplain to the 5th Kresowa Infantry Division (part of the Polish Second Corps in Italy) with the rank of colonel, and ministered to his men on the front lines during the battles of Monte Cassino, Bologna and Ancona. He moved to Britain after the war and worked as a priest in the Brompton Oratory.

5 This was probably Dr Jan Danek who had graduated from the Polish Medical School in Edinburgh.

6 The Skirmunts were an ancient and distinguished family in the former Grand Duchy of Lithuania. Most of them lived in Polesie.

7 The Polish Army had an organizational centre there, a field hospital and a centre for the women's auxiliary territorial service. There is also a Polish military cemetery in Guzar.

8 Nothing came of this. It is sad that Irena received no decorations at all from the Polish military authorities for all she had done during the war; but she was awarded British medals: the War Medal 1939–45 and the Defence Medal 1939–45. In October 1952 Irena joined the Polish Combatants Association with the member number 68649, section 348. Forty years after the war Irena joined the Association of Women Soldiers of the Polish Armed Forces in the West and was entitled to wear the Association badge (card no. 410 issued in London on 1 September 1985).

9 Dr Niedziałowski died on 29 March 1942. *Wykaz poległych i zmarłych żołnierzy Polskich Sił Zbrojnych na obczyźnie w latach 1939–1946* (London: Instytut Historyczny im. Generała Sikorskiego, 1952), 119.

10 Franciszka Bartoszewicz died on 11 April 1942, aged forty-two, and is buried in the military cemetery (CW) at Chokpak, grave no. 15: *Wykaz poległych*, 338.

11 'Sour milk' was not spoilt (or 'off') milk, but specially made into a yoghurt-like food. It is widely drunk in eastern Europe and Asia.

12 In June–July 1942: Irena's army records (MOD).

13 Józef Gawlina (1892–1964) was a field bishop of the Polish Army. During the Second World War, he was the head pastor of the Polish forces in the West. In April 1942, he travelled to the USSR and did a three-month tour of Polish units there. He visited Polish communities in the United States in 1943 and was with the Polish Army in Italy in 1944. He was chairman of the governing council of the Polish Red Cross (1945). After the war he resided in Rome where in 1946 he was appointed rector of St Stanislas House, the home of the Polish Church in Rome since the sixteenth century. In 1948 Bishop Gawlina was given special responsibility for the religious welfare of Polish exiles in the West.

14 Estera Laja (Leah) Witkowska was born in 1907 in Konin, a town in central Poland with a lively Jewish community. In 1933 she and her family moved to Łódź where Estera qualified and worked as a nurse. When war broke out she escaped to the Soviet zone, but ended up as a slave labourer in a Soviet copper mine in the Urals. After the war she went to the United States where she married Natan Szafran, a fellow Bundist. Estera's parents died before the war, but her three brothers and their families perished in the Holocaust. See the moving section on Estera Witkowska (under her married name Lola Szafran) in Theo Richmond, *Konin: A Quest* (London: Jonathan Cape, 1995), 173–81, 281. Richmond met Estera in December 1987 in a Manhattan hospital where she being treated for leukaemia. Despite her illness, she still possessed 'natural dignity and finesse'. Estera died on 29 December 1988.

15 Polish policemen apprehended by the Soviets in 1939 were murdered in Kalinin (Tver) in April–May 1940 and were buried in Mednoye.

16 There were two Polish technical schools in Egypt: Signals at Tel-el-Kebir in the Nile Delta, and the other for air force ground crew at Heliopolis. After the war, Dr Roman Żyznowski was the medical officer in the Polish resettlement camp in Springhill Lodges in Gloucestershire where Irena and her family were to live between 1951 and 1956.

17 Dr Krzywański held the rank of major when he was in charge of the Polish military hospital during the battle for Monte Cassino in 1944.

18 Gunner Józef Bratkowski died on 18 July 1942 and is buried in the military cemetery in Kenimekh, grave 150–8. *Wykaz poległych*, 91.

19 Irena's parenthetical comment is misleading. Anders could not have done this without the full agreement of the Soviets and of the British. Where Anders ignored orders from London was in allowing civilian deportees to accompany the troops leaving the USSR.

20 Michał Zawadzki drank spirits; when they ran out on board the ship his condition deteriorated. Michał joined the Polish Army in the USSR (the 8th Division – the same Irena had belonged to before her illness in Chokpak) on 22 March 1942. He arrived in Palestine on 22 July 1942. MOD records.

21 Helena Zawadzka (1888–1971), née Grabowska, lived in Kowel (province of Volhynia, today in Ukraine) where her husband was a senior government official. After her husband's arrest by the NKVD, she was deported to Siberia. Michał's father, also Michał, was murdered by the NKVD somewhere in Ukraine in the spring of 1940 along with many thousands of other Polish officials. His wife and son did not know this, but must have had their suspicions. Helena reached Iran as a civilian with the Polish Army.

22 According to Sword, it was the Soviet military authorities who ordered the Poles to surrender all their remaining roubles and to reduce their personal luggage to 20 kg (44 lbs) per person. Compare Irena's account of this last leg of the journey with that of another witness, Janina Kowalska, a twelve-year-old girl (Sword, *Deportation*, 79–80).

11 From Persia to the Holy Land

1   Pahlevi (now 'Bandar-e Anzali') lies on the southwest coast of the Caspian Sea.

2   Another Polish deportee in Pahlevi, Romuald Lipiński, commented that the British, who apparently managed the camp in Pahlevi, did not realize that the Poles had not eaten regular food for a long time and that they could not digest heavy fats. As a result the diet of fatty mutton and rice brought about violent diarrhoea. See http://www. kresyfamily.com/romuald-7.html (accessed 27 April 2018).

3   General Bolesław Szarecki (1874–1960), a pioneer of Polish military surgery, was acting head of medical services in the Polish Forces in the USSR in 1941–2, and was well known among the Polish troops in the Middle East. In 1943–5 he was chief medical officer in the Second Corps in Italy. After the war he returned to Poland (one of eleven Polish generals to do so) and was appointed head of the medical department in the Ministry of Defence (1946–9) and then chief surgeon of the Polish Army until his retirement in 1959.

4   Commandante Żylińska, described affectionately as 'Aunt' (*Ciotka*) by the troops, was later the chief sister in the Polish military hospital during the battle for Monte Cassino, and inspector of the Polish military health service. She came from a landed family in the Oszmiana region in pre-war northeastern Poland.

5   Polish military convoys travelled from Pahlevi to Qazvin, then to Hamadan, Kermanshah and across the Iraqi border to Khanaqin; then via Baghdad and across the Syrian Desert (*el Hamed*) to Trans-Jordan and Palestine.

6   Allusion to the title of Józef Czapski's book *Na nieludzkiej ziemi* (1949), published in English as *The Inhuman Land* (1951). Czapski (1896–1993), a painter, author and critic, was a prisoner in the USSR (1939–41). He was commissioned by General Anders to investigate the fate of the thousands of Polish officers in Soviet captivity. The book deals with his fruitless search.

7   Rehovot is about 20 km southeast of Tel Aviv; there was also a Polish military hospital there.

8   A friendly letter from Halina Heller to Irena (of 17 January 1944) offered sound cautionary advice about an unnamed gentleman Irena had met, presumably in Palestine (IP). Halina Heller also assisted Irena in making enquiries about Captain de Latour through the Polish Red Cross; it was established that he was alive and in a German POW camp. IP: H. Heller to Irena, Ain-Karem, 1 April 1943.

9   Dr Wit Tarnawski (1894–1988), a physician by training, was also a writer, literary critic and leading authority on Joseph Conrad. Before the war he had been the director of the fashionable health resort in Kosów (founded in 1893 by his parents) in the foothills of the Carpathian Mountains (today Kosiv in Ukraine). The schools for Polish young soldiers were allowed by the British authorities on condition that they retained a military character.

10 Camp Barbara, located east of Ashqelon on the main road from Tel Aviv to Gaza, was the home of the Polish Young Soldiers Cadet School (*Junacka Szkoła Kadetów*). For a vivid account of the cadet school in Camp Barbara by one of its former cadets, see Giedroyć, *Crater's Edge*, 146–67.

11 It was difficult to get a commission in the Polish Army because of limited funds; many educated NCOs became PROs (Public Relations Officers) with access to the officers' mess to separate them from ordinary NCOs.

12 Wlastimil Hofman (born Vlastimil Hofmann in Prague in 1881; d. 1970) was a modernist painter. At the age of eight he moved to Kraków. In 1896 he enrolled as

a student, under Jacek Malczewski, at the Academy of Fine Arts in Kraków; in 1899 he studied at the École des Beaux Arts in Paris. After living in Prague and Paris in 1914–20, he returned to Kraków in 1921. In 1919 he married his partner Ada. In 1939 he and Ada fled from Poland to Istanbul, and then to Palestine. In June 1946 the Hofmans returned to Kraków, and in May 1947 moved to Szklarska Poręba (formerly Schreiberhau), a spa town in the Karkonosze Mountains (Riesengebirge) in Lower Silesia. Hofman's works still fetch good prices in Polish art houses.

13 'I remember well how you were solicitous for us in Nazareth!!' IP: Ada Hofman to Irena, 23 March 1964.

14 Jan Hus (c. 1371–1415) was a Czech religious reformer and a precursor of the Protestant Reformation. He attacked the vices of the Catholic hierarchy and called for radical reform of the church. Condemned as a heretic by the Council of Constance, he was burned at the stake.

15 Jacek Malczewski (1854–1929), a pupil of Matejko, is regarded as one of the most famous Polish Symbolist painters; many of his works contain a complement of angels and chimeras.

16 1 Corinthians 13.12: 'For now we see in a mirror dimly, but then face to face. Now I know in part; then I shall understand fully, even as I have been fully understood.'

17 Irena suggested such an article to Dom Paul de Vooght, the author of a study of Christian theologians of the fourteenth and early fifteenth centuries (published in Bruges in 1954) and of *L'Héresie de Jean Huss*, 1st edn (Louvain: Publications Universitaires de Louvain, 1960). His article, entitled 'Jan Hus: Heretic or Martyr?', appeared in the Catholic weekly *The Tablet*, 1 February 1969, 99–100; a short preview appeared in *The Times*, 30 January 1969, 8 (Times Diary).

18 Hofman's letter from Szklarska Poręba, postmark 22 February 1968 (IP).

19 But Irena did acquire several of Hofman's paintings, including a portrait of herself (in uniform) in Nazareth, painted in January 1944.

20 Hofman served briefly in March–April 1943 as chairman of a Polish-Czechoslovak Committee of Friendship and Cooperation established in Palestine.

21 After the war, the Hellers came to England and lived in a Polish resettlement camp near Fairford, in Gloucestershire, before eventually moving to Oxford.

22 Wańkowicz's visiting card has survived from that time with a message to Irena: 'I hoped very much that we should meet. I wonder what the young lady from Borki is doing amongst that gang of little monsters [young soldiers]. I trust you'll give a good account of yourself there'. (IP)

23 It is worth bearing in mind that Irena's proselytizing attitude towards Orthodoxy and views on the relations between different Christian denominations were later to change in a liberal direction.

24 Axel Munthe (1857–1949) was a Swedish physician, psychiatrist and philanthropist, best known for his book *The Story of San Michele* (1929) which contains observations about human behaviour and human foibles.

25 In many Polish landed families of the period there emerged the ideal of the 'Polish Mother' (*Matka Polka*) who, in the absence of their menfolk (who had taken up arms or who had been killed or exiled by the tsarist authorities), acted as protectors of the family hearth and as guardians of national traditions and of mementoes of the patriotic struggles. See Jolluck, *Exile and Identity*, 88–98.

26 A large deep vertical beehive, made of dry pine wood, invented by Charles Dadant (1817–1902), an American beekeeper of French origin. Dadant's hives were later improved by E. Blatt of Switzerland, hence the double name.

27 Wanda Wasilewska was the chairman of the Soviet-sponsored Association of Polish
     Patriots (ZPP) in the USSR. Indeed, it was the Soviet-backed so-called Polish
     Committee of National Liberation (PKWN) which was established in authority by
     the Red Army in Poland in 1944, and which formed the core of the later communist-
     dominated government.

28 Not that she was spared her share of suffering in the USSR. While in Kazakhstan,
     Jadzia Przybytko refused to accept Soviet citizenship. For this act of defiance she
     was sent to a penal colony (which provided labour for a breeding farm for pedigree
     pigs) near Vladivostok. There she succumbed to night-blindness (probably caused
     by malnutrition and vitamin A deficiency) and only recovered after eating sparrows'
     livers and stealing high-quality food offered to the pigs. She was released after the
     'amnesty' of 12 August 1941. Source: Her sister Halina Kostrowicka's reminiscences,
     recorded in Legnica, 25 March 1989 (and made available by Jadzia's niece
     Aleksandra Kucz).

29 The last one was the standard popular song of the Polish Army.

30 Ref-Ren (Feliks Konarski) (1907–91) was a poet, songwriter, actor and cabaret
     performer, with an established reputation in pre-war Poland. He joined Anders's
     Army in the USSR, and created a revue theatre for the troops: *Polska Parada* (The
     Polish Parade).

31 Irena Renata Bogdańska (1920–2010) was a revue artist, singer and actress; she
     married General Anders in 1948.

32 The words by Ref-Ren and the score by Alfred Schütz were written on the evening of
     the successful capture of Monte Cassino by General Anders's Polish Second Corps
     on 18 May 1944. Text of *Czerwone maki na Monte Cassino*: in F. Konarski, *Piosenki
     z plecaka Helenki* (Rome: published by the author, 1946), 147–8. The song's second
     verse roughly reads: 'Red poppies on Monte Cassino / Instead of dew, drank Polish
     blood / As the soldier crushed them in falling / For the anger was more powerful
     than death / Years will pass and ages will roll / But traces of bygone days will stay
     / And the poppies on Monte Cassino / Will be redder having been nourished by
     Polish blood.' The song was banned in communist Poland, but remained an unofficial
     anthem for most Poles; many people used to stand to attention whenever it was
     played.

33 MOD: Irena's army records (*Zeszyt Ewidencyjny*, 14) contain the following reports
     by her company commanders: 'High degree of intelligence. Very good discipline.
     Professional qualifications adequate. Very good service loyalty. Very conscientious at
     work; likes children; nervous' (dated 11 June 1943); and 'Very dutiful at work, willing
     to help' (dated 1 March 1944).

12 From Egypt to Scotland

 1 What Irena refers to as the 'English hospital' was most probably the Anglo-American
     Hospital, opened in Cairo in 1903. During the Second World War, it was a British-
     run military hospital. The Polish Red Cross establishment in Cairo was located at 30,
     Sharia Mansour.

 2 Irena brought the daggers with her to Britain. When she lived alone in Lower
     Quinton and someone knocked on her door in the evening she would reply through
     the door with a warning, uttered in a strong Polish accent: 'Eez dat teef? I haff

stiletto!' What used to happen next is not recorded. After her death, her younger son Michael handed in these dangerous weapons to the Buckinghamshire constabulary in Aylesbury.

3 Irena was seconded to the *Gimnazjum Mechaniczne Lotnicze* (Air Force Mechanical School) in Heliopolis between 1 and 21 February 1944 (MOD: Irena's army records). Bearing in mind the reception at King Farouk's aunt's residence, it is highly probable that she was sent to Heliopolis on account of her knowledge of French. It was probably during this period that Irena attended a concert in Egypt by Artur Rubinstein: 'I last heard him [Rubinstein] play in Egypt 30 years ago.' IP: Irena to Halina Skrzyńska, 20 October 1975.

4 The Second Corps (over 50,000 men) was transported from Palestine to Italy between mid-December 1943 and mid-April 1944.

5 'When I bent down to clean the floor for the first time, I felt as if the last vestige of my self-esteem had evaporated.' IP: Irena to Halina Skrzyńska, 18 July 1991.

6 Irena was transferred to the Polish military hospital in Taymouth Castle on 1 September 1944 and was appointed ward sister (*siostra salowa*); on 15 September she was formally transferred from the 1st Battalion of the Women's Auxiliary Service to the Corps of Nurses. In July 1944 the Polish government raised the status of the Women's Auxiliary Service by recognizing them formally as soldiers and members of the Polish Armed Forces.

7 Chorus no. 269 entitled 'Wide, Wide as the Ocean', in *C.S.S.M. Choruses No.1* (London: Children's Special Service Mission, 1936). The full text reads: 'Wide, wide as the ocean, / High as the heaven above; / Deep, deep as the deepest sea / Is my Saviour's love. / I, though so unworthy, / Still am a child of His care; / For His Word teaches me / That His love reaches me everywhere.' I am indebted to Jacqui Worswick for this reference.

8 A transport of nearly 200 wounded soldiers from the Second Corps arrived at Taymouth Castle from Italy on 10 October 1944. Polish Museum and Sikorski Institute (PMSI) Archives, Daily Orders 1944, vol. 4. R.1265/D, order no. 241, 16 October 1944.

9 Dr Izydor Redler held the rank of second lieutenant and features in the Taymouth Castle hospital records (PMSI Archives). He is listed in the 1939 Lwów directory (Słowacki Street no. 2).

10 There was an Orthodox branch of the family in the nineteenth century. It is worth mentioning again that Irena's own direct Protassewicz ancestors belonged to the Orthodox Church until the turn of the sixteenth and seventeenth centuries.

11 The Polish Army formally recognized the higher education received by its servicemen, even those of 'other ranks'. Michał served in the 10th Dragoons in the Polish 1st Armoured Division under the command of General Stanisław Maczek (1892–1994). He arrived at Taymouth Castle on 28 September 1944. PMSI Archives, Military Hospital no.1, Daily Orders 1944, vol. 3, R.1265/C, order no. 227, 29 September 1944.

12 For an excellent account of the role of the Polish 1st Armoured Division, see John Keegan, *Six Armies in Normandy. From D-Day to the Liberation of Paris* (London: Pimlico, 1992), Chapter 7: 'A Polish Battlefield'. <

13 Irena also received a warm letter of congratulation from Aleksandra Piłsudska, the Marshal's widow, who was then in Edinburgh. IP: letter of 24 February 1945.

14 The postscript was added by Irena in 1987.

Epilogue: Exile and resettlement in Britain

1 Cited in Keith Sword, Norman Davies and Jan Ciechanowski, *The Formation of the Polish Community in Great Britain 1939–50* (London: SSEES, 1989), 232, see also 229–34.

2 Following the agreement of September 1944, about 1.2 million former Polish citizens of Polish and Jewish ethnicity were allowed to be 'repatriated' to the new Poland in 1944–7. A later agreement of July 1945 with the Soviet government enabled over 266,000 former Polish citizens (of Polish and Jewish ethnicity) who were still in the Soviet interior to return to Poland. A million or so Poles remained within the post-1945 borders of the USSR. A further agreement in 1957 led to the return of 256,000 people to Poland. As a result of all these movements Wilno and Lwów ceased to be cities with a Polish-speaking majority. Most of the Jewish inhabitants of both cities had already perished in the Holocaust. Cf. Sword, *Deportation*, 184–99; Wojciech Roszkowski, *Historia Polski 1914–2001* (Warsaw: PWN, 2003), 252–3; Snyder, *Reconstruction of Nations*, 84–9, 158–91; Weeks, *Vilnius*, 155–88.

3 IP: letter of 27 July 1945.

4 IP: Michał to Irena, 12 February 1946.

5 IP: Irena to Halina Skrzyńska, 5 October 1991. During the war a section of the Western General Hospital housed a Polish hospital named after Paderewski. The Polish medical school attached to the University of Edinburgh functioned from 1941 to 1949.

6 IP: O. Sawies-Zabłocka to Irena, 16 September 1948.

7 See http://eastwoodhousedunkeld.com/ (accessed 21 February 2018).

8 IP: letter of 3 June 1947.

9 IP: letter from Jerusalem, 7 June 1946.

10 IP: letter from Kraków, 9 July 1947.

11 Atholl MSS: diary entry Saturday 8 June 1946.

12 Recent fragmentary studies suggest that even with this heavy intimidation the Peasant Party received between 60 and 70 per cent of the popular vote; in some areas, it was over 70 per cent. Roszkowski, *Historia Polski*, 162–8; Jerzy Lukowski and Hubert Zawadzki, *A Concise History of Poland*, 2nd edn. (Cambridge: Cambridge University Press, 2006), 284–5. Cf. Anne Applebaum, *Iron Curtain: The Crushing of Eastern Europe 1944–56* (London: Penguin, 2013), 211–19.

13 For the origins and creation of the Polish Resettlement Corps, see Sword, *The Formation of the Polish Community*, 200–55.

14 IP: Irena to Halina Skrzyńska, 25 December 1990.

15 IP: Irena to Halina Skrzyńska, 25 December 1990.

16 Katharine, Duchess of Atholl, *Working Partnership: Being the Lives of John George, 8th Duke of Atholl and of his Wife Katharine Marjory Ramsay* (London: Arthur Barker Ltd., 1958), 243. For the duchess's extensive involvement in the Polish cause, and indeed in support of other nations and individuals whose freedom was threatened, see 237–50. I am grateful to Ben Knott for drawing my attention to this book and presenting me with a copy. In 1945 the duchess also published a booklet on the 1944 Warsaw Uprising: *The Tragedy of Warsaw and its Documentation* (London: John Murray).

17 IP: Irena to Halina Skrzyńska, 18 July 1991.

18 IP: Irena to Halina Skrzyńska, 25 December 1990. The duchess's husband, John Stewart-Murray, the 8th Duke of Atholl, died in 1942 and was succeeded by his

brother James Stewart-Murray as the 9th Duke but for many years he refused to use his ducal title. Lord James Murray's deep involvement with the Poles and their cause can be followed in his letters to his cousin William Moncrieffe and his wife Edith in 1940–7 (Atholl MSS, Bundles 929 and 955). He played a leading role in establishing and running a hostel for Polish soldiers in Edinburgh and in launching the Scottish-Polish Society; he frequently visited the wounded in the hospital in Taymouth Castle, and in 1945 had almost daily contact with Polish soldiers; and also gave farewell speeches in Polish to those who opted to return to Poland in 1947.

19 The topic of their tragic separation features frequently in family correspondence of the time.

20 IP: Irena to Halina Skrzyńska, 18 July 1991.

21 As reported by Mila Kontkowska: IP: letter to Irena, 22 November [1945].

22 IP: Zofia Protassewicz to Irena, 3 December 1945.

23 IP: letter of 24 January 1946.

24 IP: letter of 24 January 1946.

25 IP: letter of 17 March 1946.

26 IP: letter of 22 April 1946.

27 IP: Hania Protassewicz to Irena, 17 March 1946.

28 IP: Julia Prange (formerly Karczewska) to Irena, 2 April 1946.

29 IP: undated letter, probably 1946.

30 IP: letter of 16 July 1946.

31 On Hela Jamontt: IP: Róża Jamontt to Irena, 18 April 1946.

32 But Irena was never to know (and her sister would not have written about it) that Hania found herself in close vicinity of the leadership of the Home Army (AK) and of the Polish Underground State in Milanówek outside Warsaw until the Polish leaders were kidnapped by the NKVD in March 1945. The Polish leaders used to meet at the café 'U Aktorek' (At the Actresses) where Hania worked as a waitress. Joanna Podgórska, 'Powrót słońca w Milanówku', *Polityka*, no. 45, 8 November 2003, 119.

33 IP: letter of 9 August 1946.

34 IP: postcard of 17 May 1946.

35 IP: letter of 13 August 1946.

36 IP: letter of 17 October 1946.

37 IP: letter of 22 November [1945].

38 IP: letter of 28 December 1945.

39 IP: Z. Kątkowski to Irena, 23 May 1946.

40 Six years after the war there was still no news of the nephew and his wife. IP: Zofia Protassewicz to Irena, 15 June 1951. Nor four years after that. IP: Julia Prange to Irena, 23 March 1956.

41 IP: Fela Hernas to Irena, 7 October 1946.

42 IP: letter from Rio de Janiero, 18 July 1947.

43 IP: letter of 19 November 1946.

44 IP: letter of 30 April 1947.

45 IP: letter of 22 February 1947.

46 Under the rule of Wilhelm Kube, the Nazi *Gauleiter* in occupied Belarus, Soviet-style collective farms in (ex-Polish) western Belarus were dissolved: former landowners (if there were still any in the region) and individual peasants were able to recover their former properties. Szybieka, *Historia Białorusi*, 340.

47 Soviet partisans did not operate in western (ex-Polish) Belarus until 1943, out of regard for the July 1941 treaty with General Sikorski's government in London; the

treaty stated that the provisions of the Nazi-Soviet Pact of 1939 were no longer valid. Szybieka, *Historia Białorusi*, 341.

48 IP: letter of 20 September 1949.

49 IP: letters of 10 February and 10 April 1947.

50 IP: letter written from Quakenbrück, 26 February 1947. The Polish-Soviet frontier established in 1921 left the Minsk region of Belarus and most of the Ukraine on the Soviet side; it finally confirmed the end of Polish landownership in those lands. Most Polish landowners there had already fled the area during the Russian Revolution and the violent political and social upheavals that followed in 1918–20.

51 IP: letter of 22 February 1947. Indeed, as a result of the war, Belarus was one of the most devastated areas of Europe, losing over a quarter of its population. Szybieka, *Historia Białorusi*, 361–4; Snyder, *Bloodlands*, 225–52, 404 et passim.

52 Peter D. Stachura, ed., *The Poles in Britain 1940–2000: From Betrayal to Assimilation* (London: Frank Cass, 2004), 51–5.

53 IP: letter from New York, 14 October 1945.

54 IP: letter of 12 December 1946.

55 IP: letters of 19 February and 2 March 1947.

56 IP: letter of 19 November 1946.

57 IP: letter of 29 August 1946.

58 IP: letter of 17 May 1946. Halina Skrzyńska knew Tadeusz Lutosławski and informed Irena that he was a stockbroker. IP: Halina Skrzyńska to Irena, 19 December 1946.

59 IP: Wincenty Lutosławski to Irena, 19 September 1950.

60 IP: letter of 7 April 1947.

61 IP: letter to Irena, 28 July 1946.

62 IP: letter to Irena, 9 October 1946.

63 IP: Witek Kontkowski to Irena, 29 January 1947.

64 IP: letter (from Leominster) of 24 January 1947.

65 IP: letter [mid-1947].

66 IP: letter of 5 August 1947.

67 In 1947–9, Witek Kontkowski worked at the head office of an agricultural cooperative in Kraków, and in 1949–58 he held various junior managerial posts in a state building enterprise. Many years later Mila Kontkowska informed Irena that Witek was not promoted any higher, 'for as someone who had returned from the west, he did not inspire confidence' (IP: letter of September/October 1975). According to their son, Witek Kontkowski was treated like 'a second-class (even a third-class) citizen' by the communist authorities in Poland. As a pre-war career army officer, as a former landowner and as a possible 'imperialist spy', he was viewed as an ideological and class enemy.

68 IP: postcard of 14 May 1947.

69 IP: letter of 10 September 1947.

70 IP: letter of 13 October 1947.

71 IP: letters of 14 and 17 October 1947.

72 IP: letter of October 1947.

73 IP: letter of Helena Zawadzka and Zofia Wyszyńska (both born Grabowska), [late 1947].

74 IP: letter of 14 October 1947.

75 IP: letter of 12 November 1947. Underlined in the original.

76 IP: letter of 2 December 1947.

77 IP: letter from Polik to Michał, 21 October 1947.

78 IP: letter no. 4 [1947].

79 IP: letter from Rednal Camp, 30 November 1947.

80 IP: letter of 22 December 1947.

81 IP: Dr Freundlich to Irena, 31 January 1948.

82 IP: draft of letter. Irena's English spellings/style.

83 On Morpeth Common camp, see Zosia Biegus and Jurek Biegus, *Polish Resettlement Camps in England and Wales 1946–1969* (Rochford, Essex: PB Software, 2013), 188–93. On the early history of the Polish camps or hostels, see also Sword, *The Formation of the Polish Community*, 270–6; and Jerzy Zubrzycki, *Polish Immigrants in Britain: A Study of Adjustment* (The Hague: M. Nijhoff, 1956), 94–131, 181–4.

84 IP: postcard of 11 April 1948.

85 IP: Helena Zawadzka to Irena, 27 June 1948.

86 IP: draft of Irena's reply to Theodosia de Lingen's letter of May 1949. Irena's English spellings/style.

87 IP: letter of 21 June 1948. The original Displaced Persons Act of 1948 (there were further amendments in 1950 and 1951) laid down that 40 per cent of the visas offered should go to persons whose place of origin or country of nationality had been '*de facto* annexed by a foreign Power'. It was intended in particular to benefit refugees from the Baltic States. Polish ex-servicemen in the United Kingdom could qualify if they applied for a US visa by 16 June 1950; by the end of 1951 11,000 visas had been issued to this group. See Jacques Vernant, *The Refugee in the Post-war World* (London: Allen & Unwin, 1953), 482–97. Two of Michał's cousins, sisters Wanda Carlton and Irena Brzozowska (both born Woyczyńska), were working at the time in the immigration department of the US Embassy in London. Whether Michał contacted them in connection with his application to go to the US is not known.

88 IP: letter with postmark 11 October 1948.

89 IP: J. Smosarska to Irena, 6 December 1948.

90 IP: letter [after October 1948].

91 IP: letter of 28 July 1950.

92 IP: Polik to Michał, [n.d.; 1950?].

93 IP: Polik to Irena and Michał, 19 May 1951; New York, Passenger Lists, 1820–1957; https://www.ancestry.co.uk/search/categories/40/?name=apoloniusz_protassewicz&name_x=s_1 (accessed 25 April 2018).

94 IP: letter of 22 November 1949.

95 IP: letter of 23 June 1949.

96 IP: postcard [1949].

97 IP: letter of 15 February 1951. The Heller family arrived from Palestine in 1947 and were placed in a Polish resettlement camp near Fairford.

98 For a brief illustrated account of the Polish Hostel at Springhill Lodges, see Biegus and Biegus, *Polish Resettlement Camps*, 20–36. For more information and photographs, see http://www.polishresettlementcampsintheuk.co.uk/springhill01.htm (accessed 28 April 2015). At the end of 1950 there were 14,500 Poles still living in twenty-six camps; they included 4,000 children of whom half were under five years of age. After taking into account the inmates' contributions for board and lodging, the cost to the British government of maintaining these camps in 1950 was £485,000. Vernant, *The Refugee*, 352–3.

99 IP: postcard of 18 September 1951.

100 IP: letter of 23 March 1952 (enclosed with Zofia Protassewicz's letter of 31 March 1952).

101 IP: letter to Henryk and Halina Skrzyński, 23 December 1955.

102 IP: letter of 22 September 1955 from Fairford.

103 IP: postcard of 1 March 1953. Four days later Stalin died.

104 IP: Marysia Karczewska to Irena, 28 November 1955.

105 IP: letter of 7 October 1955.

106 IP: letter of 25 June 1956.

107 IP: letter of 6 November 1956.

108 Irena shared her thoughts on this with Helena Heller. IP: H. Heller's letter of 24 April 1953.

109 IP: letter of 23 November 1948.

110 IP: letter of 21 March 1949.

111 IP: letter of 13 March 1954.

112 IP: postcard of 15 June 1951.

113 IP: postcard of 27 July 1951.

114 IP: Halina Skrzyńska to Irena, 22 July 1960. Her husband Henryk had attended the Marian Fathers' prestigious school in Bielany near Warsaw and his one-time tutor there Father Józef Jarzębowski was now the Superior in Fawley Court. Father Jarzębowski founded DMC in 1951 and many Poles referred to it as 'Bielany on Thames'. The school closed in 1986 and Fawley Court was sold in 2008. See the tongue-in-cheek piece on DMC by Waldemar Januszczak, a former pupil: 'Forever Poland-on-Thames', *Guardian*, 2 August 1988, education section.

115 As reported in IP: Mila Kontkowska to Irena, 20 April 1963.

116 IP: Mila Kontkowska to Irena, 8 November 1963.

117 'One can say that by visiting everyone he [Wacio] cemented the family.' IP: Mila Kontkowska to Irena, 22 October 1967.

118 IP: Irena to Mila Kontkowska, 19 November 1972.

119 IP: letter of 24 June 1963.

120 As reported by Jula to Irena in two letters, 12 March 1959 and autumn 1959, respectively (IP).

121 Aleksander Dinces, 'Naoczny świadek o Polakach w łagrach A.D. 1967', *Na Antenie: mówi Rozgłośnia Polska Radia Wolna Europa* 5, no. 50, 26 February 1967.

122 Mila Kontkowska was much amused by Irena's description of the Vatican as 'the Catholic Kremlin'. IP: letter to Irena, 23 March 1969. In a published letter, strongly critical of the Catholic Church's control of the minds of the faithful, to the Polish Catholic weekly *Gazeta Niedzielna* (London, 24 April 1962), Irena gave vent to her indignation that she had to wait thirty years 'for that marvellous and edifying book *Les Misérables* to be removed from the Index'. Victor Hugo's novel was put on the papal Index of Prohibited Books in 1864 and not removed until 1959.

123 IP: letters to Halina Skrzyńska, 1 November 1968 and 31 January 1969.

124 IP: Irena to Leszek Kontkowski, 11 January 1969 (copy),

125 IP: letter from Father Julian Chróściechowski (a Marian priest), 25 November 1971. Among the numerous British (and Irish) philosophers and writers Irena read were Bertrand Russell, Julian and Aldous Huxley, and George Bernard Shaw; the ex-Catholic theologian Charles Davis and the psychiatrist and Catholic theologian Dr Jack Dominian (with whom Irena corresponded). Of foreign thinkers the following stand out: Albert Einstein and Carl Jung. Among theologians: Hans Küng, Albert Schweitzer and Nicolas Berdyaev, and from across the Atlantic: Paul Tillich and Richard Norris (both Protestants) and the Uniate archimandrite Victor Pospishil. She followed the English Catholic press (especially *The Tablet*) and

frequently received copies of the relatively independent Catholic weekly *Tygodnik Powszechny* from Poland.

126 IP: letter to Halina Skrzyńska, 10 May 1969.

127 IP: letter to Halina Skrzyńska, 22 October 1979. Wincenty Pol's father came from a German family settled in Warmia (Ermland); in 1815 he was granted noble status (with the surname von Pollenburg) in the Congress Kingdom of Poland. Pol's mother (Eleanor Longchamps de Berier) came from a merchant family of French descent settled in Lwów. Grottger's paternal grandmother was Swiss (and it is her maiden surname that he used) while his mother (Katarzyna Blahào de Chodietow) was of Hungarian (Croatian) origin.

128 IP: letter to Halina Skrzyńska, 22 February 1963.

129 IP: written by Irena in 1968.

130 *Ilustrowany przewodnik po zabytkach kultury na Białorusi* (Warsaw: Burchard, 1997), 23–4.

Postscript: Tying up some loose ends

1 IP: Stulgiński to Irena, 28 December 1959. See *PSB*, xlv (2008), 161–3. On the other hand, Irena was never to learn that Stulgiński was saved from the gas chamber in Auschwitz by Irena's cousin Witold Pilecki who had set up a resistance cell in the concentration camp. On Pilecki, see Chapter 2.

2 Cezary Chlebowski, 'Szedyt dla "Bazy" ' [Cheddite for the 'Base'] (part 2), *Tydzień Polski* (London), 5 September 1992, 6–7 with a photo of Daniel; the article was found among Irena's papers.

3 IP: Irena to Halina Skrzyńska, 6 January 1993.

4 Father Tadeusz Krahel, 'Ksiądz Jan Goj', *Czas miłosierdzia. Białostocki Biuletyn Kościelny*, no. 166, February 2004. Available online: http://www.archibial.pl/czas/nr166/art.php?artykul=goj (accessed 10 September 2013).

5 For online entries on Dr Atlas see: http://www.eilatgordinlevitan.com/deretchin/deretchin.html and http://www.jewishvirtuallibrary.org/jechezkiel-atlas (both accessed 26 April 2018).

6 See entries on Kazimierz de Latour (Latour-Turowski) at: Janusz Stankiewicz, 'Genealogie, przodkowie, badania. Lubelszczyzna 1939r.' Available online: http://www.stankiewicze.com/index.php?kat=43 (accessed 26 April 2018); Instytut Pamięci Narodowej, 'Kompanie wartownicze 1946–1967', Special edition, *Niezależna Gazeta Polska*, 2 November 2007. Available online: http://ipn.gov.pl_data/asset/pdf_file/0005/56174 (accessed 9 September 2013); biography of de Latour on list of officers of the 'Świętokrzyska' Brigade at Polska Podziemna. Available online: http://drugiobieg.info/php/3_p_podziemna.php?ID3=358&username=&s=7&li=0&sort=K_OPS (accessed 27 April 2018).

7 Under the name of Kazimierz de Latour-Turowski. Passenger ships arriving in Western Australia: passenger list of SS *Anna Salen*, http://members.iinet.net.au/~perthdps/shipping/anasalen.htm#LIST (accessed 27 April 2018).

8 *Die sowjetische Zwölmeilenzone in der Ostsee und die Freiheit des Meeres* (Köln-Berlin: Max-Planck-Institut/Carl Heymanns Verlag, 1955).

9 H.A. Reinkemeyer's identity was confirmed via email by Dr Brzeziński, 16 October 2012, and by Dr Martin Kroeger of the German Foreign Ministry, 11 June 2013.

10 Ewa Ziółkowska, 'Polskie groby w Uzbekistanie i Kazakstanie. W 60. rocznicę polskiego wychodźstwa z ZSRR', *Wspólnota Polska. Kwartalnik poświęcony Polonii i Polakom za granicą*, nos 3–4 (2002). Available online: http://wspolnota-polska.org. pl/kwartalniki/11.html (accessed 28 April 2015); and Ewa Ziółkowska, 'Żołnierzom Generała Andersa', *Zesłaniec* (2007), 170–1. Available online: http://zeslaniec.pl/32/ kronika.pdf (accessed 28 April 2015).

Bibliography

Manuscript sources (with abbreviations used in the book)

Atholl Manuscripts in Blair Castle, Perthshire (Atholl): Correspondence of James Stewart-Murray, 9th Duke of Atholl; Diaries of Katharine, Duchess of Atholl.

Hoover Institution Archive, University of Stanford (HIA): Polish Government Collection: Irena Protassewicz's and Michał Zawadzki's depositions, 1943.

Irena Protassewicz's Correspondence and Papers (in editor's custody) (IP).

Polish Museum and Sikorski Institute (PMSI): Records of the Polish Military Hospital, Taymouth Castle.

RAF Northolt (Ministry of Defence) (MOD): Polish Army Records: Irena Protassewicz's and Michał Zawadzki's army records.

Russian State Historical Archive in St Petersburg (RGIA): Records of the *Heroldiya* of the Russian Empire.

Printed sources

Anders, Władysław. *Bez ostatniego roździału: Wspomnienia z lat 1939–1946* [Without the last chapter: Reminiscences from 1939–1946]. 6th edn. London: Gryf Publications, 1981.

Applebaum, Anne. *Gulag: A History of the Soviet Camps*. London: Allen Lane, 2003.

Applebaum, Anne. *Iron Curtain: The Crushing of Eastern Europe 1944–56*. London: Penguin Books, 2013.

Atholl, Katharine, Duchess of. *The Tragedy of Warsaw and Its Documentation*. London: John Murray, 1945.

Atholl, Katharine, Duchess of. *Working Partnership: Being the Lives of John George, 8th Duke of Atholl and of His Wife Katharine Marjory Ramsay*. London: Arthur Barker Ltd, 1958.

Biegus, Zosia, and Jurek Biegus. *Polish Resettlement Camps in England and Wales 1946–1969*. Rochford, Essex: PB Software, 2013.

Chlebowski, Cezary. 'Szedyt dla "Bazy"' [Cheddite for the 'Base'] (part 2), *Tydzień Polski* (London), 5 September 1992, 6–7.

Davies, Norman. *Trail of Hope: The Anders Army. An Odyssey Across Three Continents*. Oxford: Osprey Publishing, 2015.

Dinces, Aleksander. 'Naoczny świadek o Polakach w łagrach A.D. 1967' [An eye-witness on Poles in Soviet labour camps in 1967]. *Na Antenie: mówi Rozgłośnia Polska Radia Wolna Europa* 5, no. 50, 26 February 1967.

Foot, M. R. D. *Six Faces of Courage*. London: Eyre Methuen, 1978.

Garliński, Józef. *Fighting Auschwitz*. London: Julian Friedmann, 1975.

Giedroyć, Michał. *Crater's Edge: A Family's Epic Journey Through Wartime Russia*. London: Bene Factum Publishing, 2010.

Godlewski, Józef. *Na przełomie epok* [At the turn of epochs]. London: Polska Fundacja Kulturalna, 1978.

Gross, Jan T. *Revolution from Abroad: The Soviet Conquest of Poland's Western Ukraine and Western Belorussia*. Expanded edn. Princeton and Oxford: Princeton University Press, 2002.

Hendrykowska, Małgorzata. *Smosarska*. Poznań: Uniwersytet im. Adama Mickiewicza, 2007.

Januszczak, Waldemar, 'Forever Poland-on-Thames', *Guardian*, 2 August 1988, education section, 1.

Johnson, Roberta. *Gender and Nation in the Spanish Modernist Novel*. Nashville: Vanderbilt University Press, 2003.

Jolluck, Katherine R. *Exile and Identity: Polish Women in the Soviet Union during World War II*. Pittsburgh: Pittsburgh University Press, 2002.

Keegan, John. *Six Armies in Normandy: From D-Day to the Liberation of Paris*. London: Jonathan Cape, 1982; London: Pimlico, 1992.

Kochanski, Halik. *The Eagle Unbowed: Poland and the Poles in the Second World War*. London: Penguin, 2013.

Konarski, F. *Piosenki z plecaka Helenki* [Songs from Helenka's knapsack]. Rome: published by the author, 1946.

Kubica, Grażyna. *Siostry Malinowskiego czyli kobiety nowoczesne na początku XX wieku* [Malinowski's sisters, or modern women at the beginning of the 20th century]. Kraków: Wydawnictwo Literackie, 2006.

Kunicki, Mikołaj. *Between the Brown and the Red: Nationalism, Catholicism and Communism in Twentieth-Century Poland. The Politics of Bolesław Piasecki*. Athens: Ohio University Press, 2012.

Liszewski, Karol. *Wojna polsko-sowiecka 1939r* [The Polish-Soviet War of 1939]. London: Polska Fundacja Kulturalna, 1986.

Lukowski, Jerzy, and Hubert Zawadzki. *A Concise History of Poland*. 2nd edn. Cambridge: Cambridge University Press, 2006.

Maćkowska, Maria. *Pomocnicza Służba Kobiet w Polskich Siłach Zbrojnych w okresie 2 wojny światowej* [The Polish Women's Auxiliary Service with the Polish Armed Forces during the Second World War]. London: Veritas Foundation, 1990.

Niesiecki, Kasper. *Herbarz polski* [Polish armorial]. 10 vols, Vol. 8. Leipzig: Breitkopf & Haertel: 1839–45; repr. 1979.

Pietrzak, Jacek. *Polscy uchodźcy na Bliskim Wschodzie w latach drugiej wojny światowej. Ośrodki, Instytucje, Organizacje* [Polish exiles in the Middle East during the Second World War: Centres, institutions, organizations]. Łódź: Wydawnictwo Uniwersytetu Łódzkiego, 2012.

Podgórska, Joanna. 'Powrót słońca w Milanówku' [The sun returns in Milanówek]. *Polityka*, no. 45, 8 November 2003, 116–21.

Polonsky, Antony. *The Jews in Poland and Russia*. Vol. 3. Oxford & Portland, OR: The Littman Library of Jewish Civilization, 2010-2012.

Polski Słownik Biograficzny [Polish biographical dictionary] (*PSB*), 51 vols. (Kraków: Polska Akad. Umiejętności, 1935–).

Pyłat, Joanna, Jan Ciechanowski and Andrzej Suchcitz (eds). *General Władysław Anders: Soldier and Leader of the Free Poles in Exile*. London: Polish University Abroad, 2008.

Rąkowski, Grzegorz. *Ilustrowany przewodnik po zabytkach kultury na Białorusi* [An illustrated guide to historical buildings in Belarus]. Warsaw: Burchard Edition, 1997.

Reinkemeyer, Hans Albert. *Die sowjetische Zwölmeilenzone in der Ostsee und die Freiheit des Meeres* [The Soviet twelve-mile zone in the Baltic Sea and the freedom of the seas]. Köln-Berlin: Max-Planck-Institut/Carl Heymanns Verlag, 1955.

Richmond, Theo. *Konin: A Quest*. London: Jonathan Cape, 1995.

Roszkowski, Wojciech. *Historia Polski 1914–2001* [History of Poland 1914–2001]. Warsaw: PWN, 2003.

Sargent, E. H. G. (ed.). *C.S.S.M. Choruses No. 1*. London: Children's Special Service Mission, 1936.

Siemaszko, Zbigniew S. *Generał Anders w latach 1892–1942* [General Anders in 1892–1942]. London & Warsaw: Wydawnictwo LTW, 2012.

Siemaszko, Zbigniew S. *W sowieckim osaczeniu 1939–1943* [In Soviet entrapment 1939–1943]. London: Polska Fundacja Kulturalna, 1991.

Sienkiewicz, Witold, and Grzegorz Hryciuk (eds). *Wysiedlenia, wypędzenia i ucieczki 1939–1959. Atlas ziem Polski* [Resettlements, expulsions and escapes 1939–1959: An atlas of Polish lands]. Warsaw: Demart, 2008.

Snyder, Timothy. *Black Earth: The Holocaust as History and Warning*. London: Bodley Head, 2015.

Snyder, Timothy. *Bloodlands: Europe between Hitler and Stalin*. London: Bodley Head, 2010.

Snyder, Timothy. *The Reconstruction of Nations: Poland, Ukraine, Lithuania, Belarus, 1569–1999*. New Haven & London: Yale University Press, 2003.

Stachura, Peter D. (ed.). *The Poles in Britain 1940–2000: From Betrayal to Assimilation*. London & Portland: Frank Cass, 2004.

Sword, Keith. *Deportation and Exile: Poles in the Soviet Union, 1939–48*. London: Studies in Russia and East Europe, Macmillan in Association with SSEES, 1996.

Sword, Keith (ed.). *The Soviet Takeover of the Polish Eastern Provinces, 1939–41*. London: Studies in Russia and East Europe, Macmillan in Association with SSEES, 1991.

Sword, Keith, with Norman Davies and Jan Ciechanowski. *The Formation of the Polish Community in Great Britain 1939–50*. London: SSEES, 1989.

Szybieka, Zachar. *Historia Białorusi 1795–2000* [A history of Belarus 1795–2000]. Lublin: Instytut Europy Środkowo-Wschodniej, 2002.

Szyrmer, Jerzy. *Zebrane kartki z moich wspomnień* [Notes of my reminiscences]. Warsaw: Neriton, 2011.

Uruski, Seweryn. *Herbarz szlachty polskiej*. Vol. 14 [Armorial of the Polish nobility]. Warsaw: Gebethner & Wolff, 1917.

Vernant, Jacques. *The Refugee in the Post-War World*. London: George Allen & Unwin, 1953.

de Vooght, Paul. 'Jan Hus: Heretic or Martyr?', *The Tablet*, 1 February 1969, 99–100.

Wańkowicz, Melchior. *Bitwa o Monte Cassino* [Battle for Monte Cassino]. Rome: Publications of the Polish Second Corps, 1946-47.

Wańkowicz, Melchior. *Tędy i owędy* [Here and there]. Warsaw: Iskry, 1961.

Wańkowicz, Melchior. *Zupa na gwoździu* [Nail soup]. Warsaw: PAX, 1967.

Weeks, Theodore R. *Vilnius Between Nations 1795–2000*. De Kalb: NIU Press, 2015.

Wierzbicki, Marek. *Polacy i Białorusini w zaborze sowieckim: Stosunki polsko-białoruskie na ziemiach północno-wschodnich II Rzeczypospolitej pod okupacją sowiecką 1939–1941* [Poles and Belarusians in the Soviet sector: Polish-Belarusian relations in the northeastern lands of the Second Polish Republic under Soviet occupation 1939–41]. Warsaw: Volumen, 2000.

Wierzbicki, Marek. *Polacy i Żydzi w zaborze sowieckim: Stosunki polsko-żydowskie na ziemiach północno-wschodnich II RP pod okupacją sowiecką 1939–1941* [Poles and Jews in the Soviet Sector: Polish-Jewish relations in the northeastern lands of the Second Polish Republic under Soviet occupation 1939–41]. 2nd edn. Warsaw: Fronda, 2006.

Wykaz poległych i zmarłych żołnierzy Polskich Sił Zbrojnych na obczyźnie w latach 1939– 1946 [Roll of members of the Polish Armed Forces who fell in action or died from other causes outside Poland in the years 1939–1946]. London: Instytut Historyczny im. Generała Sikorskiego, 1952.

Zubrzycki, Jerzy. *Polish Immigrants in Britain: A Study in Adjustment.* The Hague: M. Nijhoff, 1956.

Online sources

Ancestry. 'Protassewicz, Apoloniusz, New York, Passenger Lists, 1820–1957'. Available online: <https://www.ancestry.co.uk/search/categories/40/?name=apoloniusz_ protassewicz&name_x=s_1> (accessed 25 April 2018).

Ancestry. 'Smosarska, Jadwiga, New York, Passenger Lists, 1820–1957'. Available online: <https://www.ancestry.co.uk/search/categories/40/?name=_smosarska&name_ x=s_1> (accessed 25 April 2018).

Biegus, Zosia. 'Springhill Lodges Camp. Gloucestershire'. Available online: <http://www. polishresettlementcampsintheuk.co.uk/springhill01.htm> (accessed 28 April 2015).

Eilat Gordin Levitan. 'Welcome to the Deretchin Site: Atlas, Jehezkel'. Available online: <http://www.eilatgordinlevitan.com/deretchin/deretchin.html> (accessed 26 April 2018).

Instytut Pamięci Narodowej. 'de Latour (Latour-Turowski), Kazimierz'. 'Kompanie wartownicze 1946–1967' [Guard companies 1946–1967]. Special edn. *Niezależna Gazeta Polska*, 2 November 2007. Available online: <http://ipn.gov.pl_data/asset/ pdf_file/0005/56174> (accessed 9 September 2013).

Instytut Pamięci Narodowej. 'Rotmistrz Pilecki'. Available online: <http://www.pilecki.ipn. gov.pl/rp/biogram/7081,dok.html> (accessed 27 April 2018).

Jewish Virtual Library. 'Atlas, Jechezkiel'. Available online: <http://www. jewishvirtuallibrary.org/jechezkiel-atlas> (accessed 26 April 2018)

Krahel, Tadeusz. 'Ksiądz Jan Goj' [Father Jan Goj]. *Czas miłosierdzia. Białostocki Biuletyn Kościelny*, no. 166, February 2004. Available online: <http://www.archibial.pl/czas/ nr166/art.php?artykul=goj> (accessed 10 September 2013).

Lipiński, Romuald. '"My Story": Excerpts from Romuald Lipiński's Memoir. Evacuation Spring 1942'. Available online: <http://www.kresyfamily.com/romuald-7.html> (accessed 27 April 2018).

Muzeum Powstania Warszawskiego. 'Biogramy Helena Jamontt' [Biography of Helena Jamontt]. Available online: <https://www.1944.pl/powstancze-biogramy/helena- jamontt,12712.html> (accessed 27 April 2018).

Perth DPS. 'de Latour (Latour-Turowski), Kazimierz'. 'Passenger ships arriving in Western Australia, passenger list of SS *Anna Salen*'. Available online: <http://members.iinet.net. au/~perthdps/shipping/anasalen.htm#LIST> (accessed 27 April 2018).

Polska Podziemna. 'de Latour (Latour-Turowski), Kazimierz'. Available online: http:// drugiobieg.info/php/3_p_podziemna.php?ID3=358&username=&s=7&li=0&sor t=K_OPS (accessed 27 April 2018).

Stankiewicz, Janusz. 'de Latour (Latour-Turowski), Kazimierz'. *Genealogie, przodkowie, badania. Lubelszczyzna 1939r* [Genealogies, ancestors, research, Lublin region 1939]. Available online: <http://www.stankiewicze.com/index.php?kat=43> (accessed 26 April 2018).

Ziółkowska, Ewa. 'Polskie groby w Uzbekistanie i Kazakstanie: W 60. rocznicę polskiego wychodźstwa z ZSRR' [Polish graves in Uzbekistan and Kazakhstan: On the 60th anniversary of the Polish exodus from the USSR]. *Wspólnota Polska: Kwartalnik poświęcony Polonii i Polakom za granicą* [The Polish community: A quarterly publication devoted to Poles and their descendants abroad], nos 3–4 (2002). Available online: <http://wspolnota-polska.org.pl/kwartalniki/11.html> (accessed 28 April 2015).

Ziółkowska, Ewa. 'Żołnierzom Generała Andersa' [To General Anders' soldiers]. *Zesłaniec* [The exile] (2007): 170–1. Available online: <http://zeslaniec.pl/32/kronika.pdf> (accessed 28 April 2015).

ZOA, 'O malarzu który z miłości zyskał głowę' [About a painter who, out of love, gained a head]. Available online: <https://whu.org.pl/2016/01/06/o-malarzu-ktory-z-milosci-zyskal-glowe/> (accessed 3 March 2018).

Index

Aban (Siberia) 127
Abramek (Jewish dealer) 46, 63, 110, 181
Amberg, Werner 175
'amnesty' (of 12 August 1941) 89,
    126, 131
Anna (cook in Borki) 10, 35, 64–5
Anders, General Władysław 21, 88–9, 90,
    144–5, 158
    Irena's praise of 92, 158
    See also Polish Army in USSR; Polish
    Second Corps
Arciszewski, Tomasz 170–1
Argentina 184, 187
Assisi 77–8
Association of Polish Patriots in USSR
    (*Związek Patriotów Polskich*) 91–2,
    157–8. *See also* Wasilewska, Wanda
Atholl, Katharine, Duchess of 172, 173,
    174–5
Atlas, Yehezkel (doctor) 86, 105–7, 110,
    116, 181, 204
Auchmore House (Killin) 173
Auschwitz concentration camp 21, 48, 203,
    211n.8
Australia 205
Austria-Hungary xxvii, xxxiv

Baghdad 149
bandits 11–12, 36, 130, 191
Bandurski, Władysław (bishop) 21, 49, 56,
    155
Baranowicze 75, 181
Bartoszewiczowa, Franciszka 45, 89, 132,
    133, 138, 139, 179
Bartoszewiczowa, Maria 12, 42, 45–6
Begin, Menahem 90–1
Belarus and Belarusians xxvi–xxviii, 18,
    26–7, 56, 84–5, 100, 114–15, 116,
    182, 199, 220n.1, 223n.15. *See also*
    Orthodoxy and Orthodox Church;
    peasants

Belina-Prażmowski, Zbigniew (Knight of
    Malta) 176
Berling, Colonel Zygmunt 91
Beria, Lavrentii 92
Bilczyński family 47
Blockley (Gloucestershire) 205
Bogdańska, Renata (actor and singer) 159
Boldok, Wacław (district governor) 56–7
Bolsheviks and Bolshevism xxviii, 5, 9–10,
    13, 20, 27, 41, 64, 86, 101, 114–15. *See
    also* Protassewicz, Irena, attitudes to
    Soviets and USSR; Red Army; USSR
Borey, Anna (singer; Irena's sister). *See*
    Protassewicz, Anna
Borki district xxvii
    beekeeping 47–8, 68, 70–2, 76, 95, 101
    Borki manor and estate 3, 6, 13, 14–15,
        60, 70, 74–5, 199
    carp farm 3, 17, 65–6, 101, 223n.9
    description of house by Wańkowicz
        209n.13
    during First World War 4, 6
    under German rule (1941–44) 180–2
    hospital in xxiii, xxxv, 85, 105–8, 199
    hunting 15–16, 31
    looting of 97–99
    planned division of estate 15
    during Polish-Soviet war xxviii, 9–10, 86
    reconstruction xxix, 6, 8–9, 17
    remains of house dismantled 202
    servants 35, 38–9, 40, 98
    under Soviet rule (1939–41) 86–7, 102,
        105–20
    starch-processing plant 61, 68, 75,
        116–17, 202
    See also peasants, in Borki and district
Borodziuk, Jan (Irena's godson) 40, 199
Borodziuk, Wiera (servant and family
    friend) 40, 113, 180, 195, 199
Borowik, Augustyn (looter) 97, 98, 223n.9
Bratkowski, Józef (gunner) 144

Brazil 179, 186
Brzeziński, Dr Zbigniew 205
Brzoza, 'Lieutenant' (confidence trickster) 36–8
Buchenwald concentration camp 203
Bułyka (captain) 152
Byszewski family 25

Cairo 161
Cało (doctor) 142–3
Canada 184
Cheka (Extraordinary Commission to Combat Counterrevolution, Sabotage and Speculation) 10, 134
Chokpak (Kazakhstan) 134–5, 205
Chopin, Fryderyk xxiv, 4–5, 10, 30, 48, 60, 96, 152, 201
Churchill, Winston 89, 170, 173
collective farm (*kolkhoz*) 88, 114, 124–6, 130, 228n.19
crime and criminals 12, 35–8, 39, 73, 84, 224n.20. *See also* bandits
Cross, Father (Salesian monk) 153
Czapski, Count Emeryk. *See* Hutten-Czapski
Czechoslovakia and Czech lands 77, 153–4, 190
Czerwijowski, Faustyn (librarian) 42, 49, 216n.2

Dąbrowski (soldier in Kenimekh) 144
Danek, [Jan?] (doctor) 136
Darski, Dr (lecturer) 185
denunciations 40, 99
deportations to the Soviet interior (1940–41). *See* Polish civilians deported to USSR
depositions xii, xxv, 85, 88, 219n.13, 221n.5, 223nn.11,12, 224n.17, 227n.11, 278n.27
Dereczyn 204
Divine Mercy College 197, 239n.114
Dreyfus Affair xxvii, 63, 181
duelling 41
Dworzec 6
Dyl family 128–9
Dzhambul (Kazakhstan) 46, 89, 133–4

Eastwood House (Dunkeld) 172, 172–6
Einstein, Albert 201
'elections' under Soviet rule 85, 102
Ellaby, Dorothy (Irena's friend in Scotland) 175
El-Qassasin (Egypt) 162, 165
epidemics 91, 136–44. *See also* typhus epidemic

Fairford Park (Polish hostel) 195
Fairlie, Margaret (Irena's friend in Scotland) 176
Falaise Gap (battle) 164–5, 194
Fiodor (Irena's beekeeping assistant) 70–1, 98, 105, 181
Florence 77
food
   in Borki 64–5
   at convent school 20, 22, 23, 25, 28
   among deportees to Siberia 122–4
   at Eastwood 174, 176–7
   fasting 26, 67–8
   lack of food 86, 88, 119, 133, 202, 233n.28
   in Polish Army 138, 145, 147, 231n.2
   Polish views of English cuisine 65, 189
   resettlement camps 189, 190, 192
   sending 179
   in Siberia 123–6, 127, 128, 130–1, 132
   supply of 101, 108, 110, 114, 117
   See also hunger
France 84, 164–5, 194
Freundlich, Jan (doctor) 152, 154, 161, 188–9

Gabrielewski, Gabriel (lieutenant) 164
Gawlina, Józef (bishop) 140–1, 155–6, 230n.13
Gebel (resident of Borki) 181
Germany and Germans
   Borki under German control (1941–4) 180–2
   British Zone 177, 179, 180, 184
   during First World War xxviii, 5–6, 7
   Irena's planned visit xxxiii, 76
   relations with Poland xxxiii–xxxiv, 83
   after Second World War 171–2, 177, 187, 205
   and Poland during Second World War xxxi, 86, 96

peasant attitudes to 85–6, 101, 115
See also Reinkemeyer, Hans Albert
Giedroyć, Michael 87
Giertych, Jędrzej 111
Gnoiński family (of Wiszów) 16, 37,
    60–1
Godlewski, Józef (senator) 42–3, 70, 73, 84,
    86, 171, 214n.14
Goebel family 46
Goj, Jan (parish priest) 27, 75, 181, 204
Gołąb, Józef (parish priest) 193
Gołębiowska (Valdi-Gołębiowska),
    Irena (born Żórawska; Irena's aunt;
    'Tantesse') 7–8, 89, 179, 185, 195
Gołębiowski, Stefan 7
Gołubiew, Antoni 25
Gomulińskis, doctor husband and dentist
    wife 112, 116, 181
Gomułka, Władysław 196
Górska, Janina (Janka; born Żórawska;
    Irena's aunt) 7, 119, 177
Górski, Jan (Janina's husband) 48
Górski, Lech (farmer) 75–6
Grabowski, Maciej (military intelligence
    officer) 194
Great Britain 90
    alliance with Poland 83
    attitudes to Poles after Second World
        War 170, 171–2, 173–4, 182, 184
    and Polish Army in USSR 88–9, 90
    Polish attitudes after Second World War
        171, 175, 191, 194
Grottger, Artur 201
Gruner family 108, 117–18, 122, 123–4,
    127, 183
Gutowa, Hala (teacher) 149, 155

Haifa 157
Hanka (Jewish nurse in Chokpak) 138–9
Hejnowska (teacher) 115–16
Heliopolis (Egypt) 162
Heljasz (barnkeeper) 39, 64, 103
Heller family (Kazimierz and Halina/
    Helena) 150, 154–5, 156, 171, 173,
    179, 184, 192, 195
Helman, Mojsze (blacksmith) 109–10, 120,
    181
Hernas, Hela (born Bartoszewicz) 179
Hitler, Adolph xxxiii, 78, 83, 126

Hofman, Wlastimil and wife Ada xxxii, 33,
    152–4, 178, 199, 231n.12
Hoover, Herbert 209n.11
hunger
    in Siberia and Central Asia 125–6, 127,
        128, 131, 133, 227n.11. *See also* food
    in Taganrog 5
Hus, Jan 153–4
Hutten-Czapski, Count Emeryk 17, 55, 70
Huxley, Aldous 175

Iran 90, 147
    Poles evacuated to 90–2, 144–5, 195
Iraq 148–9
Iszora, Wacław (senior official) 20, 77
Italy xxxiii, 77–9
Iwież 35, 99

Jamontt, Halina (Irena's cousin). *See*
    Skrzyńska, Halina
Jamontt, Helena (Hela; Irena's friend) xxxii,
    54–6, 177, 217n.16
Jamontt, Jadwiga (Jadzia; Irena's aunt) 16,
    31–2, 48, 51–2, 53, 176, 178, 179
Jamontt, Janusz (judge) 36, 53, 76, 213n.2
Jamontt, Maciej (barrister) 31, 51
Jankowska, Alina (daughter of governor)
    62
Jaźwińska, Adela (senior nurse) 165
Jeśman (musician) 25
Jews
    in Anders's Army 90–1, 136–7, 138–9,
        141–2
    in Borki district xxvii, 39, 43, 46, 65–6,
        111
    fate under Nazi rule 110, 181, 204
    in interwar Poland 56, 91, 110, 112,
        226n.15
    and Irena's family 13, 48, 61, 63, 65–6,
        68, 74, 75, 86, 100, 110
    medical staff in Taymouth Castle 163–4
    in Palestine 56, 90, 149, 156–7
    during Polish–Soviet war (1920) 10
    during Soviet rule 84, 86, 99–100, 109–
        12, 115–16, 225n.13
    See also Abramek; Helman, Mojsze;
        Lejzer; Witkowska, Estera
Judycki, Wiktor (army chaplain) 135–6,
    137, 229n.4

Kamiński (commander) 175
Kansk (Siberia) 127–32
Karczewska, Jula (born Protassewicz; Irena's sister). *See* Prange, Jula
Karczewska, Marysia (Irena's goddaughter) 48
Karczewski, Jan (Irena's brother-in-law) 48, 53, 86, 96, 97, 101, 103, 152, 177
Kątkowski, Zbigniew 179
Katowice 176, 177
Katyn massacre 33, 211n.3
Kautsky, Karl 29
Kazakhstan and Kazakhs 89, 91, 133, 136, 137, 139–40, 205, 233n.28
Kazia (nurse in Kermine) 142
Kenimekh (Uzbekistan) 140–2, 144
Kermine (Uzbekistan) 142–3
Khanaqin (Iraq) 148–9
Khrushchev, Nikita 196
Kiełbiński, Adam (surgeon) 142
Kiepura, Jan 50, 216n.4
Kirgizia 91
Kluszczyński, Marian (army chaplain) 165
Koczan, Józefa (Józia; born Protassewicz; Irena's aunt) and husband Longin 62, 161
kolkhoz. *See* collective farm
Komar (bandit) 11
Konarski, Feliks (aka Ref-Ren) 158–9
Kontkowska, Emilia (Mila; born Połubińska; Irena's cousin) 24, 173, 177, 178–9, 185, 190, 192, 198
Kontkowski, Wiktor (Witek; captain of engineers; Emilia Kontkowska's husband) 16, 43, 96, 175, 178–9, 183, 184–5, 237n.67
Kopański, General Stanisław 174
Korycki family 134
Kossakowska, Bronka (nurse) 137
Kostrowicka, Hala (Halina; born Przybytko; Irena's cousin) 178, 179
Kostrowicki, Daniel (Hala Kostrowicka's husband) 179, 203
Kozak, Jan (school chaplain) 24–5
Kozłowska, Mania (nursery maid) 12–13, 96
Kozłowszczyzna 116, 204
Kraków 178, 183

Krasnovodsk (Turkmenistan) 92, 145
Krasnoyarsk (Siberia) 123
Krzyżanowski, Colonel Aleksander ('Wilk') 203
Kukiel, General Marian 194
Küng, Hans 201
Kutkowska, Lala (landowner) 43–4, 215n.23
Krzywański (doctor) 142

Ladzinki 65, 87, 102, 117
landed gentry in prewar northeastern Poland xxvii, 6–7, 11–12, 16–17, 41–8, 59–60, 86, 111. *See also szlachta*
Łaciszowa (senior nurse) 142
Latour, Kazimierz de (Kazik; army captain) 53–4, 204–5, 231n.8
languages
    in city of Wilno 207n.4
    in Słonim district xxvii, 207n.3
Lebanon 92
Lejzer (meat merchant) 100, 101, 110–11, 181
Lekis family (Wanda and Mirek) 165, 184, 187, 198
Lenino (battle) 91
Lętowski family 115
letters and letter writing xxiv, xxv, xxxiii, 87, 88, 176–7, 179, 180, 195
Lida 108–9, 181
Lingen, Theodosia de (Irena's friend in Scotland) 176, 189–90
Lisowska, Wanda. *See* Lekis family
Lithuania
    dispute over Wilno/Vilnius xxix
    Grand Duchy xxv–xxvi
    in Russian Empire xxvii–xxviii
    during Second World War 87, 97, 108, 203
Łomża, refugees from 97, 98
Long Marston (Royal Engineers Depot and Polish hostel) 193, 196
looting and anarchy (September 1939) 84, 97–102, 223n.15
Lower Quinton (Warwickshire) xxiii, 196, 197
Łoziński, Zygmunt (bishop) 56
Luba (nanny in Borki) 101
Lutosławska, Janina xxxi, 198

Lutosławski, Wincenty xxx–xxxi, 13, 73–4, 76, 79, 178, 183
Lwów (L'viv) 13, 49, 92

Maczek, General Stanisław 194, 204
Majewski (Borki resident) 117, 181
Malakanka (Siberia) 124
Malczewski, Jacek 153
Malinowska, Myszka (Irena's school friend) 24
Małkiewicz, Zdzisław (doctor) 172
Mania (Irena's servant) 40, 99, 181
Maruszkin, Antoni (law student) 25–6
Masłoniowa, Julia (commandante of nurses) 134–5, 155
Mayski, Ivan 88
medical care
  in Anders's Army 91, 135–9, 141–5
  in Borki area 38, 40–1, 105–8, 121, 219n.16
  in Polish military hospital in Scotland 163–4
  in school for young soldiers in Nazareth 152
memory xxiv–xxv, 84, 85, 141, 159, 180, 215n.23
menstruation 131, 150
Mikołajczyk, Stanisław 170, 171, 174, 187
Minasowicz, Klemens 14, 99, 210n.20
Molotov, Vyacheslav 84–5
Monte Cassino (battle) xxxii, 91, 159, 163, 233n.32
Morpeth Common (Polish hostel) 56, 186, 189
Morska, Julia 119–20
Morski, Dziutek (Irena's cousin) 96, 98, 101, 103, 119–20
Morski, Gienio (Irena's cousin) 31–2, 67
Mucha (bandit) 11
Munthe, Axel 155
Murray, Lord James 175, 235n.18

National Radical Camp (*Obóz Narodowo-Radykalny*, ONR) xxxii–xxxiii, 55, 111
Nazareth (school for Polish young soldiers) 150–2, 155
Nazi-Soviet Pact (1939) 83, 87
Niedziałowski, Captain Kamil (medical officer) 135–6, 137–8, 140

NKVD (People's Commissariat for Internal Affairs) 85, 87, 88, 92, 103, 115, 120, 123, 131–2, 170, 203, 228n.28
Normandy 164–5
Northwick Park (Polish hostel) 56–7, 193, 197
Nowojelnia 6, 99
nurses in Polish Army xxxv, 134–42, 148–9, 150, 155, 162–4, 234n.6. *See also* Polish Women's Auxiliary Service

Obelkowicze 35
ONR. *See* National Radical Camp
Orthodoxy and Orthodox Church xxv–xxvii, 53, 84, 99, 100, 101–2, 110, 127, 155, 164
Orzeszkowa, Eliza 45
Ossowiecki, Stefan 51
Ostaszewski, [Władysław] (dentist) 41
Osterwa, Juliusz 24

Paderewski, Ignacy 60
Pahlevi (Iran) 147
Palestine (British Mandate) 149–57, 161, 179
Pawulski family 134
peasants xiii, xxvii
  behaviour during Soviet invasion and occupation (1939–40) 10, 35–6, 40, 84, 97–102, 108, 116, 220n.1, 223n.15, 224n.18
  changing attitudes to Soviet rule (1940–41) 85, 114–15
  defence of Irena at public meeting 120
  in Borki and district 15, 26–7, 35–6, 39–40, 63–4, 69, 70, 73, 107–8, 120, 210n.23
  Irena's views on local 84, 112–13, 114–15
  literacy of local iii, 225n.9
  in Siberia 130
Pęski (young medic) 128
Philippines 191–2, 194, 197
Piasecki, Bolesław xxxii–xxxiii, 55, 76, 217n.14
Piasecki, Sergiusz 45, 215n.30
Pilecki, Witold (Wicio; war hero; Irena's cousin) 21, 211n.8
Piłsudska, Aleksandra (marshal's widow) 234n.13

Piłsudski, Marshal Józef xxviii, xxix, 7,
 49–50, 56, 73, 109
 Irena's views on xxxiv, 3, 105, 158
Pius XII 78–9
Plater, Emilia 11, 105, 209n.10
Pol (Pohl) Wincenty 201
Poland
 during conflicts of 1918–20 xxviii–xxix
 'Congress' Kingdom xxviii
 eve of Second World War xxxiii–xxxiv,
 83
 invasion and partition (1939) 83–5,
 220n.2
 northeastern part under German rule
 (1941–44) 180–2
 northeastern part under Soviet rule
 (1939–41) 85–7, 102, 105–20
 relations with USSR (1941–43) 88–92
 repatriation of Poles from USSR
 (1944–45) 91–2, 158, 171, 176–7, 178,
 235n.2
 under Soviet domination (after 1945)
 170–2, 174, 187–8, 190, 196, 199
Polesie 56, 169
Polish-Lithuanian Commonwealth xxvi
Polish Air Force 63, 174
Polish Army in USSR 88–90, 92, 134–5
 evacuated to Iran 90–91, 92, 144–5
 Jews in 90–1, 136–7, 138–9, 141–2
 mortality among troops 91, 136, 143–5
 See also Anders, Władysław; nurses in
 Polish Army
Polish Armed Forces in the West (after
 1945) 170, 173–4
Polish Army in Middle East 92–3, 147–50
Polish civilians deported to USSR 85, 87,
 89–90, 122–3, 195, 227n.2
 moved to British territories 92
 numbers involved 87, 221n.13
 relief arrangements after 'amnesty' 89–90,
 134
 treatment of women 88
Polish First Armoured Division 194, 204,
 234n.12
Polish government-in-exile (in London)
 xxix, 87, 88, 93, 169–70, 171,
 194, 196
Polish Insurrection (1863–4) xvii, 13, 17,
 60, 126–7

Polish Home Army (*Armia Krajowa*, AK)
 21, 180, 181, 183, 203, 211n.7, 217n.16
Polish military hospital no.1 (Taymouth
 Castle) 163–5, 234n.6
Polish Red Cross 40–1, 96, 99, 105, 124,
 134, 148, 161, 172
Polish Resettlement Corps 174, 182, 184
Polish resettlement camps (hostels) in
 Britain
 accommodation 189, 190, 192–3, 196
 cultural life 193
 education 190, 193, 197
 food 189, 190, 192
 religious life 193
 work 193
 See also Fairford Park; Long Marston;
 Morpeth Common; Northwick Park;
 St Mawgan; Springhill Lodges
Polish Second Corps 91, 92–3, 162, 173,
 175, 178, 179, 204
Polish–Soviet war (1920–1) xxviii–xxix,
 9–10
Polish 10th Dragoons 164–5, 234n.11
Polish war cemeteries in former USSR 205
Polish Women's Auxiliary Service
 (*Pomocnicza Służba Kobiet*) 90, 134,
 143, 148, 150–6, 162, 234n.6. *See also*
 nurses in Polish Army
Polish young soldiers (*junacy*) 134, 150,
 158, 162. *See also* Nazareth (school).
Połubińska, Antonina (Ninka). *See*
 Stabrowska, Antonina (Ninka)
Połubińska, Emilia (Mila; Irena's cousin).
 See Kontkowska, Emilia
Połubińska, Salomea (Salunia; born
 Protassewicz; Irena's aunt) 10, 23–4,
 67, 96, 165, 178, 185
Połubiński, Prince Mieczysław (Mieczyś;
 Salomea Połubińska's husband) 23
Pompeii 78
Potsdam Conference (1945) 171–2
Poznań 56, 62
Poznański, Dr Karol 191
Prange, Jula (born Protassewicz; 1st m.
 Karczewska; Irena's sister) 3, 22, 29,
 30, 32–3, 48, 96, 176, 177, 180, 185,
 186, 195–6, 199
Protasowicz, Jonasz (Metropolitan of Kiev)
 xxvi

Protasowicz, Walerian (Bishop of Wilno/
Vilnius) xxvi, 14, 61, 98
Protassewicz, Anna (Hania; 'Anna Borey';
Irena's sister) 3, 7, 23, 25–6, 30, 33, 40,
48, 53, 60, 75, 176–7, 178, 179, 180,
199, 236n.32
Protassewicz, Antoni (Antoś; Irena's uncle)
10–11, 59, 113
Protassewicz, Apolonia (born Żórawska;
Irena's paternal grandmother) 13, 60
Protassewicz, Apoloniusz (Polik; airman;
Irena's cousin) 12, 16, 63, 75, 169, 179,
180, 184, 187, 190–1, 199
Protassewicz, Eustachy (Irena's
grandfather) 13–14, 60
Protassewicz, Ewarysta (Wera; Irena's
aunt). *See* Przybytko, Ewarysta
Protassewicz, Helena (Hela; born
Czerwijowska; Irena's aunt) xxxiv,
49–50, 108–9, 110, 216n.3
Protassewicz, Irena (Irenka/Ireneczka/Irka;
later m. Zawadzka)
American plans thwarted 190–1
army reports 233n.33
attends convent school in Wilno xxx,
19–25, 163
attends ONR meetings 55
attends Red Cross course 40–1
attitude to Soviets and USSR xxxiv–xxxv,
85–6, 88, 93, 112–13, 123, 126,
129–31, 145, 188, 200
baptizes children in Siberia 78, 126–7
becomes a British citizen 196
beekeeping 47–8, 70–2, 76, 95, 101, 130,
157, 189, 192, 196
before a 'people's court' 99–100
birth of children 172, 189, 191, 192
during Bolshevik presence (1920) 10
childhood and upbringing 3–4, 29–30,
69
children visit Poland 198–9, 200
contact resumed with family in Poland
176–9
contracts typhus 137–40
dealings with ordinary Soviet citizens
126–30, 133–4
death of husband Michał 198, 202
demobilized 174
deported to Siberia 87–8, 121–3

discussions whether to return to Poland
182–9
education of children 190, 194, 197–8
in Egypt 161–3
employed as nurse in Borki xxxv, 41, 85,
105–8
encounters with NKVD 115, 123, 131–2
escapes from Kansk 132
escapes to Ladzinki 87, 117–18
evacuated to Iran 92, 145
experiences liberation as result of
Vatican Council 29, 200–1
on General Anders 92, 158
on ideal marriage 78, 137, 153
happy in Britain 201
hunger in Siberia and Central Asia 125–
6, 127, 128, 131, 133, 227n.11
Irena's death 205
joins Polish Women's Auxiliary Service
134
life in Eastwood House 172, 173, 174–6
life in resettlement camps in England
186, 189–95, 197
looting of the house (1939) 97–9
love of countryside and nature xxx, 22,
23, 29, 30–1, 98, 108, 143, 151, 172
marriage proposals xxxi, 20, 32, 47, 51–
2, 54, 76
marries Michał Zawadzki 164–5, 169
moves to Lower Quinton xxxiii, 196, 197
nurse in Iraq 148–9
nurse in Polish military hospital in
Scotland 162–4
nurse in USSR 91, 134–45
in Palestine 92, 131, 149–57
parcels to Poland and Germany 179–80,
185, 195
on peasants in Borki area 84, 112–13,
114–15
planned trip to Berlin xxxiii, 76
poetry 54, 65, 95
religious views and beliefs xxx, 22, 24–5,
26–9, 40, 53, 67–8, 78–9, 109, 113–14,
115, 119–20, 121, 122–3, 126–7, 129,
148–9, 153–4, 155–6, 163, 197, 200–1,
239n.122
resumes contact with Borki 199–200
romantic ideas and attitudes xxxiv, 20–1,
33, 95, 98, 113–14, 159

on Soviet 'elections' in Borki 85, 102
stays in Borki while family escapes to
    Warsaw 17, 86, 103
stiletto affair 161–2
suffers breakdown but recovers 200
in Taganrog 5–6, 64
temporary loss of faith 28–9
travels to Italy xxxiii, 76–9
views on and relations with Jews 86,
    109–12, 115, 138–9, 156–7, 181, 198.
    See also Atlas, Yezekel; Jews; Lejzer;
    Witkowska, Estera
views on Germany xxxiii, 76, 87,
    118–19. *See also* Reinkemeyer, Hans
    Albert
visitors from Poland 196, 198
work and life on *kolkhoz* 'Stalinets' 88,
    124–6
works at the school for Polish young
    soldiers in Nazareth 150–2, 155
writing memoirs xxiv–xxv
Protassewicz, Janka (born Łysak; Kazimierz
    Protassewicz's wife) 13, 178
Protassewicz, Józef (Ziuk; Leon
    Protassewicz's son) 50, 109
Protassewicz, Józefa (Józia; Irena's aunt).
    See Koczan, Józefa
Protassewicz, Jula (1st m. Karczewska;
    Irena's sister). *See* Prange, Jula
Protassewicz, Kamilla (Kama; born
    Morska; Piotr Protassewicz's wife) 10,
    19, 38, 47, 66, 108, 178
Protassewicz, Kazimierz (Kazio; Irena's
    cousin) 12–13, 20, 27–8, 96–7, 177,
    183, 209n.12
Protassewicz, Leon (Irena's uncle) xxxiv,
    28, 49–50, 60, 69, 76, 108–9
Protassewicz, Leoś (Irena's cousin) 10, 53–
    4, 62, 68, 73, 177
Protassewicz, Maria (Marynia; Irena's
    aunt). *See* Świackiewicz, Maria
Protassewicz, Maria (Marzeńka; born
    Nowakowska; wife of uncle Antoni)
    10–11, 40, 51, 177
Protassewicz, Maurycy (Irena's distant
    cousin) 96
Protassewicz, Mila (Irena's cousin). *See*
    Zbroja, Mila
Protassewicz, Narcyz (Irena's uncle) 10, 62

Protassewicz, Piotr (Piotruś; Irena's uncle)
    10, 11, 60, 62, 107
Protassewicz, Ryszard (Irena's distant
    cousin) 180–1, 182
Protassewicz, Salomea (Salunia; Irena's
    aunt). *See* Połubińska, Salomea
Protassewicz, Stanisława (Stacha; Irena's
    distant cousin) 96
Protassewicz, Stefan (Irena's cousin) 176
Protassewicz, Wacław (Wacio; Irena's
    father; 'Tatuś') xxx, 3–4, 6, 8–10, 17,
    33, 36, 46, 48, 59–72, 106, 181
    affair of Słonim funds 41–3
    beekeeping 68, 70
    bee treatment for rheumatism 219n.16
    carp farm 65–6, 101
    death of 73–4
    and farming 74–5
    fondly remembered in Borki 200
    and Jews 8, 61, 63, 65–6, 68, 74
    and medicine 40, 107
    and peasants 9–10, 48, 63–4, 114
    and religion 67
    restoration of Borki xxix, 8–9
    starch-processing plant 68, 75, 202
Protassewicz, Wilhelm (Wiluś; Irena's
    uncle) 10, 61, 218n.3
Protassewicz, Zofia (born Stabrowska;
    Wilhelm's wife) 47, 149, 178
Protassewicz, Zofia (born Żórawska; Irena's
    mother; 'Mamusia') 3, 5, 10, 29–30,
    33, 45, 48, 52, 59–60, 61, 73–5, 87,
    96–7, 99, 101, 107, 119, 176–7, 182,
    185, 186, 191, 192, 195–6, 196–7,
    221nn.11,12
Protassewicz, Zygmunt (Zygmuś; Irena's
    cousin) xxxii, 42, 50, 73, 96–7, 171, 176,
    177, 182, 190, 191, 199, 216n.4, 223n.7
Przybylski (captain) 152
Przybytko, Emil (Ewarysta's husband) 157–8
Przybytko, Ewarysta (Wera; Irena's aunt)
    110, 225n.5
Przybytko, Jadzia (Irena's cousin) 157–8,
    175, 182–3, 233n.28

Quizil Ribat (Iraq) 149

Raczyński, Count Edward 77
Radziwiłł princes 123, 124, 227n.7

Rahoza, Captain (landowner) 44
Ravensbrück concentration camp 185, 198
Red Army
    in Borki and district (1939) 84–5,
        99–100, 102, 106
    control of Poland 170
    during Polish–Soviet War xxviii–xxix,
        9–10
    during Second World War 90, 91, 122, 128
'Redhead' (vigilante leader) 99, 107–8
Redler, Izydor (doctor) 163–4
Rehovot 150
Reinkemeyer, Hans Albert (law student)
    xxxiii, 73–4, 76, 87, 118–19, 178, 205,
    220n.4
religion. *See* Orthodoxy and Orthodox
    Church; Jews; Protassewicz, Irena,
    religious views and beliefs; Roman
    Catholicism
religious denominations
    in city of Wilno/Vilnius 207n.4
    in Słonim district 207n.3
Riga, Treaty of (1921) xxix
Rodziewiczówna, Maria 17, 210n.28
Rohotna 10, 12, 70, 100, 109, 120, 181, 182
Roman Catholicism and Catholic Church
    xxv–xxvii, 78–9, 153–4, 155, 200–1
    attitudes to sex 25, 32–3, 88
    Catholic Belarusians 84, 100, 116
    clergy under Soviet rule 116
    fasting 26, 67–8
    in Poland and Polish Catholicism xxxiii,
        25–9, 56, 62, 163, 201
    See also Protassewicz, Irena, religious
        views and beliefs; Vatican Council
        (Second)
Romanowicz, Helena (born Thugutt; Irena's
    great-grandmother) 53
Rome
    St Peter's basilica 78–9
    World Catholic Youth Congress (1939)
        78
Roycewicz, Henryk 45
Roycewicz, Wanda (born Wołłowicz; 1st m.
    Strawińska) 12, 42, 45, 60, 61, 64, 75,
    109–10, 179, 186
Russia and Russians xxvi–xxviii, 31, 69
    descendants of Polish exiles 126–7
    officials 70

Russians in Siberia 126–30
    tsarist Russia xxvi
    See also NKVD; Protassewicz, Irena,
        attitudes to the Soviets; Stalin; USSR
Russian Revolution
    of 1905 xxvii
    of 1917 xxvi–xxviii, 5–6
Russo-Japanese war (1904–5) 69–70
Ryder, Sue 198

Sachsenhausen concentration camp 203
Saint Augustine 127
St Mawgan (Polish hostel) 189–90,
    191–2
Sanniki 27, 30
Savonarola, Girolamo 77
Schwetz, Antonina (Tosia) 152
sex, attitudes to 25, 30, 32–3, 125, 138–9,
    151, 155
Shakhti (Kazakhstan) 134
Shipston-on-Stour (Warwickshire) 205
Siberia 87–8, 121–32, 175
Sielicka, Regina (Irena's school friend) 115
Sienkiewicz, Henryk 97, 98
Sikh soldiers 148
Sidorowicz family (of Ladzinki) 6, 65, 66,
    75, 102, 117, 121, 178
Sikorski, General Władysław 88, 90, 126,
    144–5, 158
Sikorski–Maisky agreement (July 1941) 88,
    126, 131–2, 175
Skorochod family
    Adam (coachman) 4–5, 8–9, 16, 52, 65,
        114, 200
    Helenka 5
    Staś 5, 62, 199–200
Skotnicka, Maria 123, 124
Skrundzie 101
Skrzyńska, Halina (born Jamontt; Irena's
    cousin) 31–2, 77, 116, 177, 178, 179,
    180, 184, 198, 203
Skrzyński, Aleksander 77
Skrzyński, Henryk 77, 177, 184
Skwarczewski, Adolf (*inżynier*) 51–3,
    217nn.6,7
Słonim xxvii, 65–6, 106, 111, 121–2, 180,
    181, 204
    languages and religions in district 207n.3
    literacy in district 225n.9

Smosarska, Jadwiga (wife of Zygmunt Protassewicz) xxxii, 50, 96–7, 157, 190, 199, 223n.7
Sobakińce 8, 59
Sokołowski, Adam (provincial governor) 73
Sopot 176–7, 184, 186
Springhill Lodges (Polish hostel) 192–6, 197
Stabrowska, Antonina (Ninka; born Połubińska) 61, 180, 182, 184, 187
Stabrowski, Antoni (Tolik) 16, 61, 180, 184
Stalin, Joseph 83–4, 89, 90, 126, 157, 170, 171, 176. *See also* NKVD; USSR
Stanley, William (farmer) 196
Starczewski (policeman) 11
state farm (*sovkhoz*) 88, 123–4
Strawińska, Jadwiga (Wisia; born Zawadzka; Irena's sister-in-law) 183
Strawińska, Wanda. *See* Roycewicz, Wanda
Strawiński family (of Mirowszczyzna) 7, 17
Strawiński, Ksawery 45
Studnicki, Władysław xxxi–xxxii, 76, 184, 188, 220n.4
Stulgiński, Tadeusz 32, 53–4, 76, 178, 200, 203
Styler, S. C. (head teacher) 197
Suczek, Aleksander (smuggler) 110
Świackiewicz, Maria (Marynia; born Protassewicz; Irena's aunt) 20–2, 23, 42, 60, 177, 180
Świętokrzyska Brigade 204
Szafran, Lola. *See* Witkowska, Estera
Szarecki, General Bolesław 149
Szczecin 178, 183
Szeremiet, Adam (looter) 98, 223n.12
szlachta (Polish nobility) xiii, xxxii. *See also* landed gentry in prewar northeastern Poland
Szurlej, Stanisław 36, 213n.1

Taganrog 5–6, 64
Tarasik family 14, 37, 39, 98–99
Tarnawski, Wit 150, 152
Taymouth Castle (Polish military hospital) 136, 141–2, 162
teachers
  at Divine Mercy College 197–8
  at Irena's convent school 20, 24–5

in Lower Quinton 197
in Palestine 150, 155, 161–2
under Soviet rule 116
Tiberias 152
Tomaszewski family 122, 124, 125
Turska, Zofia (nurse) 183–4
Turzański, Jerzy (estate administrator) 74–5, 100, 103, 179
Turzański, Bolesław 96, 179
Twardowski, Pan (legendary magician) 132
typhus epidemic 91, 136–40, 145

Umiastowska, Marchioness Janina 51
USA (United States of America) 97, 182
  Labour Service Guard Companies 204
  and Poland 12, 89, 171–2
  resettlement of Poles in 190–1, 238n.87
USSR (Union of Soviet Socialist Republics) xxxiv, 205
  partition of Poland (1939) 83–5
  and Polish government-in-exile 88–92, 126
  Soviet rule in Borki area 86–7, 102, 105–20
  Soviet plans for postwar Poland 91–2
  and postwar Poland 170–2, 187, 196
  See also Bolsheviks; Protassewicz, Irena, attitudes to the Soviets; NKVD; Polish Army in the USSR; Red Army; Sikorski–Maisky pact; Stalin
Uzbekistan and Uzbeks 89, 91, 140, 143–4, 205

Valivade (Polish camp in India) 183
Vatican Council (Second) 29, 68, 127, 153–4, 200–1
Verobyova, Serafina (Kansk resident) 128
Vilnius. *See* Wilno
Volga Germans 126
Vooght, Dom Paul de 154
Vysokoe (Kazakhstan) 138, 139

Walicki family (of Sągajłowszczyzna) 13, 47
Wańkowicz, Melchior xxxii, 42–3, 61, 143, 155, 209n.13, 214nn.17,19,20, 219n.16, 232n.22
Warsaw 49–57, 64, 86, 103
  Uprising (1944) 48, 176, 177–8, 183, 211n.8

Wasilewska, Wanda 91–2, 157–8
Wasiutyński, Wojciech 55
Wasyl (carpenter in Borki) 100–1
Weiss (doctor in Chokpak) 138
Wężowszczyzna (home of Żórawski family)
    7–8, 11, 59, 74
Wilniewszczyc, Wincenty (estate
    administrator) 17–18
Wilno (Vilnius) xxvii, xxix, 23–4, 51, 59,
    61, 70, 76, 87, 177, 178, 203, 207n.4
    'repatriation' of Poles 158
Wincenty (cobbler) 27
Winczowski, Franciszek (parish priest)
    196
Witbekowa, Ala (Borki resident) 180,
    181–2
Witkowska, Estera (Lola Szafran; nurse;
    Irena's friend) 141–2, 150, 164, 198,
    230n.14
Wittlin, Józef 45, 215n.29
Wojciech family 128–9
Wolf, Czesław von (Irena's husband's uncle)
    191
Wołłowicz family (of Rohotna) 17, 44–5,
    109. *See also* Roycewicz, Wanda
Woyczyński sisters (Irena Brzozowska and
    Wanda Carlton) 195, 238n.87
Wrocław 185
Wysłouch, Franciszek and wife Basia 195
Wysock 116
Wyszyńska, Zofia (born Grabowska; 1st
    m. Zabłocka; Irena's husband's aunt)
    185, 198

Yalta Conference (1945) 170, 174
Yangi-Yul (Uzbekistan) 89

Zabłocki, Wacław (Irena's husband's
    cousin) 198
Zakopane 13, 36
Zamorski, General Kordian 55

Zawadzka, Helena (born Grabowska;
    Irena's mother-in-law) 145, 183, 185,
    196, 198, 230n.21
Zawadzka, Irena. *See* Protassewicz, Irena
Zawadzki, Michał (d.1963; Irena's husband)
    54, 68, 130, 145, 150, 164–5, 169, 172,
    173, 174, 182, 184, 185, 186, 189–92,
    193–5, 198, 202, 219n.13, 230n.20
Zawadzki, Michał (d.1940; Irena's father-
    in-law) 230n.21
Zawadzki, Stefan (Irena's husband's cousin)
    198
Zbroja, Mila (born Protassewicz; Irena's
    cousin) 19–20, 47, 61, 180, 182
Zbroja, Zygmunt 177
Żółtowska, Janina (born Countess
    Puttkamer) 42, 70
Żółtowski, Adam 70
Żórawska, Antonina (born Romanowicz;
    Irena's maternal grandmother) 7, 11,
    52–3, 60
Żórawska, Apolonia (Irena's paternal
    grandmother). *See* Protassewicz,
    Apolonia
Żórawska, Bronia (Irena's great-great-aunt)
    19
Żórawska, Ewarysta (Irena's great-great-
    aunt) 33
Żórawska, Irena (Irena's aunt). *See*
    Gołębiowska (Valdi-Gołębiowska)
Żórawska, Janina (Janka; Irena's aunt). *See*
    Górska, Janina
Żórawska, Maria (Mania; Irena's aunt) 7–8,
    52, 77, 179, 185, 195
Żórawski, Stanisław (Irena's maternal
    grandfather) 8, 59, 60
Zych, Jan (Borki resident) 39, 64, 113, 117
Zych, Wojciech (Borki resident) 39
Żylińska (commandante of nurses) 148,
    149
Żyznowski, Roman (doctor) 142, 193